Animal Ethics and Animal Law

Animal Ethics and Animal Law

Edited by Andrew Linzey and Clair Linzey

LEXINGTON BOOKS
Lanham • Boulder • New York • London

Published by Lexington Books
An imprint of The Rowman & Littlefield Publishing Group, Inc.
4501 Forbes Boulevard, Suite 200, Lanham, Maryland 20706
www.rowman.com

86-90 Paul Street, London, EC2A 4NE

British Library Cataloguing in Publication Information Available

Library of Congress Cataloging-in-Publication Data

Names: Linzey, Andrew, editor. | Linzey, Clair, editor.
Title: Animal ethics and animal law / edited by Andrew Linzey and Clair Linzey.
Description: Lanham, Maryland : Lexington Books, [2022] | Includes bibliographical references and index. | Summary: "Animal law is a growing discipline, as is animal ethics. In this wide-ranging book, scholars from around the world address the intersections between the two. A project of the Oxford Centre for Animal Ethics, this collection focuses on pressing moral issues and how law can protect animals from cruelty and abuse"— Provided by publisher.
Identifiers: LCCN 2022035750 (print) | LCCN 2022035751 (ebook) | ISBN 9781666924145 (cloth) | ISBN 9781666924169 (paper) | ISBN 9781666924152 (ebook)
Subjects: LCSH: Animal rights. | Animal welfare—Law and legislation.
Classification: LCC K3620 .A957 2022 (print) | LCC K3620 (ebook) | DDC 344.04/9—dc23/eng/20220919
LC record available at https://lccn.loc.gov/2022035750
LC ebook record available at https://lccn.loc.gov/2022035751

™ The paper used in this publication meets the minimum requirements of American National Standard for Information Sciences—Permanence of Paper for Printed Library Materials, ANSI/NISO Z39.48-1992.

This book is dedicated to
Kimberly Moore,
pioneer in the field of animal law

Contents

Introduction

Law, Ethics, and the Special Status of Animals

By Andrew Linzey and Clair Linzey

On one of the college buildings of Oxford University was sprayed the slogan "Animal Liberation." That there should be slogans daubed outside an Oxford college is not exceptional. For many years, a slogan demanding an end to the war in Vietnam existed outside the famed exterior red brick walls of Keble College. Quite why it was allowed to stay there for such a long time or what purpose it served long after the end of the war, we cannot tell. It was just there.

The "Animal Liberation" slogan, however, lasted only a few days and was quickly cleaned away. Neither is that exceptional. At the time, the university was involved (and to some degree still is) in a conflict over the building of a new animal lab (ludicrously called an "animal hotel" on the planning application). Emotions ran high, and demonstrations ensued (and still continue).[1]

What was exceptional about the animal liberation slogan was that it was accompanied by an anarchist slogan: a large circle with a prominent "A" figure protruding past its edges. Anarchists are usually associated with the rejection of political authority and resistance to the state. Perhaps their key motif is the rejection of coercive authority, which effectively means rejection of the military, the police force, and indeed all law, or at the least, the enforcement of it.[2]

Reflecting upon this juxtaposition, we were led to the sense of how the slogan itself represented an inconsistent, even self-contradictory message. How will the rejection of law and enforcement (coercive authority) help animals, let alone "liberate" them?

I

That some animal liberationists should exhibit such a cavalier attitude to law, even a public rejection of it, suggests a confusion of thought. Yes, of course, there are many bad laws—laws that perpetuate injustice through, for example, the maintenance of class, racial, or sexual discrimination. It would be impossible to say that all law is good or wise or always serves the interest of justice, not least of all because there are many conflicting, if not contradictory, laws around the world. What may be regarded as morally unexceptional in some countries may carry the death penalty in another.

What is more, there is a critique to be mounted against many laws throughout the world that allow the cruel and inhumane treatment of animals. It is not unreasonable that morally sensitive people should sometimes be appalled at how the law operates and the decisions made even by apparently reputable courts of law. Such moral concern, even occasional outrage, is entirely understandable, even in countries that sometimes pride themselves on highly developed systems of jurisprudence. Law sometimes gets it wrong—at least morally speaking.

To that extent, there is an argument to be made for anarchism, or at least some forms of it. We are reminded of that famous remark from anarchist writer Colin Ward, who, when asked why he didn't vote, replied that "the problem with voting is that the government always gets in." Or in the words of a well-known anarchist slogan: "If voting changed anything, they'd make it illegal."[3]

Despite its negative public image, anarchist thought is much more complex and nuanced than many suppose. Anarchist philosophy has not one tradition but many, incorporating elements of libertarianism, communitarianism, and (strange to say) socialism, though not state socialism. Some traditions emphasize individual freedom, and others, social engagement and collaboration. Ruth Kinna, in a sympathetic analysis, rejects the "distorting" and "disabling" cultural stereotypes that are applied to anarchists.[4] She argues that such stereotypes "conceal a history of critique and resistance that is empowering and normalize practices that are discriminatory and oppressive"[5] and that "being an anarchist means challenging the status quo to realize egalitarian principles and foster co-operative, non-dominating behaviours."[6]

In fairness, it also should be noted that the individualist strand within anarchism has sometimes been decidedly animal-friendly. Some anarchist diets have embraced vegetarianism and commended the humane and just treatment of animals. As Carl Tobias Frayne writes,

> individualist anarchists were promoting veganism as an autonomous diet and lifestyle long before the creation of the first vegan society in the UK in 1945.

> . . . For individualist anarchists, veganism was first and foremost a matter of personal emancipation through preserving one's health, gaining economic independence, and working towards moral regeneration. It was part and parcel of their aspiration to lead a simpler life, free from unnecessary possessions, and more in line with their instincts. Some individualists also defended the inherent value of animal life and opposed all forms of animal exploitation.[7]

Moreover, in addition to a moral critique of law, there is a necessary critique of the exercise of legal power, not least of all by despotic or tyrannical governments. There is a lamentable tendency among those who hold power to use law to buttress their rule. It is that government-exercised power when directed toward sheer self-preservation that results in the absolutism of government itself. Theologian Dietrich Bonhoeffer recognized this only too well when he rejected the deification of (in his case) the Nazi government. Despite believing in the "divine character of government"[8] and the duty of obedience to the state, he argued that "this duty of obedience is binding on him until government directly compels him to offend against the divine commandment, that is to say, until government openly denies its divine commission and thereby forfeits its claim."[9] As is well known, Bonhoeffer conspired with others in a plot to assassinate Adolf Hitler and was executed at Flossenbürg concentration camp in 1945.[10]

It should be obvious that law is not the same as morality. Law by its very nature is a piecemeal affair, pragmatic in orientation, and of course, constantly or nearly constantly subject to change as social sensibility itself changes. At its best, law can only approximate moral obligations. It is a blunt instrument in delivering justice. And it is often inconsistent, as public opinion is itself often inconsistent. Like philosophy and theology, law has traditionally been anthropocentric, hardly recognizing even the basics of decent humane treatment of animals. There has been a fundamental failure of Western jurisprudence to embrace the right treatment of animals or include them within the sphere of justice.

II

But why, we may ask, should animals, like humans, require legal protection? The only way to adequately answer this question is to explain why animals deserve special moral solicitude.

Many people still regard concern for animals as simply a matter of emotional attachment. The unfortunate term "animal lover" is often used in reference to people who campaign for the better treatment of animals. We say "unfortunate" because no matter how understandable, even desirable, it may be to love some animals, we cannot love them all, and if love were the only basis for moral solicitude, then we would have a very inconsistent and dichotomized view of animal protection. Probably only the cutest and most appealing animals would get the best treatment—as arguably is the case today.[11] Love or emotional attachment then (however desirable it may be in some circumstances) is unsatisfactory as a basis for moral solicitude. As one of us has written, "feelings are often good in themselves and much to be emulated in some regards, but the assumption that mere feeling ('love of animals') does the case for animals justice must be jettisoned absolutely."[12]

Some people think that friendship rather than emotion provides the basis for animal ethics. This point of view has a long history. It goes back as far as Aristotle and Aquinas, who both rejected the possibility of friendship with animals. Aristotle maintained that there can be no "friendship towards a horse or an ox, nor to a slave *qua* slave. For there is nothing common to the two parties; the slave is a living tool and the tool a lifeless slave."[13] Even today, the debate rages on, with some philosophers positing that friendship with animals not only is possible but should be the sole moral basis for caring for them.[14]

We shall not go into the long history of these points of view, except to say that what they offer are rather arbitrary, even capricious, boundaries of moral concern. After all, what "friendship" (humanly conceived) can we have with, say, frogs and crocodiles? Yes, we can and surely should have some benevolent relations with them, but basing moral concern on those we favor with friendship should properly strike us as arbitrary. After all, should we not grant human rights to individual humans even though many of them are not our friends, let alone the objects of our love? Emotion then, even in its friendliest form, cannot suffice as a basis for moral concern for animals.

But perhaps the most common ground for regarding animals as morally insignificant is that they constitute human property. This view stems from the idea that animals are not important in themselves, but rather that as property they belong to their "owners." As Saint Thomas Aquinas puts it, "he that kills another's ox, sins, not through killing the ox, but through injuring another man in his property."[15] Animals have no moral status as individuals but have status only insofar as human individuals so regard them. This view is almost entirely reflected in law worldwide.[16] However, the EU Treaty of Amsterdam did accept that animals should be classed as "sentient beings" rather than as agricultural products.[17] Disconcertingly however, the protocol also advised member states to respect "religious rites, cultural traditions and regional heritage," which means in practice that hunting, bullfighting, and blood fiestas—to take only three examples—are not affected.[18]

The issue then is this: Can animal advocates provide a strong rational basis for extending moral solicitude to animals, or will the bases offered fail to pass muster? One obvious basis is that animals are sentient, or at least many of them are. This point should not be minimized. There is now ample scientific evidence that mammals, reptiles, and even fish experience pain and pleasure.[19] That means they experience degrees of fear, foreboding, anticipation, terror, stress, and anxiety in similar ways to human beings. Although it may be technically impossible (in strict philosophical terms) to *prove* that these other-than-human creatures suffer, it is reasonable to suppose that these animals suffer as much or as little as do human beings. The evidence is out there and is mounting.[20]

In addition, one of us has set out the four major rational considerations that justify treating animals with special moral solicitude, and it is worth repeating them here:[21]

1. *Animals cannot give or withhold their consent.* It is commonly accepted that "informed consent" is required in advance from anyone who wishes to override the legitimate interests of another. The absence of this factor requires, at the very least, that we should exercise extraordinary care and thoughtfulness. The very (obvious) fact that animals cannot agree to the purposes to which they are put increases our responsibility.
2. *Animals cannot represent or vocalize their own interests.* Individuals who cannot adequately represent themselves have to depend on others to represent them. The plight of animals, like that of children or the elderly who suffer from dementia—precisely because they cannot articulate their needs or represent their interests—should invoke a heightened sense of obligation.
3. *Animals are morally innocent.* Because animals are not moral agents with free will, they cannot—strictly speaking—be regarded as morally responsible. That granted, it follows that they can never (unlike, arguably, adult humans) deserve suffering or be improved morally by it. Animals can never merit suffering; proper recognition of this consideration makes any infliction of suffering upon them problematic.
4. *Animals are relatively vulnerable and defenseless.* They are wholly, or almost wholly, within our power and entirely subject to our will. Except in rare circumstances, animals pose us no threat, constitute no risk to our life, and possess no means of offense or defense. Moral solicitude should properly relate to, and be commensurate with, the relative vulnerability of the subjects concerned, or with what might be termed "ontologies of vulnerability."[22]

Just one of these factors would be enough to make a rational case. Taken together, they provide a convincing rationale. The salient point is that all these considerations make the infliction of death and suffering on animals not *easier* but *harder* to justify.

These latter points reinforce and make necessary the strongest possible defense of animals through enactment of law. What else is going to offer them protection from sometimes greedy and cruel human beings? We know historically that appealing to human kindness (important though that is) is not enough to prevent the systematic abuse of animals.[23] Yes, law, as we have indicated, has major limitations. It cannot fully encompass the range of abuses to either animals or humans. As Martin Luther King Jr. observed, "it may be true that morality cannot be legislated, but behavior can be regulated. It may be true that the law cannot change the heart, but it can restrain the heartless."[24]

As with justice for humans, justice for animals requires much more than just the passing of laws. We need an array of measures and actions, including humane education, wise consumer choices, and ethical investment opportunities—to name just three. However vital law may be, it cannot itself be a substitute for humane and compassionate action. One distinguished jurist has argued that the purpose of law is the enforcement of morals, but it is difficult to see how any law or collection of laws could fully encompass all or even most moral imperatives.[25] In addition, legislation itself requires compliance, inspection, and enforcement in order to be effective. The latter is especially important since passed laws need to be policed. This was the crowning achievement of the first national Society for the Prevention of Cruelty to Animals (later to become the Royal SPCA), in that it didn't just campaign for legal change but also, when legislation was enacted, paid inspectors to enforce it. Without that key element it is difficult to believe that compliance would have become a reality, at least as soon as it did. The RSPCA was founded in 1824 after the passing of the 1822 Martin's Act, the first anti-cruelty law in the UK. But even the RSPCA saw the need for both kindness and legal protection.

Moreover, extending legislation to include animals does not mean that we should endorse all elements of the justice system, including imprisonment. Justin Marceau has recently challenged the long-held view in the animal movement that more prosecutions and longer sentences for animal offenders would advance the status of animals in law and society. Instead, he suggests that more systemic changes to the criminal justice system are required to bring about societal change for animals.[26] Imprisonment is just one way in which animal law can be enforced. We ourselves have endorsed the creation of an animal abusers registry that would prevent offenders from acquiring animals and working with them.[27] This would be a practical step toward preventing further animal abuse. It would not, of course, make offenders good people, but at least it could prevent further opportunities for them to harm.

In sum, then, law is fallible, inevitably selective, sometimes manifestly wrongheaded, and even morally regressive. But this does not give animal liberationists justification for a tout court rejection of all law and coercive authority. The reason is obvious: animals need law. Any protection they currently have is the direct result of law made and implemented by human beings. Without law, the currently horrible situation for animals would be worse than it is—even grossly so. Moreover, any hope for moral improvement in our treatment of animals must, to some degree, rely upon legal prescriptions and their adequate enforcement. That some (hopefully a tiny minority) of animal liberationists should not grasp this is testimony to their failure to grasp how moral and social change develops. Supporters of "direct action" often cite the militancy of the suffragette movement as an example of how militancy can be effective. In fact, Martin Pugh documents how militancy set back progress in securing women's emancipation. Although Christabel Pankhurst provocatively argued, "Women will never get the vote except by creating an intolerable situation for all the selfish and apathetic people who stand in their way,"[28] the truth is that as Pugh notes, militancy hardened opinions against women's suffrage.[29]

The fundamental weakness of anarchism is that it presupposes a ludicrously high doctrine of humans as morally responsive beings, which is belied by the evidence. Law is essential precisely because humans are not naturally good. It is also important to note that law reflects changing moral sensibility and public opinion and may even sometimes lead it. Even Ruth Bader Ginsburg, though generally cautious about the limit of jurists, accepted that the law can sometimes pronounce judgments that "reinforce or signal a green light for social change."[30] She cited *Brown v. Board of Education*, which declared "racial segregation in public schools offensive to the equal protection principle," as a necessary legal decision to advance racial equality since "blacks were confined by law to a separate sector [so] there was no . . . prospect of educating the white majority."[31]

III

This book cannot, of course, track all the ways in which ethics and law interweave, even when solely focused on animals. The purpose of this book is much more modest: to introduce readers to the relation between these subjects and open up some of the major issues that require thoughtful attention.

The book is divided into three parts. The first ("Historical Perspectives") examines some significant historical moments that have some bearing on contemporary issues, the second ("Ethical–Legal Issues") addresses issues concerning the moral status of animals and how these issues should be reflected in law, and the third ("Case Studies") examines in detail significant struggles regarding animal protection, or lack of it, drawn from around the world. A brief overview of the book's chapters may be helpful.

Despite some exceptions, traditional philosophy is not noted for its inclusion of animals within the spheres of law or ethics because of, inter alia, animals' supposed lack of rationality.[32] However, Oliver B. Langworthy ("John Philoponus's Presentation of Animal Rationality and the Law") shows how one neglected sixth-century author pioneered a more generous view of animals' rationality and their inclusion in a theory of natural law. Fast-forwarding, Robyn Hederman in her essay ("The Gallinger Bill, a Bill to Regulate Animal Experimentation in the District of Columbia: Forerunner of the 1966 Laboratory Animal Welfare Act") illustrates the conflict of ethical imperatives over animal experimentation in the battle to secure the first piece of major animal protection legislation in the United States. On the same topic, A. W. H. Bates ("The Charitable Status of English Antivivisection: How It Was Lost and Could Be Regained") shows how the continuing controversy about the ethics of experimentation resulted in the exclusion of antivivisection societies as charitable enterprises.

Moving from animal experimentation to the use of animals in film ("The 'Glass Walls' Theory: A History and Discussion of the Guidelines and Laws concerning Nonhuman Animals in the North American Film Industry"), Rebecca Stanton offers a critical examination of the role of the American Humane Association in policing the protection of animal actors in the film industry. Randall Lockwood ("Bringing Animal Cruelty Investigation into Mainstream Law Enforcement in the United States") shows how the historic role of the American Society for the Prevention of Cruelty to Animals (founded in 1866) in enforcing animal protection legislation has led to a partnership with the New York Police Department to provide system-wide training for the country's largest police department. The result has been a dramatic rise in the number of arrests and successful prosecutions. Lockwood suggests that this partnership brings animal protection into the mainstream and is a harbinger of future collaborations that other SPCAs should emulate.

In part 2, David Favre ("From Ethics into Law") indicates how problematic it is to embody in law even the simplest of moral imperatives. He shows how in an American context there are a whole range of agencies and constituencies that need to be persuaded at every level—that in addition to the complex business of writing legislation itself. Frances M. C. Robinson ("From Morally Relevant Features to Relevant Legal Protection: A Critique of the Legal Concept of Animals as 'Property'") provides a critique of the idea of animals as property and shows how this idea has bedeviled an understanding of the moral status of animals from earliest times. Further on, attorney Steven M. Wise ("The Nonhuman Rights Project's Struggles to Gain Legal Rights for Nonhuman Animals") narrates the various attempts to secure legal rights for animals. Angela Fernandez ("Animals as Quasi-Property/Persons") offers a middle way between the two previous chapters, suggesting that the property/persons distinction misleads animal rights advocates into thinking that fewer possibilities exist than do—specifically, that only personhood can generate the rights needed to protect nonhuman animals.

Solana Joy Phillips ("Housing Rights and Forever Homes: Reforms to Make Our Cities More Livable for Our Companion Animals and Ourselves") argues that animal companionship should be considered a human right and suggests ways in which the Universal Declaration of Human Rights should be expanded to protect companion animals, supported by government action. Alice Collinson ("A Legal Critique of the Putative Educational Value of Zoos") highlights the problem of enforcement even when it comes to basic zoo regulations in the UK. Mariah Rayfield Beck ("Our Costly Obsession: Animal Welfare, Plastic Pollution, and New Directions for Change") says that the need to protect free-living animals is still insufficiently recognized in the global crisis of plastic pollution. She maintains that a new paradigm is required involving international commitment and discrete actionable targets. Part 2 concludes with the reminder from Matthew J. Webber ("Why Anti-Cruelty Laws Are Not Enough") that changing the world for animals involves much more than simple promulgation of new law and requires education of both individuals and the public.

Part 3 consists of detailed studies of contentious and complex cases where ethics and law intersect. Lena Hehemann ("The European Union: Make Animal Law Work—The Direct Effect Principle in EU Law as an Instrument for Improving Animal Welfare") shows the potential of directives in the European Union to improve the lives of individual animals but demonstrates how a great amount of legislation in this area is only partially effective, especially in terms of enforcement. Danielle Duffield ("The United States and New Zealand: Farmed Animals and the Rule of Law") offers the merits and demerits of farmed animal welfare legislation in a comparative study of the United States and New Zealand.

Moving on, Ruaidhrí D. Wilson ("Africa: Crimes against Nonhumanity? The Case of the African Elephant") explores how legal arguments for nonhuman animal personhood have not included a sufficient consideration of free-living animal populations. Kenneth Valpey ("India: Whither Bovinity? Hindu Dharma, the Indian State, and Conflicting Moral Perspectives over Cow Protection") analyzes the conflict over cow protection in India between Muslims and Hindus. He suggests that a modern effort to apply state control and punitive power might—or might not—be reflective of the broader notion of law expressed by the Hindu notion of dharma. Finally, Maureen O'Sullivan and Stephanie O'Flynn ("United Kingdom and Ireland: Animal Law Compared") compare the changes in animal law in the UK and Ireland since the latter's independence. While welcoming more protective legislation, the authors show how such laws are rarely based on principle but based on convenience instead. A more thoroughgoing deontological approach is required to help animals obtain justice consistently.

IV

We intend this book to form part of a continuing and constructive dialogue between animal ethics and animal law.

In our work, we normally adhere to an ethical language policy concerning animals, since the language we choose to use about them helps construct our understanding of their lives. Thus, normally we would insist on "free-living" rather than "wild," "carer" or "keeper" rather than "owner," and "he" or "she" rather than "it." However, given the specific legal meanings of the language of, for example, "property" and "ownership," we have not always been able to adhere to our usual ethical language policy.

We are grateful to all the contributors for their excellent, innovative, and scholarly contributions. Special thanks to Kimberly Moore and Susan and Dan Boggio for their generous support of this project.

NOTES

1. See Andrew Linzey and Clair Linzey, "Oxford: The Home of Controversy about Animals," in *The Ethical Case against Animal Experiments*, ed. Andrew Linzey and Clair Linzey (Urbana: University of Illinois Press, 2018), 1–10.
2. For a classic statement, see Nicolas Walter, *About Anarchism* (London: Freedom Press, 1969). For excerpts of the major anarchist thinkers, see George Woodcock, *Anarchism: A History of Libertarian Ideas and Movements* (London: Penguin, 1970).
3. Reproduced from Colin Ward, "The Case against Voting," *Freedom* 48, no. 6 (June 1987), accessed April 26, 2021, https://theanarchistlibrary.org/library/colin-ward-the-case-against-voting. Ward's many books include *Anarchy in Action* (London: George Allen and Unwin, 1973) and *Anarchism: A Very Short Introduction* (Oxford: Oxford University Press, 2004).
4. Ruth Kinna, *The Government of No One: The Theory and Practice of Anarchism* (London: Pelican Books, 2019), 2.
5. Kinna, *Government of No One*, 2.
6. Kinna, *Government of No One*, 2.
7. Carl Tobias Frayne, "The Anarchist Diet: Vegetarianism and Individualist Anarchism in Early Twentieth-Century France," *Journal of Animal Ethics* 11, no. 2: 92–93.
8. Dietrich Bonhoeffer, *Ethics*, trans. Neville Horton Smith (London: Fontana, 1964), 339.

9. Bonhoeffer, *Ethics*, 342–43.

10. For the classic biography, see Eberhard Bethge, *Dietrich Bonhoeffer: A Biography* (Minneapolis: Fortress Press, 2000).

11. See Mark J. Estren, "The Neoteny Barrier: Seeking Respect for the Non-Cute," *Journal of Animal Ethics* 2, no. 1 (2012): 6–11.

12. Andrew Linzey, *Why Animal Suffering Matters: Philosophy, Theology and Practical Ethics* (New York: Oxford University Press, 2009), 3.

13. Aristotle, "Justice Requires Friendship," in *Animal Rights: A Historical Anthology*, ed. Andrew Linzey and Paul Barry Clarke (New York: Columbia University Press, 2004), 101.

14. See, for example, the exchange between Barbro Fröding and Martin Peterson and Mark J. Rowlands: Barbro Fröding and Martin Peterson, "Animal Ethics Based on Friendship," *Journal of Animal Ethics* 1, no. 1 (2011): 58–69; Mark J. Rowlands, "Friendship and Animals: A Reply to Fröding and Peterson," *Journal of Animal Ethics* 1, no. 1 (2011): 70–79; Barbro Fröding and Martin Peterson, "Animals and Friendship: A Reply to Rowlands," *Journal of Animal Ethics* 1, no. 2 (2011), 187–89; and Mark J. Rowlands, "Friendship and Animals, Again: A Response to Fröding and Peterson," *Journal of Animal Ethics* 1, no. 2 (2011): 190–94.

15. Thomas Aquinas, "No Friendship with Irrational Creatures," in *Animal Rights: A Historical Anthology*, ed. Andrew Linzey and Paul Barry Clarke (New York: Columbia University Press, 2004), 103.

16. See, for example, Gary L. Francione, *Animals, Property, and the Law*, foreword by William M. Kunstler (Philadelphia: Temple University Press, 1995).

17. European Union, Treaty of Amsterdam (Luxembourg: Office for Official Publications of the European Communities, 1997), 110, accessed April 26, 2021, https://www.europarl.europa.eu/topics/treaty/pdf/amst-en.pdf.

18. European Union, Treaty of Amsterdam, 110.

19. For a discussion of these issues, see Bernard E. Rollin, *The Unheeded Cry: Animal Consciousness, Animal Pain and Science* (Oxford: Oxford University Press, 1990). See also Tom Regan's chapter "The Complexity of Animal Awareness" in his book *The Case for Animal Rights* (London: Routledge and Kegan Paul, 1983): 34–81. For discussions of fish sentiency and cognition, see Jonathan Balcombe, *What a Fish Knows: The Inner Lives of Our Underwater Cousins* (New York: Scientific American, 2016); and Victoria Braithwaite, *Do Fish Feel Pain?* (Oxford: Oxford University Press, 2010). For a discussion of reptile sentiency, see Helen Lambert, Gemma Carder, and Neil D'Cruze, "Given the Cold Shoulder: A Review of the Scientific Literature for Evidence of Reptile Sentience," *Animals* (Basel, Switzerland) 9, no. 10 (2019): 821.

20. See, for example, Donald R. Griffin, *Animal Minds: Beyond Cognition to Consciousness* (Chicago: University of Chicago Press, 2001); Marc Bekoff, "Animal Emotions: Exploring Passionate Natures," *BioScience* 50, no. 10 (2000): 861–70; and Michel Cabanac, "Emotion and Phylogeny," *Journal of Consciousness Studies* 6, no. 6 (1999): 176–90. For a review of the scientific literature, see Helen S. Proctor, Gemma Carder, and Amelia R. Cornish, "Searching for Animal Sentience: A

Systematic Review of the Scientific Literature," *Animals* (Basel, Switzerland) 3, no. 3 (2013): 882–906.

21. The following paragraphs are adapted from Linzey, *Why Animal Suffering Matters*, 34–36.

22. We owe this phrase to Professor Dan Robinson of Georgetown University.

23. See Arthur W. Moss, *Valiant Crusade: The History of the R.S.P.C.A.* (London: Cassell, 1961).

24. Martin Luther King Jr., "Speech on Receipt of Honorary Doctorate in Civil Law," November 13, 1967, University of Newcastle upon Tyne, https://www.ncl.ac.uk/media/wwwnclacuk/congregations/files/Transcript%20of%20Dr%20Martin%20Luther%20King%20Jr%20speech%2013th%20November%201967.pdf.

25. See Patrick Devlin, *The Enforcement of Morals* (Oxford: Oxford University Press, 1965).

26. See Justin Marceau, *Beyond Cages: Animal Law and Criminal Punishment* (Cambridge: Cambridge University Press, 2019). For a review, see Angela Fernandez, "Review of *Beyond Cages: Animal Law and Criminal Punishment* by Justin Marceau," *Journal of Animal Ethics* (forthcoming).

27. See Oxford Centre for Animal Ethics, "Call for National Animal Cruelty Offenders' Register by Oxford Theologian," September 27, 2012, http://www.oxfordanimalethics.com/2012/09/call-for-national-animal-cruelty-offenders-register-by-oxford-theologian/.

28. Christabel Pankhurst in *The Suffragette*, 6 and 12, December 12, 1912, quoted in Martin Pugh, *The Pankhursts* (London: Allen Lane, 2001), 256.

29. Pugh, *The Pankhursts*, 299–300.

30. Ruth Bader Ginsburg, "The Madison Lecture: Speaking in a Judicial Voice," in *My Own Words*, by Ruth Bader Ginsburg with Mary Hartnett and Wendy W. Williams (New York: Simon & Schuster, 2016), 246.

31. Ginsburg, "The Madison Lecture," 245.

32. See the relevant extracts from St Thomas Aquinas in Andrew Linzey and Paul Barry Clarke, eds. *Animal Rights: A Historical Anthology* (New York: Columbia University Press, 2004).

PART I

Historical Perspectives

Chapter 1

John Philoponus's Presentation of Animal Rationality and the Law

By Oliver B. Langworthy

This chapter briefly explores the presentation of the status of animals and animal rationality in the fifth book of John Philoponus's *De opificio mundi*, or *On the Creation of the World* (*Opif*), a sixth-century commentary on Genesis.[1] *Opif* was written toward the end of a life spanning AD 470–590 and was an attempt to interpret the creation narratives of Genesis in a rigorous and, in the context of the time, scientific way. Where there is Christian thought that reflects theologically on the status of animals in late antiquity, it is in the context of commentary on the book of Genesis.[2] The creation narratives there provide a rich seam of thought on the relationship between humans and animals.[3] Crucially, the book of Genesis is one of the five books that form the Torah—the Hebrew word for law. The creation narratives in Genesis, understood by Philoponus to have been composed by Moses, do not themselves offer straightforward commandments or laws. The creation narratives are just that—narratives. They were interrogated by authors who did so on the understanding that they contained revealed truths about not just God's relationship to the world, but how God intended for humanity to relate to the world. In presenting his own interpretation of this, Philoponus presents a particularly striking image of how humans relate to animals, with animals being part of the same order of rationality as humans.

While there has been greater attention given to Philoponus thanks in large part to the increasing number of translations of his work, much of this attention, along with the translations themselves, has been concerned with his commentary and argument on Aristotle and with Philoponus's place in the history of science.[4] Given the extent to which his corpus is composed of such works and the importance of Philoponus's own reception, such an emphasis is not inappropriate. However, the only significant and recent extended interactions specifically with *Opif* come from Fladerer and Scholten, though mention should also be made of an unpublished thesis from Elweskiöld.[5] Substantial treatments in broader works also appear in Sorabji and Chadwick, and there are a number of articles and chapters of note, as well as much older works.[6] Among these, Fladerer is the only one to offer any sustained analysis of the status of animals in a monograph-length publication.[7] However, mention also must be made of the recent chapter by Pascal Mueller-Jourdan, "La question d l'âme des animaux dans le *De Opificio Mundi* de Jean Philopon (VI^e^s.): Entre revelation biblique et psychologie aristotélicienne" ("The question of the souls of animals in the *De Opificio Mundi* of John Philoponus: Between biblical revelation and Aristotelean psychology").[8] This treatment of the souls of animals (and of the animal part of humans) in *Opif* is wide-ranging and instructive, as is Fladerer's chapter on the zoological content of *Opif* V. It should be apparent at this point that much of the scholarship on Philoponus's work on animals is in non-English texts. I hope that this present study will go some way toward encouraging greater awareness not just of Philoponus but of the scholars who have written on his particular take on the status of animals in French and German.

JOHN PHILOPONUS'S *ON THE CREATION OF THE WORLD*

In *Opif* V, concerned largely with the sixth day of creation, there is an interaction of several different presentations of the proper relation of humans to animals. While some areas bear a direct resemblance to areas of Basil's *Hexaemeron*, a seminal Christian commentary on the days of creation by the fourth-century Cappadocian Basil of Caesarea, others draw on a more narrative tone, and others show extended reflections on the capacities of animals not unlike Plutarch's *On the Intelligence of Animals*. Two examples are of particular interest: the discussion of dogs and the discussion of horses and elephants. Fladerer's analysis of *Opif* V pays particular attention to the change in structure from a rigorous and ostensibly scientific consideration of Genesis to a narrative tone that strongly resembles the short stories of Herodotus when Philoponus discusses dogs.[9] Fladerer goes on to contend that this is a literary presentation of, as Philoponus understood it, factual events. Philoponus's stories of faithful dogs assisting their masters to extremes and abiding with them have parallels in many Christian commentaries on Genesis, as well as in Plutarch, Porphyry, and other ostensibly animal-friendly pagan texts. While Philoponus does not reach the conclusions of Plutarch or Porphyry, Fladerer notes that the depictions offered by Philoponus allow him to proffer dogs as the "missing link mit dem Tierreich verbindet" (missing link with the animal kingdom).[10]

This should not be over-read. Philoponus still argued that animals were not rational in the way that humans were rational. They did not possess immortal souls, and they faded with their bodies. However, Philoponus was concerned with demonstrating that the world was rational and that these animals had a place in it on their own basis. His concern was not to preach of the lessons humans should not or could derive from animals but animals' capacities as subjects in themselves. Even more instructive in this regard is an example brought up by Mueller-Jourdan: Philoponus discusses how humans are capable of teaching horses and elephants to engage in warfare.[11] While this is not an immediately animal-friendly concept, Philoponus mentions how this brings the animals closer to rationality. Other Christian authors discuss, as does Philoponus, the utility of certain animals to humans or the extensive sensory capacities of some animals, and yet others identify what virtues animals can illustrate for humans, but Philoponus specifically calls up the capacity of animals to participate in a particularly human pursuit and to learn to be skilled in it. None of this is to suggest that Philoponus was entirely out of step with his Christian near-contemporaries. He did not regard animals as being endowed with reason, which neither Fladerer nor Mueller-Jordan claims.[12] Nevertheless, in the historicization of entertainment literature identified by Fladerer discussing the loyalty and love of dogs and the ability of animals and horses to learn to participate in warfare as identified by Mueller-Jordan, Philoponus is concerned with identifying the capacity to approach reason in animals of themselves, and not solely as objects of human need or as exemplars, as in similar works by writers such as Basil.

Although Basil and Philoponus doubtless shared a similar investment in the idea of animal behavior pointing toward the disposition of God to the economy, assuming this as his principal motivation obscures some of Philoponus's uniqueness with respect to his representation of higher-order nonhuman animals.[13] Basil firmly delineated the boundaries of nonhuman animal agency in Homilies VII–IX of his *Hexaemeron*. Basil proposes that crows behave in a way that appears consistent with the laws of hospitality, but he turns this around into an indictment of humans, who can, implicitly, understand such laws while failing to follow them. Storks, whose escort by crows merits the comparison to hospitality, are said by Basil to be "very near intelligent reason" in their behavior and support of their elders, but are principally an example of why humans should not turn to evil as a result of poverty and serve as an indictment or spur to human ethical behavior.[14] The agency, or lack thereof, of animals is secondary to how it reflects on human experience of the economy. Basil argues as follows in Homily VII concerning crabs:

> Now see what tricks, what cunning, are to be found in a weak animal, and learn not to imitate wicked doers. . . . Such is the malice of these animals, deprived as they are of reason and of speech. But I would that you should at once rival the crab in cunning and industry, and abstain from harming your neighbour; this animal is the image of him who craftily approaches his brother, takes advantage of his neighbour's misfortunes, and finds his delight in other men's troubles. O copy not the damned! Content yourself with your own lot. Poverty, with what is necessary, is of more value in the eyes of the wise than all pleasures.[15]

The transition from describing natural behaviors in animals to arguing that his hearers should not copy the "damned"—and it is unlikely that Basil had in mind that crabs were damned after complimenting their industry—makes clear that his purpose in discussing animals is not the status of the animals themselves. Even where Basil pushes into areas that are proximate to what Philoponus suggests of dogs, Basil posits that dogs do not possess reason but that "instinct has the power of reason" in them. Of the love of animals, Basil writes, "If the lioness loves her cubs, . . . what shall man say who is unfaithful to the precept and violates nature herself; or the son who insults the old age of his father; or the father whose second marriage has made him forget his first children?"[16] Philoponus suggests that terrestrial mammals possess souls limited to their bodies, but that they can approach close to rationality and are guided by rational forces, are able to experience and reciprocate love, and are moreover able to volitionally manifest behavior that is virtuous. Some of this is similar to what is found in Basil, being a reflection on widespread concepts traceable to Aristotle, but there is also amplification here.

While Philoponus's familiarity with Basil's own treatments of animals contributed much to what he wrote in *Opif*, the representation of animals in *Opif* V seeks to discuss such animals in themselves, and not as a reflection of or spur to human ethical behavior. Instead, it presents animals as existing in a hierarchy of rationality that, while excluding even what Philoponus regards as the highest-order animals from equality with human reason or possession of immortal souls, locates them as proximate to it in their own right. *Opif*'s dependence on Basil's *Hexaemeron* is undeniable, but they are not identical in their assumptions about animals. Fladerer notes the differences between them, and while there is no reason to dispute his recognition of a motivation from Philoponus similar to Basil's in showing the validity of Moses's teaching, the degree to which this impacts on Philoponus's presentation of animal agency as concerning animals in themselves, rather than being something that exists for humans, should not be understated.[17] While Basil as a source of Philoponus's thought is instructive, the opponent Philoponus might have had in mind is yet more so.

Although the interpretation is not univocal, scholarship broadly contends that *Opif* was at least in part a response to flat-earth Christian cosmology espoused by Cosmas Indicopleustes, a sailor and Egyptian monk from Alexandria who lived in the sixth century.[18] The amplification of animal rationality, and a concurrent increase in the status of animals such as dogs, is consistent with Scholten's argument that Philoponus depended on Basil less out of an intellectual debt than out of a desire to draw on a source that was consistent with the tradition of an opponent.[19] While an encounter between Cosmas and Philoponus is not verifiable, it is certainly the case that Cosmas's principal concern in his *Topographia Christiana* was to litigate the shape of the world and argue for a flat earth. His interest in nonhuman animals in *Topographia Christiana* XI, or those whom he had encountered, is limited to whether he saw them himself, whether he had eaten them, and how they were killed. Cosmas's own summation of the fifth and sixth days of creation do not show even this level of interest in the status of animals. Elweskiöld, though not concerned with animals as such, delivers a cutting assessment of Cosmas's account of the fifth day of creation: "In *Christian Topography* III.34 [Cosmas] simply paraphrases the words of Genesis and says that God ordered different living animals to be produced from the waters according to their species, sea-monsters and other water animals, and at the same time also all the birds that fly in the air. That is all."[20] Even where Cosmas does comment directly on terrestrial animals, his reasoning is consistent with that of Basil:

> Then the clean quadrupeds minister to his pleasure and supply him with clothing, the cattle labour for him and afford him leisure, the wild beasts contribute the delight and terror of the chase, and so also do the reptiles; while all things serve for the exercise of his rational powers and supplying what is useful for man, who is the bond uniting all the creation in friendship—who walks upon the earth, and yet flies on the wings of thought and surveys the universe.[21]

Cosmas's reflections on animals are narrow in their concerns, perhaps even more so than those of Basil. While Philoponus certainly has a sense of animals as beneficial for humankind, he also reflects at length on their capacities in their own right. His consideration of the capacity of animals to learn, even if what they learn from humanity is not particularly good or desirable in itself, acknowledges animal capacity. Cosmas is concerned with animals insofar as they contribute to humanity. If Philoponus were seeking to counter Cosmas with his own dedicated commentary on Genesis, a digression on animals would be a sound place at which to do so. It was an area in which Cosmas was not particularly entrenched and which had been made fertile by Basil's work, and thus it was a relatively safe area for Philoponus to exceed his sources and his opponents in demonstrating the consistency of his interpretation of the narratives in Genesis with scientific principles as he understood them, presenting an accounting of the laws of nature in God's creation.

LAW AND THE LAW

While a complete analysis is not possible in a communication of this scope, there is a further point to consider in relation to Philoponus's interpretation of Genesis. Philoponus lived in a society shaped by the Theodosian Code and that was contemporary with the Code of Justinian, which built on the Theodosian Code and expanded existing prohibitions on animal sacrifice.[22] Cultural movements away from ritual food law, animal sacrifice, and the divinatory or other ritual killing of animals and the aggregation of sacrificial language around the figure of Christ were driven by primary theological investments, with any benefit to animals themselves being merely a consequence rather than an intended outcome, even when such benefits were reflected in bodies of civil law.

The codification of Roman law by the emperors Theodosius and Valentinian III in AD 429, and its publication in AD 438, does not seem immediately relevant to a text about the Hebrew Bible. However, the code is not a simple text of law as a code might be recognized today:

> The Code's aims were practical, political, and cultural. Reading between the lines, we can see that different supporters of the project had different aims in view, but on the whole the practical predominated. . . . One has to add "by the standards of the time," because the texts of the Code are not easy to read either as laws or as literary exercises. They often vex the reader by their uneasy mixture of law, rhetoric, and propaganda.[23]

Inasmuch as it was an attempt to create a legal text, it was also a cultural exercise. For the purposes of this study, it is especially notable that this codification of law affirmed Christianity as the religion of the empire and effectively banned traditional Greek and Roman religious—broadly, pagan—sacrificial practices in the empire. The success of Christians in prohibiting animal sacrifice was driven not by any investment in animals' welfare, but by a desire to criminalize traditional Greek and Roman religious practice:

> No person shall pollute himself with sacrificial animals, no person shall slaughter an innocent victim; no person shall approach shrines, shall wander through the temples, or revere the images formed by mortal labor, lest he become guilty by divine and human laws. Judges also shall be bound by the general rule that if any of them should be devoted to profane rites and enter a temple for the

> purpose of worship anywhere . . . he shall be immediately compelled to pay fifteen pounds of gold.[24]

One of the few examples of genuine protection of animals for their own sake is to be found in a section of the code from Constantine, who first legalized Christianity in the Roman empire:

> Since very many persons by means of knotty and very stout clubs force the public post animals, at the very beginning of their course, to use up whatever strength they have it is Our pleasure that no person at all shall use a club in driving, but shall employ either a switch or at most a whip in the tip of which a short prick has been inserted, by which the lazy limbs of animals may be gently tickled into action, but not force the animals to exert themselves beyond their strength.[25]

While the greatest potential benefit to animal welfare was incidental, being driven by external motivations, the code did have some elements that were genuinely aimed toward welfare. The world of the late-antiquity empire was changing, even minimally, toward one that prevented the sacrifice of animals and provided them some minor protection. That there should be those in Christian communities who reflected greater interest in animals in themselves should come as no surprise.

CONCLUSIONS

Despite being anathematized in the late seventh century, Philoponus went on to have a substantial influence on later natural scientific inquiry. Although few of Philoponus's manuscripts survived in Latin or their original Greek, his works were extensively preserved in Arabic. *Opif* itself was recovered into Greek in the 1630s and appears to have been influential on Galileo.[26] The absence of Philoponus from the study of animal ethics in English-language scholarship is therefore a notable gap, given that his works—more so than other more obscure and less intellectual, influential, or widely circulated texts—were influential on the intellectual culture of western Europe. Philoponus's desire to demonstrate the consistency of the natural philosophical principles of his time with the creation narratives of Genesis and his argument that animals were part of a hierarchy of reasonable beings, with animals such as dogs existing as what Fladerer called a missing link between the volitional virtue of humans and the animal world, plus his consideration of the capacity of horses and elephants to learn and approach closer to reason, presented an alternative model for how humans relate to animals. Philoponus has a far higher assessment of the capacities of animals, and especially of those capacities in animals for their own sake. When contrasted against the work of Basil's *Hexaemeron* or with Cosmas's *Topographia Christiana*, Philoponus's work shows a far stronger investment in the importance of animals as ethical subjects in their own right rather than solely as tutelary models for human behavior. While this study lacks the scope for a complete consideration of Philoponus's influences and interactions, his awareness of pagan authors who produced far more animal-friendly discourses, such as Porphyry, and the existence of civil law providing minor protections for animals even as animal sacrifice was increasingly illegalized suggest an intriguing set of possible trajectories for future research into the intersection of theology and law concerning animal ethics.

REFERENCES

Elweskiöld, Birgitta. "John Philoponus against Cosmas Indicopleustes." PhD diss., Lund University, 2005.

Fladerer, Ludwig. *Johannes Philoponos "De opificio mundi": Spätantikes Sprachdenken und christliche Exegese*. Leipzig: Teubner, 1999.

Gilhus, Ingvild. "Animals in Late Antique and Early Christianity." In *The Oxford Handbook of Animals in Classical Thought and Life*, edited by Gordon Campbell, 355–365. Oxford: Oxford University Press, 2014.

Honoré, Tony. *Law in the Crisis of Empire 379–455 AD: The Theodosian Dynasty and Its Quaestors*. Oxford: Oxford University Press, 1995.

Jackson, Blomfield, trans. *Nicene and Post-Nicene Fathers*. Vol. 8. Edinburgh: T&T Clark, 1895.

McCrindle, J., trans. *The Christian Topography of Cosmas, an Egyptian Monk*. London: Hakluyt Society, 1897.

Mueller-Jourdan, Pascal. "La question de l'âme des animaux dans le *De Opificio Mundi* de Jean Philopon (VI[e]s.): Entre revelation biblique et psychologie aristotélicienne." In *La restauration de la creation: Quelle place pour les animaux?*, edited by Michele Cutino, Isabel Iribarren, and Françoise Vinel, 135–56. Leiden: Brill, 2017.

Pharr, Clyde. *The Theodosian Code and Novels of the Sirmondian Constitutions*. Princeton, NJ: Princeton University Press, 1953.

Reichardt, Gualterus, trans. *Joannis Philiponi De opificio mundi libri VII*. Leipzig: Teubner, 1897.

Scholten, Clemens. *Antike Naturphilosophie und christliche Kosmologie in der Schrift "De opificio mundi" des Johannes Philoponos*. Berlin: De Gruyter, 1996.

———. "Weshalb wird die Schöpfungsgeschichte zum naturwissenschaftlichen Bericht." *Theologische Quartalschrift* 177, no. 1 (1997): 10–15.

Sorabji, Richard, ed. *Philoponus and the Rejection of Aristotelian Science*. London: Institute of Classical Studies, 2010.

Wolff, Michael. "Philoponus and the Rise of Pre-Classical Dynamics." In *Philoponus and the Rejection of Aristotelian Silence*, edited by Richard Sorabji, 125–60. London: Institute of Classical Studies, 2010.

NOTES

1. In the interest of brevity, I will refer to nonhumans animals as animals except where this could be ambiguous.

2. Ingvild Gilhus, "Animals in Late Antique and Early Christianity," in *The Oxford Handbook of Animals in Classical Thought and Life*, ed. Gordon Campbell (Oxford: Oxford University Press, 2014), 356.

3. Gilhus, "Animals in Late Antiquity," 355.

4. Richard Sorabji, *Philoponus and the Rejection of Aristotelian Science* (London: Institute of Classical Studies, 2010), preface.

5. Ludwig Fladerer, *Johannes Philoponos "De opificio mundi": Spätantikes Sprachdenken und christliche Exegese* (Leipzig: Teubner, 1999); Clemens Scholten, *Antike Naturphilosophie und christliche Kosmologie in der Schrift "De opificio mundi" des Johannes Philoponos* (Berlin: De Gruyter, 1996).

6. Birgitte Elweskiöld, "John Philoponus against Cosmas Indicopleustes" (PhD diss., Lund University, 2005). Elweskiöld also has an excellent literature review covering those smaller and older works I have omitted here. See Elweskiöld, "Philoponus," 9–10, which includes details for two sources for the Greek text of *Opif* in Reichardt and Scholten. Like Elweskiöld I have depended on Reichardt.

7. Fladerer, *Philoponos*, 355–62.

8. Pascal Mueller-Jourdan, "La question de l'âme des animaux dans le *De Opificio Mundi* de Jean Philopon (VI[e]s.): Entre revelation biblique et psychologie aristotélicienne," in *La restauration de la creation: Quelle place pour les animaux?*, ed. Michele Cutino et al. (Leiden: Brill, 2017), 135.

9. *Opif* V.1, in *Joannis Philiponi De opificio mundi libri VII*, trans. Gualterus Reichardt (Leipzig: Teubner, 1897), 209.

10. Fladerer, *Philoponos*, 358.

11. *Opif* V.2, 209.

12. Fladerer, *Philoponus*, 358; Mueller-Jourdan, "Des animaux," 150.

13. *Opif* I.1 contains numerous direct references, and others suggesting direct access to Basil's *Hexaemeron* appear throughout the work.

14. *Hexaemeron* VIII.5, in *Nicene and Post-Nicene Fathers*, vol. 8, trans. Blomfield Jackson (Edinburgh: T&T Clark, 1895), 98.

15. *Hexaemeron* VII.3, in Jackson, *Nicene and Post-Nicene*, 91.

16. *Hexaemeron* IX.4, in Jackson, *Nicene and Post-Nicene*, 104.

17. Fladerer, *Philoponos*, 362.

18. A detailed comparison of these two figures is found in Elweskiöld, who demurs from locating either Philoponus or Cosmas in any party and instead compares them individually. See Elweskiöld, "Philoponus," 11. Scholten, to whom Elweskiöld has an acknowledged debt, is also invaluable in his comparison of the two. In addition to

the Scholten monograph on Philoponus noted previously, see also Clemens Scholten, "Weshalb wird die Schöpfungsgeschichte zum naturwissenschaftlichen Bericht," *Theologische Quartalschrift* 177, no. 1 (1997): 10–15.

19. Scholten, "Naturwissenschaftlichen," 13.

20. Elweskiöld, *Philoponus*, 38.

21. *Topographia Christiana* 3, in *The Christian Topography of Cosmas, an Egyptian Monk*, trans. J. McCrindle (London: Hakluyt Society, 1897), 105.

22. The Code of Justinian 1.11 is concerned solely with the prohibition of sacrifice and pagan temples.

23. Tony Honoré, *Law in the Crisis of Empire 379–455 AD: The Theodosian Dynasty and Its Quaestors* (Oxford: Oxford University Press), 127.

24. [Emperors Gratian, Valentinians, and Theodosius Augustus to Albinus, Praetorian Prefect], 16.10.10 (AD 391), in *The Theodosian Code and Novels of the Sirmondian Constitutions*, trans. Clyde Pharr (Princeton, NJ: Princeton University Press, 1953), 473.

25. [Emperor Constantine Augustus] to Titianus, 8.5.2 (AD 316), in Pharr, *The Theodosian Code*, 195.

26. Wolff in particular highlights the complex linguistic and scholarly history of this reception. See Michael Wolff, "Philoponus and the Rise of Pre-Classical Dynamics," in *Philoponus and the Rejection of Aristotelian Silence*, ed. Richard Sorabji (London: Institute of Classical Studies, 2010), 128.

Chapter 2

The Gallinger Bill, a Bill to Regulate Animal Experimentation in the District of Columbia

Forerunner of the 1966 Laboratory Animal Welfare Act

By Robyn Hederman

In 1899 Senator Jacob Gallinger of New Hampshire introduced Senate Bill 34 regulating animal research in the District of Columbia. The Gallinger Bill ignited a battle between the medical community and opponents of vivisection. Dr. Albert T. Leffingwell, a proponent of the bill, emphasized that he was not an antivivisectionist, but instead, wished to curb animal cruelty in research. Yet American researchers resisted any efforts to impede their use of animals. Dr. William Welch of Johns Hopkins University feared the bill would obstruct medical research in the US capital and would "encourage similar restrictive laws in the states."[1]

In *Subjected to Science*, historian Susan Lederer claims that vivisection became "a potent emblem of the reforms in medical therapeutics and medical education" occurring at the end of the nineteenth century.[2] As a result, physicians and scientists linked their campaign against the antivivisectionists with their desire to attain prestige and authority in the eyes of the American public.[3] The Gallinger Bill symbolized this battle.

EARLY AMERICAN ANTIVIVISECTIONISTS

Henry Bergh's Fight against Animal Experimentation

Between 1896 and 1900, animal advocates made three attempts to pass federal legislation regulating vivisection in the District of Columbia. Senator James McMillan of Michigan introduced "A Bill for the Further Prevention of Cruelty to Animals in the District of Columbia" (Senate Bill 1552) in 1896. The legislation came before the Committee on the District of Columbia, chaired by Senator Jacob Gallinger, a homeopathic physician. Surprised by the bill, Surgeon General George M. Sternberg sought opponents to testify before the committee.

Yet this was not the first attempt by antivivisectionists to introduce legislation in the United States. When Henry Bergh established the American Society for the Prevention of Cruelty to Animals in 1866, vivisection was not widespread in the United States. Nevertheless, when Bergh spoke at New York's Clinton Hall the same year, he declared, "Of all the horrible pangs inflicted on animal creation . . . those done in the name of anatomical science are at once the most fearful and revolting, and the most plausibly defended."[4] Bergh recruited undercover agents to work in New York's largest hospitals. Equipped with "spectacles and medical books,"[5] the agents set out to expose the "remorseless inquisitors."[6]

In 1867 Bergh sought to revise New York's 1866 animal cruelty statute by attaching a clause abolishing vivisection in the state. John C. Dalton, professor of physiology at the College of Physicians and Surgeons, opposed Bergh's bill. Dalton had performed one of the first teaching demonstrations in the United States in 1854—performing a gastric fistula experiment on a dog.[7] In *The Vivisection Question*, Leffingwell stated that Dalton also discussed his practice of exposing and irritating the sensory nerves in animals, which he claimed "always causes intense pain . . . even though the animal be nearly unconscious from the influence of ether."[8] Although this procedure was first conducted by the French vivisector François Magendie, it was often repeated. Anesthesia was not always used.[9]

Dalton accused Bergh of making "extravagant misrepresentations" to the members of the New York Assembly. In a *New York Times* editorial, Bergh asked legislators if they would "close their ears to the agonizing groans of those creatures to which they owe so much of their happiness."[10] Bergh's amendment, however, was defeated. Section 10 of the 1867 anti-cruelty law provided the first exclusion for "properly conducted scientific experiments or investigations."[11] Bergh always blamed Dalton for his legislative failure.

Despite the researcher's success, the New York State Medical Society established the Committee on Experimental Medicine in 1880—its first committee to defend animal experimentation—to thwart any further efforts by Bergh to ban animal experimentation.[12] Until his death in 1888, Bergh fought to abolish vivisection in New York. Bergh hung a lithograph of the French vivisector Francois Magendie (1783–1855) in his office, writing underneath "A French physiologist, otherwise known as the 'Prince of Torturers,' who dissected, alive, 40,000 dumb animals, and ere he died confessed that vivisection was a failure."[13]

THE AMERICAN MEDICAL PROFESSION

The medical historian Ronald L. Numbers described the mid-nineteenth-century medical profession as being in "shambles," stating that it had "degenerated into little more than a trade, open to all who wished to try their hands at healing."[14] Medical schools were not accredited by the states, and few laws regulated the practice of medicine.[15] The length and quality of American medical schools, considered inferior to European schools, "virtually guaranteed mediocrity."[16] American physicians could not claim independence from European science until US medical schools improved and provided their professors with opportunities to conduct research. In 1846 the New York State Medical Society passed a resolution calling for delegates to form a national organization.[17] Dr. Nathan Smith Davis formed the American Medical Association in 1847—dedicated to raising the standard of nineteenth-century medical education and practice.[18]

States began to establish state exams and licensing boards during the last three decades of the nineteenth century. The more prestigious medical schools—for example, Johns Hopkins and Harvard—improved their curriculum and established stringent admission requirements; however, most medical schools provided inadequate education. The AMA created the Council on Medical Education in 1904, taking a more active role in medical training.[19] Yet historians claim that American physicians were less interested in science than in clinical practice, valuing "wealth over scholarly reputation." As a result, this "American obsession" with success "deterred even scientifically inclined physicians from engaging in research."[20]

Nevertheless, by the end of the century, experimental science played a pivotal role in the practice of medicine.[21] In the 1870s Henry P. Bowditch at Harvard and Henry Newell Martin at Johns Hopkins opened small physiological labs where they performed animal experiments and classroom demonstrations.[22] By the 1890s medical schools incorporated classroom courses with animal research.[23] Johns Hopkins School of Medicine, opened in 1893, "combined laboratory science with bedside training."[24] Bacteriology and immunology became significant sources of inquiry. After another outbreak of cholera, the New York City Board of Health opened the first municipal bacteriology laboratory in 1892.[25] In *Reckoning with the Beast*, historian James Turner claims that the United States became a "major center of animal experimentation" after 1890.[26]

MEDICAL CRITICISM OF ANIMAL EXPERIMENTATION

Yet not all physicians championed scientific medicine. In his essay "Divided We Stand," Gerald L. Geison looks at the division between American doctors and research physiologists in the late nineteenth century.[27] As late as the 1880s, clinicians doubted the "pragmatic value" of experimental medicine. Prominent medical schools—for example, Harvard Medical School and Columbia University—established laboratory physiology courses; however, until the turn of the century, these courses were not mandated. Geison concludes that because American medical schools did not require courses in laboratory physiology, these schools shared the belief that "practicing doctors had little or no need of it."[28]

Some clinical physicians claimed that laboratory training might "actually *damage* the practitioner's ability to treat patients effectively."[29] Daniel Webster Cathell, the author of *The Physician Himself*, warned general practitioners that if they accepted "new and unsettled theories" too quickly,[30] their "usefulness as a physician will almost surely diminish."[31] The new sciences, including bacteriology, for example, provided tools to practicing physicians. Yet historian Russel C. Maulitz asserts that clinicians feared that incorporating science into medicine "might remove them from the bedside to the bench"—causing them to pay less attention to their patients.[32]

Theophilus Parvin, the author of *The Science and Art of Obstetrics*, addressed the Academy of Medicine in 1891, concluding that the usefulness of vivisection "in relation to surgery and therapeutics has been exaggerated."[33] Parvin asserted that physicians should be "the chief apostles in preventing cruelty and proclaiming kindness to animals," or "the power of their apostleship" will be weakened by "needless, useless, and painful vivisections."[34] For these reasons, Parvin proposed that the law should restrict vivisection, and these restrictions "ought to forbid all experiments upon animals made without worthy objects; and in every case, so far as possible, the animal during and subsequent to the operation must be preserved from pain."[35]

Elizabeth Blackwell, the first woman to receive a medical degree in the United States, also opposed vivisection. Blackwell believed in a holistic approach to medicine, stating that the "ministrations to the body and soul cannot be separated by a sharply-defined line," and the "arbitrary distinction between the physician of the body and the physician of the soul . . . tends to disappear as science advances."[36] She asserted that "every branch of medicine involves moral consideration, both as regards to the practitioner and the patient."[37] In her article "Feminism, Professionalism, and Germs," historian Regina M. Morantz claims Blackwell distrusted bacteriology and experimental science because its "specific etiology" eroded her sense that right and wrong must govern the practice of medicine and medical research.[38]

Blackwell warned of the "moral danger" of training students to practice vivisection, this danger of "hardening their nature and injuring their future usefulness as good physicians."[39] She described vivisection as "an exercise of curiosity which inevitably tends to blunt the moral sense and injure that intelligent sympathy with suffering"—that is, harm fundamental qualities in a good physician.[40] This method of research, Blackwell claimed, "ignores the spiritual essence of Life and hopes to surprise its secrets by ruthless prying into the physical structure of the lower animals." Blackwell emphasized that the "basis of moral responsibility extends in kind, if not in degree, to all life" and that "we have no right, for any purpose whatever, to torture a living creature to death."[41]

Blackwell asked women physicians to discourage the practice of vivisection. In 1891 she contacted the Alumnae Association of the Women's Medical College of the New York Infirmary—which she had established in 1869—to oppose the endowment of a new experimental laboratory. Blackwell counseled women physicians that "it is not blind imitation of men, nor thoughtless acceptance of whatever may be taught by them that is required."[42] She urged "the necessity of cherishing a mild skepticism respecting the dicta of so-called medical science," stating that "the worship of the intellect, or so-called knowledge, as an end in itself, entirely regardless of the character of the means by which we seek to gain it, is the most dangerous error that science can make."[43]

Dr. Albert Leffingwell attempted to reform the worst abuses of vivisection. Leffingwell opposed "the introduction into America of the foreign ideal of scientific research; the widening opportunity for abuse."[44] In *An Ethical Problem*, Leffingwell explained that he was drawn to the issue after reading a newspaper account of Henry Bergh's attempt to pass legislation abolishing "all experiments upon living animals." Leffingwell believed that Bergh might have had greater success if he had asked for less: "That certain vivisections were atrocious was undoubtedly true; but, on the other hand, there were some experiments that were absolutely painless. Would it not be wiser to make some distinctions?"[45] Leffingwell claimed he was not against "all scientific investigation upon living creatures" but believed that a "distinct line" could be drawn, "separating what may be permitted from that which ought to be condemned."[46]

Leffingwell asserted that animal research could not be banned "until an age dawns when the sacrifice of animal life for food or raiment shall be equally abhorrent to civilization."[47] Yet he stressed that "absolute liberty in matters of painful experiments" produced "admitted abuses by physiologists of Germany, France and Italy" and led to repetition "of Magendie's extreme cruelties" before American students—demonstrations "which have been condemned by every leading English physiologist."[48]

The American Humane Society adopted Leffingwell's regulatory position and placed the issue onto its agenda in 1892. The society issued a resolution requesting states to prohibit all painful procedures conducted merely for the demonstration of established knowledge.[49] The historian Bernard Unti describes this resolution as "a change in strategy and ideology that would mark the post-Berghian challenges to vivisection."[50] Leffingwell insisted that vivisection in schools resulted in the "brutalization of childhood by including familiarity with the sacrifice of life."[51] He claimed that "in view of the dangerous impulses not infrequently awakened by the sight of bloodshed, or pain intentionally inflicted," vivisection should "be entirely forbidden before classes of students in our schools."[52] Leffingwell campaigned for the passage of the Gallinger Bill in the District of Columbia. According to Unti, "only by emulating the British example, he argued, could America avoid the well-chronicled cruelties of continental laboratories."[53]

FEDERAL LEGISLATION

The District of Columbia was considered the national center of scientific research and the location of numerous facilities conducting experimentation on animals—for example, the Bureau of Animal Industry and the US Hygienic Laboratory. Senate Bill 1552 (The "MacMillan" bill), restricting animal experimentation in the District of Columbia, was introduced in 1896. William Welch warned Daniel Coit Gilman, the president of Johns Hopkins University, that the antivivisectionist movement was "thoroughly organized and powerful," and "a petition signed by judges of the Supreme Court, bishops, distinguished clergyman and lawyers, numerous homeopathic physicians and other citizens urging the adoption of this bill by Congress must be met with vigorous action."[54] Yet the Committee on National Legislation, the national lobby group of the AMA, did not become a standing committee of the AMA until 1900.[55] As late as 1901, the president of the AMA acknowledged that the organization "exerted relatively little influence on legislation, either state or federal."[56]

Senate Bill 1552 required researchers to be licensed by the Commissioners of the District of Columbia, and it limited the types of facilities where experiments could be conducted. The bill prohibited all painful experiments on living animals in public schools and at public exhibitions. Senate Bill 1552 restricted animal experiments to those procedures constituting a discovery or to those "useful for saving or prolonging life or alleviating suffering."[57] The legislation mandated anesthesia to be used during experiments. If the animal was likely to experience pain after the procedure, the legislation required that the animal be humanely killed before recovery. Finally, certain animals—the cat, dog, horse, ass, and mule—"were excluded from use unless the experimenter could certify that no other animal would do."[58]

The Senate Committee on the District of Columbia conducted a hearing on the bill and unanimously recommended it to be heard by the full Senate. In a pamphlet titled *Defense of Vivisection*, the American Medical Association circulated a statement from the National Academy of Sciences arguing the necessity of animal experimentation.[59] As previously noted, the AMA had not yet established a standing committee on national legislation; thus, William Welch, along with William Keen, the president of the AMA, volunteered to help defeat the bill.[60] Welch and William Osler from Johns Hopkins convinced Senator Arthur Pugh Gorman, with "the help of Welch's Yale classmate, Senator Wolcott of Colorado, to defer the bill."[61]

The legislation was reintroduced in 1898 (Senate Bill 1063) and passed favorably out of committee—but stalled when it reached the full Senate because Congress was focused on the Spanish-American War.[62] According to Simon and James Flexner in *William Henry Welch and the Heroic Age of American Medicine*, the bill was allowed "to drift along," and Welch dropped his other activities and "changed himself into a political lobbyist."[63] Welch, the president of the American Congress of Physicians and Surgeons, worked to prevent the passage of this "misleading" legislation.[64] He mobilized physicians and their patients to overwhelm the Senate with protests, focusing on the "family doctors and personal friends of individual Senators."[65] As a result, Welch provided Senator Gorman with a list of twenty senators opposed to the bill.

William Keen spoke and wrote extensively on the benefits of vivisection, claiming that antivivisectionists fostered "a spirit of cruelty to human beings" and were the "enemies of animals and the whole human race."[66] Keen asserted that this question "aroused and fostered" "the most violent and vindictive passions . . . especially among women—the very flower of our modern civilization."[67] In his 1885 address to graduates of the Women's Medical College of Pennsylvania, Keen claimed that "vivisection is as humane to animal life and suffering as it is to human."[68] He described the medical profession as "conspicuously humane" but concluded it would be cruel "both to man and animals—if we refused to pain or even to slay a few animals, that thousands, both of men and animals, might live."[69]

Keen insisted that any outside regulation would thwart the progress of science, claiming that Dr. Joseph Lister, who had discovered antiseptics, would have been prevented from his experiments had he been subjected to the 1876 British Cruelty to Animals Act. According to Keen, Lister was forced to go to a veterinary school in France to conduct further research because the laws in England were "so stringent."[70]

THE 1900 SENATE COMMITTEE HEARINGS

When Senator Gallinger introduced Senate Bill 34 in 1899—titled "For the Further Prevention of Cruelty to Animals in the District of Columbia"—the AMA opposed the legislation. Welch coordinated the campaign asking Keen and other physicians to testify at the Senate hearing.[71]

Keen testified that "if the sum total of the suffering of all human beings is diminished by vivisection, not only is vivisection right, but it is our duty to perform it."[72] Keen recounted that in the past, he had been unable to obtain a dog, from Caroline Earle White, the president of the Women's Branch of the Pennsylvania SPCA, for his tumor experiments. He claimed his difficulty would increase if Senate Bill 34 passed. Senator Gallinger asked, "Do you mean to say that you could not get a dog in the city of Philadelphia to perform an experiment upon?" Keen replied, "I was refused a dog at the place where I knew I could get a dog, even though I wanted to help a human being. It shows the profound cruelty of our opponents."[73]

Dr. Mary Putman Jacobi of New York, the only woman physician to testify before the committee, claimed the provisions of the bill were "deliberately planned for the domination of knowledge by ignorance," while the "authors of the bill had no acquaintance with the study of physiological science."[74] If a "crude and clumsy system of 'regulation' by untrained officials were allowed to come into force," she stated, it would "fatally cripple the work of those who devote themselves to the science of life."[75]

Welch asserted that he "could spend the entire time allotted to [him] in enumerating useful experiments absolutely prohibited by this bill"[76] because "the objections to the bill are so numerous."[77] He believed local officials should not regulate vivisection because "scientific and medical men alone can fully know the dangers to science and humanity which lurk in what may seem to some of you this unimportant bit of legislation." He appealed to the Senate "not only in the name of science, but in the truest and widest sense in the name of humanity."[78]

Leffingwell responded, "This is not a bill for the abolition of vivisection, but for the prevention of its abuses."[79] The "restriction of the privilege of vivisection to proper persons will not injure the interests of science," he claimed, but "the practice of vivisection should be forbidden absolutely to individuals of such depraved and degenerate minds."[80] Leffingwell concluded that "all this verbal criticism of details is meaningless; that no improvements would make it acceptable to those men who demand absolute and unrestricted freedom to do exactly as they like in the vivisection of animals."[81]

THE ROCKEFELLER INSTITUTE

After the defeat of the Gallinger Bill, animal welfare organizations such as the American Humane Association abandoned the vivisection issue. But antivivisectionist organizations launched state legislative campaigns. New York was targeted after the opening of the Rockefeller Institute. Susan Lederer describes the Rockefeller Institute for Medical Research in New York as a "magnet for malignity."[82] The Rockefeller Institute was incorporated in 1901 to establish a research institute for the study of scientific medicine. Simon Flexner, a physician in scientific medicine, became the director of the institute. The main building, complete with an animal house, opened in New York City in 1906. From its inception, the public believed the institute was implicated in the theft of their companion animals. The New York Anti-Vivisection Society, formed by Diana Belais in 1908, opened a nearby booth for lost companion animals and encouraged "owners" to seek their missing companions at the institute.

When the Rockefeller Institute purchased a New Jersey farm to breed animals for experimentation, a journalist from the *New York Herald* visited the premises to investigate allegations of animal cruelty. The journalist commented on the secrecy of the institute and suggested that stolen dogs were being sold to the laboratories in New York City.[83] He correctly predicted, "It is by no means improbable that the Rockefeller Institute and its animal farm will become the antivivisection storm centre of the world."[84]

Two antivivisection groups emerged in New York. The Society for the Prevention of Abuse in Animal Experimentation (SPAAE) was formed in Brooklyn in 1907, while the aforementioned New York Antivivisection Society (NYAVS) was established the next year by Diana Belais. Both organizations campaigned for regulatory legislation.[85] It is beyond the scope of this chapter to address the campaigns initiated by these organizations or to develop fully the medical profession's tactics to halt all antivivisection legislation. Yet from 1908 to 1914, the SPAAE and the NYAVS continued to propose laws limiting animal experimentation.

The AMA established the Council for the Defense of Medical Research in 1908 to counter antivivisectionists' arguments. Walter Bradford Cannon, chair of physiology at Harvard Medical School, directed the council for the next eighteen years. In his article "Medical Control of Vivisection," Cannon claimed that medical research should be self-regulated because outside state inspectors were "untrained in observing animal reactions" and lacked "any insight whatever into the extraordinary complexities of medical investigation."[86] During the "relatively rare intervals" where "the solution of an important problem may require that animals shall suffer," Cannon asked, should not this critical decision "rest preferably with the person of training and insight, the laboratory director" whose position "is itself a warrant of trustworthiness"?[87]

CONCLUSION

In 1925 Cannon informed Simon Flexner, "I no longer fear the outcome of any hearing which may be given to these people, but I still think it is important to keep a watchful eye on them."[88] Moreover, in 1926 William Welch described antivivisection to be "a lost cause," and the adherents "pathetic."[89] Some historians have claimed that the antivivisection movement was incapacitated by 1930. In *Reckoning with the Beast*, James Turner asserts that new medical developments—for instance, the discovery of the diphtheria antitoxin in 1894—eventually "crushed" antivivisection.[90] Similarly, Harriet Ritvo claims that "the antivivisection movement collapsed suddenly in the first part of the 20th century"; it "lost its ability to mobilize public sympathy and came to occupy a position on the outer fringes of respectable opinion."[91]

Nevertheless, Susan Lederer asserts that twentieth-century American antivivisectionists continued to exert pressure on the medical research community.[92] Between 1929 and 1933, animal activists continued to introduce bills regulating vivisection—for instance, they submitted bills prohibiting the use of dogs in research. Although these bills failed, the medical profession took nothing for granted. The National Society for Medical Research was formed in 1945 to propose legislation and counter negative press.[93]

Walter Cannon continued to monitor antivivisection literature, stating that he was "wearied not so much by the monotonous recurrence of the same old stories as by the constant attempt to horrify by epithets."[94] In her article "Political Animals," Susan Lederer asserts that antivivisectionists documented animal abuse by reprinting research reports from medical journals to muster public support for restricting vivisection. In response, the *Journal of Experimental Medicine*—the journal of the Rockefeller Institute—changed its editorial policy.[95] Francis Peyton Rouse, editor of the journal from 1921 through 1946, limited the content of the journal to "placate critics of animal experimentation" and to "preclude loss of public support for the research enterprise."[96]

The medical profession marginalized the antivivisection movement, portraying the adherents as unstable. Physicians explicitly targeted women, claiming they were hysterical and suffering from "zoophil-psychosis"—described as an excessive concern for animals.[97] Moreover, scientists attributed medical discoveries to animal research and convinced Americans of the necessity of vivisection. According to historian Diane Beers, the medical profession "positioned themselves as modern heroes and fostered public acceptance of experimentation."[98] Yet antivivisectionists persisted in their campaigns to restrict research through the mid-twentieth century. In the 1950s and 1960s, the Animal Welfare Institute and the Humane Society of the United States exposed abuse of animals in laboratories. Further, these organizations exposed unscrupulous dog dealers who stole companion animals to sell to laboratories. According to Beers, the antivivisectionists "attacked rather than retreated"—challenging the public's attitudes toward nonhumans.

In the early twentieth century, antivivisectionists were attacked as anti-modern and unhinged, yet the passage of the 1966 Laboratory Animal Welfare Act vindicated the regulatory reforms they sought in 1900. Examining the early battles between the antivivisectionists and the proponents of animal experimentation may reveal the best way to move forward from the legacy of the Laboratory Animal Welfare Act. In his final work, *An Ethical Problem*, Albert Leffingwell reviewed his nearly forty years working to restrict animal experiments. As he looked to the future, Leffingwell proposed, "As one man drops the torch, another hand will grasp it; and where now is darkness and secrecy, there will one day be knowledge and light."[99]

REFERENCES

Animal Welfare Institute. *Animals and Their Legal Rights: A Survey of American Laws from 1641 to 1990*. Washington, DC: AWI, 1990.

Beers, Diane L. *For the Prevention of Cruelty: The History and Legacy of Animal Rights Activism in the United States*. Athens: Swallow Press/Ohio University Press, 2006.

Beuttinger, Craig. "Antivivisection and the Charge of Zoophil-Psychosis in the Early Twentieth Century." *Historian* 55, no. 2 (1993): 277–88.

Blackwell, Elizabeth. *Essays in Medical Sociology*. Vol 2. London: Earnest Bell, 1902.

Burrow, James G. *AMA: Voice of American Medicine*. Baltimore: Johns Hopkins University Press, 1963.

Cannon, Walter B. "Medical Control of Vivisection." *North American Review* 191, no. 655 (1910): 814–21.

Cathell, D. W. *The Physician Himself and What Should Add to His Scientific Acquirements*. 3rd ed. Baltimore: Cushing and Bailey, 1883. http://archive.org/details/physicianhimsel06cathgoog/mode/2up.

Corner, George W. *A History of the Rockefeller Institute, 1901–1953: Origins and Growth*. New York: Rockefeller Institute Press, 1964.

Dana, Charles L. "The Zoophil-Psychosis: A Modern Malady." *Medical Record* 75, no. 10 (March 1909): 381–83.

Duffy, John. "Social Impact of Disease in the Late 19th Century." In *Sickness and Health in America: Readings in the History of Medicine and Public Health*, edited by Judith Walzer Leavitt and Ronald L. Numbers, 414–21. Madison: University of Wisconsin Press, 1985.

Favre, David, and Vivien Tsang. "The Development of Anti-Cruelty Laws during the 1800s." *Detroit College of Law Review* (Spring 1993): 1–35.

Fishbein, Morris. *A History of the American Medical Association: 1847–1947*. Philadelphia: W. B. Saunders, 1947.

Flexner, Simon, and James Thomas Flexner. *William Henry Welch and the Heroic Age of Modern Medicine*. New York: Viking Press, 1942.

French, Richard D. *Antivivisection and Medical Science in Victorian Society*. Princeton, NJ: Princeton University Press, 1975.

Geison, Gerald L. "Divided We Stand: Physiologists and Clinicians in the American Context." In *The Therapeutic Revolution: Essays in the Social History of American Medicine*, edited by Morris J. Vogel and Charles E. Rosenberg, 67–90. Philadelphia: University of Pennsylvania Press, 1979.

Gossel, Patricia Peck. "William Henry Welch and the Antivivisection Legislation in the District of Columbia, 1896–1900." *Journal of the History of Medicine and Allied Science* 40, no. 4 (1985): 397–419.

Hearing before the Senate Committee on the District of Columbia, S. 34: For the Further Prevention of Cruelty to Animals in the District of Columbia. 56th Cong., 1st sess., February 21, 1900.

Hederman, Robyn. "Gender and the Animal Experiments Controversy." In *The Ethical Case against Animal Experiments*, edited by Andrew Linzey and Clair Linzey, 112–19. Urbana: University of Illinois Press, 2018.

Hudson, Robert P. "Abraham Flexner in Perspective: American Medical Education, 1865–1910." In *Sickness and Health in America: Readings in the History of Medicine and Public Health*, edited by Judith Walzer Leavitt and Ronald L. Numbers, 148–58. Madison: University of Wisconsin Press, 1985.

Keen, William Williams. *Animal Experimentation and Medical Progress*. Boston: Houghton Mifflin, 1914.

Lederer, Susan E. "The Controversy over Animal Experimentation in America, 1880–1914." In *Vivisection in Historical Perspective*, edited by Nicolaas A. Rupke, 236–58. London: Croom Helm, 1987.

———. "Political Animals: The Shaping of Biomedical Research Literature in Twentieth-Century America." *Isis* 83, no. 1 (1992): 61–79.

———. *Subjected to Science: Human Experimentation in America before the Second World War*. Baltimore: Johns Hopkins University Press, 1995.

Leffingwell, Albert. *An Ethical Problem*. New Haven, CT: C. P. Farrell, 1914.

———. "Physiology in Our Public Schools." *Journal of Education* 40, no. 2 (1894), 45–46.

———. *The Vivisection Controversy: Essays and Criticisms*. London: The London and Provincial Anti-Vivisection Society, 1908. https://archive.org/details/b2086806/mode/2up.

———. *The Vivisection Question*. New Haven. The Tuttle, Moorehouse, and Taylor Company, 1901. http://archive.org/details/vivisectionquest00leffrich/mode/2up.

Maulitz, Russel C. "'Physician versus Bacteriologist': The Ideology of Science in Clinical Medicine." In *The Therapeutic Revolution: Essays in the Social History of American Medicine*, edited by Morris J. Vogel and Charles E. Rosenberg, 91–107. Philadelphia: University of Pennsylvania Press, 1979.

Morantz, Regina Markell. "Feminism, Professionalism, and Germs: The Thought of Mary Putman Jacobi and Elizabeth Blackwell." *American Quarterly* 34, no. 5 (1982): 459–78.

Numbers, Ronald L. "The Fall and Rise of the American Medical Profession." In *Sickness and Health in America: Readings in the History of Medicine and Public Health*, edited by Judith Walzer Leavitt and Ronald L. Numbers, 185–96. Madison: University of Wisconsin Press, 1985.

Numbers, Ronald L., and John Harley Warner. "The Maturation of American Medical Science." In *Sickness and Health in America: Readings in the History of Medicine and Public Health*, edited by Judith Walzer Leavitt and Ronald L. Numbers, 113–25. Madison: University of Wisconsin Press, 1985.

Parvin, Theophilus A. *A Physician on Vivisection: Extracts from the Annual Address before the American Academy of Medicine, Washington, May 4, 1891*. 1895. Reprint, India: Facsimile Press, 1990.

Ritvo, Harriet. "*Plus Ça Change*: Antivivisection Then and Now." *Science, Technology and Human Values* 9 (1984): 57–66.

Ruacille, Deborah. *The Scalpel and the Butterfly: The Conflict between Animal Research and Animal Protection*. Berkeley: University of California Press, 2000.

Shultz, William. *The Humane Movement in the United States, 1910–1922*. New York: AMS Press, 1924.

Smith-Rosenberg, Carrol. "The Hysterical Woman: Sex Roles and Role Conflict in Nineteenth-Century America." In *Disorderly Conduct: Visions of Gender in Victorian America*, 167–81. New York: Oxford University Press, 1985.

Steele, Zuma. *Angel in the Top Hat*. New York: Harper & Brothers, 1942.

Turner, James. *Reckoning with the Beast: Animals, Pain, and Humanity in the Victorian Mind.* Baltimore: Johns Hopkins University Press, 1980.

Unti, Bernard Oreste. "The Doctors Are So Sure That They Only Are Right: The Rockefeller Institute and the Defeat of Vivisection Reform in New York, 1908–1914." In *Creating a Tradition of Biomedical Research: Contributions to the History of the Rockefeller University*, edited by Darwin H. Stapleton, 175–89. New York: Rockefeller University Press, 2004.

———. "The Quality of Mercy: Organized Animal Protection in the United States, 1866–1930." PhD diss., American University, 2002.

Veith, Ilza. *Hysteria: The History of a Disease.* Chicago: University of Chicago Press, 1965.

Welch, William H. "Argument against Senate Bill 34, Fifty-Sixth Congress, First Session, Generally Known as the 'Antivivisection Bill.'" *Journal of the American Medical Association* 34 (1900): 1242–1244, 1322–1327.

Westermann-Cicio, Mary L. "Of Mice and Medical Men: The Medical Profession's Response to the Vivisection Controversy at the Turn of the Century." PhD diss., State University of New York at Stony Brook, 2001.

White, Caroline Earle. *An Answer to Dr. Keen's Address Entitled "Our Recent Debts to Vivisection."* 1885. Reprint, n.p.: Nabu Public Domain Reprints, n.d.

Wirtschafter, Jonathan Dine. "The Genesis and Impact of the Medical Lobby: 1896–1906." *Journal of the History of Medicine and Allied Sciences* 13, no. 1 (1958): 15–49.

NOTES

1. Jonathan Dine Wirtschafter, "The Genesis and Impact of the Medical Lobby: 1896–1906," *Journal of the History of Medicine and Allied Sciences* 13, no. 1 (1958): 17.

2. Susan E. Lederer, *Subjected to Science: Human Experimentation in America before the Second World War* (Baltimore: Johns Hopkins University Press, 1995), 54.

3. Mary L. Westermann-Cicio, "Of Mice and Medical Men: The Medical Profession's Response to the Vivisection Controversy at the Turn of the Century" (PhD diss., State University of New York at Stony Brook, 2001), 159.

4. Zuma Steele, *Angel in the Top Hat* (New York: Harper & Brothers, 1942), 271.

5. Steele, *Angel in the Top Hat*, 272.

6. Steele, *Angel in the Top Hat,* 271. See also, "Vivisection," *New York Post*, November 7, 1866, and "Vivisection," *New York Post*, November 9, 1866.

7. Susan E. Lederer, "The Controversy over Animal Experimentation in America, 1880–1914," in *Vivisection in Historical Perspective*, ed. Nicolaas A. Rupke (London: Croom Helm, 1987), 237.

8. Albert Leffingwell, MD, *The Vivisection Question* (New Haven: The Tuttle, Moorehouse and Taylor Company, 1901), 16,https://archive.org/details/vivisectionquest00leffrich/page/16/mode/2up.

9. Leffingwell, *The Vivisection Question*, 16.

10. "Prevention of Cruelty to Animals: A Card from Mr. Bergh," *New York Times*, February 24, 1867, 5.

11. An Act for the More Effective Prevention of Cruelty to Animals, N.Y. Rev. Ch 375, §§1–10 (1867), in David Favre and Vivien Tsang, "The Development of Anti-Cruelty Laws during the 1800s," *Detroit College of Law Review* (Spring 1993): 1–35, appendix A: The 1867 New York Anti-Cruelty Law. See also Animal Welfare Institute, *Animal and Their Legal Rights: A Survey of American Laws from 1641 to 1990* (Washington, DC: AWI, 1990), 5.

12. Lederer, *Subjected to Science*, 56.

13. Bernard Oreste Unti, "The Quality of Mercy: Organized Animal Protection in the United States, 1866–1930" (PhD diss., American University, 2002), 331.

14. Ronald L. Numbers, "The Fall and Rise of the American Medical Profession," in *Sickness and Health in America: Readings in the History of Medicine and Public Health*, ed. Judith Walzer Leavitt and Ronald L. Numbers (Madison: University of Wisconsin Press, 1985), 185.

15. Wirtschafter, "The Genesis and Impact of the Medical Lobby," 16.

16. Ronald L. Numbers and John Harley Warner, "The Maturation of American Medical Science," in *Sickness and Health in America: Readings in the History of Medicine and Public Health*, ed. Judith Walzer Leavitt and Ronald L. Numbers (Madison: University of Wisconsin Press, 1985), 114–15. The authors note that European schools mandated attendance for four years with thirty-seven to forty-one weeks per year. In contrast, the University of Pennsylvania—considered to be one of the best at the time—required only twenty-five weeks per year for two years. Yet most American schools offered annual terms for sixteen weeks.

17. Westermann-Cicio, "Of Mice and Medical Men," 158; Morris Fishbein, *A History of the American Medical Association: 1847–1947* (Philadelphia: W. B. Saunders, 1947), 7–8; James G. Burrow, *AMA: Voice of American Medicine* (Baltimore: Johns Hopkins University Press, 1963), 1–2.

18. Westermann-Cicio, "Of Mice and Medical Men," 158; Fishbein, *A History of the American Medical Association*, 7–8; Burrow, *AMA*, 1–2.

19. Robert P. Hudson, "Abraham Flexner in Perspective: American Medical Education, 1865–1910," in *Sickness and Health in America: Readings in the History of Medicine and Public Health*, ed. Judith Walzer Leavitt and Ronald L. Numbers (Madison: University of Wisconsin Press, 1985), 152.

20. Numbers and Warner, "The Maturation of American Medical Science," 115.

21. Lederer, *Subjected to Science*, 54.

22. Patricia Peck Gossel, "William Henry Welch and the Antivivisection Legislation in the District of Columbia, 1896–1900," *Journal of the History of Medicine and Allied Science* 40, no. 4 (1985): 399.

23. Gossel, "Welch and the Antivivisection Legislation," 401n11.

24. Gossel, "Welch and the Antivivisection Legislation," 401; Simon Flexner and James Thomas Flexner, *William Henry Welch and the Heroic Age of Modern Medicine* (New York: Viking Press, 1942), 211–13.

25. John Duffy, "Social Impact of Disease in the Late 19th Century," in *Sickness and Health in America: Readings in the History of Medicine and Public Health*, ed. Judith Walzer Leavitt and Ronald L. Numbers (Madison: University of Wisconsin Press, 1985), 419; Gossel, "Welch and the Antivivisection Legislation," 401n11.

26. James Turner, *Reckoning with the Beast: Animals, Pain, and Humanity in the Victorian Mind* (Baltimore: Johns Hopkins University Press, 1980), 92; Deborah Ruacille, *The Scalpel and the Butterfly: The Conflict between Animal Research and Animal Protection* (Berkeley: University of California Press, 2000), 50.

27. Gerald L. Geison, "Divided We Stand: Physiologists and Clinicians in the American Context," in *The Therapeutic Revolution: Essays in the Social History of American Medicine*, ed. Morris J. Vogel and Charles E. Rosenberg (Philadelphia: University of Pennsylvania Press, 1979), 67–90.

28. Geison, "Divided We Stand," 72.

29. Geison, "Divided We Stand," 73–74.

30. D. W. Cathell, *The Physician Himself and What He Should Add to His Scientific Acquirements,* 3d. ed. (Baltimore: Cushing and Bailey, 1883), 55, https://archive.org/details/physicianhimsel06cathgoog/page/n60/mode/2up.

31. Cathell, *The Physician Himself, 56.*

32. Russel C. Maulitz, "'Physician versus Bacteriologist': The Ideology of Science in Clinical Medicine," in *The Therapeutic Revolution: Essays in the Social History of American Medicine*, ed. Morris J. Vogel and Charles E. Rosenberg (Philadelphia: University of Pennsylvania Press, 1979), 92.

33. Theophilus Parvin, *A Physician on Vivisection: Extracts from the Annual Address before the American Academy of Medicine, Washington, May 4, 1891* (1895; reprint, India: Facsimile Press, 1990), 5.

34. Parvin, *A Physician on Vivisection*, 13.

35. Parvin, *A Physician on Vivisection*, 15

36. Elizabeth Blackwell, "The Influence of Women in the Profession of Medicine," in Blackwell, *Essays in Medical Sociology*, vol. 2 (London: Earnest Bell, 1902), 5–6; Regina Markell Morantz, "Feminism, Professionalism, and Germs: The Thought of Mary Putman Jacobi and Elizabeth Blackwell," *American Quarterly*, 34, no. 5 (1982): 465.

37. Blackwell, "The Influence of Women," 6.

38. Morantz, "Feminism, Professionalism, and Germs," 465–66.

39. Blackwell, "Erroneous Method in Medical Education," in *Essays in Medical Sociology*, 41.

40. Blackwell, "Erroneous Method," 42–43.

41. Blackwell, "Scientific Method in Biology," in *Essays in Medical Sociology*, 99–100.

42. Blackwell, "The Influence of Women in the Medical Profession" in *Essays in Medical Society*, 8–9.

43. Blackwell, "The Influence of Women," 20–22.

44. Albert Leffingwell, "A Reply to Professor H. C. Wood," in Leffingwell, *The Vivisection Question*, Appendix, 236.

45. Albert Leffingwell, introduction to *An Ethical Problem* (New Haven, CT: C. P. Farrell, 1914).

46. Leffingwell, preface to *The Vivisection Question.*

47. Leffingwell, preface to *The Vivisection Question.*

48. Albert Leffingwell, MD. "Certain Dangers of Vivisection," in Leffingwell, *The Vivisection Controversy: Essays and Criticisms* (London: The London and Provincial Anti-Vivisection Society, 1908), 32–33, http://archive.org/details/b2086806/page/32/mode/2up. According to Richard French, Magendie's public demonstrations were viewed with disgust when he visited London in 1824. In 1829, the *London Medical Gazette* stated that Magendie was "unnecessarily torturing and sacrificing the lives of rabbits, frogs, dogs and cats." Richard D. French, *Antivivisection and Medical Science in Victorian Society* (Princeton, NJ: Princeton University Press, 1975), 20n13, citing "Dissection of the Living," *London Medical Gazette* 3 (1829): 644–45.

49. Unti, "The Quality of Mercy," 618.

50. Unti, "The Quality of Mercy," 618–19. Henry Bergh, the founder of the American Society for the Prevention of Cruelty to Animals, proposed the abolition of vivisection.

51. Albert Leffingwell, "Physiology in our Public School," *Journal of Education* 40, no. 2 (1894): 45–46.

52. Leffingwell, "Certain Dangers of Vivisection," in *The Vivisection Controversy*, 33.

53. Unti, "The Quality of Mercy," 620.

54. Quoted in Flexner and Flexner, *William Henry Welch*, 256.

55. Wirtschafter, "The Genesis and Impact of the Medical Lobby," 23–24.

56. Numbers, "The Fall and Rise of the American Medical Profession," 191.

57. Gossel, "Welch and the Antivivisection Legislation," 406.

58. Gossel, "Welch and the Antivivisection Legislation," 406.

59. Gossel, "Welch and the Antivivisection Legislation," 410.

60. Lederer, *Subjected to Science*, 56–57. The Council of Legislation was established in 1900, and in 1908, the Council on the Defense of Medical Research was created.

61. Gossel, "Welch and the Antivivisection Legislation," 411; Flexner and Flexner, *William Henry Welch*, 257.

62. Gossel, "Welch and the Antivivisection Legislation," 413; Diane L. Beers, *For the Prevention of Cruelty: The History and Legacy of Animal Rights Activism in the United States* (Athens: Swallow Press/Ohio University Press, 2006), 138.

63. Flexner and Flexner, *William Henry Welch*, 257.

64. Westermann-Cicio, "Of Mice and Medical Men," 153.

65. Flexner and Flexner, *William Henry Welch*, 257.

66. William Williams Keen, "The Antivivisection Exhibition in Philadelphia in 1914," in Keen, *Animal Experimentation and Medical Progress* (Boston: Houghton Mifflin, 1914), 290.

67. Keen, "The Influence of Antivivisection on Character," in *Animal Experimentation and Medical Progress*, 234.

68. Keen, "Our Recent Debts to Vivisection," in *Animal Experimentation and Medical Progress*, 20.

69. Keen, "Our Recent Debts to Vivisection," 2–3. Caroline Earle White, in her response to Keen's speech on the benefits of vivisection, claimed a "few" animals were really "millions." Caroline Earl White, *An Answer to Dr. Keen's Address Entitled "Our Recent Debts to Vivisection"* (1885; reprint, n.p.: Nabu Public Domain Reprints, n.d.), 4.

70. Keen, "Modern Antiseptic Surgery and the Role of the Experiment in Its Discovery and Development," in *American Experimentation and Medical Progress*, 208. See also Lederer, *Subjected to Science*, 58; Westermann-Cicio, "Of Mice and Medical Men," 97. This claim has been challenged. In *Antivivisection and Medical Science in Victorian Society*, French asserts that "experimental medicine "enjoyed a spectacular growth" in the years following the passage of the Act. French, *Antivivisection and Medical Science in Victorian Society*, 392.

71. Unti, "The Quality of Mercy," 625; Lederer, "The Controversy over Animal Experimentation," 241.

72. *Hearing before the Senate Committee on the District of Columbia, S. 34: For the Further Prevention of Cruelty to Animals in the District of Columbia*, 56th Cong., 1st sess., February 21, 1900, 24.

73. *Hearing before the Senate Committee*, 28.

74. *Hearing before the Senate Committee*, 58, 59.

75. *Hearing before the Senate Committee*, 61.

76. William H. Welch, "Argument against Senate Bill 34, Fifty-Sixth Congress, First Session, Generally Known as the 'Antivivisection Bill,'" *Journal of the American Medical Association* 34 (1900): 1323; Unti, "The Quality of Mercy," 626; William Shultz, *The Humane Movement in the United States, 1910–1922* (New York: AMS Press, 1924), 149.

77. Welch, "Argument against Senate Bill 34," 1325.

78. Welch, "Argument against Senate Bill 34," 1327.

79. Leffingwell, "The Regulation of Vivisection," in *The Vivisection Question*, 191.

80. Leffingwell, "The Regulation of Vivisection," 193.

81. Leffingwell, "The Regulation of Vivisection," 199.

82. Susan E. Lederer, "Political Animals: The Shaping of Biomedical Research Literature in Twentieth-Century America," *Isis* 83, no. 1 (1992): 67.

83. George W. Corner, *A History of The Rockefeller Institute, 1901–1953: Origins and Growth* (New York: Rockefeller Institute Press, 1964), 84. For more on the Rockefeller Institute, see Bernard Unti, "The Doctors Are So Sure That They Only Are Right: The Rockefeller Institute and the Defeat of Vivisection Reform in New York, 1908–1914," in *Creating a Tradition of Biomedical Research: Contributions to the History of the Rockefeller University*, ed. Darwin H. Stapleton (New York: Rockefeller University Press, 2004), 175–89.

84.*84. New York Herald*, October 20, 1907.

85. The SPAAE was influenced by the ideology of Leffingwell. The director of the SPAAE, Frederick Bellamy, wished to legally control vivisection in New York State.

86. Walter B. Cannon, "Medical Control of Vivisection," *North American Review* 191, no. 655 (1910): 820.

87. Cannon, "Medical Control of Vivisection," 821.

88. Unti, "The Quality of Mercy," 654.

89. Flexner and Flexner, *William Henry Welch*, 262.

90. Turner, *Reckoning with the Beast*, 115–21.

91. Harriet Ritvo, "*Plus Ça Change*: Anti-Vivisection Then and Now," *Science, Technology and Human Values* 9, no. 2 (1984): 62.

92. Susan E. Lederer, "Political Animals," 62.

93. The NSMR devoted its efforts to enacting state seizure laws, which required shelters and public pounds to surrender dogs and cats to research institutions. See Animal Welfare Institute, *Animals and Their Legal Rights*, 67.

94. Cannon, "Medical Control of Vivisection," 814.

95. Lederer, "Political Animals," 61.

96. Lederer, "Political Animals," 61, 68.

97. For more on zoophil-psychosis, see Charles L. Dana, "The Zoophil-Psychosis: A Modern Malady," *Medical Record* 75, no. 10 (March 1909): 381–83; Craig Beuttinger, "Antivivisection and the Charge of Zoophil-Psychosis in the Early Twentieth Century," *Historian* 55, no. 2 (1993): 277–88; Robyn Hederman, "Gender and the Animal Experiments Controversy," in *The Ethical Case against Animal Experiments*, ed. Andrew Linzey and Clair Linzey (Urbana: University of Illinois Press, 2018), 112–19. For more on hysteria and women, see Carrol Smith-Rosenberg, "The Hysterical Woman: Sex Roles and Role Conflict in Nineteenth-Century America," in *Disorderly Conduct: Visions of Gender in Victorian America* (New York: Oxford University Press, 1985), 167–216; Ilza Veith, *Hysteria: The History of a Disease* (Chicago: University of Chicago Press, 1965).

98. Beers, *For the Prevention of Cruelty*, 120.

99. Leffingwell, introduction to *An Ethical Problem*.

Chapter 3

The Charitable Status of English Antivivisection

How It Was Lost and Could Be Regained

By A. W. H. Bates

CHARITY LAW AND ENGLISH ANTIVIVISECTION SOCIETIES

In England and Wales, charitable trusts must by law be able to demonstrate both public benefit and charitable purpose.[1] The advantages of charitable status include freedom from taxation and enhanced public approval, while jurisdiction over charity disputes is shared between the High Court and the Charities Commission: with the latter rests the power to revoke charitable status, which it may do if, for example, a fund is mismanaged or if the trust's aims are deemed not charitable. Certain types of organizations are excluded from holding charitable status under English law, the most obvious being those that campaign for political or legal change, though a charity may facilitate political or legal discussion in a balanced manner. In practice, organizations whose purpose is primarily to stop vivisection are not accorded charitable status. This essay considers the legal background for this state of affairs and asks whether historical judgments are likely to be binding on contemporary courts.

Organized antivivisection societies in England came into being in response to a proposed change in the law. Frances Power Cobbe and others founded the

Victoria Street Society (which in 1897 became the National Antivivisection Society) in 1875, in anticipation of the report from the first Royal Commission on Vivisection, which appeared the following year. The commission's report informed the drafting of the Cruelty to Animals Act, which became law on August 15, 1876.[2] Both experimenters and antivivisectionists found the act unsatisfactory: the former complained of unnecessary government regulation, and the latter thought it ineffectual, not unreasonably, since there was no successful prosecution in the 110 years it remained in force.

The controversial act soon became a focus for pro- and antivivisection lobbying. The experimentalists were represented by the Physiological Society, which acted for their "mutual benefit and protection." The society, which had started life as a dining club, relied on membership subscriptions from researchers and medical students to cover the expenses of promoting experiments on animals, which it did very effectively. Though the majority of vivisectionists joined, membership was small, and the physiologists looked enviously at the income available to antivivisection groups, whose wealthy supporters gave generously while alive and left substantial legacies in their wills.[3] The physiologists could not hope to compete on equal terms and began to question the charitable status of the "antis."

In the twenty years following passage of the Cruelty to Animals Act, the courts generally accepted that antivivisection societies were legitimate charities, notwithstanding the fact that they were at least implicitly trying to get an existing law repealed. In the case of *Obert v. Barrow* in 1887, Kay J and Lindley LJ (on appeal) ruled that a gift to the Society for the Protection of Animals Liable to Vivisection was charitable.[4] This ruling went unchallenged the following year in *Purday v. Johnson*, and two years later, in *Armstrong v. Reeves*, a court again held that legacies to English antivivisection societies were charitable.[5]

Re Foveaux (1895)

In 1895, one Miss Foveaux, who had the authority under her mother's will to appoint £6,000 for some charitable purpose, made gifts of £300 each to three antivivisection societies, two of which were subject to English law: the Victoria Street Society and the London Anti-Vivisection Society.[6] Both were committed to ending vivisection completely, which in practice would have required the repeal of the Cruelty to Animals Act. The trustees of the will therefore questioned whether these antivivisection societies satisfied the legal requirements for holding charitable status.[7] In his judgment, Mr. Justice Chitty noted that the law had customarily taken a "liberal" view of charitable purposes; he cited a case from 1862, in which a trust for the publication of the works of Joanna Southcott, the soi-disant Devonshire prophetess, had been deemed a lawful charity, noting that as long as the *intention* of a trust was to benefit the public (in the Southcott trust case, by promoting religion), it did not matter if in practice it did not succeed in doing so.[8]

Vivisectionists and antivivisectionists both claimed that their activities were beneficial to society, by alleviating human illness in the former case and by reducing cruelty in the latter: it was a question, according to Chitty, on which "men's minds might reasonably differ" and on which the court properly "stands neutral." Provided an antivivisection society *sought* to benefit the public by its actions, it was not for the court to take a view on whether a total ban on vivisection would, if realized, be of public benefit. Furthermore, although the repeal of an act of Parliament was in practice part of the antivivisection societies' agenda, in order to completely put a stop to experiments on living animals, they might be judged by the court on their overarching aim, which was to bring about moral improvement in society as a whole. In his judgment, Chitty stated that "cruelty is degrading to man; and a society for the suppression of cruelty to the lower animals, whether domestic or not, has for its object, not merely the protection of the animals themselves, but the advancement of morals and education among men."[9]

Allen v. Wedgewood (1915)

Twenty years later, this principle was upheld in a judgment handed down by the Court of Appeal in the case of *Allen v. Wedgewood*, in which Swinfen Eady LJ ruled, "A gift for the benefit and protection of animals tends to promote and encourage kindness towards them, to discourage cruelty, and to ameliorate the condition of the brute creation, and thus to stimulate humane and generous sentiments in man towards the lower animals, and by these means promote feelings of humanity and morality generally, repress brutality, and thus elevate the human race."[10]

Re Grove-Grady (1929)

In 1926, Mrs. Sarah M. Grove-Grady, described in the *Times* as "a lonely widow," died at the age of eighty-four, leaving gifts totaling almost £100,000 in her will to various organizations for the benefit of animals, with the residue of her estate to be held in trust for the Beaumont Animals' Benevolent Society, "for the purpose of providing a refuge or refuges for the preservation of all animals, birds or other creatures not human . . . and so that all such animals, birds and other creatures not human shall there be safe from molestation or destruction by man."[11]

The residual bequest was challenged on behalf of the trustees of the will, and the House of Lords ruled the trust unlawful because it was of no benefit to the public. Lord Hanworth questioned the usefulness of the proposed sanctuary:

> It is not a sanctuary for any animals of a timid nature whose species is in danger of dying out: nor is it a sanctuary for birds which have almost entirely left our shores and may be attracted once more. . . . The one characteristic of the refuge is that it is free from the molestation of man, while all the fauna within it are to be free to molest and harry one another.
>
> Such a purpose does not, in my opinion, afford any advantage to animals that are useful to mankind in particular, or any protection from cruelty to animals generally. It does not denote any elevating lesson to mankind.[12]

Lord Justice Lawrence, mindful of other charitable refuges for animals, gave a dissenting judgment, believing his fellow judges to be making too fine a distinction between one form of animal sanctuary and another. The judgment given, however, established the principle in law that a trust for animals ought to benefit humans in some way, a point still relevant to charities such as animal hospitals and zoos.

References to the Grove-Grady case in law textbooks usually consider the Beaumont Animals' Benevolent Society only with regard to its remit to provide a wilderness where animals could roam—an objective, incidentally, that, though unusual in 1929, might be viewed more sympathetically in these times of vanishing habitats. Among its other purposes, however, was the distribution of money to other societies acting for the "benefit" of animals, which included "establishing endowing supporting maintaining or providing . . . hospitals or homes for animals in Great Britain having no vivisectionist upon the governing body."[13] The court did not specifically rule on whether such distributions would have been deemed charitable, since it concluded that the testatrix's intention in this regard was too loosely expressed for charitable status to be granted: it is unclear, for example, whether the hospitals referred to were those for animals or humans, though the Research Defence Society (RDS), which followed the case closely, believed it meant the latter.

The RDS was a select group of physiologists founded in 1908 in order to prevent legislation on animal experimentation from being tightened following the report of the Second Royal Commission on Vivisection. Most RDS members were active researchers, and many had academic links with University College London, then one of England's principal centers for vivisection.[14] The few "antivivisection" hospitals that tolerated no vivisectors on their staff were particularly loathed by the RDS, and the society's secretary, Dr. G. P. Crowden, expressed relief at the judgment in the Grove-Grady case, fearing that the boost the trust would have given antivivisection bodies would have caused experimenters "endless trouble."[15]

Commissioners of Inland Revenue v. National Anti-Vivisection Society (1942–1947)

Though under-resourced compared to antivivisectionists, the RDS was adept at lobbying Parliament to ensure that attempts to change the law on vivisection—such as the many attempts to pass a Dogs' Protection Bill to render dogs safe from laboratory experimentation—were blocked. During World War II, the RDS saw an opportunity to mount a legal challenge to the charitable status of antivivisection organizations. With Crowden away on active service, Sir Leonard Rogers, who had stepped in as secretary, drew up a memorandum titled "Are Anti-Vivisection Societies Good Charities?," which he sent on behalf of the RDS to the Treasury. The implication was that such societies were not worthy of charitable status at all, and the Commissioners of the Inland Revenue duly refused the application by the National Anti-Vivisection Society (NAVS) for exemption from income tax in the 1942–1943 tax year.[16]

Given that the NAVS's objectives were unchanged, it was clearly the RDS's intervention that had prompted the revenue commissioners to act. The RDS had astutely capitalized on a waning of public sympathy for the wartime antivivisection movement, owing to its imprudent association with the anti-vaccination campaign (which was perceived as hampering the war effort) and the links between some prominent antivivisectionists and the British Union of Fascists (Wilfred Risdon, the secretary of the London and Provincial Anti-Vivisection Society, had been Sir Oswald Mosley's director of propaganda and was briefly interned as a Nazi sympathizer).[17] The RDS further assisted the Inland Revenue with expert advice from medical and veterinary scientists, whose evidence was presented to the Special Commissioners for Income Tax in July 1945.

The stated objects of the antivivisectionists were to awaken the public conscience "to the iniquity of torturing animals for any purpose whatever," draw public attention "to the impossibility of any adequate protection from torture being afforded to animals under the present law," and lead the people "of this country to call upon Parliament totally to suppress the practice of vivisection."[18] The case presented by the Inland Revenue concentrated on the medical benefits of animal experiments, and a total of nineteen medical men "of great eminence" gave testimony to the efficacy of vivisection and its necessity for medical progress. One particularly influential witness was Major-General Leopold Thomas Poole, director of pathology at the War Office, honorary physician to His Majesty the King, and opponent of antivivisection, who testified that the NAVS was encouraging recruits to refuse vaccinations and so was putting lives at risk and forcing the army to squander time and resources justifying its vaccination policy.

Not surprisingly, given the mood of the times, the commissioners concluded that "upon the evidence, even after taking into account any public benefit (if any) by way of improvement of morals, the objects and activities of the society were not for the public benefit, but, on the contrary, were, in peace, a menace to the human race and animals, and, in war, a disaster."[19] However, they felt bound by legal precedent to grant the NAVS tax-exempt status: *In re Foveaux* had indicated that anti-cruelty campaigners were acting charitably by attempting to elevate public morals and that the relative merits of morality and medical progress were not for any court to judge. That judgment not only had never been overruled but also had been positively referenced by the Court of Appeal in *In re Wedgwood* (1915).[20]

"In these circumstances," the commissioners went on, "we have come to the conclusion that so far as we are concerned we are bound by the authorities to hold that the society is a body of persons established for charitable purposes only and entitled to exemption from Income Tax under Section 37 of the Income Tax Act, 1918." This grudging conclusion (which was made public only after the case had gone to the High Court) reads like an invitation to the higher courts to overrule the commissioners, and on July 27, 1945, Macnaghten J duly reversed the judgment in favor of the Crown, ruling that "the main object of the Society was the total abolition of vivisection, and that the attainment of that object, so far from being beneficial, would be gravely injurious to the community." The NAVS, and by implication other antivivisectionist organizations, therefore could not be treated as a charity, since it had failed the test of public benefit.

The Court of Appeal upheld the High Court's decision but gave leave for a final appeal to the House of Lords, which was heard in February 1947. In their judgment, the Law Lords agreed with the appeal court's decision that the public benefit of a bequest was for the courts to decide, adding that "advances in medicine now seemed to the court conclusively to demonstrate the public benefit of animal research."[21] Their lordships also held that changing the law was in fact a primary purpose of the NAVS, thus disqualifying it from charitable status.

UTILITARIAN CALCULUS

Animal welfare remained, of course, an important part of the charitable sector, and it is clearly acceptable under English law for a charitable trust to exist for the alleviation of animal suffering. According to Jamieson, for a trust to be valid, there must be some "tangible net benefit to society" from its execution.[22] In many of the nineteenth-century cases that he discusses—for example, an animal hospital and a home for lost dogs—the animals assisted were among those deemed most useful to humankind, and so it can be argued that trusts promoting animal welfare had always, in fact, served "purposes beneficial to the community": the fourth and final catchall category in Lord Macnaghten's seminal classification of "charity" for legal purposes.[23] Thus, any kind of animal used or enjoyed by humans might reasonably become the beneficiary of their charity.

Lord Wright's opinion in the NAVS tax case was that *Foveaux* had been wrongly decided and ought to be reversed because the interests of animals could never be allowed to compete with those of humans: "Mankind, of whatever race or breed, is on a higher plane and a different level from even the highest of the animals who are our friends, helpers and companions."[24]

The wording of the judgment makes clear that it was based on a kind of utilitarian calculus that any educated person might reasonably perform: "To my mind the scale of the anti-vivisectionist mounts up and kicks the beam. A statesman is constantly weighing conflicting moral and material utilities." The NAVS, however, argued that this was "an illegitimate method of reasoning" and that the charitable nature of its program to suppress cruelty was independent of any consequential disadvantages to medicine that would flow from the society achieving its aim. "The Court," it said, "has no scales in which to weigh material against moral benefits."[25]

The Law Lords disagreed: "There is not, so far as I can see, any difficulty in weighing the relative value of what is called the material benefits of vivisection against the moral benefit which is alleged or assumed as possibly following from the success of the Appellant's project."[26] In legal practice, the merits of a charitable trust are not uncommonly assessed by the courts according to utilitarian principles: will it benefit humankind, or at least a significant portion of humankind?[27] When it comes to those cases that Jamieson claims invoke a "doctrine of moral improvement," however, difficulties can arise, since "moral elevation" is, while undoubtedly desirable, not easily measured.

CONCLUSION

Seventy years have passed since antivivisection groups in England lost their charitable status, perhaps for good, as the result of an action prompted by the pro-vivisection lobby, which took advantage of the antivivisectionists' unprecedented wartime unpopularity. The courts' decision to overturn the status quo was based on a reevaluation of the benefits of vivisection, in the light of the many developments in medical science that had taken place since the nineteenth century, and on the presumption that earlier judges had given undue weight to the antivivisectionists' claim that the suppression of cruelty would improve the public's morals. Since both medical science and utilitarian ethics have changed at least as much in the last seventy years as they had between 1875 and 1945, one might wonder if the time has come for the charitable status of antivivisection organizations to be reconsidered in the courts.

The House of Lords ruling in 1947 depended on the assumption that utilitarian calculus overwhelmingly favored the vivisectionists, hardly a view that could be unquestioningly accepted now that there exists a substantial body of work by utilitarian ethicists advocating improved animal protection.[28] The potential medical benefits anticipated from experiments on animals in 1947 and the nature of the experiments also differ from the situation today. Many basic therapeutic agents were still being developed: antibiotics were in their infancy, the first chemotherapeutic agents were still being tested, and there was no reliable treatment for hypertension. The number of experimental procedures performed on animals in Britain was just over a million in 1947, and high though this figure was, it is about a quarter of the present-day figure. Much of the subsequent rise has been due to so-called LD50 testing—determination of the dose of a candidate drug that kills half the animals to which it is administered—which became a legal requirement in the 1950s, though it is arguably of little medical value. Furthermore, there are now alternatives to animal testing, such as in vitro cell cultures and computer modeling, which were not previously available. If changes in experimental medicine between 1895 and 1945 were sufficient to alter significantly the value that the courts placed on animal experimentation, may not the diminishing returns of the last sixty years prompt a further review?

But perhaps justice is not best served by considering animal welfare and human health as competing interests. If the courts continue to apply a utilitarian yardstick to charity, they discount not only the arguments that prompted antivivisectionists to begin their campaign—that cruelty is demoralizing to society and that to act out of compassion for those weaker than ourselves is of itself a virtue—but also the developments in animal rights theory that prompted a resurgence of the English antivivisection movement in the 1970s. The legal situation would be considerably clearer if, as Pearce and Barr suggest, England followed the same principle as Irish law, where trusts are accepted as charitable if they benefit the animals themselves.[29]

REFERENCES

Bates, A. W. H. *Anti-Vivisection and the Profession of Medicine in Britain: A Social History.* London: Palgrave Macmillan, 2017.

Edwards, Richard, and Nigel Stockwell. *Trusts and Equity*. 8th ed. Harlow, UK: Pearson Longman, 2007.

Francione, Gary L. "Animal Rights Theory and Utilitarianism: Relative Normative Guidance." *Between the Species* 13, no. 5 (2011). https://doi.org/10.15368/bts.2003v13n3.5.

Jamieson, Philip. "On Charity's Edge—The Animal Welfare Trust." *Monash University Law Review* 13 (1987): 1–36.

Kean, Hilda. *Animal Rights: Political and Social Change in Britain since 1800*. London: Reaktion Books, 1998.

Maurice, S. G., and D. B. Parker. *Tudor on Charities*. 6th ed. London: Sweet & Maxwell, 1984.

Pearce, R., and W. Barr. *Pearce and Stevens' Trusts and Equitable Obligations*. Oxford: Oxford University Press, 2015.

Risdon, J. L. *Black Shirt and Smoking Beagles: The Biography of Wilfred Risdon, an Unconventional Campaigner*. Scarborough, UK: Wilfred Books, 2013.

NOTES

1. Richard Edwards and Nigel Stockwell, *Trusts and Equity*, 8th ed. (Harlow, UK: Pearson Longman, 2007), 205.

2. Hilda Kean, *Animal Rights: Political and Social Change in Britain since 1800* (London: Reaktion Books, 1998), 105–6.

3. A. W. H. Bates, *Anti-Vivisection and the Profession of Medicine in Britain: A Social History* (London: Palgrave Macmillan, 2017), 135–37.

4. *Obert v. Barrow*, [1887] 35 Ch 472.

5. *Purday v. Johnson*, [1888] 60 LT 175; *Armstrong v. Reeves*, [1890] 25 LR 325.

6. *Re Foveaux*, [1895] 2 Ch 501.

7. High Court of Justice, *Times*, July 24, 1895, 13.

8. *Thornton v. Howe*, [1862] 31 Beav 14.

9. *Re Foveaux*, [1895] 2 Ch 501.

10. *Allen v. Wedgewood*, [1915] 1 Ch 113. This reasoning was accepted without question by Nourse J in *Re Green's Will Trust*, [1985] 3 All ER 455.

11. "Widow's £100,000 for the Care of Animals," *Times*, January 22, 1926, 6.

12. *Re Grove-Grady*, [1929] 1 Ch 557.

13. Chancery Division, *Times*, July 11, 1928, 5.

14. Bates, *Anti-Vivisection*, 137–47.

15. Memo from GP Crowd, September 9, 1934, Wellcome Library, London, SA/RDS/C2.

16. "Anti-Vivisection Societies and Income Tax," *BMJ* 2 (1945): 291–92.

17. J. L. Risdon, *Black Shirt and Smoking Beagles: The Biography of Wilfred Risdon, an Unconventional Campaigner* (Scarborough, UK: Wilfred Books, 2013).

18. *Zoophilist*, July 1, 1898, 60.

19. *Commissioners of Inland Revenue v. National Anti-Vivisection Society*, [1942–48] 28 TC 311.

20. *Re Wedgwood*, [1915] 1 Ch. 113 (see especially the judgment of Swinfen Eady LJ, at page 122).

21. *National Anti-Vivisection Society v. Inland Revenue Commissioners*, [1947] Parliamentary Archives HL/PO/JU/4/3/986.

22. Philip Jamieson, "On Charity's Edge—The Animal Welfare Trust," *Monash University Law Review* 13 (1987): 1–36.

23. *Commissioners for Special Purposes of Income Tax v. Pemsel*, [1891] AC 531.

24. *National Anti-Vivisection Society v. Inland Revenue Commissioners*, [1947] Parliamentary Archives HL/PO/JU/4/3/986.

25. Ibid.

26. *Commissioners of Inland Revenue v. National Anti-Vivisection Society*, [1942–48] 28 TC 311.

27. S. G. Maurice and D. B. Parker, *Tudor on Charities*, 6th ed. (London: Sweet & Maxwell, 1984), 87.

28. See, for example, Gary L. Francione, "Animal Rights Theory and Utilitarianism: Relative Normative Guidance," *Between the Species* 13, no. 5 (2011), https://doi.org/10.15368/bts.2003v13n3.5.

29. R. Pearce and W. Barr, *Pearce and Stevens' Trusts and Equitable Obligations* (Oxford: Oxford University Press, 2015), 404.

Chapter 4

The "Glass Walls" Theory

A History and Discussion of the Guidelines and Laws Concerning Nonhuman Animals in the North American Film Industry

By Rebecca Stanton

A Dog's Purpose (2017) is a big-budget film adaptation of a popular novel about a man and his dog; therefore, it should have had a glitzy Hollywood premiere like similar films before it.[1] However, a few days before this movie's planned premiere, something happened that would haunt its release. On January 18, 2017, the entertainment website TMZ posted a minute-long clip of a German shepherd being dragged and dipped into rushing water in order to film a scene for the movie.[2] During the clip, an unidentified voice shouts, "Well, he ain't going to calm down until he goes in the water. Just got to throw him in."[3] The offstage voice then guffaws a few moments later as the dog (Hercules) is forced into the artificial rapids, seemingly against his will. The clip appears to show Hercules as visibly distressed throughout the incident.[4] For example, he is scrambling against the trainer, trying to get away from the water he is being lowered into. The video quickly went viral, after which many people and organizations, such as PETA, immediately called for the film to be boycotted.[5] As a result, the premiere of the film (which had been due to take place just a few days later) was canceled, along with much of the movie's planned promotion.[6] In addition, some of the film's own cast and crew spoke out in defense of the dog, rather than the film, during this controversy.[7]

Because the movie was a Screen Actors Guild production, the use of animals on set had been monitored by the American Humane Association throughout filming.[8] However, the AHA's independent investigation of the video, which was swiftly completed in just over two weeks, concluded that the leaked footage was "misleading" and "manipulated."[9] Furthermore, the AHA's official statement did not condemn the actions of those involved in the incident but instead questioned the "motives and ethics" of whoever leaked the footage.[10] The AHA proudly concluded its investigation by stating that "no animals were harmed in the making of this film."[11]

One of the best-known and most-repeated sayings from the animal rights movement is the one proposing that if slaughterhouses had glass walls, everyone would be vegetarian (often attributed to Paul McCartney).[12] The film industry shows why this axiom holds so much merit: when animal abuse is seen or known, it often drastically changes how people feel about the end product. For example, the leaked footage from the filming of *A Dog's Purpose* greatly changed how the public felt about this movie. Additionally, for very similar reasons, the American meat industry has tried to stop the production of videos and photography in its slaughterhouses and farms.[13] This is because documented instances of animal abuse can (and have) put companies that use animals out of business.[14] Animal rights activists have used this sensitivity to further their cause.[15] For example, a modern tactic of the animal rights movement is to go undercover at slaughterhouses and film the worst instances of abuse that they see. These videos are often met with outrage toward the farms or equivalent.[16] This demonstrates that while people may be happy to buy products that involve animal abuse during production, they do not want to be faced with the reality of these processes. When consumers are faced with the production methods involved, this often results in a drastic change of opinion. For example, *A Dog's Purpose* would have had its planned Hollywood premiere if the alleged animal abuse on set had remained hidden from the public.

Throughout this chapter, the "glass walls" theory will be used to refer to the evident hypocrisy humans have around animal abuse, particularly animal actors. The original saying that "if slaughterhouses had glass walls, everyone would be vegetarian"[17] implies that animal abuse can exist comfortably only when it is hidden. Without veneers of good animal welfare, companies that use and/or abuse animals, such as Amblin and Universal, do not have the public's support.

It is documented that people are much more sensitive to animal abuse when it is in filmic form.[18] This especially applies to fictional films using animal actors who score highly on the socio-zoological scale, such as dogs.[19] The full suspension of disbelief is just not possible with animal actors because audiences know that animals are not *really* actors and are unable to consent to performance in the same way that humans can.[20] As a result of this sensitivity from viewers, many film companies often boast that their animal actors are treated just as well as their human stars. For example, after the viral clip from *A Dog's Purpose* spread, Universal and Amblin (the film's production companies) quickly responded by claiming, "While we are all disheartened by the appearance of an animal in distress, everyone has assured us that Hercules the German Shepherd was not harmed throughout the filmmaking."[21] It is clear that Universal and Amblin were keen to reassure potential audiences that the dog involved was unharmed, despite the filmic evidence to the contrary. Because of this unique concern for animal performers, film companies have to follow certain rules when using live animals. This is essentially why the AHA exists and why it has widespread public support.

This chapter aims to give a history and discussion of the AHA and the laws surrounding animal actors in the film industry, using case studies from Disney's live-action films. The first part will give a history of the AHA, the organization that monitors the use of animal actors in around 70 percent of all professional filming in North America. Next, this chapter will explore the laws that exist, or rather do not exist, to protect animal actors in the United States. Third, this chapter will look at how the AHA, American laws, and the "glass walls" theory work alongside Disney's live-action films. I will conclude by arguing that while the AHA originally may have had good intentions, the association is not doing enough today to protect animal actors. Evidence suggests that the AHA's main purpose is to minimize animal abuse on film sets, rather than stop it altogether. Additionally, there are too few laws to protect animal actors from being abused. This will be proven by the Disney case studies and a detailed analysis of the AHA's practices and guidelines.

THE AMERICAN HUMANE ASSOCIATION

The AHA was founded in 1877 to advocate on behalf of animals and children. Its first animal-focused aim was to improve the treatment of farmed animals during their transportation.[22] Today, the AHA is a nonprofit organization that mainly monitors the use of animals on American film sets.[23] The association's website proudly claims that it supports the welfare of all animal actors, from ants to zebras.[24]

Before the AHA began monitoring animals in the film industry, animal abuse was much more common on film sets.[25] The AHA first started investigating animal abuse within the film industry in the 1920s, after seeing how many horses were injured and killed during the production of "Wild West" films. For example, during the production of *Jesse James* (1939), a blindfolded horse was intentionally ridden over a seventy-foot drop into a river.[26] While the stuntman lost only his hat, the horse lost his life.[27] After this particular incident, there was increased public concern about the use of animals in the film industry.[28] This subsequently helped the AHA gain the authority to monitor film sets in 1941.[29] Since 1980, the Screen Actors Guild (SAG) has given the AHA the sole authority for overseeing animal welfare in Hollywood films.[30] SAG (also sometimes known as SAG-AFTRA) is an American labor union that represents a large number of professional media performers, such as film actors.[31] All SAG films that use animals and are filmed in North America are required to give the AHA full access to their sets.[32] However, films that are not part of SAG are under no obligation to follow the AHA's guidelines if they do not wish to.[33] If a non-SAG film chooses not to follow the AHA's guidelines, all this means is that it will not be eligible for any of the AHA's disclaimers.

Today, the AHA claims to be an independent group with no conflict of interest.[34] Currently, it monitors around 70 percent of professional American film sets, which is around two thousand productions annually.[35] However, in 2013, the *Hollywood Reporter* released an article that questioned the practices and ethics of the modern AHA, concluding that it is today "inadequate."[36] The author of this detailed exposé interviewed six AHA staff members and reviewed a large number of internal AHA documents, such as logs, emails, and meeting minutes. The article claimed that the AHA "distorts its film ratings, downplays or fails to publicly acknowledge harmful incidents and sometimes doesn't seriously pursue investigations."[37]

The AHA's "No animals were harmed . . . " slogan was first used in 1972 on *The Doberman Gang*.[38] Since then, it has become a reassuring disclaimer for film audiences worldwide.[39] It is a persuasive reassurance that connotes the good treatment of any animals involved.[40] As with "organic" meat and "free-range" eggs, humans are much more comfortable with animal abuse when it is neatly hidden from them behind comforting labels such as "no animals were harmed." This relates back to the "glass walls" theory presented at the beginning of this chapter. Basically, widespread animal abuse exists much more comfortably behind veneers (i.e., solid walls) of good animal welfare, such as "no animals were harmed" or "free-range." However, just like organic meat and free-range eggs, the AHA's label may not be entirely accurate, since it evidently has been given to films that have had questionable incidents involving animals, such as *A Dog's Purpose*. This is because a film can still receive the disclaimer even if an animal was harmed or killed, as long as it was following the AHA's guidelines when the incident occurred.[41] For example, *Life of Pi* (2012) was awarded the "No animals were harmed" disclaimer even though there was strong evidence to suggest that a tiger nearly drowned during filming.[42]

Whether or not a film can receive the AHA's disclaimer is decided once a production is finished. Once the final edit of a film is complete, it is viewed by the AHA to ensure that the scenes involving animals are the same ones that the AHA's set monitor viewed.[43] The AHA is allowed to view scripts before filming, and the AHA's set monitors can show up on set at any time during the filming of any scene involving animals. Moreover, they have the right to intervene during scenes involving animals at any point.

There are currently six different grades that films can receive from the AHA:

1. Monitored: Outstanding[44]
2. Monitored: Acceptable
3. Monitored: Special Circumstances
4. Monitored: Unacceptable
5. Not Monitored: Production Compliant
6. Not Monitored[45]

Only films rated as "Outstanding" are permitted to use the full "No animals were harmed . . . " disclaimer. Films graded as "Monitored: Acceptable" can use only the AHA's modified disclaimer: "American Humane Association monitored some of the animal action. No animals were harmed in those scenes."[46]

Critics have suggested that this rating system is too broad and ambiguous, especially since the vast majority of AHA-monitored films are claimed to be safe for animals.[47] The AHA proudly announced in 2013 that around 99.98 percent of AHA-monitored film sets are graded as safe for animals.[48] However, this statistic accounts only for animals physically on set.[49] It does not include any animals harmed in training, transit, or holding. The AHA even admits that some of its "outstanding" or "acceptable" films may have included animal deaths, but the association insists that in these cases, the animals' deaths happened off set and/or were not the fault of the production company or the AHA.[50]

Over five hundred points are made in the AHA's remarkably strict, 131-page guideline book (*Guidelines for the Safe Use of Animals in Filmed Media*). For example, on-set sedation is banned, except in veterinary emergencies.[51] However, again, these guidelines mostly apply only to animals who are physically on set, meaning that the AHA seemingly has little concern for what happens to animals before or after they arrive on a film set. Additionally, the introduction to the *Guidelines* claims, "At its most fundamental level, American Humane Association's role is to prevent legally defined cruelty to animal actors. In reality, the industry today is primarily composed of *caring and responsible* individuals"[52] (emphasis added). This statement seems somewhat naive. After all, the film industry was notoriously cruel toward animals before the AHA began monitoring film sets. Moreover, this statement seems to imply an overwhelming amount of support and bias toward the industry that the AHA claims to be impartial toward. After the controversy surrounding *A Dog's Purpose*, the AHA did not condemn the questionable actions of those who were apparently forcing Hercules underwater. Instead, it criticized the person(s) who released the footage. This suggests, along with the AHA's guidebook introduction, that the AHA is not entirely impartial and in fact sometimes support filmmakers before it supports animals.

It is also worth noting that the AHA refuses to comment on a film's content and message.[53] Therefore, if the storyline of a film supports animal abuse, it can still receive the full AHA disclaimer. For example, 2011's *We Bought a Zoo* received the full "No animals were harmed" disclaimer and was later awarded a "Pawscar" for having the "best ensemble cast."[54] However, given that *We Bought a Zoo* is a film that promotes zoo animals as mostly happy, its message is questionable within the ethics of animal rights. Nevertheless, the AHA still awarded the movie as "outstanding." This point, along with the other points raised in this section, brings up questions about where the AHA's loyalties really lie.

ANIMAL ACTORS AND THE LAW

The majority of professional American filmmaking takes place in two states: Louisiana and California.[55] This is significant because each state in America has different laws and regulations on animal welfare and abuse. Looking at the United States as a whole, both the federal government and individual states have yet to implement any laws specifically for the welfare of animals used in the film industry.[56] A few federal enactments, such as the federal Animal Welfare Act, the Marine Mammal Protection Act, and the federal Endangered Species Act (ESA), can be used to make specific applications against animal abuse in the film industry indirectly.[57] However, these acts apply only to certain species and specific situations. For example, the ESA covers only around 2,300 species, which is not many considering that there are approximately 8.7 million species worldwide.[58]

While there are no specific laws to protect animal actors, all states do have laws against general animal abuse and neglect.[59] Because these laws are quite broad, they can be applied to animal actors. Interestingly, several of these state laws prohibit animal cruelty depictions, and a few of these laws do mention any animal actors involved.[60] This is significant because it suggests that there is more concern about images of animal abuse than about actual animal abuse.

Additionally, six states (Alabama, Arkansas, Iowa, Kansas, Missouri, and North Carolina) have "ag-gag" laws—that is, laws that make undercover filming or photography in animal agriculture facilities illegal.[61] These laws mostly exist to deter and prevent animal welfare activists from filming slaughterhouses and the like.[62] However, these controversial laws have been overturned in many states. For example, in Utah, these laws were declared unconstitutional on the grounds that they violate the First Amendment's free speech protections.[63] Ag-gag laws are relevant here because they further suggest that there is often more concern and legal protection for the industries that abuse animals than for abused animals.

If an animal gets a paid acting job in any state, the animal's "owner" must get an exhibitor's permit from the US Department of Agriculture.[64] However, this process is done entirely in writing. The Department of Agriculture does not check the "owner's" living conditions for the animal and so forth. Therefore, there is currently very little being done to stop animal actors from coming from abusive homes or even puppy mills and the like.

However, despite these broad and ambiguous laws, bald and golden eagles are two animals who are offered full countrywide protection from the film industry. There are strict federal regulations specifically for these breeds of eagles that have made it almost impossible for filmmakers to use them for entertainment purposes: "It is illegal to sell, purchase, barter, trade, import, export, or offer for sale, at any time or in any manner, any bald eagle or any golden eagle, or the parts, nests, or eggs of these birds, and the Department of the Interior will not issue a permit to authorize these acts."[65] This remarkably strict regulation makes it incredibly complex for filmmakers to legally use eagles, and hence they are very rarely used in films.

Since 1997, the AHA's set monitors have been licensed law enforcement officers within the state of California. This means that they can write citations and even make arrests.[66] Despite this, the AHA has never used either of these legal powers, even though it is estimated to have monitored over 35,000 film sets in this time.[67] California currently has some of the toughest animal cruelty laws in America.[68] For example, anyone who maliciously or intentionally kills, tortures, neglects, or wounds a live animal can be fined up to $20,000 or imprisoned.[69] However, for this penalty to be imposed, the state must prove willfulness or malice. This perhaps helps explain why the AHA has never arrested a filmmaker; enforcing the law is possible only if abusive intentions can be proven.

Despite the association's legal powers, it has been claimed that the AHA has more of a coaching role on film sets.[70] Its monitors suggest what filmmakers should do, but they do not demand that film sets follow their instructions. Therefore, ultimately, the welfare of the animals involved is up to the filmmakers, not the AHA. The AHA's own guidelines even specifically state that "production is always ultimately responsible for the well-being of any animal (or person) on a set."[71] This statement seems to absolve the AHA of any wrongdoing before a film's production has begun.

Therefore, other than a few token laws and acts, animal actors are not offered much legally to protect them from the dangers of the film industry. What they seem to have instead is the AHA's guidelines and disclaimers. When the AHA states that "no animals were harmed," one could reasonably expect that to mean that no animals were harmed. However, if this label is awarded in cases where some animals were harmed, that is clearly misleading. As evidenced earlier, this disclaimer seems to be given quite liberally to films, even ones that may have involved animal abuse.

ANIMAL ACTORS AND DISNEY

The animal identity is arguably celebrated throughout Disney media, even with animals who score low on the socio-zoological scale, such as mice.[72] Moreover, Disney's animated animal characters are actually less likely to experience violence or abuse than Disney's human characters are.[73] Interestingly, this often contrasts with the fairy tales and other stories from which Disney frequently adapts its films. For example, the abuse toward animals in Carlo Collodi's original *Pinocchio* is far worse than in the later Disney animated adaptation.[74] As evidenced earlier, animal welfare issues have surrounded the film industry for many years. Disney has undoubtedly been aware of this since its very beginnings, which perhaps helps explain the animal-friendly image it often promotes.

From 1948 to 1960, Disney produced its "True-Life Adventures" films, a series of animal-focused documentaries.[75] However, these movies were criticized for manipulating natural animal footage in order to create plots and characters.[76] For example, it was claimed that the narratives presented in these films were purposefully reflective of middle-class American families and reinforced human notions of gender.[77] Additionally, there is strong evidence that the films' production methods involved animal abuse. One of these documentaries, 1958's *White Wilderness*, is today remembered primarily for the animal abuse that is believed to have occurred during production.[78] This documentary contains a scene that implies a group of lemmings committed mass suicide after leaping into the Arctic Ocean.[79] However, it was later revealed that this scene was filmed not in the Arctic Ocean, but actually at a river in Calgary, Canada.[80] Moreover, experts claimed that the specific breed of lemming shown is not one that migrates or commits suicide[81] (that is supposing that lemmings do commit suicide, rather than simply die from accidents or accidental drowning). This has led many people to accuse the filmmakers of trapping the animals, transporting them to Calgary, and forcing them into jumping, which obviously killed them.[82] To this day, Disney has yet to release any official statement on the production methods used in this documentary.

This event took place before the AHA had the authority to monitor all SAG film sets; additionally, documentary films are not SAG productions since no human performers are involved. Therefore, the *White Wilderness* incident did not fall within the AHA's purview, but it is highlighted here because it demonstrates that even though Disney has an animal-friendly image, it also has a questionable history when it comes to using live animals.

Despite their suspicious filming methods, the "True-Life" documentaries were said to have had a positive effect on animal welfare and environmental issues.[83] Moreover, these films were hugely successful both financially and with critics.[84] For example, eight of these films won Academy Awards.[85] Their financial and critical success inspired Walt Disney to make live-action fictional films with real animals, the first of which was 1957's *Perri*.[86]

The strong relationship between Disney and the AHA began in the 1940s and continues to the present day.[87] The AHA has proudly monitored many Disney films and television shows. At one of the Disney theme parks, there is even a plaque that was presented to Walt Disney by the AHA.[88] However, this partnership is today questionable because there is substantial evidence of animal abuse in several of Disney's recent AHA-monitored live-action films.

In 1999, the AHA gave a "believed acceptable"[89] grade to the live-action film *The 13th Warrior*. This was because a horse had to be euthanized after having a tendon and artery sliced by some loose wire. The AHA described the horse's death as an "industrial accident."[90] Additionally, Disney claimed that it had never been informed about the incident; thus, the company very much distanced itself from it.[91] Disney's response suggests that it placed the welfare of the animal actors entirely in the care of other organizations. Its response also suggests a lack of communication between Disney and the AHA.

During the filming of 2003's *Pirates of the Caribbean: The Curse of the Black Pearl*, thousands of fish and other marine animals died and washed up onshore. This happened after crew members set off several explosions underwater to film battle scenes without taking any precautions to protect any animals in the area.[92] Despite this, the film got AHA's "acceptable" rating (the highest possible rating at that time) and therefore the "No animals were harmed" disclaimer. When later questioned about the deaths, the AHA said, "It was never determined that the cause of the fish washing up was due to the explosions."[93] Additionally, the AHA's official web page for this film does not mention this incident at all.[94] Instead, the web page focuses on the "healthy" animal actors in the film who went on to live with the people who had first supplied them.[95] The web page also claims that the fish seen in the film were "all computer generated" and fails to mention the fish who washed up onshore during filming.[96]

During the production of 2006's Antarctic sledding film *Eight Below*, a husky dog was repeatedly punched in the diaphragm after a fight broke out between the dogs on set. The AHA's incident report stated, "The hero dog seriously got into a fight with two other dogs. The trainer beat the dog harshly, which included five punches to its diaphragm."[97] The AHA later added, "The trainer had to use force to break up the fight. As a result, the dogs were not injured."[98] This film received a grade of "acceptable." Interestingly, as with 2003's *Pirates of the Caribbean*, the AHA's official web page on the film focuses on the production's positive instances of animal welfare and does not mention the dogfight at all.[99]

It seems clear that although these incidents were questionable, both Disney and the AHA were able to distance themselves from any wrongdoing. The AHA did this by promoting the instances of good welfare, and Disney did this by not commenting on any documented instances of animals being harmed. It was probably also helpful that in most of the cases, the incidents seemed to be the result of negligence rather than purposeful abuse. In 2008, however, there would be a series of incidents on a film too serious for the AHA to ignore.

Snow Buddies (2008), the fifth film in Disney's ever-popular *Air Bud* film series, received an "unacceptable" rating after at least three dogs died on set.[100] For the purpose of the film, twenty-five six-week-old puppies were transported from New York (where they had been bred) to Canada (where they were filming). During this 3,000-mile journey, many of the puppies fell ill. Once on set, at least three puppies died from contagious viral diseases that they were too young to handle in the extremely cold Canadian weather. The AHA later claimed that the puppies were younger than the AHA had previously been told; as a result, they were too young to have been vaccinated for the viruses they had caught.[101] PETA claimed that the puppies had come from an unlicensed commercial breeder.[102] As highlighted earlier, there are currently no laws in place to stop animal actors from coming from abusive homes. Additionally, the fact that these puppies were underage suggests that the AHA does not check the ages of animal actors before allowing them on set. It has been claimed that as the crew tried to control the on-set disaster, the situation became so bad that some of the puppies were on drips between filming scenes.[103]

Interestingly, in a statement, the AHA seemed to distance both itself and Disney from blame: "It is speculated that the unhealthy puppies arrived on the set underage and already ill. The contagious nature of their illness and the stress of their journey compounded the situation."[104] This statement is problematic because it seems to blame the puppies and external influences for the deaths and illnesses. The reason the puppies took the journey, and thus became "unhealthy," was precisely for the film. The AHA then added:

> American Humane would like to acknowledge that the production cooperated in every way with the Animal Safety Representative's recommendations, and once

> the unhealthy puppies were removed from the set to receive veterinary care, healthy puppies were then brought in—using proper procedures and following all guidelines regarding age limits, vaccinations, illness prevention methods and other safety protocol—to ensure that healthy puppies were ultimately used during filming.[105]

The AHA's full statement does not mention Disney at all. However, it does mention that the "production" was cooperative without specifying whom this refers to. Therefore, it seems fair to suggest that the AHA was trying to avoid giving Disney any bad publicity by not directly associating the company with the incidents that occurred on set.

Once the film was finally completed, PETA publicly asked Disney not to distribute it.[106] Disney never responded to PETA's request. Moreover, the film's on-set incidents barely made the news at all, despite the "unacceptable" rating from the AHA. Upon its eventual release, *Snow Buddies* made over fifty million dollars in DVD sales alone.[107] The final cut of the film simply states that "American Humane monitored the animal action."[108] However, this statement gives little clue to the deaths and illnesses that evidently occurred on set. In fact, it could even be argued that this statement potentially misleads viewers into believing that since the AHA monitored the animal action, the animals came to no harm, which obviously is not true.

Disney has since released five more films in the dog-filled *Air Bud* film series, and there have been no further reports of poor animal welfare, with all five subsequent films achieving the AHA's "No animals were harmed" disclaimer.[109] It is also worth noting here that the *Air Bud* film series is said to be Disney's second-most profitable film series.[110] Therefore, it is likely to continue being produced.

Ironically, in 2008, the same year as *Snow Buddies*' release, Disney released another dog-filled film, *Bolt*. *Bolt* is a CGI-animated film about the ethics of using animals, specifically dogs, as actors in the entertainment industry. The film's dog protagonist, Bolt, is a television star who gets confused between his acting and his real life. The film ends with Bolt giving up acting and living happily ever after with his human best friend, whom he met on set. The storyline of this film contrasts greatly with the ethics Disney evidently has with animal actors. It is clear from *The 13th Warrior*, *Eight Below*, and *Snow Buddies* that Disney does use animal actors, which goes against the message of *Bolt*. In addition to this, the majority of Disney's films that oppose animal abuse are animated. For example, *Bambi*, *Dumbo*, and *The Fox and the Hound* are all films that center around animal abuse issues, and they are all animations. This suggests that while Disney is keen to release films that condemn animal abuse, it is much more likely to do so in animated form, which helpfully distances the company from any difficult questions surrounding the animals involved.

Additionally, as has been highlighted here, Disney rarely releases statements on the animal abuse involved in its filmmaking, unless the message is positive. For example, in 2012, Disney responded to the growing backlash against ape actors by announcing that they would no longer be using apes or large primates in any of its live-action films.[111] A statement like this obviously makes Disney appear animal-friendly. However, any negative instances, such as the deaths on *Snow Buddies*, are left up to the AHA, which, as evidenced here, avoids using Disney's name negatively.

CONCLUSION

The film industry shows why the axiom featured at the start of this chapter—"If slaughterhouses had glass walls, everyone would be vegetarian"—has merit. The American film industry walls its questionable use of animals behind the AHA's trusted disclaimers. When things go wrong, and animals are harmed, films are boycotted and condemned, but only if the public knows about the harm, which is not always the case. Similarly, when slaughterhouse footage is leaked, there is often outrage over the treatment of farmed animals; however, there is little outrage when no footage is leaked, even though there is almost certainly animal abuse taking place. Therefore, it seems that film may be one of the animal rights movement's most powerful tools, since it evidently has a widespread effect on how many consumers feel about a product involving animals.

The AHA was set up to protect animals, but today it does not seem to be doing enough to achieve its aims. Rather, it seems to minimize animal suffering and deflect blame toward the animals and external sources when things go wrong, such as in *Snow Buddies* and *A Dog's Purpose*. The reality is that the laws, guidelines, and disclaimers that are in place purportedly to protect animals exist for consumers only (i.e., humans). They exist to shield consumers from the uncomfortable truths about animal abuse. Slaughterhouses do not have glass walls for an obvious reason: to protect humans from being uncomfortable. If slaughterhouses did have glass walls, then animal welfare would likely improve significantly. Similarly, for the same reason, many of the dangers of the film industry are neatly hidden from consumers behind labels such as "No animals were harmed." However, as the evidence presented here suggests, this label may not be an accurate reflection of the reality faced by some animal actors.

REFERENCES

American Humane. "Governance." Accessed September 7, 2018. https://www.americanhumane.org/about-us/governance-and-finances/.

———. *Guidelines for the Safe Use of Animals in Filmed Media.* Accessed September 28, 2018. https://www.americanhumane.org/app/uploads/2016/08/Guidelines2015-WEB-Revised-110315-1.pdf.

———. "History." Accessed September 7, 2018. https://www.americanhumane.org/about-us/history/.

———. "Humane Hollywood." Accessed September 7, 2018. https://www.americanhumane.org/about-us/history/.

———. "Independent Investigative Report on *A Dog's Purpose* Finds Edited Video Mischaracterized What Happened on the Set." Accessed September 12, 2018. https://www.americanhumane.org/press-release/independent-investigative-report-on-a-dogs-purpose-finds-edited-video-mischaracterized-what-happened-on-the-set/.

———. "'No Animals Were Harmed' Frequently Asked Questions." Accessed September 7, 2018. https://www.americanhumane.org/fact-sheet/no-animals-were-harmed/.

———. "'No Animals Were Harmed': We Help Keep the Cameras Rolling and the Animals Safe." Accessed September 7, 2018. https://www.americanhumane.org/initiative/no-animals-were-harmed/.

Animal Legal Defense Fund. "Animal Protection Laws of the United States of America." Accessed September 7, 2018. https://aldf.org/article/animal-protection-laws-of-the-united-states-of-america/.

Arluke, Arnold, and Clinton R. Sanders. *Regarding Animals*. Philadelphia: Temple University Press, 1996.

Baum, Gary. "Animals Were Harmed." *Hollywood Reporter*, November 25, 2013. https://www.hollywoodreporter.com/news/general-news/animals-were-harmed-hollywood-reporter-investigation-on-set-injury-death-cover-ups-659556/.

———. "*Life of Pi* AHA Monitor Leaves Job after THR Email Exposes Tiger 'Damn Near Drowned.'" *Hollywood Reporter*, November 26, 2013. https://www.hollywoodreporter.com/news/life-pi-aha-monitor-leaves-660369.

BBC News. "*A Dog's Purpose* Premiere Cancelled Amid Animal Rights Concerns." January 20, 2017. https://www.bbc.com/news/world-us-canada-38695074.

Bender, Kelli. "*A Dog's Purpose* Controversy: What Does It Mean When Movies Claim 'No Animals Were Harmed' during Filming?" *People*, January 19, 2017. https://people.com/pets/a-dogs-purpose-controversy-what-does-it-mean-when-movies-claim-no-animals-were-harmed-during-filming/.

Bocking, Stephen. "Science and Spaces in the Northern Environment." *Environmental History* 12, no. 4 (2007): 867–94. http://www.jstor.org/stable/25473165.

Brucculieri, Julia. "Josh Gad Responds to 'Disturbing' Leaked Video from *A Dog's Purpose* Set [UPDATE]." *Huffington Post*, January 19, 2017. https://www.huffingtonpost.com/entry/josh-gad-a-dogs-purpose-video-response_us_5880be0ae4b04b69667e9e09.

Burt, Jonathan. *Animals in Film*. London: Reaktion Books, 2002.
"California Code, Penal Code, PEN 597." FindLaw. Accessed September 7, 2018. https://codes.findlaw.com/ca/penal-code/pen-sect-597.html.
Campbell, Duncan. "Hollywood Shoot Horses, Don't They?" *Guardian*, February 10, 2001. https://www.theguardian.com/world/2001/feb/10/filmnews.film.
Chester, Sharon. *The Arctic Guide: Wildlife of the Far North*. Princeton, NJ: Princeton University Press, 2015.
Child, Ben. "*Life of Pi* Tiger Nearly Drowned on Set, Report Alleges." *Guardian*, November 27, 2013. https://www.theguardian.com/film/2013/nov/27/life-of-pi-tiger-nearly-drowned-report-animals-hollywood.
Frammalino, Ralph, and James Bates. "Questions Raised about Group That Watches Out for Animals in Movies." *Los Angeles Times*, February 9, 2001. http://articles.latimes.com/2001/feb/09/news/mn-23161/3.
Glazer, Sophia. "Now Is the Time to Fight for the Endangered Species Act." *Jane Goodall's Good for All News*. Accessed September 7, 2018. http://news.janegoodall.org/2017/09/05/now-time-fight-endangered-species-act/.
Gruttadaro, Andrew. "The Insane Story behind Disney's *Snow Buddies*, the Movie That Killed 5 Puppies." *Complex*, December 16, 2016. https://www.complex.com/pop-culture/2016/12/snow-buddies-killed-five-puppies?utm_campaign=popculturetw&utm_source=twitter&utm_medium=social.
Harrington, Sean. *The Disney Fetish*. Bloomington: Indiana University Press, 2015.
Humane Hollywood. "About the Film and Television Unit: No Animals Were Harmed." Accessed September 7, 2018. http://humanehollywood.org/index.php/component/content/article/10-reviews/30-about-the-film-television-unit.
———. "Certification Definition." Accessed September 7, 2018. http://humanehollywood.org/index.php/on-the-set/certification-definition.
———. "*Eight Below*." Accessed September 11, 2018. http://humanehollywood.org/index.php/movie-archive/item/eight-below.
———. "Eligibility for the 'No Animals Were Harmed' Certification." Accessed September 7, 2018. http://humanehollywood.org/index.php/component/content/article/11-film-makers/32-eligibility-no-animals-were-harmed.
———. "A Long History of Ensuring Safety." Accessed September 11, 2018. http://www.humanehollywood.org/index.php/end-credits/end-credit-evolution.
———. "*Pirates of the Caribbean: Curse of the Black Pearl*." Accessed September 11, 2018. http://humanehollywood.org/index.php/movie-archive/item/pirates-of-the-caribbean-the-curse-of-the-black-pearl.
———. "*Snow Buddies*." Accessed September 8, 2018. http://humanehollywood.org/index.php/movie-archive/item/snow-buddies.
Humane Society of the United States. "Ag-Gag Laws Keep Animal Cruelty Behind Closed Doors." Accessed September 19, 2018. http://www.humanesociety.org/issues/campaigns/factory_farming/fact-sheets/ag_gag.html.
Jones, Amy. "Sir Paul McCartney Narrates 'Glass Walls.'" PETA UK. November 30, 2009. https://www.peta.org.uk/blog/glass-walls/.

Kilday, Greg. "Universal Cancels Premiere of *A Dog's Purpose*." *Hollywood Reporter*, January 19, 2017. https://www.hollywoodreporter.com/news/a-dogs-purpose-premiere-cancelled-controversy-966354.

Lancaster, Kendra, and Josh Boyd. "Redefinition, Differentiation, and the Farm Animal Welfare Debate." *Journal of Applied Communication Research* 43, no. 2 (2015): 185–202.

Lengyel, Kerry. "The Best and Worst States for Animal Safety." *American Veterinarian*. Accessed September 7, 2018. https://www.americanveterinarian.com/news/the-best-and-worst-states-for-animal-safety.

Lippit, Akira Mizuta. "The Death of an Animal." *Film Quarterly* 56, no. 1 (2002): 9–22.

Loughrey, Clarisse. "*A Dog's Purpose*: Terrified Dog Filmed Being Pushed into Water during Shooting." *Independent*, January 19, 2017. https://www.independent.co.uk/arts-entertainment/films/news/a-dogs-purpose-dog-pushed-into-water-peta-boycott-german-shepherd-a7534741.html.

MacDonald, Scott. "Up Close and Political: Three Short Ruminations on Ideology in the Nature Film." *Film Quarterly* 59, no. 3 (2006): 4–21. doi:10.1525/fq.2006.59.3.4.

McClintock, Pamela. "How Tinker Bell Became Disney's Stealthy $300 Million Franchise." *Hollywood Reporter*, April 3, 2014. https://www.hollywoodreporter.com/news/how-tinker-bell-became-disneys-692559.

Nicholls, Henry. "The Truth about Norwegian Lemmings." *BBC*, November 21, 2014. http://www.bbc.com/earth/story/20141122-the-truth-about-lemmings.

The Numbers. "*Snow Buddies* (2008)." Accessed September 8, 2018. https://www.the-numbers.com/movie/Snow-Buddies#tab=summary.

The Official Disney Fan Club. "Disney's Decades of Work with American Humane Association." Accessed September 8, 2018. https://d23.com/disney-aha-historic-milestones/.

Paul, Ellen, and Robert S. Sikes. "Wildlife Researchers Running the Permit Maze." *ILAR Journal* 54, no. 1 (2013): 14–23. https://doi:10.1093/ilar/ilt013.

PETA. "Animal Actors: Command Performers." Accessed September 7, 2018. https://www.peta.org/issues/animals-in-entertainment/animals-used-entertainment-factsheets/animal-actors-command-performances/.

———. "Disney Gets Sketchy." Accessed September 8, 2018. https://www.peta.org/blog/disney-gets-sketchy/.

———. "In a Win for Animals, Federal Judge Declares Utah 'Ag-Gag' Law Unconstitutional." Accessed September 27, 2018. https://www.peta.org/blog/victory-peta-aldf-challenge-utahs-ag-gag-law/.

Polone, Gavin. "Gavin Polone on *A Dog's Purpose* Outcry, What Really Happened and Who Is to Blame." *Hollywood Reporter*, January 23, 2017. https://www.hollywoodreporter.com/news/gavin-polone-a-dogs-purpose-outcry-what-happened-whos-blame-967160.

Pomerantz, Dorothy. "Camera Rolling—Away from California: State Falls to Fourth in Film Production." *Forbes*, March 6, 2014. https://www.forbes.com/sites/

dorothypomerantz/2014/03/06/local-film-industry-in-deep-trouble-in-california/#5377f5c32f5d.

PR Newswire. "American Humane Association Responds to *The Hollywood Reporter*." Accessed September 12, 2018. https://www.prnewswire.com/news-releases/american-humane-association-responds-to-the-hollywood-reporter-233398221.html.

———. "And the PAWSCAR Goes to . . . " Accessed September 7, 2018. https://www.prnewswire.com/news-releases/and-the-pawscar-goes-to-139040659.html.

Rees, Paul A. *The Laws Protecting Animals and Ecosystems*. Hoboken, NJ: Wiley, 2017.

Rizzo, Vincent. "Brief Summary of Laws concerning Animals in Film Media." *Animal Law*. Accessed September 7, 2018. https://www.animallaw.info/intro/animals-film.

———. "Detailed Discussion of the Legal Protections of Animals in Filmed Media." Animal Legal and Historical Center, Michigan State University. Accessed September 7, 2018. https://www.animallaw.info/article/detailed-discussion-legal-protections-animals-filmed-media.

Rollin, Lucy. "*Pinocchio*: An American Commedia." In *Walt Disney, from Reader to Storyteller: Essays on the Literary Inspirations*, edited by Kathy Merlock Jackson and Mark I. West, 31–44. Jefferson, NC: McFarland, 2014.

Rust, S. "Ecocinema and the Wildlife Film." In *The Cambridge Companion to Literature and the Environment*, edited by L. Westling, 226–40. Cambridge: Cambridge University Press, 2013.

SAG-AFTRA. "About." Accessed September 12, 2018. https://www.sagaftra.org/about.

Shea, Matthew. "Punishing Animal Rights Activists for Animal Abuse: Rapid Reporting and the New Wave of Ag-Gag Laws." *Columbia Journal of Law and Social Problems* 48, no. 3 (2015): 338–71.

Shoard, Catherine. "*A Dog's Purpose* Premiere Cancelled after Video of Stunt Dog 'in Distress.'" *Guardian*, January 20, 2017. https://www.theguardian.com/film/2017/jan/20/a-dogs-purpose-premiere-video-german-shepherd.

Stanton, Rebecca. *The Disneyfication of Animals*. Basingstoke: Palgrave Macmillan, 2021.

Strodder, Chris. *The Disneyland Book of Lists*. Santa Monica, CA: Santa Monica Press, 2015.

Taylor, Drew. "How Walt Disney Invented the Nature Film." *ABC Chicago*, August 12, 2016. https://abc7chicago.com/entertainment/how-walt-disney-invented-the-nature-film/1407077/.

The Telegraph. "Paul McCartney Narrates PETA Video on Slaughterhouses." December 7, 2009. https://www.telegraph.co.uk/news/celebritynews/6750881/Paul-McCartney-narrates-Peta-video-on-slaughterhouses.html.

US Department of Agriculture Animal and Plant Health Inspection Service. "Regulated Businesses (Licensing and Registration)." Accessed September 7, 2018. https://www.aphis.usda.gov/aphis/ourfocus/animalwelfare/ct_awa_regulated_businesses.

Walt Disney Company. "Disney's Use of Live Animals in Entertainment Policy." Accessed September 8, 2018. https://www.thewaltdisneycompany.com/wp-content/uploads/Disneys-Use-of-Live-Animals-in-Entertainment-Policy.pdf.

Wills, John. "Felix Salten's Stories: The Portrayal of Nature in *Bambi*, *Perri* and *The Shaggy Dog*." In *Walt Disney, from Reader to Storyteller: Essays on the Literary Inspirations*, edited by Kathy Merlock Jackson and Mark I. West, 45–61. Jefferson, NC: McFarland, 2014.

NOTES

1. An earlier version of this chapter was published in Rebecca Stanton, *The Disneyfication of Animals* (Basingstoke: Palgrave Macmillan, 2021), 119–51.

2. Clarisse Loughrey, "*A Dog's Purpose*: Terrified Dog Filmed Being Pushed into Water during Shooting," *Independent*, January 19, 2017, https://www.independent.co.uk/arts-entertainment/films/news/a-dogs-purpose-dog-pushed-into-water-peta-boycott-german-shepherd-a7534741.html.

3. Loughrey, "*A Dog's Purpose*."

4. Gavin Polone, "Gavin Polone on *A Dog's Purpose* Outcry, What Really Happened and Who Is to Blame," *Hollywood Reporter*, January 23, 2017, https://www.hollywoodreporter.com/news/gavin-polone-a-dogs-purpose-outcry-what-happened-whos-blame-967160.

5. Polone, "*A Dog's Purpose* Outcry."

6. Catherine Shoard, "*A Dog's Purpose* Premiere Cancelled after Video of Stunt Dog 'in Distress,'" *Guardian*, January 20, 2017, https://www.theguardian.com/film/2017/jan/20/a-dogs-purpose-premiere-video-german-shepherd.

7. Julia Brucculieri, "Josh Gad Responds to 'Disturbing' Leaked Video from *A Dog's Purpose* Set [UPDATE]," *Huffington Post*, January 19, 2017, https://www.huffingtonpost.com/entry/josh-gad-a-dogs-purpose-video-response_us_5880be0ae4b04b69667e9e09.

8. "*A Dog's Purpose* Premiere Cancelled Amid Animal Rights Concerns," *BBC News*, January 20, 2017, https://www.bbc.com/news/world-us-canada-38695074.

9. American Humane, "Independent Investigative Report on *A Dog's Purpose* Finds Edited Video Mischaracterized What Happened on the Set," accessed September 12, 2018, https://www.americanhumane.org/press-release/independent-investigative-report-on-a-dogs-purpose-finds-edited-video-mischaracterized-what-happened-on-the-set/.

10. American Humane, "Independent Investigative Report."

11. American Humane, "Independent Investigative Report."

12. Amy Jones, "Sir Paul McCartney Narrates 'Glass Walls,'" PETA UK, November 30, 2009, https://www.peta.org.uk/blog/glass-walls/.

13. Matthew Shea, "Punishing Animal Rights Activists for Animal Abuse: Rapid Reporting and the New Wave of Ag-Gag Laws," *Columbia Journal of Law and Social Problems* 48, no. 3 (2015): 349.

14. Shea, "Punishing Animal Rights," 349.

15. Kendra Lancaster and Josh Boyd, "Redefinition, Differentiation, and the Farm Animal Welfare Debate," *Journal of Applied Communication Research* 43, no. 2 (2015): 186.

16. Lancaster and Boyd, "Redefinition," 186.

17. "Paul McCartney Narrates PETA Video on Slaughterhouses," *Telegraph*, December 7, 2009, https://www.telegraph.co.uk/news/celebritynews/6750881/Paul-McCartney-narrates-Peta-video-on-slaughterhouses.html.

18. Jonathan Burt, *Animals in Film* (London: Reaktion Books, 2002), 165–67.

19. The socio-zoological scale determines how important a species is, or is not, to humans. A species' rank is determined by the following criteria: usefulness, human relationship, appearance, danger factor, and how "demonic" the animal seems to humans. For example, cats score very highly on this scale, whereas cockroaches do not. Further information can be found in Arnold Arluke and Clinton R. Sanders, *Regarding Animals* (Philadelphia: Temple University Press, 1996), 167–86.

20. Burt, "Animals in Film," 137.

21. Greg Kilday, "Universal Cancels Premiere of *A Dog's Purpose*," *Hollywood Reporter*, January 19, 2017, https://www.hollywoodreporter.com/news/a-dogs-purpose-premiere-cancelled-controversy-966354.

22. American Humane, "History," accessed September 7, 2018, https://www.americanhumane.org/about-us/history/.

23. American Humane, "Humane Hollywood," accessed September 7, 2018, https://www.americanhumane.org/about-us/history/.

24. American Humane, "'No Animals Were Harmed' Frequently Asked Questions," accessed September 7, 2018, https://www.americanhumane.org/fact-sheet/no-animals-were-harmed/.

25. Paul A. Rees, *The Laws Protecting Animals and Ecosystems* (Hoboken, NJ: Wiley, 2017), 355.

26. American Humane, "History."

27. Gary Baum, "*Life of Pi* AHA Monitor Leaves Job after THR Email Exposes Tiger 'Damn Near Drowned,'" *Hollywood Reporter*, November 26, 2013, https://www.hollywoodreporter.com/news/life-pi-aha-monitor-leaves-660369.

28. Gary Baum, "Animals Were Harmed," *Hollywood Reporter*, November 25, 2013, https://www.hollywoodreporter.com/news/general-news/animals-were-harmed-hollywood-reporter-investigation-on-set-injury-death-cover-ups-659556/.

29. American Humane, "History."

30. American Humane, *Guidelines for the Safe Use of Animals in Filmed Media*, accessed September 28, 2018, https://www.americanhumane.org/app/uploads/2016/08/Guidelines2015-WEB-Revised-110315-1.pdf.

31. SAG-AFTRA, "About," accessed September 12, 2018, https://www.sagaftra.org/about.

32. Humane Hollywood, "Certification Definition," September 7, 2018, http://humanehollywood.org/index.php/on-the-set/certification-definition.

33. American Humane, "Frequently Asked Questions."

34. American Humane, "Governance," accessed September 7, 2018, https://www.americanhumane.org/about-us/governance-and-finances/.

35. American Humane, "'No Animals Were Harmed': We Help Keep the Cameras Rolling and the Animals Safe," accessed September 7, 2018, https://www.americanhumane.org/initiative/no-animals-were-harmed/.

36. Baum, "Animals Were Harmed."

37. Baum, "Animals Were Harmed."

38. American Humane, "History."

39. Humane Hollywood, "About the Film and Television Unit: No Animals Were Harmed," accessed September 7, 2018, http://humanehollywood.org/index.php/component/content/article/10-reviews/30-about-the-film-television-unit.

40. Akira Mizuta Lippit, "The Death of an Animal," *Film Quarterly* 56, no. 1 (2002): 9.

41. Humane Hollywood, "Certification Definition."

42. Ben Child, "*Life of Pi* Tiger Nearly Drowned on Set, Report Alleges," *Guardian*, November 27, 2013, https://www.theguardian.com/film/2013/nov/27/life-of-pi-tiger-nearly-drowned-report-animals-hollywood.

43. Humane Hollywood, "Eligibility for the 'No Animals Were Harmed' Certification," accessed September 7, 2018, http://humanehollywood.org/index.php/component/content/article/11-film-makers/32-eligibility-no-animals-were-harmed.

44. The "outstanding" grade was added in 2004. Before then, "acceptable: monitored" was the highest possible grade. Humane Hollywood, "A Long History of Ensuring Safety," accessed September 11, 2018, http://www.humanehollywood.org/index.php/end-credits/end-credit-evolution.

45. Humane Hollywood, "Certification Definition."

46. Humane Hollywood, "A Long History of Ensuring Safety."

47. PETA, "Animal Actors: Command Performers," accessed September 7, 2018, https://www.peta.org/issues/animals-in-entertainment/animals-used-entertainment-factsheets/animal-actors-command-performances/.

48. "American Humane Association Responds to *The Hollywood Reporter*," PR Newswire, accessed September 12, 2018, https://www.prnewswire.com/news-releases/american-humane-association-responds-to-the-hollywood-reporter-233398221.html.

49. American Humane, "We Help Keep the Cameras Rolling."

50. Baum, "Animals Were Harmed."

51. American Humane, *Guidelines for the Safe Use of Animals in Filmed Media*, 6.

52. American Humane, *Guidelines for the Safe Use of Animals in Filmed Media*, 5.

53. American Humane, "Frequently Asked Questions."

54. "And the PAWSCAR Goes to . . . ," PR Newswire, accessed September 7, 2018, https://www.prnewswire.com/news-releases/and-the-pawscar-goes-to-139040659.html.

55. Dorothy Pomerantz, "Camera Rolling—Away from California: State Falls to Fourth in Film Production," *Forbes*, March 6, 2014, https://www.forbes.com/sites/dorothypomerantz/2014/03/06/local-film-industry-in-deep-trouble-in-california/#5377f5c32f5d.

56. Kelli Bender, "*A Dog's Purpose* Controversy: What Does It Mean When Movies Claim 'No Animals Were Harmed' during Filming?," *People*, January 19,

2017, https://people.com/pets/a-dogs-purpose-controversy-what-does-it-mean-when-movies-claim-no-animals-were-harmed-during-filming/.

57. Vincent Rizzo, "Brief Summary of Laws concerning Animals in Film Media," *Animal Law*, accessed September 7, 2018, https://www.animallaw.info/intro/animals-film.

58. Sophia Glazer, "Now Is the Time to Fight for the Endangered Species Act," *Jane Goodall's Good for All News*, accessed September 7, 2018, http://news.janegoodall.org/2017/09/05/now-time-fight-endangered-species-act/.

59. Animal Legal Defense Fund, "Animal Protection Laws of the United States of America," accessed September 7, 2018, https://aldf.org/article/animal-protection-laws-of-the-united-states-of-america/.

60. Vincent Rizzo, "Detailed Discussion of the Legal Protections of Animals in Filmed Media," Animal Legal and Historical Center, Michigan State University, accessed September 7, 2018, https://www.animallaw.info/article/detailed-discussion-legal-protections-animals-filmed-media.

61. Shea, "Punishing Animal Rights Activists," 337–71.

62. Humane Society of the United States, "Ag-Gag Laws Keep Animal Cruelty Behind Closed Doors," accessed September 19, 2018, http://www.humanesociety.org/issues/campaigns/factory_farming/fact-sheets/ag_gag.html.

63. PETA, "In a Win for Animals, Federal Judge Declares Utah 'Ag-Gag' Law Unconstitutional," accessed September 27, 2018, https://www.peta.org/blog/victory-peta-aldf-challenge-utahs-ag-gag-law/.

64. US Department of Agriculture Animal and Plant Health Inspection Service, "Regulated Businesses (Licensing and Registration)," accessed September 7, 2018, https://www.aphis.usda.gov/aphis/ourfocus/animalwelfare/ct_awa_regulated_businesses.

65. Ellen Paul and Robert S. Sikes, "Wildlife Researchers Running the Permit Maze," *ILAR Journal* 54, no. 1 (2013): 14–23, https://doi:10.1093/ilar/ilt013.

66. Baum, "Animals Were Harmed."

67. Baum, "Animals Were Harmed."

68. Kerry Lengyel, "The Best and Worst States for Animal Safety," *American Veterinarian*, accessed September 7, 2018, https://www.americanveterinarian.com/news/the-best-and-worst-states-for-animal-safety.

69. "California Code, Penal Code, PEN 597," FindLaw, accessed September 7, 2018, https://codes.findlaw.com/ca/penal-code/pen-sect-597.html.

70. Baum, "Animals Were Harmed."

71. American Humane, *Guidelines for the Safe Use of Animals in Filmed Media*, 12.

72. Arluke and Sanders, *Regarding Animals*, 167–86.

73. Stanton, *The Disneyfication of Animals*, 165–68.

74. Lucy Rollin, "*Pinocchio*: An American Commedia," in *Walt Disney, from Reader to Storyteller: Essays on the Literary Inspirations*, ed. Kathy Merlock Jackson and Mark I. West (Jefferson, NC: McFarland, 2014), 36.

75. Sean Harrington, *The Disney Fetish* (Bloomington: Indiana University Press, 2015), 193–220.

76. Scott MacDonald, "Up Close and Political: Three Short Ruminations on Ideology in the Nature Film," *Film Quarterly* 59, no. 3 (2006): 7, doi:10.1525/fq.2006.59.3.4.

77. MacDonald, "Up Close and Political," 7.

78. Stephen Bocking, "Science and Spaces in the Northern Environment," *Environmental History* 12, no. 4 (2007): 870, http://www.jstor.org/stable/25473165.

79. S. Rust, "Ecocinema and the Wildlife Film," in *The Cambridge Companion to Literature and the Environment*, ed. L. Westling (Cambridge: Cambridge University Press, 2013), 226–40.

80. Sharon Chester, *The Arctic Guide: Wildlife of the Far North* (Princeton, NJ: Princeton University Press, 2015), 47.

81. Rust, "Ecocinema," 226.

82. Henry Nicholls, "The Truth about Norwegian Lemmings," BBC, November 21, 2014, http://www.bbc.com/earth/story/20141122-the-truth-about-lemmings.

83. MacDonald, "Up Close and Political," 8.

84. MacDonald, "Up Close and Political," 7.

85. Drew Taylor, "How Walt Disney Invented the Nature Film," ABC Chicago, August 12, 2016, https://abc7chicago.com/entertainment/how-walt-disney-invented-the-nature-film/1407077/.

86. John Wills, "Felix Salten's Stories: The Portrayal of Nature in *Bambi*, *Perri* and *The Shaggy Dog*," in *Walt Disney, from Reader to Storyteller: Essays on the Literary Inspirations*, ed. Kathy Merlock Jackson and Mark I. West (Jefferson, NC: McFarland, 2014), 51–55.

87. The Official Disney Fan Club, "Disney's Decades of Work with American Humane Association," accessed September 8, 2018, https://d23.com/disney-aha-historic-milestones/.

88. Chris Strodder, *The Disneyland Book of Lists* (Santa Monica, CA: Santa Monica Press, 2015), 21.

89. "Believed acceptable" is given when the AHA did not monitor all of the scenes involving animals. This grade is no longer used by the AHA. Humane Hollywood, "A Long History of Ensuring Safety."

90. Duncan Campbell, "Hollywood Shoot Horses, Don't They?," *Guardian*, February 10, 2001, https://www.theguardian.com/world/2001/feb/10/filmnews.film.

91. Ralph Frammalino and James Bates, "Questions Raised about Group That Watches Out for Animals in Movies," *Los Angeles Times*, February 9, 2001, http://articles.latimes.com/2001/feb/09/news/mn-23161/3.

92. Baum, "Animals Were Harmed."

93. Baum, "Animals Were Harmed."

94. Humane Hollywood, "*Pirates of the Caribbean: Curse of the Black Pearl*," accessed September 11, 2018, http://humanehollywood.org/index.php/movie-archive/item/pirates-of-the-caribbean-the-curse-of-the-black-pearl.

95. Humane Hollywood, "*Pirates of the Caribbean: Curse of the Black Pearl*."

96. Humane Hollywood, "*Pirates of the Caribbean: Curse of the Black Pearl*."

97. Baum, "Animals Were Harmed."

98. Baum, "Animals Were Harmed."

99. Humane Hollywood, "*Eight Below*," accessed September 11, 2018, http://humanehollywood.org/index.php/movie-archive/item/eight-below.

100. Humane Hollywood, "*Snow Buddies*," accessed September 8, 2018, http://humanehollywood.org/index.php/movie-archive/item/snow-buddies.

101. Humane Hollywood, "*Snow Buddies*."

102. PETA, "Disney Gets Sketchy," accessed September 8, 2018, https://www.peta.org/blog/disney-gets-sketchy/.

103. Andrew Gruttadaro, "The Insane Story behind Disney's *Snow Buddies*, the Movie That Killed 5 Puppies," *Complex*, December 16, 2016, https://www.complex.com/pop-culture/2016/12/snow-buddies-killed-five-puppies?utm_campaign=popculturetw&utm_source=twitter&utm_medium=social.

104. Humane Hollywood, "*Snow Buddies*."

105. Humane Hollywood, "*Snow Buddies*."

106. PETA, "Disney Gets Sketchy."

107. The Numbers, "*Snow Buddies* (2008)," accessed September 8, 2018, https://www.the-numbers.com/movie/Snow-Buddies#tab=summary.

108. Gruttadaro, "The Insane Story."

109. Gruttadaro, "The Insane Story."

110. Pamela McClintock, "How Tinker Bell Became Disney's Stealthy $300 Million Franchise," *Hollywood Reporter*, April 3, 2014, https://www.hollywoodreporter.com/news/how-tinker-bell-became-disneys-692559.

111. Walt Disney Company, "Disney's Use of Live Animals in Entertainment Policy," accessed September 8, 2018, https://www.thewaltdisneycompany.com/wp-content/uploads/Disneys-Use-of-Live-Animals-in-Entertainment-Policy.pdf.

Chapter 5

Bringing Animal Cruelty Investigation into Mainstream Law Enforcement in the United States

By Randall Lockwood

A BRIEF HISTORY OF THE ASPCA AND LAW ENFORCEMENT

The American Society for the Prevention of Cruelty to Animals (ASPCA) was founded in 1866 by Henry Bergh and a small group of prominent New Yorkers, becoming the first animal protection organization in the Western Hemisphere. Bergh had been moved by the plight of working animals he observed while serving as a diplomat in Russia. He stopped in London prior to his return to America to meet with leaders of the Royal Society for the Prevention of Cruelty to Animals (RSPCA), which had been founded in 1824 and received a Royal Charter in 1840. He recognized the need for a similar organization in America.

Soon after his return from London, Bergh drafted a charter for the ASPCA that listed many prominent New Yorkers as supporters, including the mayor of New York City and members of the Rockefeller family. The original patrons also included the police board president (the equivalent of the current police commissioner) and the district attorney for New York County.[1]

Nine days after the ASPCA charter was granted by the New York State legislature, Bergh convinced this body to pass an anti-cruelty law that gave the new society the authority to enforce the new law. Under this law animal fighting was made illegal—including bull, bear, dog-, and cockfighting—as was the keeping of fighting animals and the management of fights. The law also imposed a duty to provide "sufficient quality of good and wholesome food and water" to many animals and empowered any persons to enter premises to provide for animals' needs. It also made it illegal to transport any creature in a cruel or inhumane manner. The legislation establishing the ASPCA not only empowered ASPCA agents to enforce the animal cruelty laws but also required that the police force of New York City "as well as all other places where police organizations exist [in New York State]" aid the ASPCA in enforcing the law. Police superintendent John Kennedy issued an order to police captains to inform their men of the requirement to assist ASPCA agents when asked.[2]

Bergh also succeeded in being appointed to the New York Bar and was given authority to act as an assistant district attorney to help prosecute the cases that came under the ASPCA's jurisdiction. These arrangements did not go smoothly. Bergh often complained about a lack of cooperation from some police and the city's magistrates, who frequently simply refused to hear animal cases.

This broad authority and Bergh's aggressive enforcement alienated many of those who exploited animals, including carting and transport companies (which often overloaded horses), dogfighters, fox hunters, and animal exhibitors, including legendary showman P. T. Barnum.

Over the next century the relationship between the ASPCA and the NYPD was cordial, but officers tended to rely on ASPCA humane law enforcement officers to deal with any animal-related cases and were generally less informed about existing animal cruelty laws and their enforcement. In the 1980s, law enforcement interest in animal cruelty began to increase significantly, in part fueled by the proliferation of research into the association between animal cruelty and interpersonal violence,[3] including domestic violence. This interest was further driven by the dramatic growth in size and political impact of animal protection and animal rights groups in the United States, who often demanded action against those who abused animals. This development was mirrored in the strengthening of animal cruelty laws and the inclusion of felony penalties for some forms of animal cruelty in every state's law by 2016;[4] dogfighting, for example, was made a felony offense in every state and at the federal level.[5]

HUMANE LAW ENFORCEMENT IN THE TWENTY-FIRST CENTURY

Public interest in law enforcement's response to animal cruelty cases surged starting in 2001 with the launch of the television program *Animal Precinct*, a popular weekly show following the activities of the Humane Law Enforcement Division of the ASPCA. The show ran until 2008 and spawned many similar programs, including *Animal Cops: Detroit*; *Animal Cops: Houston*; *Animal Cops: San Francisco*; *Animal Cops: Phoenix*; *Animal Cops: Philadelphia*; *Animal Cops: Miami*; *Miami Animal Police*; and even *Animal Cops: South Africa*.[6]

Despite their popularity, these shows pointed out several serious issues surrounding how animal crimes were being addressed. First, most of the agencies involved in humane law enforcement were, and continue to be, charitable animal protection organizations rather than publicly funded law enforcement or animal control agencies. Although the organizations' cases of responding to animal cruelty are popular with potential donors, the financial and time costs of becoming involved in often complex and lengthy legal proceedings can be a considerable drain on the resources of these charities.[7] Second, such humane law enforcement teams tend to be relatively small. At the peak of *Animal Precinct*, the ASPCA's Humane Law Enforcement Division had only about twenty officers to cover cases in a city of nearly eight million people. Response times were often very slow, and nonemergency cases would often receive little or no response.

Another problem was the fact that animal cruelty offenses often co-occur with other serious crimes, often violent ones. Crimes such as dogfighting usually involve illegal drugs, illegal weapons, and other serious crimes beyond the scope of training or the enforcement powers of humane agents. Animal cruelty was also increasingly recognized as a frequent component of domestic violence and child abuse, where humane agents had limited training and authority.[8] Humane law enforcement officers also often lacked training or access to up-to-date forensic resources such as DNA and trace evidence collection that are increasingly an important part of animal cruelty investigations.[9]

ASPCA research found that nearly half of law enforcement officers encounter animal cruelty at least several times a year, nearly a quarter of them on a monthly basis. Although animal cruelty clearly violates many laws nationwide, the investigation and prosecution of such crimes usually was not seen as a core component of law enforcement training or activity. The leadership of the ASPCA thought that it was time to facilitate a shift in this thinking that could parallel changing approaches to police response to interpersonal violence. In the recent past, domestic violence often had been viewed by police as the purview of social services or victim advocacy groups—a family problem that was best addressed outside of law enforcement. As awareness grew about the severity—and often lethality—of interpersonal violence, it came to be seen as a serious law enforcement issue. Today all law enforcement officers receive training on laws related to domestic violence and other forms of interpersonal violence, as well as training on the dynamics of this abuse and appropriate law enforcement investigation and response. In addition, most police departments have special units devoted to such crimes. Given the growing recognition of the significance of animal cruelty as a serious crime in and of itself and as both an indicator and predictor of other crimes, it seemed timely to push for law enforcement changes echoing those that had taken place for interpersonal violence.

In mid-2013 the ASPCA entered into a four-month pilot partnership with the New York Police Department in the Bronx. The agreement for this partnership identified the responsibilities of the two agencies.

The NYPD would:

- Create an animal cruelty squad of specially trained officers to serve as the primary contact for animal cruelty cases
- Provide rapid response to animal cruelty calls made to emergency (911) and nonemergency (311) police lines
- Use its resources, including forensic teams, to investigate and document animal crimes as needed
- Participate in community outreach efforts to encourage the public to report crimes against animals
- Provide criminal case data to the ASPCA for analysis of animal-related crimes

The ASPCA would:

- Provide animal cruelty response training to all officers and managers
- Provide for immediate care of all animals brought in by NYPD
- Conduct veterinary forensic exams and prepare reports on animals involved in cases where charges might be filed
- Provide long-term housing, care, treatment, and placement of animals
- Work with prosecutors and police to provide legal expertise and assistance for cruelty case management
- Assist in public information and awareness campaigns and events
- Provide additional resources to facilitate responses to animal cruelty crimes

The pilot project proved to be successful and popular with NYPD officers and leadership and was expanded to the entire NYPD in January 2014, with the goal of eventually reaching all 34,000 officers of the nation's largest police force. In the first two years of operation, arrests for animal cruelty crimes rose 18 percent, and the number of animals rescued from harm by the NYPD rose 58 percent, to over 1,000. As of 2020, the ASPCA had documented and treated more than 4,300 animals from nearly 2,000 cruelty cases brought to it by the NYPD.

The partnership continues to grow and develop. In 2018 the ASPCA and NYPD began a partnership with Crimestoppers to encourage the reporting of suspected animal cruelty and provide rewards of up to $2,500 for information leading to arrests for such crimes. The ASPCA also donated microchip scanners to each of the eighty-six NYPD precincts to allow more rapid identification of "owned" animals who may have been the victim of cruelty. The ASPCA and NYPD also launched a new series of social media videos to encourage New Yorkers to report animal cruelty throughout the city's five boroughs. In August 2018 the NYPD unveiled a $500,000 mobile command post vehicle donated by the ASPCA that will be used to help fight animal abuse. The command center has a full conference room and space to carry collapsible cages, portable lights, leashes, and microchip readers. It will be sent to the scene of major crimes or incidents and is expected to help improve the work already being done by the department's animal cruelty investigation squad.

OTHER PROMISING TRENDS IN ANIMAL LAW ENFORCEMENT IN THE UNITED STATES

The ASPCA–NYPD partnership is just one indicator of the growing commitment that mainstream law enforcement has shown to responding to animal cruelty. Major law enforcement organizations, including the International Association of Chiefs of Police[10] and the National Sheriffs' Association,[11] have distributed information to their members on the importance of responding to animal abuse and neglect. A growing number of police departments have sought additional training on dogfighting and other animal crimes and have established special units to handle animal-related crimes. Professional associations for prosecutors also have developed tools for helping support those who bring such cases to trial. The National District Attorneys Association has provided such resources,[12] and the Association of Prosecuting Attorneys maintains a library of webinars on animal abuse prosecution as a resource for prosecutors.[13] Many prosecutor's offices also have designated a particular individual or team to become specialized in handling all animal-related cases in their jurisdiction. This has significantly improved the efficiency of handling such cases since such prosecutors become familiar with the applicable laws and nature of the special evidence that is likely to be of importance.

Although there is currently no centralized record-keeping for all animal cruelty cases in the United States,[14] a major indicator of new interest in such crimes is the fact that the Federal Bureau of Investigation (FBI) added animal cruelty to the crimes tracked within the National Incident-Based Reporting System (NIBRS) beginning in 2016. The NIBRS uses a generic definition of animal cruelty as

> intentionally, knowingly, or recklessly taking an action that mistreats or kills any animal without just cause, such as torturing, tormenting, mutilation, maiming, poisoning, or abandonment. Included are instances of duty to provide care, e.g., shelter, food, water, care if sick or injured; transporting or confining an animal in a manner likely to cause injury or death; causing an animal to fight with another; inflicting excessive or repeated unnecessary pain or suffering, e.g., uses objects to beat or injure an animal.[15]

The NIBRS further categorizes animal cruelty cases as intentional abuse/torture, organized abuse (dogfighting and cockfighting), animal sexual abuse, or simple/gross neglect, defined as "the failure of a person to provide for the needs of an animal (lack of food, water, shelter, grooming or veterinary care)."[16]

Unfortunately, the NIBRS system does not identify the species or numbers of animals involved in each incident, so there is no capability within NIBRS reports to easily identify the nature of the crime or the specifics of the animal victim or victims. The NIBRS considers the victim in each incident to be "society." In addition, current participation in reporting animal cruelty cases to the NIBRS is low. The 2016 NIBRS report listed only 1,126 animal cruelty cases from thirteen states, with only three states accounting for nearly 75 percent of reports.[17] By 2018, reports of 5,201 cases had been received from twenty-nine states, representing only 36 percent of the US population.[18]

The potential for involvement in animal abuse to predict other acts of interpersonal violence has reached the attention of the nation's top anti-terrorism forces. In July 2018 the Joint Counterterrorism Assessment Team, a collaboration of the National Counterterrorism Center, the Department of Homeland Security, and the FBI, published a report describing animal cruelty as a possible warning behavior for terrorism.[19]

These are all promising signs that animal cruelty is now widely recognized as a significant crime impacting thousands of people and animals and that mainstream law enforcement at local, state, and national levels are seeking effective ways to respond. Challenges remain in the United States. Few communities have the resources of the NYPD and the ASPCA to launch the kind of large-scale coordinated response to animal abuse and neglect that has been possible in New York City. But many components of this innovative partnership, including training, community coordination, and public awareness campaigns, can be adapted for use in many more areas, hopefully aiding in the reduction of violence and suffering of animals and the people who care about them.

REFERENCES

Arkow, Phil, and Randall Lockwood. "Defining Animal Cruelty." In *Animal Cruelty: A Multidisciplinary Approach to Understanding*, edited by Cassandra L. Reyes and Mary P. Brewster, 3–24. Durham, NC: Carolina Academic Press, 2013.

Ascione, Frank R., and Randall Lockwood. "Cruelty to Animals: Changing Psychological, Social, and Legislative Perspectives." In *The State of the Animals 2001*, edited by Deborah J. Salem and Andrew N. Rowan, 39–54. Washington, DC: Humane Society of the United States, 2001.

Association of Prosecuting Attorneys. "Animal Abuse Prosecution." Accessed February 18. 2022, https://apat.mclms.net/en/package/1568/course/2546/view.

Bernstein, Madeline, and Barry M. Wolf. "Time to Feed the Evidence: What to Do with Seized Animals." *Environmental Law Reporter* 35, no. 10 (2005): 10679–89.

DeSousa, Dan. *NIBRS User Manual for Animal Control Officers and Humane Law Enforcement*. 2016. Accessed March 1, 2017. http://www.nacanet.org/page/NIBRS_Manual.

Federal Bureau of Investigation. "2016 National Incident-Based Reporting System." Accessed November 1, 2017. https://ucr.fbi.gov/nibrs/2016.

Gupta, Maya. "Functional Links between Intimate Partner Violence and Animal Abuse: Personality Features and Representations of Aggression." *Society & Animals* 16, no. 3 (2008): 223–42.

Joint Counterterrorism Assessment Team. "First Responder's Toolbox." Accessed June 20, 2018. https://www.sheriffs.org/sites/default/files/First%20Responders%20Toolbox%20Animal%20Cruelty.pdf.

Lane, Marion S., and Stephen L. Zawistowski. *Heritage of Care: The American Society for the Prevention of Cruelty to Animals*. Westport, CT: Praeger, 2008.

Linzey, Andrew, ed. *The Link between Animal Abuse and Human Violence*. Sussex, UK: Sussex Academic Press, 2009.

Lockwood, Randall. *Animal Cruelty Prosecution: Opportunities for Early Response to Crime and Interpersonal Violence*. Alexandria, VA: American Prosecutors Research Institute, 2006.

———. "Counting Cruelty: Challenges and Opportunities in Assessing Animal Abuse and Neglect in America." In *International Handbook of Theory and Research on Animal Abuse and Cruelty*, edited by Frank R. Ascione, 87–110. West Lafayette, IN: Purdue University Press, 2008.

———. "Cruelty to Animals and Interpersonal Violence: An Update." Training Key #689. Arlington, VA: International Association of Chiefs of Police, 2014.

———. *Dogfighting Toolkit for Law Enforcement: Addressing Dogfighting in Your Community.* Washington, DC: Community Oriented Policing Services, US Department of Justice, 2011.

———. "Investigating Animal Cruelty: The Past, Present and Future." Maddie's Fund Shelter Medicine Conference, Cornell University School of Veterinary Medicine Ithaca, NY, July 28, 2017.

Lockwood, Randall, and Frank R. Ascione, eds. *Animal Cruelty and Interpersonal Violence: Readings in Research and Application.* West Lafayette, IN: Purdue University Press, 1998.

Merck, Melinda. *Veterinary Forensics: Animal Cruelty Investigations.* 2nd ed. Ames, IA: Wiley-Blackwell, 2013.

Palais, J. "Animal Cruelty in the U.S." *Animal Care and Control Today* (Summer 2020): 19–23.

Phillips, Allie, and Randall Lockwood. *Investigating & Prosecuting Animal Abuse: A Guidebook on Safer Communities, Safer Families & Being an Effective Voice for Animal Victims.* Alexandria, VA: National District Attorneys Association, 2013.

Ponder, Claire, and Randall Lockwood. "Cruelty to Animals and Family Violence." Training Key #526. Arlington, VA: International Association of Chiefs of Police, 2001.

Sinclair, Leslie, Melinda Merck, and Randall Lockwood. *Forensic Investigation of Animal Cruelty: A Guide for Veterinary and Law Enforcement Professionals.* Washington, DC: Humane Society of the United States, 2006.

Thompson, John. "NSA's Deputy Executive Director, John Thompson, Supports Animal Cruelty Laws." *Deputy and Court Officer* 3 (2013): 8–9.

Touroo, Rachel, and Amanda Fitch. "Identification, Collection, and Preservation of Veterinary Forensic Evidence: On Scene and during the Postmortem Examination." *Veterinary Pathology* 53, no. 5 (2016): 880–87.

Zawistowski, Stephen L. "The American Society for the Prevention of Cruelty to Animals (ASPCA)." In *Encyclopedia of Animal Rights and Animal Welfare*, 2nd ed., edited by Marc Bekoff, 13–16. Santa Barbara, CA: Greenwood Press, 2010.

NOTES

1. Stephen L. Zawistowski, "The American Society for the Prevention of Cruelty to Animals (ASPCA)," in *Encyclopedia of Animal Rights and Animal Welfare*, 2nd ed., ed. Marc Bekoff (Santa Barbara, CA: Greenwood Press, 2010), 13–16.

2. Marion S. Lane and Stephen L. Zawistowski, *Heritage of Care: The American Society for the Prevention of Cruelty to Animals* (Westport, CT: Praeger, 2008), 15–21.

3. Andrew Linzey, ed., *The Link between Animal Abuse and Human Violence* (Sussex, UK: Sussex Academic Press, 2009); Randall Lockwood and Frank Ascione, eds., *Animal Cruelty and Interpersonal Violence: Readings in Research and Application*

(West Lafayette, IN: Purdue University Press, 1998); Frank R. Ascione and Randall Lockwood, "Cruelty to Animals: Changing Psychological, Social, and Legislative Perspectives," in *The State of the Animals 2001*, ed. Deborah J. Salem and Andrew N. Rowan (Washington, DC: Humane Society of the United States, 2001), 39–54.

4. Randall Lockwood, *Dogfighting Toolkit for Law Enforcement: Addressing Dogfighting in Your Community* (Washington, DC: Community Oriented Policing Services, US Department of Justice, 2011).

5. Phil Arkow and Randall Lockwood, "Defining Animal Cruelty," in *Animal Cruelty: A Multidisciplinary Approach to Understanding*, ed. Cassandra L. Reyes and Mary P. Brewster (Durham, NC: Carolina Academic Press, 2013), 3–24.

6. Randall Lockwood, "Investigating Animal Cruelty: The Past, Present and Future" (Maddie's Fund Shelter Medicine Conference, Cornell University School of Veterinary Medicine, Ithaca, NY, July 28, 2017).

7. Madeline Bernstein and Barry M. Wolf, "Time to Feed the Evidence: What to Do with Seized Animals," *Environmental Law Reporter* 35, no. 10 (2005): 10679.

8. Maya Gupta, "Functional Links between Intimate Partner Violence and Animal Abuse: Personality Features and Representations of Aggression," *Society & Animals* 16, no. 3 (2008): 223–42.

9. Leslie Sinclair, Melinda Merck, and Randall Lockwood, *Forensic Investigation of Animal Cruelty: A Guide for Veterinary and Law Enforcement Professionals* (Washington, DC: Humane Society of the United States, 2006); Rachel Touroo and Amanda Fitch, "Identification, Collection, and Preservation of Veterinary Forensic Evidence: On Scene and during the Postmortem Examination," *Veterinary Pathology* 53, no. 5 (2016): 880–87; Melinda Merck, *Veterinary Forensics: Animal Cruelty Investigations*, 2nd ed. (Ames, IA: Wiley-Blackwell, 2013).

10. Claire Ponder and Randall Lockwood, "Cruelty to Animals and Family Violence," Training Key #526 (Arlington, VA: International Association of Chiefs of Police, 2001); Randall Lockwood, "Cruelty to Animals and Interpersonal Violence: An Update," Training Key #689 (Arlington, VA: International Association of Chiefs of Police, 2014).

11. John Thompson, "NSA's Deputy Executive Director, John Thompson, Supports Animal Cruelty Laws," *Deputy and Court Officer* 3 (2013): 8–9.

12. Randall Lockwood, *Animal Cruelty Prosecution: Opportunities for Early Response to Crime and Interpersonal Violence* (Alexandria, VA: American Prosecutors Research Institute, 2006); Allie Phillips and Randall Lockwood, *Investigating & Prosecuting Animal Abuse: A Guidebook on Safer Communities, Safer Families & Being an Effective Voice for Animal Victims* (Alexandria, VA: National District Attorneys Association, 2013).

13. Association of Prosecuting Attorneys, "Animal Abuse Prosecution," accessed February 18, 2022, https://apat.mclms.net/en/package/1568/course/2546/view.

14. Randall Lockwood, "Counting Cruelty: Challenges and Opportunities in Assessing Animal Abuse and Neglect in America," in *International Handbook of Theory and Research on Animal Abuse and Cruelty*, ed. Frank R. Ascione (West Lafayette, IN: Purdue University Press, 2008), 87–110.

15. Dan DeSousa, *NIBRS User Manual for Animal Control Officers and Humane Law Enforcement* (2016), accessed March 1, 2017, http://www.nacanet.org/page/NIBRS_Manual.

16. DeSousa, *NIBRS User Manual.*

17. Federal Bureau of Investigation, "2016 National Incident-Based Reporting System," accessed November 1, 2017, https://ucr.fbi.gov/nibrs/2016.

18. J. Palais, "Animal Cruelty in the U.S.," *Animal Care and Control Today* (Summer 2020): 19–23.

19. Joint Counterterrorism Assessment Team, "First Responder's Toolbox," accessed June 20, 2018, https://www.sheriffs.org/sites/default/files/First%20Responders%20Toolbox%20Animal%20Cruelty.pdf.

PART II

Ethical–Legal Issues

Chapter 6

From Ethics into Law

By David Favre

Let us begin with a simple ethical proposition. It is unethical to beat your dog, or any other dog for that matter. That is a personal, ethical judgment that comes easily and most likely is held by a strong majority of people within our society. But is the act illegal? Could we not simply pass a law that says it is a crime to beat your dog? It certainly is possible, but it is unlikely to happen. Passing a law is a very complex process. We do not have a philosopher-king who simply makes things happen. Many individuals, with differing views, are part of the process of law adoption. While ethics is a personal decision, law is a group decision in a process not unlike that of herding dogs (I am not sure cats can be herded, but with dogs at least there is hope). Therefore, the first step in moving toward the adoption of a law is to find out if others share your ethical view—in particular, those who will have a voice in the adoption process, collectively referred to as the legal decision-makers.

Our political process in the United States intentionally contains significant sharing of political power. The adoption of a law is a majority-vote activity, but before it even gets to a vote, the legislative committee process gives power to those who chair committees and who are party leaders to stop, start, and modify proposed laws. These individuals have a chain of other people linked to them who influence what the decision-makers might do. Our sample issue most likely would not give rise to adverse lobbying from economic interests seeking to protect their profit, as is the case with so many animal issues. So we set aside that complexity for this simple example.

Now, not everyone in this political process will hold the same view of how to treat a companion animal. A few might hold that it is necessary to have the right to beat a dog for purposes of discipline. Some will say, "We don't need more laws that the police have no time to enforce." Others (often lawyers with expertise in criminal law) will ask, "Well, what is a beating—when does it rise to the level of crime? One strike with a shoe or belt? Perhaps ten strikes? How can the state prove when a violation has occurred?" A few might say, "Why are we wasting our time talking about dogs?" Some will hold that although they do not approve of beating a dog, the state should not interfere with events that happen within the home, within the family. These are road-blocks to change, sometimes overcome, sometimes not, usually resolved by compromise.

The discussion among the legislators of draft language for the law will quickly focus on the difference of striking a dog versus viciously beating a dog, which hopefully all would oppose. How do you describe exactly which acts should be a crime? Why should the prohibition be limited to dogs? What about cats, horses, or lizards? Is it reasonable to impose a criminal record and possible jail time on someone for such acts? Those with different views will seek compromise. And compromise language is usually intentionally vague, allowing both sides to declare victory. In our example the language most likely to be adopted would be this: "It is a misdemeanor crime for any individual to unnecessarily beat their dog or the dog of another." The word "beat" might be defined as "the striking of a dog with an object with sufficient force as to break the skin or cause harm to an organ of the dog." Most likely, this outcome would not be exactly what those with the initial ethical concern had in mind.

Consider some examples from the real world of law. The first example is the historical beginning point for the United States. This anti-cruelty law was adopted in New York in 1867. Section 1 of the law reads,

> If any person shall . . . torture, torment, deprive of necessary sustenance, or *unnecessarily or cruelly beat*, or needlessly mutilate or kill . . . any living creature [no ownership statement], every such offender shall, for every such offence, be guilty of a misdemeanor.[1]

The qualifier "unnecessary" has been part of animal law from the beginning. Think about how the word would be acceptable to the elected representative considering a new law. It would not be difficult to convince the lawmaker to make unnecessary beating illegal. It is by definition unnecessary. However, the term "unnecessary" is never actually defined, so the responsibility to define the term is shifted to a court proceeding.

The second example is from the most recent law adopted in England.

> 4 Unnecessary suffering
>
> (1) A person commits an offence if—
>
> (a) *an act* of his, or a failure of his to act, *causes an animal to suffer*,

(b) he knew, or ought reasonably to have known, that the act, or failure to act, would have that effect or be likely to do so,
(c) the animal is a protected animal, and
(d) *the suffering is unnecessary*.[2]

In this law the key word is not "beat" but "suffering." This term is also a very difficult one to define. However, assuming an act is deemed to cause suffering, it is a crime only if it is unnecessary. Clearly, much is being left to the courts to decide on a case-by-case basis.

Setting aside our specific issue, consider some of the more general issues that arise in the crafting of a new criminal law provision. Criminal laws put individuals at the risk of loss of money and liberty. We want the state to be very careful about the words it uses to define crimes. Vague laws allow the state to engage in arbitrary enforcement, often for reasons not related to the actions of the individual. Perhaps those in power are simply looking for an excuse to harass someone. On the other side of the equation, lawyers who represent a defendant will use all their skill to show how the actions of the defendant did not fall under the specific words. Words matter—a whole lot—in both common-law and civil-law countries, for the words shape what an individual may or may not do in their society.

Another policy consideration in the adoption of new criminal law is that it is a bad idea to adopt laws that will not be enforced, cannot be enforced, or would be a waste of state resources to enforce. Will the police be able to find and arrest those who violate the law, will the prosecutors be willing to file criminal charges, and will the judges take the offense seriously?

In the United States we have some newly adopted laws to deal with a recently arising problem of individuals falsely claiming that their dogs are service animals, who by federal law are allowed in public places as an accommodation for health problems such as blindness or seizures or for conditions such as PTSD.[3] A number of states have made it illegal to represent falsely that your dog is a service animal in order to obtain access to public places such as restaurants with a untrained companion animal.[4] While the legislatures should be commended for trying to address the problem, such laws are not going to work, for they are basically unenforceable. The crime is a lie told to someone like a building guard or headwaiter of a restaurant, and it is impossible to know it is a lie at the time of the statement. Businesses don't want the hassle of calling the police, and the police have more important things to do. Finally, I cannot imagine a prosecutor believing it is worth their time and resources to file a legal action in such a case and bring it before a judge. News stories suggest that people continue to make this false claim, and yet I am unaware of any prosecutions in any of the states that have adopted a related new law.

A fundamental issue that a legislature will address for each animal law it drafts is who should make the determination as to whether a specific act is illegal. There are three possibilities:

1. The legislature itself: "It is a crime to strike a dog with an object weighing more than ten pounds/kilos."
2. The courts, by jury or judge: "It is a crime to unnecessarily beat a dog."
3. State agencies by the adoption of regulations: Since it is unlikely the state would regulate the striking of dogs, this would not apply in our example case. But regulations are adopted for the control of puppy mills.[5]

Under option one, it is the legislature that draws a clear line, easy to understand and enforce with objective evidence: either the object is ten pounds, or it is not. The motivation for the act is not an issue. The problem, of course, is that sometimes we do want to know what the actor was thinking, and lots of objects weighing less than ten pounds can be used to beat an animal. Finally, there is the reality that avoidance of the law is very easy.

If the legislature chooses option two, then there is an additional level of vagueness inserted into the law. Some critical words in the adopted language are not defined (this is intentional, not an oversight). What is "unnecessary," and what does "beat" mean? This uncertainty is an additional level of grayness. How is this resolved? In our legal system, it is resolved by a jury in a particular case. Prosecutors do not like this type of language because it does not make clear exactly what set of action is a crime. This means that prosecutors are reluctant to file cases against bad actors unless the prosecutors have a high degree of certainty that a particular set of facts will be found by a jury to constitute an "unnecessary beating." Otherwise, it is a waste of time and resources.

For example, consider a hypothetical case brought to the attention of the police: A dog is in the midst of biting a visiting child. The "owner" of the dog strikes the dog to make him stop and continues to strike the dog to make sure the dog understands that the action of biting was unacceptable. Afterward, it is observed that the dog has a large black bruise and a one-inch break in the skin, but the wound does not need to be stitched up by a veterinarian. Was the person's action unethical? Some say yes; some say no. Was it a crime? We do not know until the jury returns with a verdict. So the ultimate question is: how does a jury decide if a particular act of beating is "unnecessary"? This is the ultimate fuzzy point. Making matters even more difficult to understand or predict, a jury does not have to explain its thinking. The defendant is either guilty of a crime or not guilty. It is a collective social judgment from a group of average people from the local community. And different societies in different places and times may well reach different conclusions from the same laws and facts.

Not every ethical position is so difficult to transform into law. For example, another ethical position might be that it is unethical to cut off the tails of dogs, regardless of "breed standards" or the whim of the "owner." In this case the legislature has before it a very clear and clean path it could take. The law might say, "It is illegal for any person, except a veterinarian, to cut off any portion of a dog's tail." This requires no future judgment of whether it was a necessary act. The legislature is using an "option one" approach. The legislature has decided that it is never necessary to cut off a dog's tail, and no defense or belief will justify the act. The act is illegal regardless of motivation. It is a simple fact determination. Did the defendant cut off a portion of a tail, or did they not? Necessariness is not part of the discussion. The ethical position is a public policy position, clearly stated in the language of the law.

Very briefly consider the third option of the legislature—that of delegation to a regulatory agency. This option usually arises when the problem is complex, involving multiple facts and a need for scientific information beyond the capabilities of most legislatures. For example, consider the complexity and level of fuzziness that arises when the law seeks to regulate a commercial activity such as that of zoos. Let us assume that the public position is that the use of animals in zoos is acceptable by the public, but that the animals are expected to be kept in good animal welfare. (The issue of just what is good animal welfare has to be ignored for this discussion.)

First, there is the language used by the legislature. In the United States, the federal Animal Welfare Act directs an agency to develop regulations for the keeping of animals in zoos: "(1) The Secretary shall promulgate standards to govern the humane handling, care, treatment, and transportation of animals by dealers, research facilities, and exhibitors."[6] The problem is that the law does not define "humane." Additionally, the social definition will change over time, depending on evolving social attitudes toward groups of animals. In more recent time, the definition has been expanded to take into account mental well-being, not just physical. However, the US Department of Agriculture has chosen to keep regulations adopted in 1989 dealing with temperature extremes, cage size, and access to food and water.[7] This creates a neat checklist for inspectors. It does not determine the quality of life or mental state of the animals in confinement. I think these objective standards fail to assess whether the treatment of the animals is humane. Congress has chosen not to try to correct this state of affairs. The ethics of good care for zoo animals has not yet been fully realized in the law.

Given all the complexities suggested here concerning the adoption of animal protection laws, how can the individual make an impact on the legal status of animals? Consider the following options:

1. Is there some social consensus that there is a problem that needs to be addressed? If not, perhaps you start with a program to education the public about the nature and scope of the problem. Work with an organization. Get the press interested. Go to social media.
2. Work with a lawyer to see what is possible.
3. Have a clear, concise statement of the problem and possible solutions.
4. If the decision-makers do not seem to be motivated by your ethical concerns, find other reasons to motivate the legislators:
   a. An economic decision.
   b. A positive PR event—politically positive.
   c. A negative PR event.
   d. Trading political support with another legislator.

Most individuals find it impossible to move from their personal ethical concerns directly into adopted law. Instead, individuals can join organizations that deal with pieces of this process. Decide which issues concern you the most. Find organizations that are willing to deal with this issue, and work with those to which your abilities and talents will be most useful.

We are at the beginning, not the end, of the changing status of animals in our legal system. There is much to be done and room in the process for all who are interested.

REFERENCES

Barnes, Kimberly. "Detailed Discussion of Commercial Breeders and Puppy Mills." Animal Legal and Historical Center, Michigan State University College of Law, 2017. https://www.animallaw.info/article/detailed-discussion-commercial-breeders-and-puppy-mills-0.

Ensminger, John, and Frances Breitko. "Evolving Functions of Service and Therapy Animals and the Implications for Public Accommodation Access Rules." Animal Legal and Historical Center, Michigan State University College of Law, 2009. https://www.animallaw.info/article/evolving-functions-service-and-therapy-animals-and-implications-public-accommodation-access.

Mele, Christopher. "Is that Dog (or Pig) on Your Flight Really a Service Animal?" *New York Times*, May 1, 2018. https://www.nytimes.com/2018/05/01/travel/service-animals-planes.html.

Wisch, Rebecca. "Table of State Assistance Animal Laws." Animal Legal and Historical Center, Michigan State University College of Law, 2016. https://www.animallaw.info/topic/table-state-assistance-animal-laws.

NOTES

1. N.Y. Rev. Stat. §§ 375.2–.9 (1867), available at https://www.animallaw.info/article/development-anti-cruelty-laws-during-1800s, Appendix A; emphasis added.
2. Animal Welfare Act 2006, sec. 4, available at https://www.animallaw.info/statute/england-and-wales-cruelty-animal-welfare-act-2006; emphasis added.
3. John Ensminger and Frances Breitko, "Evolving Functions of Service and Therapy Animals and the Implications for Public Accommodation Access Rules," Animal Legal and Historical Center, Michigan State University College of Law, 2009, https://www.animallaw.info/article/evolving-functions-service-and-therapy-animals-and-implications-public-accommodation-access; Christopher Mele, "Is that Dog (or Pig) on Your Flight Really a Service Animal?," *New York Times*, May 1, 2018, https://www.nytimes.com/2018/05/01/travel/service-animals-planes.html.
4. Rebecca F. Wisch, "Table of State Assistance Animal Laws," Animal Legal and Historical Center, Michigan State University College of Law, 2016, https://www.animallaw.info/topic/table-state-assistance-animal-laws (right-hand column in the fifty-state table).
5. Kimberly Barnes, "Detailed Discussion of Commercial Breeders and Puppy Mills," Animal Legal and Historical Center, Michigan State University College of Law, 2017, https://www.animallaw.info/article/detailed-discussion-commercial-breeders-and-puppy-mills-0.
6. Animal Welfare Act, 7 U.S.C. § 2143.
7. 54 Fed. Reg. 36112–01 (1989).

Chapter 7

From Morally Relevant Features to Relevant Legal Protection

A Critique of the Legal Concept of Animals as "Property"

By Frances M. C. Robinson

Should one be concerned about human judicial decisions involving nonhuman animals? The following examples of human judicial decisions give rise to this question being asked. The first example concerns a case (*Seehunde v. Bundesrepublik Deutschland* [1988]) in which German environmental lawyers took the West German government to court over the deaths of approximately fifteen thousand seals. The reason for the suit was that the government had issued permits that had resulted in the sea becoming polluted with heavy metals. The bodies of the seals had washed up on the beaches of both the North Sea and the Baltic Sea. Paul Rees points out that the environmental lawyers lost their case, and the reason given by the court was that "the court rejected the seals' standing on the grounds that they were not 'persons' and no specific legislation had authorized standing on their behalf."[1]

The second example concerns a case (*The Nonhuman Rights Project, Inc. v. Stanley* [2015]) in which the Nonhuman Rights Project petitioned the Supreme Court of New York State for a writ of habeas corpus (under the common law) on behalf of two chimpanzees, Hercules and Leo. The petitioner wanted the respondent (State University of New York at Stony Brook) to release the chimpanzees and transfer them to a sanctuary in Florida. The petition was denied. According to Rees, the reason given by the court was that "the court did not recognize the chimpanzees as legal persons and only a legal person is entitled to bring a writ of habeas corpus"[2] under the common law.

The third example concerns a case (*Predator Breeders Association v. Minister of Environmental Affairs and Tourism*) involving "canned hunting" in South Africa. The Predator Breeders Association challenged the Threatened or Protected Species Regulations (2007) regarding the prohibition of "canned hunting"—in particular, the exception clause—on the grounds that it was not clear that a lion could be rehabilitated into his or her free natural habitat at all and that the twenty-four-month period allotted for rehabilitation was without a justifiable basis.

David Bilchitz points out that the judge, Heher J, argued that it was not clear how either ethical hunting or fair chase fitted into the legislative structure of the Biodiversity Act, "which is designed to promote and conserve biodiversity in the wild and, more especially in relation to captive-bred predators that are not bred or intended for release into the wild."[3] The court agreed that the twenty-four-month period given for rehabilitation of a captive "listed large predator" was indeed arbitrary and without a justifiable basis.[4] Bilchitz notes,

> The court found that "if there was no real prospect that such lions will be able to look after themselves then there will be as little prospect of hunting being permitted" (*PBA* case, para 40). Regulation 24(2) thus purported to create an exception which would never be capable of being invoked and thus was meaningless and irrational. On these grounds, the court ruled that the regulations in their present form were irrational and would be invalid should lions be included in the definition of a "listed large predator."[5]

Bilchitz later writes,

> Whilst the court's conclusion relating to the irrationality of the exception in the regulations was justifiable, its final remedy—simply to declare the regulations invalid should they be applied to lions—was not. Merely declaring the regulations invalid allowed canned lion hunting to continue unabated and left the room open for the government to fail to regulate at all.[6]

Pertinently, Bilchitz also points out that "the environmental laws which were passed in post-apartheid South Africa largely avoid directly addressing the interests of individual animals."[7] In these laws an animal is considered to be a biological resource, and sentience and welfare are not explicitly mentioned. Thus, in this particular case, it was the legislative framework that was ill-suited to address the extremely important question of the regulation of hunting.[8]

Although these examples differ in many respects, there are some common features. There is a lack of concern for the individual animal subject, and there is a sense that justice is not being served. This leads one to question the legal processes by which these decisions were reached. What one is actually questioning is the relationship between the law and justice, and this particular relationship is central to the academic field of jurisprudence.

Suri Ratnapala has noted that the term "jurisprudence" is not a precise term because it can refer to three different things.[9] First, it can refer to "a body of substantive legal rules, doctrines, interpretations and explanations that make up the law of a country."[10] Second, it can refer to "the interpretations of the law given by a court," such that it "signifies the juristic approaches and doctrines associated with particular courts."[11] Third, it can refer to "scientific and philosophical investigations of the social phenomenon of law and of justice generally."[12] Pertinently, Ratnapala writes, "Law is normative in the sense that it lays down rules of conduct—what ought to be done and what ought not to be done. Basic laws of society, such as the rules against harming person and property and the rule that promises must be performed, are also moral rules."[13] If the problem lies with the first sense of jurisprudence, then one can say that the problem exists in the legal systems of more than one country. If the problem lies with the second sense of jurisprudence, then one can say that each of those countries has at least one court that arguably has rendered an unjust judicial decision. However, the crux of the matter is that these examples of judicial decisions are not exceptional cases; rather, they are symptomatic of a much deeper problem within the law itself. So it is the third sense of jurisprudence to which attention should be drawn—to scientific and philosophical investigations of the social phenomenon of law and of justice generally.

A number of academic lawyers have already identified a serious problem within the law, and this problem has been very succinctly described by David Favre, who writes, "The concept of property exists and is well-entrenched in our legal thinking. . . . Property law is an institution with four component parts: the persons who hold the rights, the relationships between persons, the objects to which property concepts attach, and sanctions for violations of the rules."[14] Favre later continues,

> Animals are like infant children in that they can be recognized as legal persons, but do not have the capacity to understand or knowingly exercise any legal rights allocated to them. This has been particularly difficult for the animals as, unlike children, they are property and one of the legal mantras often repeated is that property cannot be the holder of legal rights.[15]

A critical examination of this problem reveals that there are actually several problems. The first is that whether or not a nonhuman animal subject is categorized as a "legal person" appears to depend either on the laws of a particular country or on the interpretation of the law by a particular court or courts within the country. Second, the question arises as to why nonhuman animal subjects are categorized as "objects" to which "property" concepts attach. Third, according to Kant's deontological moral theory—the theory on which the protection of the basic moral rights of an individual person is based—one cannot be both a person and a property. These concerns expose a lack of clarity in legal thinking, and in order to understand where this confusion has arisen, it is necessary to critically examine the foundations of the law in general and the foundations of property law in particular.

FIRST CONCERN

The first concern is that property law is an institution, in which at least some nonhuman animal subjects are categorized as "property." What is of concern is that the humans who make the rules, the humans who interpret the rules, and the humans who abide by the rules have an unfair advantage over the nonhuman animal subjects whom they have categorized as property and who may suffer harm as a result of this categorization. In short, property law supports human self-interest at the expense of nonhuman animals.

Taking a more general view of institutions, it can be seen that there is a tendency to form in-groups based on some shared characteristic or interest, and belonging to a particular group may mean that there are certain obligations to the members of the group, but not to those outside the group. In addition, there may be some agreed-upon rules of behavior or some binding social contract involved, such that the rules and/or the binding social contract help to connect members of the group. There is nothing wrong with group-forming in itself. Rather, problems can arise when a group, once formed, closes its boundaries to others and then either intentionally or unintentionally causes harm to those outside the group. Indeed, ethical arguments are often geared to breaking down the boundaries that have been created. The crux of the matter is that decisions made by group members may appear to be just decisions to the members of the group, but they may appear to be unjust decisions to those outside the group. A just decision should be both fair and impartial.

Amartya Sen has recognized that there are two different ways in which impartiality can be invoked.[16] He points out,

> The procedures involve disparate interpretations of the demands of impartiality, and can correspondingly have rather dissimilar substantive implications. The two approaches will be called *closed* and *open* impartiality, respectively. . . .
>
> With *closed impartiality*, the procedure of making impartial judgments invokes only members of the focal group itself. For example, the Rawlsian

> method of "justice as fairness" uses the device of an "original contract" between the citizens of a given polity. . . .
>
> In contrast, in the case of *open impartiality*, the procedure of making impartial judgments can (and in some cases, must) invoke judgments from outside the focal group. For example, in Adam Smith's use of the device of "the impartial spectator," the demands of impartiality require the invoking of disinterested judgments of "any fair and impartial spectator," not necessarily (indeed sometimes ideally not) belonging to the focal group. Both approaches demand impartiality, but through different procedures, which can substantially influence the reach as well as the results of the respective methods.[17]

Thus, Sen explains why this distinction between the two approaches matters; namely, that each procedure may have a substantial influence on both the reach and the results. He continues,

> Indeed, it may emerge that what is taken to be perfectly natural and normal in a society cannot survive a broad-based and less limited scrutiny. . . .
>
> Smith's insistence that we must *inter alia* view our sentiments from "a certain distance from us" is, thus, motivated by the object of scrutinizing not only the influence of vested interest, but also the impact of entrenched tradition and custom. . . . An impartial assessment requires not only the avoidance of the impact of individual vested interests, but an exact scrutiny of parochial moral and social sentiments, which may influence the ideas and outcomes in locally separated "original positions."[18]

Crucially, Sen points out that partiality can give rise to a number of problems. Indeed, he identifies some of the potentially serious consequences of the closed impartiality approach as follows:

> The procedure of closed impartiality, particularly exemplified by contractarian devices applied to closed groups, can involve a strictly partial approach to impartiality. It suffers, as a result, from a number of distinct problems, of which "exclusionary neglect" is one.. . . . [It] can suffer from other serious problems as well, including "procedural parochialism" and "inclusionary incoherence." Since these limitations have not yet received much examination at all, they demand greater—and clearer—recognition. . . . In tackling each of these problems, the alternative of open impartiality has some merit.[19]

In many cases both our ethical and our legal decision-making processes are examples of closed impartiality. Thus, in order to avoid the problems that are associated with closed impartiality and act more cooperatively and more socially within a much wider framework, it is necessary to include the interests of those outside the human group in our decision-making processes, in order to be able to decide more impartially how we are to act.

SECOND CONCERN

The second concern is the inconsistent way in which different legal systems categorize nonhuman animals. The pertinent point is that whether or not a nonhuman animal subject is categorized both as a person and as a legal person will have substantial consequences for the welfare of the nonhuman animal subject in terms of both ethical and legal protection. Thus, it is necessary to clarify whether a nonhuman animal subject should be categorized as a person and to identify why most legal systems deny that a nonhuman animal subject be categorized as a legal person. Thus, we must critically examine the historical roots of the categorization of nonhuman animals, not only with particular regard to the classification of the nonhuman animal subject per se, but also with regard to the influence of the concept of instrumental value on the evolution of the English common law.

Brian Bix has pointed out that the traditional common-law subjects taught at most English and American law schools are contracts, torts, criminal law, and property.[20] Notably, Favre observes, "The common law legal system has its conceptual roots in the Roman law period. The Roman view of the world produced two fundamental categories: persons and things. Persons had access to the law, and property law was written about things."[21] Thus, of central importance to this inquiry is the following question: Why were humans categorized as persons in the common law and all other animals categorized as things? In order to understand why this likely happened, it is necessary to look at the philosophical debates that took place in ancient Greece.

Richard Sorabji writes that in ancient Greece the motives for drawing distinctions between different capacities of mind were as follows: (1) ancient skepticism, (2) "concern with man and his place in nature above the animals," and (3) the moral question of how humans should treat animals.[22] Indeed, the question of animal rationality came to play a central role in both moral philosophy and the philosophy of mind.[23] However, Sorabji points out, a crisis arose for both moral philosophy and the philosophy of mind when Aristotle reverted to a position in the debate that was closer to the position that had been held by an earlier thinker—namely, the medical writer Alcmaeon (late sixth century BCE). In this position, Aristotle denied that animals had reason (*logos*), reasoning (*logismos*), thought (*dianoia*, *nous*), intellect (*nous*), and belief (*doxa*).[24] Indeed, Gary Steiner writes that Aristotle believed animals had "sensitive souls," as opposed to "rational souls," because he believed that animals responded to external objects of desire *without* any free-thinking or deliberation.[25] Steiner notes, "For Aristotle and [later] Aquinas, because animals are governed by the sensitive soul, they cannot discriminate between different objects of desire and make informed choices among them, but instead can only be caused to move toward the objects of their desires by the sheer presence of the objects to the animals' perception."[26] Aristotle's belief has had a significant influence on the way humans treat other animals. Thus, of central importance is the question of whether or not Aristotle's belief is correct.

The Three Moral Theories

Three distinct moral theories underpin our ethical decision-making processes: theories known as virtue ethics, utilitarianism, and deontology. Virtue ethics was developed by the Greek philosopher Aristotle (384–322 BCE), who argued that a virtuous person would be able to find the correct mean between opposing extremes of behavior.[27] For example, a virtuous person would be generous (neither mean nor a spendthrift) and brave (neither cowardly nor foolhardy).[28] Aristotle also argued that a virtuous person would be able to determine whether or not a particular goal was fine, and to do this, one required both intelligence and virtue.[29] A virtuous person has been described as generous; however, for someone to be generous, there has to be a recipient of that generosity. Thus, the virtuous person is described in terms of how that person interacts with his or her social and/or physical context. Of central importance is that a virtuous person should consider not only the goal itself but also the interactions between self and others who may be affected by the self striving to reach his or her goal. Problems often arise when there is a failure to recognize the others who may be affected during the process. Thus, it is necessary for a virtuous person to consider not only the goal itself but also the means by which that goal is to be reached.

The utilitarian moral theory was developed by the English lawyer Jeremy Bentham (1748–1832 CE). As noted by Peter Singer, Bentham wrote the following passage in relation to nonhuman animals: "The question is not, Can they reason? Nor can they talk? But, Can they suffer?"[30] Bentham thus highlights the capacity to suffer as being of central importance in moral considerations. Bentham's theory claims that the right action is the one that produces the greatest happiness for the greatest number or—for consequentialism, which is a form of utilitarianism—the best consequences. The practical application of the utilitarian moral theory is the use of a cost-benefit analysis. However, there are a number of problems associated with the utilitarian moral theory in practice, and they are as follows:

1. There is a risk of tyranny by the majority.
2. There is a lack of restrictions on actions.
3. The theory is impersonal.
4. It is questionable that all of the consequences are predictable.

5. And of particular concern, there is a lack of protection for the individual subject.

The deontological moral theory was developed principally by the German philosopher Immanuel Kant (1724–1804 CE). Kant's moral theory underpins the protection of the basic moral rights of individual persons and is a duty-based theory founded on the moral law known as the "categorical imperative."[31] However, Kant's argument includes the following passage:

> Beings whose existence depends, not on our will, but on nature, have none the less, if they are non-rational beings, only a relative value as means and are consequently called *things*. Rational beings, on the other hand, are called *persons* because their nature already marks them out as ends-in-themselves—that is, as something which ought not to be used merely as a means—and consequently imposes to that extent a limit on all arbitrary treatment of them (and is an object of reverence).[32]

This particular passage creates some serious problems for Kant's moral theory in practice. First, as Tom Regan has pointed out, it creates a serious problem for irrational humans—such as very young children, the mentally challenged, and the elderly.[33] Second, it creates serious problems for nonhuman animals because of the prevailing culture that was and is based on the belief that only humans have the capacity for reason. Indeed, Regan observes that Kant argued that humans have only indirect duties toward nonhuman animals, as is illustrated in the following passage: "we have no direct duties. Animals are not self-conscious and are there merely as a means to an end. That end is man."[34]

Aristotle's Belief: True or False?

Bentham argued that having the capacity to suffer entitles an organism to be included in the moral community. However, the problems that are associated with the utilitarian moral theory remain, and of particular concern is the lack of protection for the individual subject. Kant failed to provide protection for individual nonhuman animal subjects because he believed that nonhuman animals were not self-conscious—a belief that can be traced back to Aristotle. Hence, as noted previously, the question of whether Aristotle's belief is correct is of central importance.

The present understanding is that nonhuman animals should be classed as *persons* because we now know from the scientific evidence available that (1) nonhuman animals have the capacity to suffer; (2) nonhuman animals have emotions; (3) nonhuman animals can experience both stress and distress; (4)

nonhuman animals have the capacity to communicate, at least within their own species; and (5) notably, nonhuman animals have the capacity for reason in terms of goal-directed behavior. Indeed, Giovanni Pezzulo et al. point out,

> The brain has evolved to act in a complex and unpredictable world, and it must continuously select among many goals and action options. In the past 20 years, research in neuroscience and robotics has principally focused on the neural underpinnings of *habitual* choice, linked to stimulus-response mechanisms in restricted contexts. However, a recent trend of research is to focus on *goal-directed* choice mechanisms that select among anticipated action outcomes in a context-dependent way. These goal-oriented processes provide the foundations of many everyday human and animal decisions.
>
> Goal-directed decision-making relies on multiple sources of information beyond immediately available sensory stimuli, such as representations of (proximal and distal) goal states and their utility, memory and predicted future states. Furthermore, it has to take into consideration the specific behavioural context in which a decision is to be made rather than just activate habits. . . . We need to understand the specific contributions of goals, episodic memory, working memory and cognitive control to decisions, and to analyse the neural substrates of these brain processes and how they link to flexible forms of computation (e.g. model-based methods of reinforcement learning, which consider specific action outcomes and not only stimulus-response pairs).[35]

In particular, Pezzulo et al. note,

> Goals are multifarious constructs that include at minimum affective and motivational components along with predictive state representations that guide action specification and selection. . . . During choice, cognitive processing is orchestrated to serve the identification and selection of goals, including perception and attention (to goal- and task-relevant aspects of the sensorium), memory (to retrieve goal-related information), prediction and valuation (of action outcomes), selection and monitoring (of actions that achieve goals while also caring about effort).[36]

The answer to a question will depend on the question being asked. Notably, there has been an important development in the question being asked with regard to neural functioning. Pezzulo et al. point out,

> [There is] a new breed of studies that not only ask how the brain learns to link sensory stimuli to stereotyped actions (habitual system), but also ask how it integrates multiple information streams (e.g. internal needs and external opportunities) and coordinates them in time to formulate, maintain and achieve goals. . . .
>
> [Notably,] consensus is growing on how neuronal circuits for goal-directed choice link to specific computations and learning mechanisms.[37]

They then ask the crucial question: “How do animals choose their actions in ecologically valid contexts, in social and in potentially risky environments?” [38]

Pezzulo et al. write,

> Cisek & Pastor-Bernier[39] discuss the challenges of embodied decision-making faced by animals interacting with their environment in real time. The evidence they review points towards an embodied architecture in which multiple processes of action specification, selection and execution all run in parallel and sensorimotor processes are part and parcel of the decision-making process.[40]

Notably, this more recent information gives us some insight into why confined animals may develop stereotypic behavior. The confined environment in which the animals are kept may not only lack sufficient external stimuli for the animals and, as a result, limit both their learning opportunities and their learning processes, it also will ensure that their patterns of behavior are necessarily restricted. The tragedy of this situation is that we create the restricted conditions for the animals and then we misjudge both their capacities and their capabilities. The current scientific evidence shows that nonhuman animals have the capacity for reason, and therefore Aristotle’s belief is incorrect. Indeed, Aristotle’s belief is a *false* belief.

Personal Property

As noted by Favre, there are three basic categories of property within the law: real property, personal property, and intellectual property.[41] Favre also points out, “Some animals are, and have always been, categorized as personal property. However, as the English common law developed, not all animals had equal presence or status within the law.”[42] Favre follows this with a quote from Frank Hall Childs: “The common law regards and gives the greatest protection to those designated as ‘useful,’ and the least protection to those *ferae naturae*.”[43] To understand why this is the case, one has to return once again to Aristotle’s false belief.

Based on his *false* belief, Aristotle held two further beliefs. The first belief was that because the actions of animals were governed by the “sensitive soul,” as opposed to the “rational soul,” it made no sense to hold animals responsible for their actions. He then argued that because animals have no moral obligations, they have no moral rights.[44] However, it does not logically follow from the premise that animals cannot be held morally responsible for their actions that animals have no moral rights. For example, it is reasonable to argue that very young children cannot be held morally responsible for their actions because very young children have to learn to act in a morally responsible way. However, the fact that very young children cannot be held morally responsible for their actions does not and should not imply that very young children have no moral rights. Indeed, to the contrary, it implies that they require protection from morally responsible adults. The crux of the matter is that if an organism possesses morally relevant features, then the organism should be considered morally.

The second of Aristotle's beliefs was that animals have only instrumental value, and he expresses this explicitly in the following passage, as related by Gary Steiner:

> After the birth of animals, plants exist for their sake, and . . . the other animals exist for the sake of man, the tame for use and food, the wild, if not all, at least the greater part of them, for food, and for the provision of clothing and various instruments. Now if nature makes nothing incomplete, and nothing in vain, the inference must be that she has made all animals for the sake of man.[45]

Aristotle's somewhat controversial conclusion is based on premises that are no more than biased assumptions. Thus, rather than believing that animals have only instrumental value, it is more accurate to acknowledge that it was Aristotle who valued animals only instrumentally. However, the concept of animals as having only instrumental value is reflected in the evolution of the English common law. Again, as noted by Childs, the greatest protection is given to those designated as "useful"; the least protection is given to those who are *ferae naturae*.

Third Concern

Objectification

The concerns over property law being an institution and the concerns over the inconsistent way in which different legal systems categorize nonhuman animals have been discussed. However, perhaps of greatest concern is the human attitude toward nonhuman animals that is so deeply embedded within legal systems globally. This attitude manifests itself in the categorization of nonhuman animal subjects as objects to which property concepts attach. Objectification (the treating of a person as an object) is of central concern in feminist theory. Indeed, Martha Nussbaum has set out the following list of the features of objectification:

1. *Instrumentality*: The objectifier treats the object as a tool of his or her purposes.
2. *Denial of autonomy*: The objectifier treats the object as lacking in autonomy and self-determination.

3. *Inertness*: The objectifier treats the object as lacking in agency, and perhaps also in activity.
4. *Fungibility*: The objectifier treats the object as interchangeable (a) with other objects of the same type, and/or (b) with objects of other types.
5. *Violability*: The objectifier treats the object as lacking in boundary-integrity, as something that it is permissible to break up, smash, break into.
6. *Ownership*: The objectifier treats the object as something that is owned by another, can be bought or sold, etc.
7. *Denial of subjectivity*: The objectifier treats the object as something whose experience and feelings (if any) need not be taken into account.[46]

Of particular relevance in this context is ownership; the person is treated as property. One can readily identify the power structure that exists between the one who is empowered (the one who "owns") and the one who is vulnerable (the one who is "owned"). This type of relationship can be viewed in terms of both liberty and a lack of liberty. Indeed, it is this distinction between having liberty and lacking liberty that highlights the central problem in the relationship between the law and justice, as far as both human and nonhuman animals are concerned.

The Relationship between the Law and Justice

The *Belmont Report* was published in 1979 in the United States, and it sets out the three basic ethical principles for the protection of human subjects of biomedical and behavioral research, plus guidelines for the application of those principles.[47] The first basic ethical principle, "respect for persons," states that "individuals should be treated as autonomous agents" and that "persons with diminished autonomy are entitled to protection."[48] Notably, an autonomous agent is defined in the report as "an individual who is capable of deliberation about personal goals and of acting under the direction of such deliberation."[49] The pertinent point is that this definition of an autonomous agent is applicable not only to humans but also to nonhuman animals, since we now know from the scientific evidence that goal-oriented processes provide the foundations of many everyday human and animal decisions.

In his book *A Theory of Justice*, John Rawls sets out two principles of justice, and the first principle states, "Each person is to have an equal right to the most extensive total system of equal basic liberties compatible with a similar system of liberty for all."[50] Notably, Rawls also sets out two priority rules, and the first priority rule is that the first principle of justice has priority over the second principle of justice, "and therefore liberty can be restricted only for the sake of liberty."[51] Thus, liberty has top priority in Rawls's theory of justice. Hence, the lack of liberty associated with a person being "owned" is completely at odds not only with the *Belmont Report*'s first basic ethical principle (respect for persons) but also with Rawls's first principle of justice. In short, the legal concept of the animal subject as an "object" to which property concepts attach denotes a totally inappropriate relationship between the law and justice.

Voluntary Informed Consent

The practical application of the *Belmont Report*'s first basic ethical principle (respect for persons) is in voluntary informed consent. There is a marked difference between the view of a nonhuman animal as an autonomous agent from whom voluntary informed consent is required and the view of a nonhuman animal as an object to which property concepts attach. Indeed, markedly different consequences arise for nonhuman animals as a direct result of these different perspectives. In the first case, the nonhuman animal is categorized as a *person* who is to be protected by basic moral rights; in the second case, the nonhuman animal is categorized as *property*, and a legal mantra often repeated is that property cannot be the holder of legal rights. The current scientific evidence supports the first perspective that a nonhuman animal subject is an autonomous agent and therefore is a *person* to be protected by basic moral rights. This raises the question of why most legal systems deny that nonhuman animal subjects should be categorized as legal persons and thus be protected by legal rights. However, it is now apparent that if a nonhuman animal subject has no legal rights within the laws of a country, it is because the humans responsible for making the laws and the humans responsible for interpreting laws have *objectified* the nonhuman animal subjects by categorizing them as objects to which property concepts attach.

In exchange for the right to practice veterinary medicine and surgery in the United Kingdom, every veterinary surgeon has to make a declaration,[52] and since April 1, 2012, that declaration has been as follows:

> I PROMISE AND SOLEMNLY DECLARE that I will pursue the work of my profession with integrity and accept my responsibilities to the public, my clients, the profession and the Royal College of Veterinary Surgeons and that, ABOVE ALL, my constant endeavour will be to ensure the health and welfare of animals committed to my care.[53]

However, a significant problem arises for veterinary surgeons in practice in the form of two counteracting forces. The first concerns veterinary ethics, and the second concerns the legal status of the animal as property.

As Vanessa Ashall, Kate Miller, and Pru Hobson-West have pertinently pointed out, voluntary informed consent is required from the patient in medical ethics,[54] whereas in veterinary ethics, voluntary informed consent is required from the "owner" of the animal patient, because the animal patient is not able to express his or her wishes in terms of voluntary informed consent.[55] The problem is that the wishes of the "owner" are not always consistent with the wishes and the welfare of the animal patient, because the wishes of the "owner" will necessarily be value-laden in terms of both economic interests and the various ways in which he or she values the animal.[56]

The legal status of the nonhuman animal subject as "property" is completely at odds with the nonhuman animal subject's fundamental interests. Indeed, it also can be at odds with the veterinary surgeon's ethical requirement to ensure the health and welfare of the animals committed to his or her care. It is absolutely necessary both to recognize and to respect the autonomy of the individual animal subject in order to be able to provide adequate ethical and legal protection for the animal subject. It is also necessary to think in terms of relationships between persons, rather than thinking in terms of "ownership."

MAKING A JUST DECISION

The utilitarian moral theory strives for the greater good, but there are serious problems associated with this moral theory in practice. Thus, the basic moral rights of individual autonomous agents are used in practice to address the problems associated with the utilitarian moral theory. This counterbalancing relationship is mirrored in legal processes; legal rights are used to address the problems associated with legal welfarism, because legal welfarism is based on the utilitarian moral theory. The crux of the matter is that individual nonhuman animal subjects either are given no legal rights or are given minimal legal rights in comparison to those given to humans,[57] because of a *category error* in the classification of nonhuman animal subjects by those responsible for making the laws and by those responsible for interpreting the laws. As a result, there is virtually no counterbalance in place to address the problems that are associated with legal welfarism.

In order to make a *just* decision, it is necessary to balance the goal of achieving the greater good with the protection of the basic moral rights of the individual autonomous agents who may be affected by the process through which one reaches for that goal. The greater good may involve many complex relationships, including those between sentient and non-sentient life-forms and those between biotic and abiotic systems. Problems arise for the following reasons: we fail to recognize, to respect, and to protect (1) the complexity of those relationships and (2) the basic moral rights of the individual autonomous agents who may be affected by the processes by which we reach for our goals. The means by which a worthy goal is reached should ensure that the basic moral rights of the individual autonomous agents affected during the process are protected—particularly when those individual autonomous agents are not able to express their wishes in terms of voluntary informed consent. In many, if not all, countries, the law fails to recognize the basic moral rights of individual nonhuman animal subjects, and as a result of this failure, the law fails to comply with the first basic ethical principle to respect the autonomy of individual nonhuman animal subjects. As a consequence of this failure, the law not only fails to protect nonhuman animal subjects; it also fails to comply with its top priority—the first principle of justice.

REFERENCES

Aristotle. *Nicomachean Ethics*. Translated by Terence Irwin. Indianapolis: Hackett Publishing, 1985.

Ashall, Vanessa, Kate M. Miller, and Pru Hobson-West. "Informed Consent in Veterinary Medicine: Implications for the Profession and the Animal 'Patient.'" *Food Ethics* 1, no. 3 (March 2018): 247–58.

Bilchitz, David. "Animal Interests and South African Law: The Elephant in the Room?" In *Animal Law and Welfare—International Perspectives*, edited by Deborah Cao and Steven White, 131–55. Cham, Switzerland: Springer International Publishing, 2016.

Bix, Brian H. *Jurisprudence: Theory and Context*. 7th ed. London: Sweet & Maxwell/Thomas Reuters, 2015.

Childs, Frank Hall. *Principles of the Law of Personal Property, Chattels and Choses*. Chicago: Callaghan, 1914.

Cisek, Paul and Pastor-Bernier, Alexandre. "On the Challenges and Mechanisms of Embodied Decisions." *Philosophical Transactions of the Royal Society B* 369, no. 20130479 (2014).

Favre, David S. "Living Property: A New Status for Animals within the Legal System." *Marquette Law Review* 93, no. 3 (2010): 1021–71. http://scholarship.law.marquette.edu/mulr/vol93/iss3/3.

Francione, Gary L. *Animals as Persons: Essays on the Abolition of Animal Exploitation*. New York: Columbia University Press, 2008.

———. *Animals, Property, and the Law*. Philadelphia: Temple University Press, 2007.

Kant, Immanuel. *The Moral Law: Groundwork of the Metaphysic of Morals*. Translated and analyzed by H. J. Paton. London: Routledge, 1991.

———. "Duties to Animals and Spirits." In *Lectures on Ethics*, trans. Louis Infield, 239–41, New York: Harper & Row, 1963.

Linzey, Andrew, and Clair Linzey, eds. *The Ethical Case against Animal Experiments*. Urbana: University of Illinois Press, 2018.

National Commission for the Protection of Human Subjects of Biomedical and Behavioral Research. *The Belmont Report: Ethical Principles and Guidelines for the Protection of Human Subjects of Research*. US Department of Health and Human Services, April 18, 1979. https://www.hhs.gov/ohrp/regulations-and-policy/belmont-report/index.html.

Nussbaum, Martha C. "Objectification." *Philosophy and Public Affairs* 24, no. 4 (Fall 1995): 249–91. https://www.mit.edu/~shaslang/mprg/nussbaumO.pdf.

Pezzulo, Giovanni, Paul F. M. J. Verschure, Christian Balkenius, and Cyriel M. A. Pennartz. "The Principles of Goal-Directed Decision-Making: From Neural Mechanisms to Computation and Robotics." *Philosophical Transactions of the Royal Society B* 369, no. 1655 (2014): 1–6.

Radford, Mike. *Animal Welfare Law in Britain: Regulation and Responsibility*. Oxford: Oxford University Press, 2001.

Ratnapala, Suri. *Jurisprudence*. 3rd ed. Cambridge: Cambridge University Press, 2017.

Rawls, John. *A Theory of Justice*. Oxford: Oxford University Press, 1973.

Rees, Paul A. *The Laws Protecting Animals and Ecosystems*. Chichester, UK: John Wiley & Sons, 2018.

Regan, Tom. *The Case for Animal Rights*. London: Routledge, 1988.

———. *The Case for Animal Rights*. Berkeley and Los Angeles: University of California Press, 2004.

Royal College of Veterinary Surgeons. *Code of Professional Conduct for Veterinary Surgeons*. Accessed on February 6, 2022. https://www.rcvs.org.uk/setting-standards/advice-and-guidance/code-of-professional-conduct-for-veterinary-surgeons/.

Sen, Amartya. "Open and Closed Impartiality." *Journal of Philosophy* 99, no. 9 (September 2002): 445–69.

Singer, Peter. *Animal Liberation*. 2nd ed. London: Pimlico, 1995.

Sorabji, Richard. *Animal Minds and Human Morals: The Origins of the Western Debate*. London: Gerald Duckworth, 1993.

Steiner, Gary. "Descartes, Christianity, and Contemporary Speciesism." In *A Communion of Subjects: Animals in Religion, Science & Ethics*, edited by Paul Waldau and Kimberley Patton, 117–31. New York: Columbia University Press, 2006.

NOTES

1. Paul A. Rees, *The Laws Protecting Animals and Ecosystems* (Chichester, UK: John Wiley & Sons, 2018), 55.

2. Rees, *Laws Protecting Animals and Ecosystems*, 318.

3. David Bilchitz, "Animal Interests and South African Law: The Elephant in the Room?," in *Animal Law and Welfare—International Perspectives*, edited by Deborah Cao and Steven White (Cham, Switzerland: Springer International Publishing, 2016), 145.

4. Bilchitz, "Animal Interests," 145.

5. Bilchitz, "Animal Interests," 145.

6. Bilchitz, "Animal Interests," 148.
7. Bilchitz, "Animal Interests," 145.
8. Bilchitz, "Animal Interests," 146.
9. Suri Ratnapala, *Jurisprudence*, 3rd ed. (Cambridge: Cambridge University Press, 2017).
10. Ratnapala, *Jurisprudence*, 3.
11. Ratnapala, *Jurisprudence*, 3.
12. Ratnapala, *Jurisprudence*, 3.
13. Ratnapala, *Jurisprudence*, 2.
14. David S. Favre, "Living Property: A New Status for Animals within the Legal System," *Marquette Law Review* 93, no. 3 (2010): 1024–25, http://scholarship.law.marquette.edu/mulr/vol93/iss3/3.
15. Favre, "Living Property," 1032.
16. Amartya Sen, "Open and Closed Impartiality," *Journal of Philosophy* 99, no. 9 (September 2002): 445–69.
17. Sen, "Open and Closed Impartiality," 445–46.
18. Sen, "Open and Closed Impartiality," 458–59.
19. Sen, "Open and Closed Impartiality," 469.
20. Brian H. Bix, *Jurisprudence: Theory and Context*, 7th ed. (London: Sweet & Maxwell/Thomas Reuters, 2015), 155.
21. Favre, "Living Property," 1024.
22. Richard Sorabji, *Animal Minds and Human Morals: The Origins of the Western Debate* (London: Gerald Duckworth, 1993), 7.
23. Sorabji, *Animal Minds and Human Morals*, 7.
24. Sorabji, *Animal Minds and Human Morals*, 12.
25. Gary Steiner, "Descartes, Christianity, and Contemporary Speciesism," in *A Communion of Subjects: Animals in Religion, Science & Ethics*, ed. Paul Waldau and Kimberley Patton (New York: Columbia University Press, 2006), 121.
26. Steiner, "Descartes, Christianity, and Contemporary Speciesism," 121.
27. Aristotle, *Nicomachean Ethics*, trans. Terence Irwin (Indianapolis: Hackett Publishing, 1985).
28. Aristotle, *Nicomachean Ethics*, 71–79, 85–93.
29. Aristotle, *Nicomachean Ethics*, 169.
30. Quoted in Peter Singer, *Animal Liberation*, 2nd ed. (London: Pimlico, 1995), 7. The passage originally appeared in Jeremy Bentham, *An Introduction to the Principles of Morals and Legislation*, chap. 17.
31. Immanuel Kant, *The Moral Law: Groundwork of the Metaphysic of Morals*, trans. H. J. Paton (London: Routledge, 1991).
32. Kant, *The Moral Law*, 90–91.
33. Tom Regan, *The Case for Animal Rights* (London: Routledge, 1988), 152–55.
34. Immanuel Kant, "Duties to Animals and Spirits," in *Lectures on Ethics*, trans. Louis Infield (New York: Harper and Row, 1964), 239–41; reprint in *The Case for Animal Rights*, Tom Regan (Berkeley and Los Angeles: University of California Press, 2004), 177.

35. Giovanni Pezzulo et al., "The Principles of Goal-Directed Decision-Making: From Neural Mechanisms to Computation and Robotics," *Philosophical Transactions of the Royal Society B* 369, no. 1655 (2014): 1.

36. Pezzulo et al., "The Principles of Goal-Directed Decision-Making," 1–2.

37. Pezzulo et al., "The Principles of Goal-Directed Decision-Making," 2.

38. Pezzulo et al., "The Principles of Goal-Directed Decision-Making," 4.

39. Paul Cisek and Alexandre Pastor-Bernier, "On the Challenges and Mechanisms of Embodied Decisions," *Philosophical Transactions of the Royal Society B* 369, no. 20130479 (2014).

40. Pezzulo et al., "The Principles of Goal-Directed Decision-Making," 4.

41. Favre, "Living Property," 1025.

42. Favre, "Living Property," 1026.

43. Frank Hall Childs, *Principles of the Law of Personal Property, Chattels and Choses* (1914), 35–36, quoted in Favre, "Living Property," 1026.

44. Steiner, "Descartes, Christianity, and Contemporary Speciesism," 121.

45. Aristotle, quoted in Steiner, "Descartes, Christianity, and Contemporary Speciesism," 122.

46. Martha C. Nussbaum, "Objectification," in *Philosophy and Public Affairs* 24, no. 4 (Fall 1995): 257, https://www.mit.edu/~shaslang/mprg/nussbaumO.pdf.

47. National Commission for the Protection of Human Subjects of Biomedical and Behavioral Research, *The Belmont Report: Ethical Principles and Guidelines for the Protection of Human Subjects of Research* (US Department of Health and Human Services, April 18, 1979), https://www.hhs.gov/ohrp/regulations-and-policy/belmont-report/index.html.

48. National Commission, *Belmont Report*, 4.

49. National Commission, *Belmont Report*, 4.

50. John Rawls, *A Theory of Justice* (Oxford: Oxford University Press, 1973), 302.

51. Rawls, *Theory of Justice*, 302.

52. Royal College of Veterinary Surgeons, *Code of Professional Conduct for Veterinary Surgeons*, https://www.rcvs.org.uk/setting-standards/advice-and-guidance/code-of-professional-conduct-for-veterinary-surgeons/.

53. Royal College of Veterinary Surgeons, *Code of Professional Conduct*, 2.

54. Vanessa Ashall, Kate M. Miller, and Pru Hobson-West, "Informed Consent in Veterinary Medicine: Implications for the Profession and the Animal 'Patient,'" *Food Ethics* 1, no. 3 (March 2018): 247–58.

55. Voluntary informed consent should include the following three elements: information, comprehension, and voluntariness (National Commission, *Belmont Report*, 7–8). It is not possible to obtain voluntary informed consent from nonhuman animal subjects, with all that such consent should entail, for the following reasons:

"1. It is not possible to communicate the relevant information to them. 2. It is reasonable to argue that they may not fully comprehend the information, even if it were possible to communicate the information to them. 3. Therefore, they are not in a position to make sound judgments between alternative (long-term) future optional courses of action."

Andrew Linzey and Clair Linzey, eds., *The Ethical Case against Animal Experiments* (Urbana: University of Illinois Press, 2018), 39–40.

56. Ashall et al., "Informed Consent," 249–51.

57. Gary L. Francione, *Animals, Property, and the Law* (Philadelphia: Temple University Press, 2007), 3–14.

Chapter 8

The Nonhuman Rights Project's Struggles to Gain Legal Rights for Nonhuman Animals

By Steven M. Wise

For more than two thousand years, Western law has bifurcated all physical entities into "persons," with the capacity for legal rights, and "things" that lack that capacity. Until recently, all nonhuman animals everywhere had always been legal "things." But for much of those two millennia, millions of human beings also were "things" who attained personhood only after protracted struggles inside and outside courtrooms and parliaments. The manner in which personhood for enslaved humans was established in England in 1772 remains a model for the work of the Nonhuman Rights Project (NhRP).

Edith Hamilton, arguably the premier classical scholar of the mid-twentieth century, reminded us of the initial turning point in the struggle to abolish human thinghood. The words she used to describe the status of enslaved humans in ancient Greece resonate with the modern legal rule that excludes all nonhuman animals from eligibility for even the most fundamental legal rights: "When the Greek achievement is considered, what must be remembered is that the Greeks were the first to think about slavery. To think about it was to condemn it and by the end of the second century, two thousand years before our Civil War, the great school of the Stoics, most widely spread of Greek philosophies, was denouncing it as an intolerable wrong."[1] The "personhood" of all human beings now has been won; everywhere, treating humans as things constitutes an international wrong. The NhRP has turned to another intolerable wrong: the continuing rightslessness and legal thinghood of all nonhuman animals.

An initial task of the NhRP has been to encourage judges, who likely have never encountered the question, to begin to think about the injustice of the legal thinghood of all nonhuman animals, for to think about their thinghood, their utter rightlessness, is to condemn it as well. For those who have never thought about it or have thought it impossible, the required psychological shift must begin with being able to imagine that an entity that has long been considered a legal "thing" might *possibly* be seen as a legal "person."

Most people understand what Churchill meant when he said of the 1942 British victory over the Nazis at El Alamein, "It is not the end. It is not even the beginning of the end. But it is, perhaps, the end of the beginning."[2] Reaching "the end of the beginning" is an initial goal of the work of the Nonhuman Rights Project. For us "the end of the beginning" is helping judges to imagine that at least some nonhuman animals need not continue to be legal "things" and can be legal "persons" and persuading them to establish the capacity of at least some nonhuman animals for legal rights. That will open the road to the fleshing out of the specific rights to which justice entitles them.

The NhRP prepares to accomplish this by studying the fundamental values and principles of any jurisdiction in which it seeks to litigate. In the United States these are typically autonomy, liberty, and equality. The fundamental values and principles in other countries may be the same, or there may be other qualities that courts believe constitute justice. We then gather every relevant scientific fact from the world's most respected experts in their fields and fashion our legal arguments in favor of the personhood and right to bodily liberty of our nonhuman animal clients in terms of those fundamental values and principles.

This approach leaves courts the ability to choose among four roads when confronted with our nonhuman clients' arguments that autonomy, liberty, and equality constitute the fundamental values and principles of justice that entitle them, at minimum, to the right to bodily liberty protected by habeas corpus.

The first road leads courts to deny that autonomy, liberty, and equality, or some other fundamental values, are actually the fundamental values and principles the courts believe constitute justice. This response has the benefit of allowing the NhRP to file new lawsuits that invoke the correct values and principles. No American court has done this.

Following the second road, courts may try to narrow some, or all, of their fundamental values and principles of justice by arbitrarily insisting, without any support, that they apply to all, but only, human beings. For example, in 2014, in a case involving Tommy the chimpanzee, New York's Third Appellate Department stated that an entity has to have the capacity to bear legal duties in order to have the capacity for any legal rights. But recognizing that hundreds of thousands of New Yorkers, including infants, children, the severely cognitively disabled, and others, cannot bear duties yet still have legal rights, the court wrote, "To be sure, some humans are less able to bear legal duties or responsibilities than others. These differences do not alter our analysis, as it is undeniable that, collectively, human beings possess the unique ability to bear legal responsibility. Accordingly, nothing in this decision should be read as limiting the rights of human beings in the context of habeas corpus proceedings or otherwise."[3] In other words, for some unexplained reason, the ability to bear duties is a necessary prerequisite for having any legal right, and only humans collectively bear that ability.

In 2018, New York's First Appellate Department, in a case involving two chimpanzees, Tommy and Kiko, noted that the NhRP "argues that the ability to acknowledge a legal duty or legal responsibility should not be determinative of entitlement to habeas relief, since, for example, infants cannot comprehend that they owe duties or responsibilities and a comatose person lacks sentience, yet both have legal rights. This argument ignores the fact that these are still human beings, members of the human community."[4] This court similarly offered no explanation for its conclusion.

These sorts of pronouncements severely undermine justice as the courts themselves define it and may have serious consequences for humans in both the short and long term. Because, as Martin Luther King Jr. noted, "justice denied anywhere diminishes justice everywhere," the negative effects of such ad hoc undermining of the rationale for granting fundamental rights to extraordinarily cognitively complex autonomous nonhuman animals will inevitably severely undermine any rationale for fundamental human rights.

American courts have not infrequently passed through periods in which they similarly initially undermined their own fundamental values and principles rather than acknowledge their application to entities long excluded from justice.

These courts once limited legal rights to white people and refused to grant them to black people. In the infamous Dred Scott case, the US Supreme Court, holding that black people could never become citizens of the states or of the United States, referred to them as "beings of an inferior order, and altogether unfit to associate with the white race either in social or political relations, and so far inferior that they had no rights which the white man was bound to respect, and that the negro might justly and lawfully be reduced to slavery for his benefit."[5] The California Supreme Court refused to allow Chinese people to testify against a white person, calling them "a race of people whom nature has marked as inferior, and who are incapable of progress or intellectual development beyond a certain point, as their history has shown."[6] Other courts have limited personhood and legal rights to men, refusing to grant them to women. When Lavinia Goodell tried to become a lawyer in 1886, the Supreme Court of Wisconsin refused her request solely because she was a woman, stating that "the law of nature destines and qualifies the female sex for the bearing and nurture of the children of our race and for the custody of the homes of the world and their maintenance in love and honor. And all life-long callings of women, inconsistent with these radical and sacred duties of their sex, as is the profession of the law, are departures from the order of nature; and when voluntary, treason against it."[7]

Perhaps the most unfortunate way in which some courts undermine their own fundamental values and principles of justice is by grounding their decisions in their implicit bias. As I have written elsewhere,

> present judges have been raised in a culture that pervasively views all nonhuman animals as "things." As are most of their fellow citizens, most judges are daily and routinely involved in the widespread exploitation of nonhuman animals, eating them, wearing them, hunting them, and engaging in other of the numerous exploitive ways that the culture has long accepted. When thinking about humans, different clusters of neurons are subconsciously triggered depending upon the degree to which one identifies with the subject. Imagine how differently a judge is likely to view even such a close relative to humans as a chimpanzee.[8]

Judges are therefore likely, automatically and unconsciously, to be biased against the personhood arguments the NhRP presents—just as they are likely to be implicitly biased on the basis of race, gender, sexuality, religion, weight, age, and ethnicity—because "our minds have been shaped by the culture around us. In fact, they have been invaded by it."[9] We therefore expected to encounter puzzling and diverse judicial reactions to our early cases. We were not disappointed.

In 2014 New York's Third Appellate Department issued a confused decision that dismissed Tommy's habeas corpus case, becoming the first English-speaking court in history to find that personhood could be lodged only in an entity with the capacity to shoulder not just rights, but duties.[10] To accomplish this, the court had to ignore centuries of law that uniformly held that a "person" is an entity able to possess either rights or duties, not rights and duties. For example, Harvard Law School professor John Chipman Gray stated in his 1921 treatise *The Nature and Sources of the Law* that "one who has rights but not duties, or who has duties but not rights, is, I suppose, a person . . . [and] if there is anyone who has rights though not duties, or duties though not rights, he is, I take it, a person in the eyes of the law."[11] Directly to the NhRP's point, Professor Gray wrote that "animals may conceivably be legal persons. First, legal persons because possessing legal rights. . . . Secondly, animals as legal persons, because subject to legal duties."[12]

In Tommy's case the Third Appellate Department grounded its holding upon the principle of the "social contract," which it erroneously believed posed an impassable barrier to rights for a nonhuman animal. The judges claimed that "society extends rights in exchange for an express or implied agreement from its members to submit to social responsibilities."[13] However, a philosophers' group would explain in its amicus curiae brief to another New York appellate court,

> Among the most influential of social contract philosophers are Thomas Hobbes, John Locke, and Jean-Jacques Rousseau, who maintain that all persons have "natural rights" that they possess independently of their willingness or ability to take on social responsibilities (Hobbes 1651; Locke 1698; Rousseau 1762). These rights, which we possess in the state of nature, include the right to absolute freedom and liberty. Upon contracting with our fellows, we do not become "persons," but rather "citizens"; and we do not suddenly acquire rights, but rather give up our natural rights, sometimes in exchange for civil and legal rights.
>
> [The Third Appellate Department] advances the argument that persons are those who have rights by virtue of their capacity to bear responsibilities. They acquire those responsibilities the moment they assent to an "express or implied" social contract. The social contract, according to this line of thought, is the mechanism whereby persons take up societal duties and responsibilities, receiving rights in exchange. But this is not how political philosophers have understood the meaning of the social contract historically or in contemporary times.[14]

Put another way, the Connecticut Supreme Court once noted that "the social contract theory posits that all individuals are born with certain natural rights and that people, in freely consenting to be governed, enter a social contract with their government by virtue of which they relinquish certain individual liberties in exchange for the mutual preservation of their lives, liberties, and estates."[15] Even those humans who are expressly excluded from any "social contract," as enslaved black people once were, and people from foreign countries, including those imprisoned at Guantanamo, have the right to habeas corpus. In other words, the Third Appellate Department appellate court got the meaning of "social contract" backward, for however it may be precisely defined, it presupposes that individuals are born with certain fundamental rights that are not given to the individuals by the state.

Perhaps of greatest concern was that the Third Appellate Department never said why the ability to bear legal duties should have anything to do with whether an autonomous being, such as a chimpanzee, should have the fundamental right to bodily liberty that habeas corpus protects.

Some courts appear so determined to rule that our nonhuman animal clients cannot have the right to bodily liberty protected by habeas corpus that they dismiss our cases without assessing the merits of our claims or even hearing our arguments, even if this action violates their own rules.

In New York this has sometimes taken the form of interfering with our absolute right to appeal. In 2014, the NhRP brought an appeal in the Second Appellate Department on behalf of two chimpanzees, Hercules and Leo, who had been imprisoned for years in the basement of a computer building at Stony Brook University. Remarkably, that court on its own motion immediately notified the NhRP that it had no right to appeal and dismissed our appeal without giving us the opportunity either to file a brief or to engage in oral argument. The judges took this action despite a statute that explicitly gives any party the right to appeal a refusal to issue a habeas corpus order.[16] The legal commentator analyzing New York habeas corpus statutes later found that the court must have "overlooked" that statute. That is unlikely considering that the NhRP asked the court to reconsider its decisions while pointing out the statute that gave us the absolute right to appeal to the court.[17]

When the Niagara Falls trial court in Kiko the chimpanzee's case refused in 2014 to rule on a ministerial motion that was formally necessary to allow the NhRP to appeal, the NhRP sought a highly unusual writ of mandamus in New York's Fourth Appellate Department.[18] A mandamus is a demand that a court order a public official to do his nondiscretionary public duty. That court immediately set a hearing date. Then two days later, our cases appeared as the cover story in that week's Sunday *New York Times Magazine*. Immediately, the lower court allowed our appeal to proceed.

When the NhRP tried to appeal cases we had filed on behalf of Tommy and Kiko to New York's First Appellate Department in 2017, the clerk informed us that we had no right to appeal, just as New York's Second Appellate Department had done three years before. This time the NhRP fought back. We filed a motion that demanded that the First Appellate Department hear our appeal. A single judge of that court said no. We then demanded a rehearing. Now five judges of that court said no. And so we were required to bring a second highly unusual writ of mandamus in the very same court, demanding that the court order *itself* to follow the law—which, belatedly, it did.

Fourth, courts may apply their fundamental values and principles of justice to the claims the NhRP brings on behalf of its nonhuman animal clients and recognize the justice of acknowledging their personhood and rights. No American court has fully taken this road, but some have traveled a distance down, and some foreign courts have gone even farther.

In 2015, Manhattan trial court justice Barbara Jaffe issued the first habeas corpus order for a nonhuman animal in the history of English-speaking courts. She recognized that being a person is not synonymous with being a human and that cases brought on behalf of chimpanzees may someday succeed, but she felt bound "for now" by the 2014 decision of New York's Third Appellate

Department court in Tommy's case, noting that a lower court is bound by the ruling of a higher court "even though they may disagree."[19]

On May 8, 2018, in one of Tommy's and Kiko's joint appeals, New York's Court of Appeals refused, as it does 95 percent of the time, without comment and without considering the merits of the NhRP's appeal, to review a lower court's adverse ruling. Then something extraordinary occurred.

Writing separately, Associate Judge Eugene Fahey, who had twice voted in 2015 to refuse to review the decisions of the Third Appellate Department in Tommy's case and the Fourth Appellate Department in Kiko's case, became the first American judge in any court of last resort in any state to give his opinion on the merits of the NhRP's arguments. His opinion was that we were correct.[20]

Judge Fahey specifically rejected both courts' refusal to recognize that chimpanzees cannot be "persons" because they lack "the capacity or ability . . . to bear legal duties, or to be held legally accountable for their actions."

> Petitioner and amici law professors Laurence H. Tribe, Justin Marceau, and Samuel Wiseman question this assumption. Even if it is correct, however, that nonhuman animals cannot bear duties, the same is true of human infants or comatose human adults, yet no one would suppose that it is improper to seek a writ of habeas corpus on behalf of one's infant child [citation omitted] or a parent suffering from dementia [citation omitted]. In short, being a "moral agent" who can freely choose to act as morality requires is not a necessary condition of being a "moral patient" who can be wronged and may have the right to redress wrongs (*see generally* Tom Regan, *The Case for Animal Rights* 151–156 [2d ed 2004]).[21]

Judge Fahey then argued that the First Appellate Department's "conclusion that a chimpanzee cannot be considered a 'person' and is not entitled to habeas relief is in fact based on nothing more than the premise that a chimpanzee is not a member of the human species." "I agree," Judge Fahey said, "with the principle that all human beings possess intrinsic dignity and value . . . but, in elevating our species, we should not lower the status of other highly intelligent species."[22]

Judge Fahey recognized that chimpanzees "are autonomous, intelligent creatures" and urged his fellow judges to address the "manifest injustice" of depriving a nonhuman animal such as a chimpanzee of the right to bodily liberty.[23] "The question will have to be addressed eventually," and judges will "have to recognize its complexity and confront it."[24] The answer to the question of whether a being has the "right to liberty protected by a writ of habeas corpus," Fahey wrote,

> will depend on our assessment of the intrinsic nature of chimpanzees as a species. The record before us in the motion for leave to appeal contains unrebutted evidence, in the form of affidavits from eminent primatologists, that chimpanzees have advanced cognitive abilities, including being able to remember the past and plan for the future, the capacities of self-Awareness and self-Control, and the ability to communicate through sign language. Chimpanzees make tools to catch insects; they recognize themselves in mirrors, photographs, and television images; they imitate others; they exhibit compassion and depression when a community member dies; they even display a sense of humor. Moreover, the amici philosophers with expertise in animal ethics and related areas draw our attention to recent evidence that chimpanzees demonstrate autonomy by self–Initiating intentional, adequately informed actions, free of controlling influences.[25]

The judge concluded,

> In the interval since we first denied leave to the Nonhuman Rights Project [citation omitted], I have struggled with whether this was the right decision. . . . The issue whether a nonhuman animal has a fundamental right to liberty protected by the writ of habeas corpus is profound and far-reaching. It speaks to our relationship with all the life around us. Ultimately, we will not be able to ignore it. While it may be arguable that a chimpanzee is not a "person," there is no doubt that it is not merely a thing.[26]

The following month, New York's Fourth Appellate Department signaled that it might have heard Judge Fahey in the process of rejecting the argument that an auto dealership was not a person. It was, said the court, "*common knowledge* that personhood can and sometimes does attach to nonhuman entities like corporations or *animals* [citations omitted]."[27]

Five months later, New York trial court justice Tracey A. Bannister, sitting in rural Albion, granted the NhRP's request to issue the world's first habeas corpus order on behalf of an imprisoned elephant, then transferred the case to the Bronx.[28] There trial court justice Alison Tuitt heard arguments for three days. On February 18, 2020, she issued her decision. "The arguments advanced by the NhRP are extremely persuasive for transferring Happy from her solitary, lonely one-acre exhibit at the Bronx Zoo to an elephant sanctuary," she said. Based on the unrebutted affidavits filed by some of the world's most eminent elephant experts, Justice Tuitt found that Happy is "an extraordinary animal with complex cognitive abilities, an intelligent being with advanced analytical abilities akin to human beings" and "an intelligent, autonomous being who should be treated with respect and dignity, *and* who may be entitled to liberty."[29]

The reason Justice Tuitt did not order Happy's immediate release to a sanctuary was that "regrettably," in her view, she was bound by the that 2014 decision of the Third Appellate Department, despite the fact that Judge Fahey had made his dissatisfaction with that decision clear, writing, as noted previously, that "even if it is correct, however, that nonhuman animals cannot bear duties, the same is true of human infants or comatose human adults, yet no one would suppose that it is improper to seek a writ of habeas corpus on behalf of one's infant child."[30] In 2021, New York's Court of Appeals became the first English-speaking highest court in any jurisdiction to hear any case that demands the personhood of a nonhuman animal.[31]

On the other hand, several courts outside the United States have followed this road to its end. The first such decision came in 2014, when the Indian Supreme Court, in *Nagarajah v. Animal Welfare Board*, said that all nonhuman animals have legal rights under India's Prevention of Cruelty Act, though these rights are subject to human necessity, which excludes entertainment, exhibitions, and amusement. But animals also have rights under Article 56(g) of the Indian Constitution, which the court called the "magna carta of animal rights" even if it does not disturb their status as property. The court said that Article 21 of the Indian Constitution grants every species a right to life and security, with "life" being given an expansive meaning that includes intrinsic worth, honor, and dignity, and not merely "survival or existence or instrumental value for human beings." The article also protects the fundamental rights of humans to a healthy and wholesome environment in which nonhuman animals are treated with dignity and honor.[32]

The second decision came in 2016 from a Mendoza, Argentina, trial court in the case "Presented by A.F.A.D.A. about the Chimpanzee 'Cecilia'—Nonhuman Individual." Here the court granted a writ of habeas corpus to a chimpanzee named Cecilia, who was imprisoned in the Mendoza city zoo. The court found that anyone could seek a habeas corpus writ on behalf of a detained "person." Characterizing nonhuman animals as "involuntary actors in the theater of human law," the court stated that Cecilia was not a thing, but a cognitively complex and sentient being who possessed both emotions and metacognitive abilities. She therefore was a legal person possessed of inherent nonhuman legal rights even though she might not be able to follow law-based rules of conduct, since some human beings cannot do that either. The court found that these animals may not be granted the same rights humans have, but they still have legal personhood and possess, among other rights, the fundamental rights to be born, live, grow, and die in the proper environment for their species.[33]

The third decision came in 2020 when the Superior Court of Islamabad, Pakistan, ruled that Kaavan, an Asian elephant, was an extraordinary, cognitively complex being and, along with other nonhuman animals at the zoo, was being kept in captivity in disregard of his natural habitat and was suffering pain, distress, and agony that violated the Anticruelty Act of 1890.[34]

That court stated that Article 9 of the Pakistani Constitution guarantees the life of every person and that cruel treatment and neglect of the well-being of a captive animal or exposing the animal to conditions that do not meet his or her behavioral, social, and physiological needs infringes the right to life of humans. This human right to life is dependent on the welfare, well-being, preservation, and conservation of all animal species, and any treatment that violates the provisions of the Act of 1890, or that subjects an animal to unnecessary pain or suffering, violates the right to life guaranteed under Article 9 of the Constitution.

In addition, the court stated that Article 31 of the Pakistani Constitution provides that "steps shall be taken to enable the Muslims of Pakistan, individually and collectively, to order their lives in accordance with the fundamental principles and basic concepts of Islam" and noted that the Prophet Mohammed had stated that "a good deed done to an animal is as meritorious as a good deed done to a human being, while an act of cruelty to an animal is a bad as an act of cruelty to a human being."[35]

In the court's opinion, both human and nonhuman animals' rights are inherent and stem from being alive; life is the premise for the existence of a right. It is each animal's right to live in an environment that meets their behavioral, social, and physiological needs and to be respected and not to be tortured or unnecessarily killed, because the animal's gift of life is precious and disrespect of this gift undermines the respect of the Creator.[36]

Even when demands for legal change are based on scientific discovery, evolution in morality, and good public policy, as are the NhRP's demands, they inevitably encounter strong headwinds. The long and painful struggles for the personhood and legal rights of enslaved humans, women, children, gay people, and other traditionally disenfranchised human groups demonstrate that catalyzing a gestalt shift from "thing" to "person" will demand a clear and unshakable long-term strategy, smart and flexible tactics, effective networking, a broad political base, and perhaps most importantly, sheer persistence in the face of multiple rejections.

The NhRP persists in catalyzing judicial imaginations by bringing scientific discovery to courts' attention and by giving American judges opportunities to vindicate their own ideals of justice by recognizing that at least some nonhuman animals—certainly those the NhRP's experts can prove are autonomous—should be entitled to the basic right of bodily liberty. Those who fail to take this opportunity to end this nonhuman animal slavery may one day be judged as harshly as those judges who once failed to end human slavery, "earnest, well-meaning pillars of legal respectability" who "collaborat[ed] in a system of oppression."[37]

REFERENCES

Alexander, Vincent C. "Practice Commentaries—Articles 70 (Habeas Corpus) in General."

Banaji, Mahzarin R., and Anthony G. Greenwald. *Blindspot*. Cambridge, MA: Harvard University Press, 2013.

Churchill, Winston. Speech at Lord Mayor's Luncheon. Mansion House, London. November 10, 1942.

Cover, Robert M. *Justice Accused—Anti-Slavery and the Judicial Process*. New Haven: CT, Yale University Press 1975.

Gray, John Chipman. *The Nature and Sources of the Law*. 2nd ed. New Orleans, LA: Quid Pro, 2012 [1921].

Hamilton, Edith. *The Echo of Greece*. W. W. Norton & Company, U.S.A. 1964.

Wise, Steven M. "Introduction to Animal Law Book." 67 *Syracuse Law Review* 7 (2017).

NOTES

1. Edith Hamilton, *The Echo of Greece* (1964), 24.
2. Winston Churchill, speech at Lord Mayor's Luncheon (Mansion House, London, November 10, 1942).
3. *People ex rel. Nonhuman Rights Project v. Lavery*, 124 A.D. 3d 148, 152 (3rd. Dept. 2014).
4. *Matter of Nonhuman Rights Project, Inc. v. Lavery*, 152 A.D. 3d 73, 78 (1st Dept. 2017).
5. *Dred Scott v. Sandford*, 60 U.S. 393, 407 (1857).
6. *People v. Hall*, 4 Cal. 399, 404 (1854).
7. *In the Matter of the Motion to Admit Miss Lavinia Goodell*, 39 Wis. 232 (1875).
8. Steven M. Wise, "Introduction to Animal Law Book," *Syracuse Law Review* 67 (2017): 7, 13.
9. Mahzarin R. Banaji and Anthony G. Greenwald, *Blindspot* (Cambridge, MA: Harvard University Press, 2013), 98.
10. *People ex rel. Nonhuman Rights Project v. Lavery*, 124 A.D. 3d 148.
11. John Chipman Gray, *The Nature and Sources of the Law*, 2nd ed. (New Orleans, LA: Quid Pro, 2012 [1921]), 27.
12. Gray, *The Nature and Sources of the Law*, 42–43, 44.
13. *People ex rel. Nonhuman Rights Project*, 124 A.D. 3d at 151.
14. *Philosophers' Amicus Brief*, https://www.nonhumanrights.org/content/uploads/Notice-of-Motion-for-Leave-Philosophers-Amicus-Happys-Case-1.pdf, at 12–13.
15. *Moore v. Ganim*, 233 Conn. 557, 598 (1995).
16. Nonhuman Rights Project vs. Stanley, Decision, https://www.nonhumanrights.org/content/uploads/4.-Dismissal-of-Appeal-4-3-14-Hercules-Leo.pdf.
17. Vincent C. Alexander, "Practice Commentaries—Articles 70 (Habeas Corpus) In General."

18. https://www.nonhumanrights.org/content/uploads/4.-Petition-for-Mandamus-Kikos-Appeal.pdf.

19. *In the Matter of a Proceeding under Article 70 of the CPLR for a Writ of Habeas Corpus, the Nonhuman Rights Project, Inc, on Behalf of Hercules and Leo v. Stanley*, 16 N.Y.S. 3d 898 (Supr. Ct. 2015).

20. *Nonhuman Rights Project, Inc. on Behalf of Tommy v. Lavery*, 31 N.Y. 3d 1054 (2018) (Fahey, J., concurring).

21. *Fahey Concurrence,* 31 N.Y. 3d at 1057.

22. (*Fahey Concurrence,* 31 N.Y. 3d at 1057).

23. *Fahey Concurrence,* 31 N.Y. 3d at 1058.

24. *Fahey Concurrence,* 31 N.Y. 3d at 1059.

25. *Fahey Concurrence,* 31 N.Y. 3d at 1057.

26. *Fahey Concurrence,* at 1059.

27. *People v. Graves*, 163 A.D. 3d 16 (4th Dept. 2018); emphases added.

28. https://www.nonhumanrights.org/content/uploads/Order-to-Show-Cause-Happy.pdf.

29. The Nonhuman Rights Project v. Breheney, 2020 WL 1670735 (Bronx Supreme Ct. 2020), at *10.

30. https://www.nonhumanrights.org/content/uploads/HappyFeb182020.pdf.

31. Fahey Concurrence, at 1057.

32. *Animal Welfare Board of India v. Nagarajah*, Civil Appeal No. 5387 of 2014, 6 SCALE 468, https://indiankanoon.org/doc/39696860/.

33. Cecilia the Chimpanzee's Case, File No. P-72, 254/15 (Mendoza, Argentina, November 3, 2016), https://www.nonhumanrights.org/content/uploads/2016/12/Chimpanzee-Cecilia_translation-FINAL-for-website.pdf.

34. *Islamabad Wildlife Mmgt. Bd. v. Metropolitan Corp. Islamabad*, W.P. No. 1155/2019 (H.C. Islamabad, Pakistan May 21, 2020)

35. *Islamabad Wildlife Management Board v. Metropolitan Corporation*, W.P. No. 1155/2–19 (April 2020), https://www.nonhumanrights.org/content/uploads/Islamabad-High-Court-decision-in-Kaavan-case.pdf.

36. *Islamabad Wildlife Management Board*, W.P. No. 1155/2–19.

37. Robert M. Cover, *Justice Accused—Anti-Slavery and the Judicial Process* (New Haven, CT: Yale University 1975), 6.

Chapter 9

Animals as Quasi-Property/ Persons

By Angela Fernandez

There are a number of examples of symbolic name changes in the animal law movement. Companion animal "owners," for example, are designated "guardians" in some jurisdictions in order to track the idea that many people think of companion animals as members of the family, not as property.[1] Abolitionists would point out that as long as a guardian/"owner" can kill a perfectly healthy animal, nothing (or little) has been accomplished by a name change. The legal property status is what permits the guardian/"owner" to make that choice, even if it does not justify that choice morally or socially. As recently as the 1960s, it was not unheard of for a family to kill the family dog before going on vacation, with plans to get a new dog when they returned home, which was cheaper than paying to board the dog during their holiday. Presumably, the dognapping that went on to provide household animals for laboratory experiments and that helped to incite the passage of the US Animal Welfare Act (1966) indicated that there was a range of societal views about the value of the family dog, one of which saw dogs as a poachable commodity.[2]

Many dog lovers today would be shocked to hear that such practices occurred in such recent memory. The family-member view now seems to be the dominant position.[3] It would be horrific to think about killing an animal family member to facilitate taking a vacation and difficult to think that any member of society (including laboratories purchasing animals for testing) would countenance those animals' theft for research experiments and that a law to prohibit that theft would be necessary. Yet unwanted but healthy dogs are euthanized at shelters in alarmingly high numbers every day, and beagles are commonly bred for use in animal research testing laboratories. The family-member view, in other words, exists alongside the view of dogs as disposable, and in an animal testing context, it is viewed as permissible to subject them to routine acts of violence. Such are the contradictions in human attitudes toward nonhuman animals.[4]

The property status of nonhuman animals has come under attack by Gary Francione and other abolitionists for decades. One might infer from the strength with which he and Steven Wise attack the property status of nonhuman animals that they think the primary problem for nonhuman animals is that we humans (backed up by the legal system) see nonhuman animals as (disposable) property. Yet surely Wendy Adams is correct when she writes, "Human beings do not treat animals harshly because they are classified as property; animals are classified as property so that human beings can legally treat them harshly."[5] So long as people still want to treat animals badly—to use them, eat them, and test on them—animals will continue to be categorized as property. The legal category facilitates that use and abuse and reinforces it; however, the legal category does not *itself* create the desire to hurt animals, even if it permits the harm and is strengthened when people who are born into that legal system use it to pattern their ethical beliefs.

At least two things are important about the fact that the law does not itself create the desire to use and abuse nonhuman animals by considering them property. First, the property status itself does not justify anything about the treatment of nonhuman animals, positive or negative.[6] Second, abolishing the property status by, say, establishing a move into personhood would leave those societal desires (and accompanying customs and habits) intact, at least in the short term (not to discount that there might be eventual gain from a shift from property to personhood for some nonhuman animals, just as there might be with the idea of animal guardian).

What follows from saying "this animal is mine"? In the case of nonhuman animals, you cannot treat them however you want. Domesticated animals should be protected by animal welfare laws against unnecessary cruelty. Codes relating to animals farmed for food are written by industry and do not protect against practices that are often both cruel and unnecessary, but legally even farmed animals should not be treated in any way a sadistic person would want.[7] Similarly, animals used in research should be treated in accordance with guidelines and standards drafted and overseen by members of the scientific research community. Animal advocates routinely point out how weak and ineffective these protections are, and in the case of code and industry-drafted guidelines, they are arguably not even really law.[8] However, as "living property" or "sentient property," nonhuman animals cannot legally be treated in any way a property owner desires.[9] They are "quasi-property" in the sense that they have some rights. And if they have some (albeit limited) rights, they also are already a kind of legal person, a "quasi-person."[10]

Abolitionists like Francione and Wise hammer home the property status of nonhuman animals because they want to blame that status for the bad ways in which nonhuman animals are treated, in order to argue, especially in the case of Wise and the Nonhuman Rights Project, that we should move nonhuman animals into the category of persons through habeas corpus court cases for individual chimpanzees and elephants.[11] Such approaches presuppose that "property" and "person" are mutually exclusive categories[12] and further that personhood would require abolishment of property status. Yet the legal classifications of persons and property do not definitively demarcate the legal possibilities for recognizing rights and protections for other animals. At least some rights (including rights we now ascribe only to persons) could be extended to nonhuman animals even as they retain the status of property, and conversely, not all rights of persons need to be extended to nonhuman animals, even though they may hold some of the rights of personhood.[13]

It is true that civil law codes, based on Roman law's Gaian triad, persons–things–actions, use the distinction between property and persons in a central way. However, these demarcations have never precluded overlap. Roman law's treatment of slavery itself showed that one could be considered property and at the same time have some of the rights of personhood.[14] Following Roman law, married women and children were never classified in the common law as property per se, although the authority of the patriarch certainly made them vulnerable to being treated *as if* they were property, specifically in the sense that their labor belonged to him.[15] Indeed, women, children, and enslaved individuals are all included in the "law of persons" (not "things") in Gaius's *Institutes*, the first topic of which is the distinctions between different kinds of free men.[16]

Being owned by another is the rock base of indignity even when that ownership is exercised in a benevolent manner. We think of it as inconsistent with any entity's ability to bear rights and look out for their own interests. Yet personhood, apart from the kind that adult white propertied men possess, tends to be splintered or fragmented in actual fact. Enslaved people, married women, children, and racialized and poor individuals tend to carry (and have carried) a mixed bag of things they can and cannot do, either as a formal legal matter or in terms of practical reality. In other words, their personhood is already in a "quasi" state, split between different, more specific capacities and incapacities.[17] The background against which human inequality operates puts outright human ownership beyond the pale, and by extension, empathy for the plight of nonhuman animals makes us think that they cannot continue to be classified as property. Hence, Richard Posner's claim that nonhuman animals should continue to be commodified in order for us to protect them (given what he calls the "'liberating' potential" of private property) falls deafeningly flat in a world in which the vast majority of nonhuman animals are treated as they are.[18] Yet it is important, I think, to not blame property status itself for that treatment and to watch for the ways in which the contestation of the property status of nonhuman animals might be standing in for other concerns that have less to do with the property status of animals per se and more to do with issues such as transparency relating to nonhuman animal treatment and the representation of their interests in political life.

So much animal abuse takes place on private property away from those who could see and report it, both in domestic contexts and in industrial factory farm settings. "Ag-gag" laws are making it increasingly difficult to gain access to places where that abuse takes place, when just coming onto the property can result in a trespass or other criminal charge. This important concern is much more about the private property upon and in which nonhuman animals are kept, not about their own status as private property. Similarly, the voicelessness of nonhuman animals, their inability to object to their poor treatment, and the absence of direct representation of their interests in our legal and political processes are exacerbated by their property status and lack of legal personhood. Yet one can imagine ways in which that situation might be improved that do not involve making them legal persons or abolishing their status as property.[19] The private nuclear family as a location of domestic violence and other forms of abuse and the historic inability of women to vote (and of children, who are still unable to vote until quite an old age) track generally similar concrete concerns that have less to do with property status per se than with being physically located inside private property that belongs to another without any kind of direct political representation or other effective protection. Framing the concern as one relating to the property status of these groups themselves misunderstands what needs to be done to correct the situation. Attaining "personhood" (e.g., voting rights) is a shorthand way to make things better; however, what is really needed is attitude change. People need to view locking up vulnerable individuals in settings with minimal oversight and systematically cruel treatment as unacceptable, whether it is for food production (especially in countries that are food-secure and can use other options) or for animal testing (most of which is actively misleading and unhelpful).[20]

Insofar as "property" means "not person," and "not person" means no rights, property status operates as a reason to treat nonhuman animals *as if* they have no rights.[21] We might think of this as what Cass Sunstein has identified as the rhetorical value of speaking about nonhuman animals as property and, conversely, the power in changing that rhetoric.[22] Yet the truth is that nonhuman animals do have *some* rights, and so we would not be entitled to make that deductive leap even if conclusions about treatment flowed from the property status, which they do not. The sharks whose fins are cut off to make shark fin soup are not private property. The long, slow death for them that results from this practice has its roots in other legal permissions and attitudes toward the value of their lives, pain, and suffering balanced against human desire for this specialized (and unnecessary) "luxury" food.[23] Free-living animals generally are not private property. Yet they nonetheless suffer massively from a lack of representation of their interests in decisions about so-called conservation and "wildlife management," as well as in mainstream political processes, where economic drivers result in their habitat loss and impacts on biodiversity. The problem for them is a disregard of their interests, not their property status.

It is now well established that at least some nonhuman animals, particularly companion animals, are no longer seen as "mere property." They are "more than property."[24] However, recognition of their quasi-property status does not push them into the category of full legal persons equivalent to human beings. As "quasi-property," animals would have some (mostly negative) rights not to be interfered with, tortured, and so on, but they would lack a wide array of positive rights that would not be appropriate to their situation, such as the right to vote (at least as individuals, even if species interests might someday form a more robust part of our political process), the right to drive, or the right to an education. They would not, at least not without the help of a legal trustee or guardian, be able to own property or make contracts or sue or be sued, the traditional indicia of legal personhood.

Having some rights (not to be interfered with) but not all the rights of (male propertied) humans or other kinds of legal persons lands us immediately in "quasi" territory (arguably, corporations also should be there, having as they do some rights but not others that humans have, such as the right to vote). Property with some rights makes animals, in my view, quasi-property *and* quasi-persons.[25] Quasi-hood, in other words, is a hybrid space that already exists and has existed from at least Gaius on. Animal advocates themselves relentlessly reinforce the idea that the categories operate in a mutually exclusive way, unnecessarily simplifying the options we feel we have before us.[26]

Cobbling together aspects of concepts that are already familiar to us may be less revolutionary than creating a totally new category, but this approach could be very powerful in terms of symbolic cognitive structuring, as with companion animal guardianship. Moreover, it could help us start to tell the story in a new way. Rather than declaring that law is bad because it classifies nonhuman animals as property and that the solution is to move nonhuman animals from property to personhood, we might think instead that law is neutral, or at least it can be good or bad for nonhuman animals, and that nonhuman animals already are different from other forms of property (as most people would acknowledge), already have some rights (a point around which there is less social recognition), and to that extent, are already quasi-persons.

The law should promote and protect their interests and further recognize their quasi-hood status.

Jonathan Safran Foer has written eloquently about the importance of the stories we tell about nonhuman animals.[27] George Monbiot, thinking primarily about issues relating to the environment, also has written extensively about the way that political inspiration and motivation requires a positive animating narrative.[28] The aim with the quasi-hood idea is not to run a public relations campaign for law, to argue that it is not that bad or that private property has received an undeservedly bad rap; history shows the multiple ways in which the legalization of force has effected dispossession and colonization beyond calculation, especially over the last four hundred years in North America.[29] I am not trying to undermine (or underestimate) the large role that law and legal categories play in structuring ethics and human beliefs about what is right and wrong and what can be done about that. What is clear is that the story needs to be told another way, wherein *law at least has the opportunity* to do the right thing, using concepts already known and familiar in it, recombined perhaps in only a slightly different way, a strategy designed to appeal to incrementalists, which most lawyers are, at least in common law jurisdictions or parts of the world in which English law continues to be relevant.

The idea that nonhuman animals should be thought of as "quasi-property/quasi-person" faces the same objection that the move toward adopting the nomenclature of companion animal guardianship faces—namely, what power ultimately does a name contain when, at the end of the day, everything stays the same (e.g., the healthy animal can be killed with impunity)? What difference does it make to think of nonhuman animals in this way, especially if it is the status they already possess, one that has proven to be woefully inadequate at protecting them? What are the downsides of moving to this way of thinking, specifically in retaining anything about "property," especially if the goal is to promote a recognition that animal lives matter in themselves, intrinsically, and if only personhood (because it connotes human personhood) can do that? These are all questions worth further thought.

REFERENCES

Adams, Wendy A. "Human Subjects and Animal Objects: Animals as 'Other' in Law." *Animal Law & Ethics* 31, no. 1 (2009): 29–51.

Alter, Lloyd. "'Why Love One but Eat the Other' Ads Stir Controversy in Toronto Subway System." *Treehugger*, October 27, 2011. https://www.treehugger.com/green-food/why-love-one-eat-other-ads-stir-controversy-toronto-subway-system.html.

Anderson, Virginia DeJohn. *Creatures of Empire: How Domestic Animals Transformed Early America*. New York: Oxford University Press, 2004.
Balcombe, Jonathan. *What a Fish Knows: The Inner Lives of Our Underwater Cousins*. New York: Scientific American / Farrar, Straus and Giroux, 2016.
Beatty, Stephen J., Mark G. Allen, Jeff M. Whitty, Alan J. Lymbery, James J. Keleher, James R. Tweedley, Brendan C. Ebner, and David L. Morgan. "First Evidence of Spawning Migration by Goldfish (*Carassius auratus*): Implications for Control of a Globally Invasive Species." *Ecology of Freshwater Fish* 26 (2017): 444–55.
Berg, Jessica. "Owning Persons: The Application of Property Theory to Embryos and Fetuses." *Wake Forest Law Review* 40, no. 1 (2005): 159–219.
Berman, Morris. *Coming to Our Senses: Body and Spirit in the Hidden History of the West*. New York: Bantam Books, 1989.
Black, Henry Campbell. *Black's Law Dictionary*. 6th ed. St. Paul: West Publishing, 1990.
Blackstone, William. *Commentaries on the Law of England*. Vol. 2, *The Rights of Things*. Oxford: Clarendon Press, 1766.
Blattner, Charlotte E. "The Recognition of Animal Sentience by the Law." *Journal of Animal Ethics* 9, no. 2 (2019): 121–36.
Boyd, David R. *The Rights of Nature: A Legal Revolution That Could Save the World*. Toronto: ECW Press, 2017.
Brown, Culum. "Fish Intelligence, Sentience and Ethics." *Animal Cognition* 18 (2015): 1–17.
Cassuto, David N., and Amy M. O'Brien. "You Don't Need Lungs to Suffer: Fish Suffering in the Age of Climate Change with a Call for Regulatory Reform." *Canadian Journal of Comparative and Contemporary Law* 5 (2019): 31–75.
Chitty, Joseph. *A Treatise on the Games Laws, and on Fisheries: With an Appendix Containing All the Cases and Statutes on the Subject*. Vol 1. London: W. Clarke, 1812.
Cochrane, Alasdair. *Should Animals Have Political Rights?* Cambridge, UK: Polity, 2020.
Donaldson, Sue, and Will Kymlicka. *Zoopolis: A Political Theory of Animal Rights*. Oxford: Oxford University Press, 2013.
Epstein, Richard A. "The Dangerous Claims of the Animal Rights Movement." *Responsive Community* 10, no. 2 (2000): 28–37.
Favre, David. "Animals as Living Property." In *The Oxford Handbook of Animal Studies*, edited by Linda Kalof, 65–80. New York: Oxford University Press, 2017.
———. "Equitable Self-Ownership for Animals." *Duke Law Journal* 50, no. 2 (2000): 473–502.
———. "Living Property: A New Status for Animals within the Legal System." *Marquette Law Review* 93 (2010): 1021–71.
———. "A New Property Status for Animals: Equitable Self-Ownership." In *Animal Rights: Current Debates and New Directions*, edited by Cass R. Sunstein and Martha C. Nussbaum, 234–50. New York: Oxford University Press, 2004.
Fernandez, Angela. "Already Artificial: Legal Personality and Animal Rights." In *Human Rights after Corporate Personhood: An Uneasy Merger?*, edited by Jody Greene and Sharif Youssef, 211–58. Toronto: University of Toronto Press, 2020.

———. "Legal History and Rights for Nonhuman Animals: An Interview with Steven M. Wise." *Dalhousie Law Journal* 41, no. 1 (Spring 2019): 197–218.

———. "Not Quite Property, Not Quite Persons: A 'Quasi' Approach for Nonhuman Animals." *Canadian Journal of Comparative and Contemporary Law* 5 (2019): 155–231.

———. *Pierson v. Post, the Hunt for the Fox: Law and Professionalization in American Legal Culture*. New York: Cambridge University Press, 2018.

Foer, Jonathan Safran. *Eating Animals*. New York: Little, Brown, 2009.

Graham, Courtney, Marina A. G. Von Keyserlingk, and Becca Franks. "Zebrafish Welfare: Natural History, Social Motivation, and Behaviour." *Applied Animal Behaviour* 200 (2018): 13–22.

Hankin, Susan J. "Making Decisions about Our Animals' Health Care: Does It Matter Whether We Are Owners or Guardians?" *Stanford Journal of Animal Law & Policy* 2, no. 1 (2009): 1–51.

Herzog, Hal. *Some We Love, Some We Hate, Some We Eat: Why It's So Hard to Think Straight about Animals*. New York: HarperCollins, 2010.

Ingham, John H. *The Law of Animals: A Treatise on Property in Animals, Wild and Domestic, and the Rights and Responsibilities Arising Therefrom*. Philadelphia: T & J. W. Johnson, 1900.

Jacquet, Jennifer, Becca Franks, Peter Godfrey-Smith, and Walter Sánchez-Suárez. "The Case against Octopus Farming." *Issues in Science and Technology* (Winter 2019): 37–45.

Kent, James. *Commentaries on American Law*. Vol. 2. New York: O. Halsted, 1827.

Kramer, Lisa, and Ray Greek. "Human Stakeholders and the Use of Animals in Drug Development." *Business and Society Review* 123, no. 1 (2018): 3–58.

Kurki, Visa A. *A Theory of Legal Personhood*. Oxford: Oxford University Press, 2019.

Kymlicka, Will. "Social Membership: Animal Law beyond the Property/Personhood Impasse." *Dalhousie Law Journal* 40, no. 1 (2017): 123–55.

Labchuk, Camille. "The Creeping Privatization of Animal Protection Lawmaking and Enforcement." Presented at the Oxford Centre for Animal Ethics, Fifth Annual Oxford Summer School on Animal Ethics, "Animal Ethics and Law: Creating Positive Change for Animals," St Stephen's House, Oxford, England, July 23, 2018.

Matlack, Carolyn B. *We've Got Feelings Too: Presenting the Sentient Property Solution*. Winston-Salem, NC: Log Cabin Press, 2006.

McRobbie, Linda Rodriguez. "Should We Stop Keeping Pets? Why More and More Ethicists Say Yes." *Guardian*, August 1, 2017. https://www.theguardian.com/lifeandstyle/2017/aug/01/should-we-stop-keeping-pets-why-more-and-more-ethicists-say-yes.

Monbiot, George. *Feral: Rewilding the Land, the Sea, and Human Life*. Toronto: Allen Lane, 2013.

———. *How Did We Get into This Mess? Politics, Equality, Nature*. London: Verso, 2016.

———. *Out of the Wreckage: A New Politics for an Age of Crisis*. London: Verso, 2017.

Nagel, Thomas. "What Is It Like to Be a Bat?" *Philosophical Review* 83, no. 4 (1974): 435–50.

Perry, Nancy V. "Ten Years of Animal Law at Lewis & Clark Law School." *Animal Law* 9 (2003): ix–xv.

Pietrzykowskis, Tomasz. "The Idea of Non-Personal Subjects of Law." In *Legal Personhood: Animals, Artificial and the Unborn*, edited by Visa A. J. Kurki and Tomasz Pietrzykowskis, 49–67. Cham, Switzerland: Springer, 2017.

Posner, Richard A. "Animal Rights." Review of *Rattling the Cage*, by Steven Wise. *Yale Law Journal* 110, no. 3 (2000–2001): 527–41.

Saint-Exupéry, Antoine. *The Little Prince*. Paris: Éditions Gallimard, 1943.

Shannon-Missal, Larry. "More Than Ever, Pets Are Members of the Family." *Harris Poll*, July 16, 2015. https://www.theharrispoll.com/whether-furry-feathered-or-flippers-a-flapping-americans-continue-to-display-close-relationships-with-their-pets-2015-is-expected-to-continue-the-pet-industrys-more-than-two-decades-strong/.

Singer, Peter. "Fish: The Forgotten Victims on Our Plate." *Guardian*, September 14, 2010. https://www.theguardian.com/commentisfree/cif-green/2010/sep/14/fish-forgotten-victims.

Sirois, Lauren. "Recovering from the Loss of a Beloved Pet: Rethinking the Legal Classification of Companion Animals and the Requirements for Loss of Companionship Tort Damages." *University of Pennsylvania Law Review* 163, no. 4 (2014–15): 1199–239.

Steneck, R. S., T. P. Hughes, J. E. Cinner, W. N. Adger, S. N. Arnold, F. Berkes, S. A. Boudreau, et al. "Creation of a Gilded Trap by the High Economic Value of the Maine Lobster Fishery." *Conservation Biology* 25, no. 5 (2011): 904–12.

Studemund, Wilhelm, and James Muirhead. *The Institutes of Gaius and Rules of Ulpian*. Edinburgh: T. & T. Clark, 1880.

Sunstein, Cass R. "Standing for Animals (with Notes on Animal Rights)." *University of California Los Angeles Law Review* 47 (2000): 1333–68.

Sykes, Katie. "Rethinking the Application of Canadian Criminal Law to Factory Farming." In *Canadian Perspectives on Animals and the Law*, edited by Peter Sankoff, Vaughan Black, and Katie Sykes, 33–56. Toronto: Irwin Law, 2015.

Sykes, Katie, Joanna Langille, and Robert Howse. "Whales and Seals and Bears, Oh My! The Evolution of Global Animal Law and Canada's Ambiguous Stance." In *Canadian Perspectives on Animals and the Law*, edited by Peter Sankoff, Vaughan Black, and Katie Sykes, 209–36. Toronto: Irwin Law, 2015.

Tomlins, Christopher L. *Freedom Bound: Law, Labor and Civic Identity in Colonizing English America, 1580–1865*. Cambridge: Cambridge University Press, 2010.

Treves, A., F. Santiago-Ávila, and W. S. Lynn. "Just Preservation." *Biological Conservation* 229 (2018): 134–41.

Tse, M. H. "Animals and the Rule of Force." Presented at the Canadian Animal Law Conference, Dalhousie University, Halifax, Nova Scotia, October 5, 2019.

Wadiwel, Dinesh Joseph. "Do Fish Resist?" *Cultural Studies Review* 22, no. 1 (2016): 196–242.

Wise, Steven M. "Animal Thing to Animal Person—Thoughts on Time, Place, and Theories." *Animal Law* 5 (1999): 61–68.
———. *Rattling the Cage: Towards Legal Rights for Animals*. Boston: Da Capo Press, 2000; with a new foreword by Jane Goodall and a new preface, 2014.
Ziff, Bruce. "The Law of Capture, Newfoundland Style." *University of Toronto Law Journal* 63, no. 1 (2013): 53–72.

NOTES

1. See, e.g., Susan J. Hankin, "Making Decisions about Our Animals' Health Care: Does It Matter Whether We Are Owners or Guardians?," *Stanford Journal of Animal Law & Policy* 2, no. 1 (2009): 1.

2. Laboratory Animal Welfare Act, Pub. L. No. 89–544 (1966).

3. See Linda Rodriguez McRobbie, "Should We Stop Keeping Pets? Why More and More Ethicists Say Yes," *Guardian*, August 1, 2017, https://www.theguardian.com/lifeandstyle/2017/aug/01/should-we-stop-keeping-pets-why-more-and-more-ethicists-say-yes (reporting that "90% of pet-owning Britons" consider their pet a family member, "with 16% listing their animal in the 2011 census"); and Larry Shannon-Missal, "More Than Ever, Pets Are Members of the Family," *Harris Poll*, July 16, 2015, https://www.theharrispoll.com/whether-furry-feathered-or-flippers-a-flapping-americans-continue-to-display-close-relationships-with-their-pets-2015-is-expected-to-continue-the-pet-industrys-more-than-two-decades-strong/ (reporting that 95 percent of Americans consider their animal companions to be members of the family).

4. See Hal Herzog, *Some We Love, Some We Hate, Some We Eat: Why It's So Hard to Think Straight about Animals* (New York: HarperCollins, 2010). The Toronto subway system has carried a powerful advertising campaign capitalizing on the contradiction by asking, "Why love one but eat the other?" alongside images that show a dog next to a pig and a fluffy kitten next to a baby chick. See Lloyd Alter, "'Why Love One but Eat the Other' Ads Stir Controversy in Toronto Subway System," *Treehugger*, October 27, 2011, https://www.treehugger.com/green-food/why-love-one-eat-other-ads-stir-controversy-toronto-subway-system.html.

5. Wendy A. Adams, "Human Subjects and Animal Objects: Animals as 'Other' in Law," *Animal Law & Ethics* 31, no. 1 (2009): 29.

6. M. H. Tse, "Animals and the Rule of Force" (presented at the Canadian Animal Law Conference, Dalhousie University, Halifax, Nova Scotia, October 5, 2019), arguing that property status and rules are an important clue to the legal source of permission human beings give themselves to exercise enterprising and predatory force against other animals; but property status and entitlements do not explain as a general matter why human beings are permitted to inflict violence on nonhuman animals.

7. For an argument that the "cruel" and "unnecessary" requirements under the Canadian Criminal Code should be interpreted to include routine cruelty involved in factory farming, see Katie Sykes, "Rethinking the Application of Canadian Criminal

Law to Factory Farming," in *Canadian Perspectives on Animals and the Law*, ed. Peter Sankoff, Vaughan Black, and Katie Sykes (Toronto: Irwin Law, 2015), 33–56.

8. Camille Labchuk, "The Creeping Privatization of Animal Protection Lawmaking and Enforcement," presented at the Oxford Centre for Animal Ethics, Fifth Annual Oxford Summer School on Animal Ethics, "Animal Ethics and Law: Creating Positive Change for Animals," St Stephen's House, Oxford, England, July 23, 2018.

9. See David Favre, "Living Property: A New Status for Animals within the Legal System," *Marquette Law Review* 93 (2010): 1021–71; David Favre, "Animals as Living Property," in *The Oxford Handbook of Animal Studies*, ed. Linda Kalof (New York: Oxford University Press, 2017), 65–80; and Carolyn B. Matlack, *We've Got Feelings Too: Presenting the Sentient Property Solution* (Winston-Salem, NC: Log Cabin Press, 2006). See also Lauren Sirois, "Recovering for the Loss of a Beloved Pet: Rethinking the Legal Classification of Companion Animals and the Requirements for Loss of Companionship Tort Damages," *University of Pennsylvania Law Review* 163, no. 4 (2014–15): 1227 (using the term "semi-property" for a "more than just property" status for nonhuman companion animals).

10. See Angela Fernandez, "Not Quite Property, Not Quite Persons: A 'Quasi' Approach for Nonhuman Animals," *Canadian Journal of Comparative and Contemporary Law* 5 (2019): 155–231. For a similar argument, see Cass R. Sunstein, "Standing for Animals (with Notes on Animal Rights)," *University of California Los Angeles Law Review* 47 (2000): 1335n9 ("Statutes protecting animal welfare protect a form of animal rights"), 1337 ("As a matter of positive law, animals have rights in the same sense that people do, at least under many statutes that are enforceable only by public officials"), and 1363–64. See also David Favre, "A New Property Status for Animals: Equitable Self-Ownership," in *Animal Rights: Current Debates and New Directions*, ed. Cass R. Sunstein and Martha C. Nussbaum (New York: Oxford University Press, 2004), 239 ("Animals presently have some legal rights, notwithstanding their existing property status. . . . These rights, however, are imperfect in that enforcement is limited to actions by the state in criminal court").

11. For an overview of Wise's work, see Angela Fernandez, "Already Artificial: Legal Personality and Animal Rights," in *Human Rights after Corporate Personhood: An Uneasy Merger?*, ed. Jody Greene and Sharif Youssef (Toronto: University of Toronto Press, 2020), 211–58. See also Angela Fernandez, "Legal History and Rights for Nonhuman Animals: An Interview with Steven M. Wise," *Dalhousie Law Journal* 41, no. 1 (Spring 2019): 197–218.

12. Wise tends to describe the distinction between humans and all other animals, rooted in the Roman law distinction between property and persons, as "the great legal wall." See, e.g., Steven M. Wise, "Animal Thing to Animal Person—Thoughts on Time, Place, and Theories," *Animal Law* 5 (1999): 61. See also Steven M. Wise, *Rattling the Cage: Towards Legal Rights for Animals* (Boston: Da Capo Press, 2000; with a new foreword by Jane Goodall and a new preface, 2014), xviii, 270 ("the ancient Great Wall").

13. For a similar argument in a different context, see Jessica Berg, "Owning Persons: The Application of Property Theory to Embryos and Fetuses," *Wake Forest Law Review* 40, no. 1 (2005): 162 (arguing that "'person' and 'property' are not

mutually exclusive designations, and one might recognize both property interests in, and personhood interests of, certain entities") and 218 (noting that the concept could be applied to nonhuman animals).

14. Richard A. Epstein, "The Dangerous Claims of the Animal Rights Movement," *Responsive Community* 10, no. 2 (2000): 30 ("From the earliest time they [enslaved people] were governed by a set of rules that treated them as legal hybrids, part property and part human beings").

15. This is contrary to what Wise says about Roman law—specifically that women, children, and enslaved individuals were all classified as "things" in Gaius's tripartite division. See Wise, *Rattling the Cage*, 31–32.

16. See Wilhelm Studemund and James Muirhead, *The Institutes of Gaius and Rules of Ulpian* (Edinburgh: T. & T. Clark, 1880), 21–75 (on women and children) and 4–21 (on different kinds of unfree men).

17. See Visa A. J. Kurki, *A Theory of Legal Personhood* (Oxford: Oxford University Press, 2019) (arguing that legal personhood is best understood as a "cluster" property consisting of distinct incidents).

18. See Richard A. Posner, "Animal Rights," review of *Rattling the Cage*, by Steven Wise, *Yale Law Journal* 110, no. 3 (2000–2001): 539 ("One way to protect animals is to make them property, because people tend to protect what they own").

19. See, e.g., Alasdair Cochrane, *Should Animals Have Political Rights?* (Cambridge, UK: Polity, 2020).

20. See Lisa Kramer and Ray Greek, "Human Stakeholders and the Use of Animals in Drug Development," *Business and Society Review* 123, no. 1 (2018): 3–58 (on how the nonhuman animal testing requirement in the United States actually misleads, telling us that certain drugs are safe when they are not, leading us to be able to cure cancer in mice but not humans, and resulting in missed opportunities for drugs that might not work on rats but do on human beings).

21. The first legal definition of "quasi" is "as if; almost as it were; analogous to." *Black's Law Dictionary*, 6th ed. (St. Paul, MN: West Publishing, 1990), s.v. "quasi." The entry continues, "This term is used in legal phraseology to indicate that one subject resembles another, with which it is compared, in certain characteristics, but that there are intrinsic and material differences between them."

22. Sunstein, "Standing for Animals," 1363 ("The rhetoric does matter. In the long term, it would indeed make sense to think of animals as something other than property, partly in order to clarify their status as beings with rights of their own").

23. Lobsters are another luxury food, the intensive fishing for which creates what is referred to as a "gilded trap," "a type of social trap in which collective actions resulting from economically attractive opportunities outweigh concerns over associated social and ecological risks or consequences," specifically the creation of an aquatic monoculture that lacks resilience to weather changes in the coastal marine ecosystem such as climate-change triggered disease. R. S. Steneck et al., "Creation of a Gilded Trap by the High Economic Value of the Maine Lobster Fishery," *Conservation Biology* 25, no. 5 (2011): 904. Farmed octopuses are yet another, eaten in largely food-secure "upscale outlets in Japan, Korea, northern Mediterranean countries, the

United States, China, and Australia." Jennifer Jacquet et al., "The Case against Octopus Farming," *Issues in Science and Technology* (Winter 2019): 44.

24. I understand the "not things" provisions in countries such as Germany, Austria, and Spain to be saying that nonhuman animals are not *mere* things. See Fernandez, "Not Quite Property, Not Quite Persons," 183 (quoting from a Nonhuman Rights Project case in which a sympathetic judge wrote, "While it may be arguable that a chimpanzee is not a 'person,' there is no doubt that it is not *merely* a thing").

25. See Fernandez, "Not Quite Property, Not Quite Persons."

26. See, e.g., Will Kymlicka, "Social Membership: Animal Law beyond the Property/Personhood Impasse," *Dalhousie Law Journal* 40, no. 1 (2017): 123–55 (arguing for a "third option" based on the social recognition rights for domesticated animals based on family membership and workers' rights).

27. Jonathan Safran Foer, *Eating Animals* (New York: Little, Brown, 2009).

28. George Monbiot, *Out of the Wreckage: A New Politics for an Age of Crisis* (London: Verso, 2017).

29. See, e.g., Christopher L. Tomlins, *Freedom Bound: Law, Labor and Civic Identity in Colonizing English America, 1580–1865* (Cambridge: Cambridge University Press, 2010).

Chapter 10

Housing Rights and Forever Homes

Reforms to Make Our Cities More Livable for Our Companion Animals and Ourselves

By Solana Joy Phillips

ANTHROPOMORPHISM MAKES THE MAN

Discussions of animal habitats often focus on regions of the world with little to no human population: rain forest, tundra, ice floe, et cetera. But there are many places where the habitats of humans and animals can and should overlap. Among the most common are the spaces where animals live among us in our human-built dwellings, as our domesticated companions.

For much of human history, bringing animals into the domestic realm required capturing them, usually as infants, from their free habitats, often after hunting and killing their parents. These animals were then raised among human children but often would end up being released back into the wild—or indeed eaten—when they grew bigger and more unruly.[1] But we found a couple of species that didn't need perpetual recapturing. Wolves started to hang around us about thirty thousand years ago and slowly became dogs.[2] About ten thousand years ago, shortly after we had taken up agriculture, free-ranging cats started hunting the rodents that were thriving in the concentrated filth and food stores of our new settlements, and by about three and a half thousand years ago, these felines had evolved into so-called house cats.[3]

What is important to note about the domestication of both cats and dogs is that research across many fields of natural and social science seems to show that *they* came to *us*; they had an interest in sharing our lives and living spaces with us and came to us with innate traits that enabled them, with many thousands of years of encouragement, to evolve into domesticated companions.[4] One recent study out of Emory University showed that the majority of dogs respond to human praise as strongly as or more strongly than they do to food.[5] Another study out of Oregon State University found that half of the cats in the study (both from shelters and from private homes) were more interested in human interaction than in food, toys, or catnip.[6] If these species are as interested in human interaction as they are in food, or even more interested, that says a great deal about our importance in their lives.

Equally important to note is that the feeling is mutual. It isn't just animals who have evolved to live with humans; *we* also have evolved to live with them, and very much so. One of the defining features of our human brains is our ability and desire to anthropomorphize. Anthropomorphizing often gets a bad rap, and indeed, it's a skill we don't always use very cleverly. But we can. Anthropologists believe that the ability to anthropomorphize may have been one of the key differences between *Homo sapiens* and the Neanderthals—one of the key reasons we're still here, and they aren't.[7] One of the most obvious benefits is that anthropomorphizing allowed our ancestors to predict the habits of animals and thus hunt with greater success.[8] But they used their anthropomorphic brains to nurture animals too, and this habit has continued around the world up to the present day. Anthrozoologist John Bradshaw has conducted extensive studies of the human habit of keeping companion animals and has found "a powerful and apparently near-universal instinct amongst hunter-gatherers to extend their most intimate caring to, and expend essential resources on, young animals."[9] As he describes in detail, this caring has frequently included the practice of tribal women nursing baby animals (including monkeys and even bear cubs) at their own breasts—so when Bradshaw says intimate, he *means* intimate.

Our fascination with animals predates almost every other thing our species does. To quote Bradshaw once more, "we kept dogs before we invented writing, before we had permanent homes, before we grew crops."[10] There is also an argument that the human impulse to invent religions is in fact a side effect of our anthropomorphic tendencies. The fact that most of the religions we have ever invented have been either animistic (i.e., had animal gods) or therianthropic (i.e., involved gods composed of both human and animal components) seems to support this idea.[11]

DEVASTATING DECISIONS

When I adopted my cat from the San Francisco SPCA eight years ago, I signed papers taking on legal responsibility for her. I also promised that I was going to be her "forever home." "Forever home" is the idea that when you adopt an animal, you're not just in it until the novelty or cuteness wears off; you're making a commitment to do your absolute best to take care of the animal for the rest of her life—whether that's two years or twenty. Not all adopters take that commitment seriously, but many of us take it very seriously indeed.

But being a forever home requires more than sentiment and goodwill. You need an actual physical dwelling to live in that both is suitable for and allows the animal in question—which is not so easy to come by when we are in the midst of what is commonly referred to as a global housing crisis. The cost of housing in cities everywhere is soaring, out of sync with wages, and there are shortages of decent units that anyone but the richest members of society can afford.[12] Around the world, whole communities are being displaced, and homelessness is on the rise.[13] With a market entirely in their favor, landlords in such cities can afford to be choosy about tenants. Very few places legally require landlords to allow animals in their properties, and so a lot of them simply don't.[14]

One recent study of the housing market in Australia found that only 1.59 percent of the properties listed in Sydney were listed as animal-friendly.[15] Over half of the postcodes had zero animal-friendly listings, and over a quarter had only one. The same study found that around half the tenants who declared their companion animals on applications had been told at least once that their application was being rejected specifically because of their animals. But the researchers point out that even those who weren't told they were being turned down because of their companion animals very well may have been, because landlords and property managers aren't obliged to explain their decisions.[16] The researchers surveyed leasing agents as well and concluded, "These agents did not recognise the importance of companion animals to applicants, instead viewing them as a form of property that could be disposed of as needed to secure a house. This reflects broader framings of pets as property."[17]

Companion animals are *not* disposable property. They are important members of our families. A report from the Pew Research Center in 2006 titled "Gauging Family Intimacy" found that 94 percent of Americans who lived with dogs felt they had a "close" relationship with their dog, and 84 percent of cat caregivers felt they had a close relationship with their cats.[18] Only 87 percent said they felt close to their moms, and only 74 percent felt close to their dads. That's 20 percent more people close to their dogs than people close to their fathers, and even moms barely squeezed in ahead of cats. While it's probably not fair to say that relationships with companion animals are *more* important than relationships with parents, they are certainly not "disposable."

The willful failure of housing markets around the world to recognize the individuality of companion animals and the uniqueness of their relationships with their caregivers, and those markets' failure to find suitable ways to accommodate them, has increasingly forced animals and their human caregivers into difficult, sometimes devastating situations.

Some people opt to remain in substandard rental situations. But there are many circumstances where people *have* to relocate: changes in employment, changes in property management, changes in the family such as death and divorce. A lot of people who are unable to find new, suitable, animal-friendly housing that they can afford try to rehome their animals with friends or family, or even strangers. But even when they are able to pass their animals on to safe new homes, there can still be real trauma. As ethologist Mark Bekoff says, "animals have families and friends, and they know when they are missing."[19] They "can suffer monumentally over a separation or loss."[20]

Some people who can't find affordable, animal-friendly housing are so dedicated to their animals that they choose homelessness over parting with them.[21] Unfortunately, others just abandon their animals. The American Pet Products Association estimates that 1 percent of all cats and dogs—or *a quarter of a million*—are "set free" from US households every year.[22]

The other option is to surrender the animal to a shelter. One survey of animal surrenders in the United States found that "for those that rented, housing problems were the number one reason for re-homing."[23] The Humane Society of the United States estimates that in the United States, "problems finding and keeping rental housing lead to the surrender of half a million pets to shelters each year."[24] There *are* some shelters that are "no kill," meaning they have a policy to never euthanize an animal unless the animal has an incurable condition that will cause him or her acute suffering. But those shelters are the minority and have limited intake capacities and therefore often must refer people surrendering animal companions to other animal control facilities. The majority of those *do* kill for space, because they lack either the resources or the vision to do anything else. As such, an animal's admission to one of these shelters—in the United States and in many other countries—is quite likely to be his or her death sentence.

The displacement of companion animals has implications for other animal species too. According to Bradshaw, "people who grow up around pets aren't just more likely to own pets later in life; they are more likely to be concerned about animal welfare in general. They are also more likely to have an interest in wildlife and animal conservation, and to be vegetarians."[25]

These claims about the correlation between having companion animals and having empathy with the larger animal kingdom are reinforced by historian Katherine Shrevelow, who argues that the entire modern animal welfare movement grew out of the proliferation of urban animal-keeping after industrialization:

> In the history of the changes in attitude that underlay the rise of the animal protection movement, arguably the most powerful force countering Cartesian mechanism, Christian anthropocentrism, and the long traditions of exploiting animals in every way was not the philosophical discourse of unorthodox intellectuals. Rather, it was something much more mundane: the fact that many people were sharing their lives with animal companions.[26]

This is a big deal for anyone who cares about animal welfare in any context. If we cannot even take seriously the commitments we make to the animals we keep in our own homes, and if we openly tolerate their distress and death en masse, we can't possibly expect people to take the needs, dignity, and suffering of other nonhuman species seriously.

DEATH BY LONELINESS

Humans aren't doing well in this deal either. For one thing, we are lonely—very, very lonely, so lonely that many are discussing it as a loneliness "epidemic."[27] The Conservative government in Britain even appointed the first-ever Minister of Loneliness.[28] In an article for the *New Statesman*, George Monbiot summarized statistics from many recent studies of loneliness:

> The stress response triggered by loneliness raises blood pressure and impairs the immune system. Loneliness enhances the risk of depression, paranoia, addiction, cognitive decline, dementia, heart disease, stroke, viral infection, accidents and suicide. It is as potent a cause of early death as smoking 15 cigarettes a day, and can be twice as deadly as obesity.[29]

If the definition of loneliness is lack of companionship, and our lack of companionship has reached an epidemic level of concern, surely one approach to reducing loneliness that we should be discussing involves the very creatures who have "companion" in their name. Obviously, the relationships we have with other humans and human institutions are very important. But human interactions and community building can be prompted and greatly improved by the presence of animals. Walking a dog or cat markedly increases the likelihood of the animal's caregiver engaging in conversation. The responsibilities of caring for animals give neighbors a reason to ask each other for help. There is even a program in the UK called HenPower, whose mission is to "hengage" "older people in arts activities and hen-keeping to promote health and wellbeing and reduce loneliness."[30]

The news abounds with stories about children with autism, soldiers with PTSD, and civilians with drug addiction and schizophrenia who have really been able to open up to other humans only after they've experienced a deep, trusting bond with a cat or dog. There are even new studies finding that exposure to animals in utero and in infancy can significantly reduce a child's odds of developing a range of allergies and illnesses and even obesity.[31] If these relationships can not only fix what is most damaged in us but also help us ward off maladies in the first place, we shouldn't accept housing laws that disappear them from our lives.

POSSIBLE ROUTES TOWARD PAWSITIVE CHANGE

If both humans and companion animals have evolved over tens of thousands of years to bond and cohabitate with each other, then we in fact *belong* together. We are a fundamental feature in each other's welfare and habitats. This should be reflected in the laws that regulate how and where we live. Anyone wishing to work on improving the law for companion animals and their human caregivers needs to answer four basic questions.

Question #1: What Animals Should be Included within the Legal Definition of "Companion Animals"?

As many thousands of books and Instagram accounts can confirm, humans have the fortunate ability to make friends with all manner of critters: raccoons, foxes, hedgehogs, horses, deer, pigs, gerbils, birds. But is it reasonable, or plausible, to require landlords to accommodate all of these species in their buildings, regardless of location and square footage? Would it be the best thing for the animals themselves—particularly in dense urban areas? In many cases, probably not.

The Humane Society of the United States says that in order to be truly "pet-friendly," a property should allow cats and dogs, regardless of breed or size.[32] These two species make sense. For one thing, they are the most popular companion animals. A 2016 survey of UK households found that 17 percent had a cat, and 24 percent had a dog.[33] Other species, such as exotic birds, snakes, amphibians, gerbils, and mice, were present in only 1 or 2 percent of households. Even in the United States, where the percentages of households with cats and dogs are nearly double those in the UK, other species aren't found in much larger percentages.[34]

Focusing on cats and dogs also makes sense because these two species have changed, on a genetic level, to communicate with us and even love us like family.[35] The fact that they are so much more popular than any other species of animal indicates that we are able to form bonds with them in ways we can't with other animals. It also means that they can be trained to follow some basic guidance that makes them better tenants than most other nonhumans—most notably, to not defecate at random around the dwelling. Other species ought to be considered as and when suitable to the particular animal and building in question. But as a baseline, anywhere suitable for a human to live ought to be suitable for a cat or a dog as well, and landlords should be able and willing to accommodate them.

Question #2: How Can We Take into Account the Legitimate Concerns of Landlords and Neighbors Regarding Issues such as Noise, Hygiene, and Safety?

It would be wildly negligent to ignore the fact that many humans are not nearly as responsible as they should be. Many do not take proper care in cleaning up after their animals or in offering them sufficient stimulation, training, grooming, and affection. Some are downright abusive. Others, despite good intentions, find that the animals they adopt have medical or temperamental issues they did not anticipate. There are any number of reasons that rental situations may become problematic for human and animal neighbors alike, and any laws designed to include companion animals in residential spaces must make sure that the landlords, tenants, and animals involved will be protected when bad situations pop up.

The first thing is to have laws that put liability squarely on animals' legal "owners" for the welfare of their animal and for their animal's behavior both in public and in common areas of shared rental buildings. Laws along these lines do already exist; under British law, for example, animals' legal "owners" are supposed to be explicitly responsible for animal nuisance and animal negligence.[36] Even still, landlords can get drawn into legal disputes around their tenants' animals and their actions—for example, if one tenant's animal injures another tenant. Also, because animals are technically seen as property, they can get mixed up in other property laws. For example, in British Columbia, landlords are responsible for safekeeping any personal property left behind by a former tenant for thirty days. Apparently, if a tenant were to leave behind any animals, the landlord also would be responsible for taking care of them for a month.[37] So cleaning up laws in order to protect landlords from such liability and emphasizing clear "owner" accountability could go a long way toward alleviating landlords' sometimes justifiable worries.

Also important is crafting tenancy contracts that very explicitly outline the tenant's responsibilities and liabilities and what outcomes will be punishable by eviction or fine. One possibility would be to require prospective tenants to prove that their animals are well looked after. The introduction of animal abuse registries could enable landlords to run checks similar to the way they now routinely run credit checks. Landlords might ask for a current certificate of health from a veterinarian, as many airlines and ferry companies do before allowing an animal on board. Of course, the latter idea would prove problematic for animals who are old or unwell, so perhaps the better option would be proof of the animal's upkeep rather than current health status. Across the EU, there is a "pet passport" scheme in which the microchip number and vaccinations of an animal are recorded by vets in one booklet. Landlords might ask to see animals' passports or other similar veterinary records.

Part of the bigger picture in making cities livable for companion animals, as well as humans and free-living animals, is planning them with sufficient open, communal spaces. Animals are less likely to damage rental units when they have sufficient stimulation. Dogs need somewhere to walk, run, sniff, and pee. Cats are increasingly being walked as well. Backyards and courtyards are good when buildings can accommodate them, but parks, gardens, and other green and open spaces are important for the health and sociability of *everyone* in a city.

Question #3: What Kinds of Existing Laws Might be Built On?

There are a variety of animal protection and anti-cruelty laws that could be extended to protect companion animals in housing. In the UK, the Protection of Animals Act 1911 made "wantonly or unreasonably causing unnecessary suffering to an animal" an offense.[38] As we've discussed, separating a companion animal from a responsible and beloved human caregiver causes the animal to suffer and potentially leads to his or her death. So there must be a way to extend the Protection Act (or indeed, its more recent iteration, the Animal Welfare Act 2006) and other laws like it, to include the arbitrary refusal and expulsion of companion animals from domestic rentals as inducing "unreasonable" suffering. Landlords should be required to prove sufficient cause for denying or expelling a companion animal from their rental, such as bad references from prior landlords or a petition of complaint from current neighbors.

Civil rights actually is an area of law that has put companion animals into many rental housing systems that otherwise would have excluded them. In the United States, a series of acts have slowly expanded the rights of public housing tenants to keep animals. The 1993 Housing and Urban–Rural

Recovery Act included the provision that "owners and managers of federally assisted rental housing for the elderly or handicapped cannot prohibit or prevent a tenant from owning common household pets."[39] A subsequent law in 1999 expanded that allowance to *all* residents of public housing agencies.[40]

The problem is that these kinds of acts don't provide comprehensive protection to renters across a given locality. They are conditional, including only people and animals who fall into specific schemes and categories. This perpetuates an overall atmosphere of insecurity and anxiety, which is exacerbated by vague definitions. For example, landlords of both public and private housing are required to offer people with disabilities "reasonable accommodation," which means allowing, among other things, service animals. But what constitutes a service animal? What certifications does the animal need? There aren't standardized requirements. And because mental health issues can be counted as disabilities in some places, many people are now getting medical certification that they need "emotional support" animals in the same way that a blind person would rely on a seeing-eye dog. But what is an emotional support animal? Many legal cases have been fought over this. In one case, *Zatopa v. Lowe*, expert evidence included a physician's note stating that "an emotional support animal is a pet—an animal whose function is to provide affection and companionship, and does not need any special training."[41] In other words, people are getting "prescription pets," often quite simply to get around housing and travel restrictions.[42] This may seem like fair play to those who can take advantage of loopholes in an inhumane system, but gaming the system doesn't actually change it. And indeed, by saying that only certifiably afflicted people really *need* the companionship of animals, this practice pathologizes a basic, universal human need—which is an ethical travesty.

The best and fairest way to protect and support all animal caregivers, and to assert the overlapping interests of humans and companion animals, is to protect animal companionship for *everyone*, without qualification. The preamble of the UN's Universal Declaration of Human Rights says that any rights it sets out are for all human beings, regardless of location or social group.[43] So it seems worth advocating that animal companionship be declared a universal human right.

There are two ways to pursue this change. The first would be to put an entirely new article into the Universal Declaration of Human Rights, just about animals. This might include more than just companion animals, because we do share habitats around the world with animals of all kinds. For many years now, organizations set up to protect the habitats of free-living animal communities, from the Jane Goodall Institute to the World Wildlife Fund, have known that they cannot hope to protect the habitats of other species without taking into account the needs of the people living in the vicinity. And the UN itself has spent a great deal of time and money considering problems of deforestation and climate change, which affect all species. So it seems only appropriate for the UN's declaration to explicitly say a few words about the relationship between human rights and the species and landscapes with which we exist.

The second way would be to take existing articles and tweak them. Article 12 says, "No one shall be subjected to arbitrary interference with his privacy, family, home or correspondence."[44] And Article 16 says, "The family is the natural and fundamental group unit of society and is entitled to protection by society and the State."[45] People who live with companion animals widely speak of "adopting" their animals and consider them integral parts of their family. And that is by no means a new sentiment; families in ancient Egypt shaved their eyebrows off as a sign of mourning when a cat died,[46] and Victorians held funerals for their deceased animal friends.[47] So these articles would much better reflect our lived reality if they made explicit that "family" can include nonhumans.

Question #4: At What Level are Legislative Change and Implementation Most Effective or Plausible?

In a recent volume of the *Journal of Animal Ethics*, Kathy Archibald argued that emphasizing the *human* cost of using animals in biomedical research will be the key to successfully ending the practice.[48] Similarly, emphasizing the global human rights approach discussed previously may be one of the strategies with the greatest potential efficacy for changing the conversations—and laws—regarding how we live with animals.

But even if the UN were to get on board, it would still be up to actual governments to make and enforce the laws that people—and animals—live by. In terms of housing laws and enforcement, the bigger the geographic area covered by a set of laws, the easier it is for citizens to know what the laws are and how to navigate them. So change at the national level is highly desirable. But change at the county, provincial, or district levels is, of course, desirable as well. And while governments at these levels often focus on *public* housing, it is entirely possible for them to regulate *private* housing as well. They do this all the time to address issues of health and safety, as well as housing discrimination against particular human demographics. And they have the capacity to do it on behalf of animals too. California has a lot of private condominium developments, and it's been common practice for those to prohibit animals, full stop. However, in 2014 the state passed the Davis–Stirling Act, which says condominium associations can restrict the number and size but have to allow residents at least *one* companion animal.[49]

But the actual implementation and enforcement of animal welfare regulations tend to happen at the local level. Local authorities have their own rules on matters such as companion animal registration, licensing, microchipping, and vaccination. And it often comes down to city animal-control authorities, and even individual shelters and veterinarians, to watch out for, investigate, and deal with the many forms of animal suffering. It is these people who are best placed to help individuals understand their rights and responsibilities both as carers for animals and as tenants. Therefore, reforms to protect the human–companion animal bond through improved access to housing should be pursued as much at the grassroots level as at the global level.

NOW, MORE THAN EVER

The majority of humanity is, for the first time in history, now living in cities. This has many implications for how we humans live and for the animals who have evolved to live with us. It makes having companion animals in our lives more precious because our animal companions often are—as we become increasingly alienated from our ecosystems and traditional communities—our only opportunity to directly engage with, learn about, and bond with other species.

Unfortunately, at the same time that people are gaining greater appreciation for companion animals, our ability to care for them is being made increasingly precarious by housing policies that are grossly insufficient for human tenants and devastating for companion animals. As this chapter has noted, we have some rough statistics on how many people rehome, surrender, and otherwise abandon animals *not* because the animals are unwanted, but solely and explicitly because they cannot access animal-friendly housing. Those numbers run into the millions. What we can't know is how many people never adopt animals in the first place for lack of adequate housing. Those numbers could easily be just as substantial. Altogether, this makes for a very serious bottleneck in any effort to deal with animal homelessness. Animal welfare groups can run the best adoption, education, and spay/neuter campaigns in the world, but if the public is unable to access affordable, animal-friendly housing, on a sustained basis, they will never be able to offer the kind of forever homes these organizations envision—or that these animals absolutely deserve. There needs to be comprehensive housing reform on this issue, or this already acute problem will simply keep getting worse.

REFERENCES

Archibald, Kathy. "Animal Research Is an Ethical Issue for Humans as Well as for Animals." *Journal of Animal Ethics* 8, no. 1 (Spring 2018): 1–11.

ASPCA. "Pet Statistics." Accessed September 24, 2018. https://www.aspca.org/animal-homelessness/shelter-intake-and-surrender/pet-statistics.

BBC News. "Minister for Loneliness Appointed to Continue Jo Cox's Work." January 17, 2018. https://www.bbc.com/news/uk-42708507.

Bekoff, Marc. *The Emotional Lives of Animals: A Leading Scientist Explores Animal Joy, Sorrow, and Empathy—and Why They Matter.* Novato, CA: New World Library, 2007.

Bosworth, Kay. "Condo Association Pet Rules." *SF Gate*. Accessed September 24, 2018. http://homeguides.sfgate.com/condo-association-pet-rules-71790.html.

Bradshaw, John. *The Animals among Us: The New Science of Anthrozoology.* London: Penguin Random House UK, 2017.

Cooper, Margaret E.. *An Introduction to Animal Law.* London: Academic Press Limited, 1987.

Delisle, Raina. "Another Reason to Get That Cute Puppy: Pets Make for Healthier Babies." *Today's Parents*, April 10, 2017. https://www.todaysparent.com/baby/baby-health/pets-make-for-healthier-babies.

Dreifus, Claudia. "Gregory Berns Knows What Your Dog Is Thinking (It's Sweet)." *New York Times*, September 8, 2017. https://www.nytimes.com/2017/09/08/science/gregory-berns-dogs-brains.html.

Easton, Mark. "How Should We Tackle the Loneliness Epidemic?" *BBC*, February 11, 2018. https://www.bbc.com/news/uk-42887932.

Equal Arts. "HenPower." Accessed September 24, 2018. https://www.equalarts.org.uk/our-work/henpower.

Fahey, Mark. "No Dogs Allowed: San Francisco's Pet Housing Crisis." *CNN*, February 20, 2015. https://money.cnn.com/2015/02/20/real_estate/pets-san-francisco/index.html.

Foster, Charles. *Being a Beast: An Intimate and Radical Look at Nature.* London: Profile Books, 2016.

Grandin, Temple, and Catherine Johnson. *Animals Make Us Human: Creating the Best Life for Animals.* New York: Mariner Books, 2010.

Harris, Scarlett. "Comment: I Can't Get a Rental Because I Own a Dog. So Now I'm Homeless." *SBS*, June 23, 2017. https://www.sbs.com.au/topics/life/culture/article/2017/06/19/comment-i-cant-get-rental-because-i-own-dog-so-now-im-homeless.

Humane Society of the United States. "Increasing Housing Options for Renters with Pets." Accessed September 24, 2018. http://www.humanesociety.org/animals/resources/pets-are-welcome-renting-with-pets.html.

Huss, Rebecca J. "No Pets Allowed: Housing Issues and Companion Animals." *Animal Law Review at Lewis & Clark Law School* 11 (2005): 69–129.

Kirk, Mildred. *The Everlasting Cat.* London: Faber and Faber Limited, 1977.

Madden, David, and Peter Marcuse. *In Defense of Housing.* London: Verso Books, 2016.

Matthews, Mimi. "These Victorian Cat Funerals Put Your Cat Funeral to Shame." *Bust*, May 11, 2016. https://bust.com/living/16284-cat-funerals-in-the-victorian-era.html.

Meltzer, Marisa. "Prescription Pets: 'I Got a Doctor's Note to Fly with My Dog.'" *Guardian*, May 12, 2018. https://www.theguardian.com/world/2018/may/12/doctors-note-dog-on-plane-emotional-support-animals.

Monbiot, George. "The Age of Loneliness." *New Statesman*, October 24, 2016. https://www.newstatesman.com/politics/health/2016/10/age-loneliness.

Pet Food Manufacturer's Association. "Pet Population 2016." Accessed September 24, 2018. https://www.pfma.org.uk/pet-population-2016.

Pew Research Center. "Gauging Family Intimacy." March 7, 2006. http://www.pewsocialtrends.org/2006/03/07/gauging-family-intimacy.

Power, Emma R. "Renting with Pets: A Pathway to Housing Insecurity?" *Housing Studies* 32, no. 3 (2017): 336–60.

Sheppard, Jenni. "1,700 Pets Were Surrendered Due to Lack of Pet-Friendly Housing in BC in 2017." *Daily Hive*, January 11, 2018. http://dailyhive.com/vancouver/pet-friendly-housing-pets-surrendered-bc-2017.

Shreve, Kristyn R. Vitale, Lindsay R. Mehrkam, and Monique A. R. Udell. "Social Interaction, Food, Scent or Toys? A Formal Assessment of Domestic Pet and Shelter Cat (*Felis silvestris catus*) Preferences." *Behavioural Processes* 141 (2017): 322–28.

Shrevelow, Katherine. *For the Love of Animals: The Rise of the Animal Protection Movement.* New York: Holt Paperbacks, 2008.

United Nations. *Universal Declaration of Human Rights.* New York: United Nations, 2015. http://www.un.org/en/udhrbook/pdf/udhr_booklet_en_web.pdf.

Weiss, Emily, Shannon Gramann, C. Victor Spain, and Margaret Slater. "Goodbye to a Good Friend: An Exploration of the Re-Homing of Cats and Dogs in the U.S." *Open Journal of Animal Sciences* 5 (2015): 435–65.

NOTES

1. John Bradshaw, *The Animals among Us: The New Science of Anthrozoology* (London: Penguin Random House UK, 2017).

2. Bradshaw, *Animals among Us*.

3. Temple Grandin and Catherine Johnson, *Animals Make Us Human: Creating the Best Life for Animals* (New York: Mariner Books, 2010).

4. Grandin and Johnson, *Animals Make Us Human.*

5. Claudia Dreifus, "Gregory Berns Knows What Your Dog Is Thinking (It's Sweet)," *New York Times*, September 8, 2017, https://www.nytimes.com/2017/09/08/science/gregory-berns-dogs-brains.html.

6. Kristyn R. Vitale Shreve, Lindsay R. Mehrkam, and Monique A. R. Udell, "Social Interaction, Food, Scent or Toys? A Formal Assessment of Domestic Pet and Shelter Cat (*Felis silvestris catus*) Preferences," *Behavioural Processes* 141 (2017): 322–28.

7. Bradshaw, *Animals among Us*.

8. Marc Bekoff, *The Emotional Lives of Animals: A Leading Scientist Explores Animal Joy, Sorrow, and Empathy—and Why They Matter* (Novato, CA: New World Library, 2007).

9. Bradshaw, *Animals among Us*, 50.

10. Bradshaw, *Animals among Us*, 37.

11. Charles Foster, *Being a Beast: An Intimate and Radical Look at Nature* (London: Profile Books, 2016).

12. David Madden and Peter Marcuse, *In Defense of Housing* (London: Verso Books, 2016).

13. Madden and Marcuse, *In Defense of Housing*.

14. Mark Fahey, "No Dogs Allowed: San Francisco's Pet Housing Crisis," CNN, February 20, 2015, https://money.cnn.com/2015/02/20/real_estate/pets-san-francisco/index.html.

15. Emma R. Power, "Renting with Pets: A Pathway to Housing Insecurity?," *Housing Studies* 32, no. 3 (2017): 336–60.

16. Power, "Renting with Pets."

17. Power, "Renting with Pets," 350.

18. Pew Research Center, "Gauging Family Intimacy," March 7, 2006, http://www.pewsocialtrends.org/2006/03/07/gauging-family-intimacy.

19. Bekoff, *The Emotional Lives of Animals*, 157.

20. Bekoff, *The Emotional Lives of Animals*, 63.

21. Scarlett Harris, "Comment: I Can't Get a Rental Because I Own a Dog. So Now I'm Homeless," *SBS*, June 23, 2017, https://www.sbs.com.au/topics/life/culture/article/2017/06/19/comment-i-cant-get-rental-because-i-own-dog-so-now-im-homeless.

22. Emily Weiss et al., "Goodbye to a Good Friend: An Exploration of the Re-Homing of Cats and Dogs in the U.S.," *Open Journal of Animal Sciences* 5 (2015): 445.

23. Weiss et al., "Goodbye to a Good Friend," 445.

24. Humane Society of the United States, "Increasing Housing Options for Renters with Pets," accessed September 24, 2018, http://www.humanesociety.org/animals/resources/pets-are-welcome-renting-with-pets.html.

25. Bradshaw, "Animals among Us," 69.

26. Katherine Shrevelow, *For the Love of Animals: The Rise of the Animal Protection Movement* (New York: Holt Paperbacks, 2008), 54.

27. Mark Easton, "How Should We Tackle the Loneliness Epidemic?," BBC, February 11, 2018, https://www.bbc.com/news/uk-42887932.

28. "Minister for Loneliness Appointed to Continue Jo Cox's Work," BBC News, January 17, 2018, https://www.bbc.com/news/uk-42708507.

29. George Monbiot, "The Age of Loneliness," *New Statesman*, October 24, 2016, https://www.newstatesman.com/politics/health/2016/10/age-loneliness.

30. Equal Arts, "HenPower," accessed September 24, 2018, https://www.equalarts.org.uk/our-work/henpower.

31. Raina Delisle, "Another Reason to Get That Cute Puppy: Pets Make for Healthier Babies," *Today's Parents*, accessed April 10, 2017, https://www.todaysparent.com/baby/baby-health/pets-make-for-healthier-babies.

32. Humane Society, "Increasing Housing Options."

33. Pet Food Manufacturer's Association, "Pet Population 2016," accessed September 24, 2018, https://www.pfma.org.uk/pet-population-2016.

34. ASPCA, "Pet Statistics," accessed September 24, 2018, https://www.aspca.org/animal-homelessness/shelter-intake-and-surrender/pet-statistics.

35. Bradshaw, *Animals among Us*.

36. Margaret E. Cooper, *An Introduction to Animal Law* (London: Academic Press Limited, 1987).

37. Jenni Sheppard, "1,700 Pets Were Surrendered Due to Lack of Pet-Friendly Housing in BC in 2017," *Daily Hive*, January 11, 2018, http://dailyhive.com/vancouver/pet-friendly-housing-pets-surrendered-bc-2017.

38. Cooper, *Animal Law*, 28.

39. Rebecca J. Huss, "No Pets Allowed: Housing Issues and Companion Animals," *Animal Law Review at Lewis & Clark Law School* 11 (2005): 90.

40. Huss, "No Pets," 93.

41. Huss, "No Pets," 81.

42. Marisa Meltzer, "Prescription Pets: 'I Got a Doctor's Note to Fly with my Dog,'" *Guardian*, May 12, 2018, https://www.theguardian.com/world/2018/may/12/doctors-note-dog-on-plane-emotional-support-animals.

43. United Nations, *Universal Declaration of Human Rights* (New York: United Nations, 2015), http://www.un.org/en/udhrbook/pdf/udhr_booklet_en_web.pdf.

44. United Nations, *Declaration*, 35.

45. United Nations, *Declaration*, 43.

46. Mildred Kirk, *The Everlasting Cat* (London: Faber and Faber Limited, 1977).

47. Mimi Matthews, "These Victorian Cat Funerals Put Your Cat Funeral to Shame," *Bust*, May 11, 2016, https://bust.com/living/16284-cat-funerals-in-the-victorian-era.html.

48. Kathy Archibald, "Animal Research Is an Ethical Issue for Humans as Well as for Animals," *Journal of Animal Ethics* 8, no. 1 (Spring 2018): 1–11.

49. Kay Bosworth, "Condo Association Pet Rules," *SF Gate*, accessed September 24, 2018, http://homeguides.sfgate.com/condo-association-pet-rules-71790.html.

Chapter 11

A Legal Critique of the Putative Educational Value of Zoos

By Alice Collinson

This chapter addresses the regulation of zoos in the UK. It provides an overview of the principal legislation, guidance, and enforcement bodies, with a focus on zoos' legal requirement to educate the public on biodiversity conservation. The educational value of zoos is a contentious issue. For example, the issue was raised in 2014 at Copenhagen Zoo, when it was questioned whether the dissecting of Marius, the "surplus giraffe," was an educational experience for visitors.

The UK has held collections of free-living animals in captivity since the 1300s. London Zoo opened in 1828 and is claimed to be the oldest scientific zoo.[1] Although there are no accurate national records available, according to the Born Free Foundation, there are estimated to be close to five hundred establishments that display animals in England.[2] For as long as animals are kept in captive zoo conditions, the existing legislation needs to be adequate and enforceable.

LEGISLATION OVERVIEW

Animal Welfare Act 2006

Animals deemed "protected" under this legislation include vertebrates who are under human control and "not living in a wild state."[3] The Animal Welfare Act focuses on the prevention of harm to animals by way of "unnecessary suffering"[4] and lists what have been coined the "five freedoms" as the duties for the promotion of animal welfare: a suitable environment, a suitable diet, the ability to exhibit normal behavior patterns, housing with or apart from other animals depending on the animal's need, and protection from pain, suffering, injury, and disease.[5]

Zoo Licensing Act 1981

Zoo licensing is managed by local authorities and entails zoo inspections both prior to the granting of a license and periodically every three to four years. Licenses often come with conditions such as the requirement to keep detailed records of all animals and to ensure public safety. A "zoo" is defined as an "establishment where wild animals are kept for exhibition to the public" other than for the purposes of a circus or a shop selling animals as "pets."[6] "Wild animals" are defined as "animals not normally domesticated in Great Britain."[7] Public exhibition involves public access for "more than seven days in any period of 12 consecutive months,"[8] with or without admission fees.

Conservation

The Zoo Licensing Act requires that zoos contribute to conservation by participating in one of five ways:

1. Research from which conservation benefits accrue to species of wild animals.
2. Training in relevant conservation skills.
3. The exchange of information relating to the conservation of species of wild animals.
4. Where appropriate, breeding of wild animals in captivity.
5. Where appropriate, the repopulation of an area with, or the reintroduction into the wild of, wild animals.[9]

Although active involvement in conservation is a requirement for all licensed zoos, only one of these preceding five measures must be met. It is also noted that the majority of zoos hold very few threatened or endangered species. In a 2011 inspection of twenty-five English zoos, the Born Free Foundation found that only 17 percent of the species held were officially classified as "threatened," and only 3 percent were "critically endangered."[10] Whether and how the measures are met is largely left to the discretion of the zoo license inspectors.

Education

The act requires zoos to educate the public on conservation. This is broadly defined as a requirement to promote awareness by "providing information about the species of wild animals kept in the zoo and their natural habitats."[11] We will consider the application of this legislation later on in the discussion.

Welfare

Zoos are required to provide animals with "conditions which aim to satisfy the biological and conservation requirements of the species to which they belong."[12] This includes providing "each animal with an environment well adapted to meet the physical, psychological and social needs" of the animal's species[13] and "a high standard of animal husbandry with a developed programme of preventative and curative veterinary care and nutrition."[14] An application to a local authority for a zoo license must detail how the conservation, education, and welfare measures are to be met,[15] failing which a license may be refused.[16] However, it is noted that exemptions can be provided in some circumstances, including for zoos holding fewer than around 120 species.[17]

European Council Directive 1999/22/EC

Directive 1999/22/EC of the European Union sets out very similar requirements, with a particular focus on conservation and public education measures. The directive states that part of its purpose is "the need to ensure that zoos adequately fulfil their important role in the conservation of species, public education, and/or scientific research."[18] The directive also stipulates that in order to obtain a license, a zoo must participate in "promoting public education and awareness in relation to the conservation of biodiversity."[19] Member states are left to implement the directive how they wish, and there is no requirement for any management committee or similar body. The UK legislation provides for regulation and enforcement bodies. Examination of the potential effects of Brexit are out of scope of this chapter, save to say that the impacts, if any, would be expected to be minimal while the EU directive's provisions continue to be implemented in the Zoo Licensing Act.

REGULATION AND ENFORCEMENT

Local Authorities

Local authorities also may conduct inspections outside of the required periodic inspections when they believe circumstances require investigation.[20] The statute wording concerns circumstances in which "in their opinion it is necessary or desirable to do so for ensuring the proper conduct of the zoo."[21]

Offenses under the Zoo Legislation Act 1981

Key offenses are operating a zoo without a license or failing to comply with any license condition, without reasonable excuse.[22] Offenses under the act carry fines, alongside potential zoo closure. The reality is that individuals tasked with assessing and granting licenses under the act are provided with limited guidance or training. Further, it is difficult to find any information to confirm whether any zoos have in fact been shut down. The recently exposed Cumbria Zoo had its license suspended and later renewed. Yet this was clearly an extreme case of animal welfare failings, along with potential criminal liability and public health and safety issues.[23] Considering that nearly five hundred animals died at this facility over a four-year period, this situation evidences the system deficiencies with zoo inspections.

Defra

Guidance to supplement the Zoo Licensing Act is provided by the Department for Environment, Food and Rural Affairs, known as Defra, and titled the *Secretary of State's Standards of Modern Zoo Practice*.[24] It must be followed by zoo inspectors and refers to requirements to participate in conservation, education, and welfare as well as matters such as record keeping.

BIAZA

The British and Irish Association of Zoos and Aquariums is a membership organization, rather than a regulating body. It does not provide formal accreditation or codes of practice. Yet membership does require inspections by the organization in addition to local authority inspections. Failed inspections would lead only to potential loss of membership since the body has no enforcement powers; there is no requirement to be registered, and no real implications come from not being a member.

EAZA and WAZA

Similar to the BIAZA, the European Association of Zoos and Aquariums and the World Association of Zoos and Aquariums are limited in their ability to influence UK zoos to adhere to the Zoo Licensing Act, and they provide minimal accreditation. They are industry-led bodies and have been accused of inconsistent application of zoo regulations.[25] In the example of Marius, the "surplus" giraffe killed at the Danish zoo, support for the zoo's actions—stated to be an important step in development of conservation breeding programs—reportedly came from the head of the EAZA.[26]

The Zoos Expert Committee

The UK's Zoos Expert Committee provides guidance to the government on zoo standards and inspections. It is made up of individuals inside the industry as well as external animal welfare and conservation experts.

THE LEGAL STANDARD FOR EDUCATION

As noted previously, the Zoo Licensing Act, echoed by the EU directive, requires that licensed zoos educate the public about conservation, specifically by "providing information about the species of wild animals kept in the zoo and their natural habitats."[27]

The 2012 *Secretary of State's Standards of Modern Zoo Practice* provides further guidance regarding education requirements as follows:

- "The measures required should be proportionate to the size and type of the zoo." (7.8)
- "A zoo must have a written education strategy and an active education programme." (7.9)
- "Suitable facilities, commensurate to the size of the zoo, should be available for education purposes." (7.10)
- "Accurate information about the species exhibited must be available. Generally, this should include, as a minimum, the species name (both scientific and common), its natural habitat and some of its biological characteristics and details of its conservation status." (7.11)
- "The zoo should be able to demonstrate: the educational role of the zoo" and "how the written education plan applies to different types of people who visit the zoo." (7.12)
- "Zoos should keep records of their . . . education activities and . . . be encouraged to evaluate the effectiveness of their contribution to these activities by collecting appropriate evidence and/or engaging in research projects to do this." (7.13)[28]

In addition, the guidance states that inspectors must be familiar with the *Zoos Expert Committee Handbook*. Although nonbinding, this guide is intended to supplement the *Secretary of State's Standards* and to be referenced by inspectors. The document provides some examples as to how the "broad term"[29] of education (as defined in this document) can be met by zoos. The suggestions take into account zoos of various sizes and ownership type. The handbook discusses ways to implement an education strategy; provides suggestions such as staff training and talks; and distinguishes the needs of school children and the general public.

Of specific note from these guidelines is that adequate education can include "on-site and local environmental action such as recycling and reducing energy use and other such initiatives,"[30] which have a tenuous link to biodiversity conservation. Of further note is the handbook's explanation of an "education facility" being broad, to include the zoo in its entirety without need for a designated room or area. In reference to signage, the minimum suggested requirement by the committee is "basic identification labels—featuring name, scientific name, range/natural habitat."[31] While this handbook is informative in its efforts to guide zoos in education strategy, providing numerous examples for establishments to consider, it is limited, and zoos are bound only by the minimal requirements under the legislation. BIAZA, EAZA, and WAZA also provide guidance and hold conferences on improving education. However, as noted, these bodies currently have no impetus to enforce legislation for their members.

The steps required to meet the education requirement of the Zoo Licensing Act are therefore minimal. In application, although some form of educational signage is required, there is no strict requirement to monitor whether such signage is an effective public education tool or to provide evidence of this. And should a zoo take steps to review the educational impact of its efforts, whether internally or externally, such evidence is difficult to obtain and quantify, and there are no clear evaluation processes in place in the guidance. A further barrier to improvement is the administrational framework for enforcing the legislation, which is far from robust. The government-issued inspection form for zoo inspectors shows general questions that require solely "yes" or "no" answers regarding education measures required by law. For example: "Is the zoo promoting public education and awareness in relation to the conservation of biodiversity, in particular by providing information about the species of wild animals kept in the zoo and their natural habitats?" (7.2).[32] This question does not require that every enclosure have appropriate signage but rather requires only general (and minimal) information about the animals across the zoo.

Second, this inspection form asks, "Are on-site education facilities adequate for the resources of the collection?" (7.4).[33] Again, this requires a general "yes" or "no" response, allowing broad discretion, particularly since legislation does not define "on-site education facilities," and guidance stipulates that "the whole zoo is an educational facility."[34]

How is the Educational Value of Zoos Quantified?

A handful of international studies addressing the general public's educational takeaway from zoos have been carried out, and broad suggestions for assessing educational value are set out in the *Secretary of State's Standards*. Yet the guidance notes that the value of education is subjective, cumulative, and thereby difficult to quantify.[35] Attempts to assess educational value include before- and after-visit questionnaires, follow-ups on these visit questionnaires, observations of how long visitors spend at information signs by enclosures, and testing of the knowledge they obtain.

In one example, an internal WAZA report assessed educational value pre- and post-zoo visit in reference to specifics, including "recycling and waste management" and "responsible purchasing and diet choices."[36] These are questionable categories for assessing takeaway knowledge of biodiversity conservation. According to the *EU Zoo Inquiry* published by the Born Free Foundation, twenty of the twenty-five zoos the organization inspected in England were found to largely meet the general education criteria set out by the Zoos Committee handbook. However, in taking a closer look at the zoos' "educational experiences," Born Free found that the majority failed to provide information specific to the species' conservation status or threats in their natural habitats.[37] This basic information is central to the Zoo Licensing Act's education requirement.

Is There a Purpose behind the Education Requirement?

Consideration of zoo education requirements raises the question of whether zoos in their current form provide a valuable learning experience for visitors, while animals are on display outside of their natural habitat and associated normal behaviors. The Zoos Expert Committee recognizes this issue in stating that while "enclosure design can simulate a 'natural' setting . . . there are limitations."[38] In fact, some question the legitimacy of this education and argue that viewing animals in these unnatural habitats constitutes miseducation.[39] There also have been a number of incidents in which these imposed unnatural conditions have led to dangerous behaviors toward nonhuman animals. Recent international incidents in which humans and animals have been harmed have raised much discussion about the educational value of zoos as balanced against the inherent dangers of keeping the animals on display.

Alternative Sources of Conservation Education

The *Zoos Expert Committee Handbook* lists the following as educational benefits of zoos in their current form:

> Introduction to the wonder of nature, developing enthusiasm and excitement, and inspiring people to action; opportunity for humans to be put into perspective as part of the natural world; broadening the appreciation, knowledge and understanding of nature and the environment; illustration of biodiversity; [and] highlighting conservation issues affecting both wildlife and wild places.[40]

Arguably, these benefits can be found and replicated, and even enhanced, in other forms, without need for today's outdated zoos. The ever-expanding world of augmented or virtual reality is one way to learn about the natural world and a technology being used increasingly in schools and elsewhere. There are many tech companies investing in the development of virtual reality experiences, which would be expected to make such experiences more accessible. One such company is Google Expeditions.[41] In order for an alternative "zoo" experience to gain traction, it may well need to encompass very similar ingredients, such as an exciting day out. In early 2018, a virtual zoo was opened in southern China.[42] Time will tell whether this experience will be successful and whether it will be perceived as comparable to, or better than, a zoo that physically holds animals. Augmented reality has the potential to offer so much more to conservation education. "Visitors" can walk among the animals in depictions of their natural habitats, such as the Serengeti and the Amazon rainforest. As envisaged by the *Guardian*, this could be "a world where 'Be a keeper for the day' schemes are replaced by 'Be an elephant ranger for the day' schemes, where zoo visitors in Regent's Park fly remote-controlled drones over elephants and rhinos in Africa, protecting them from poachers."[43]

There are also existing opportunities to view animals in their natural habitats from the comfort of home. African safari web cameras have been set up at water holes, and nonprofit organizations such as Explore.org provide live feeds of various animals all over the world. Even virtual reality is readily accessible on smartphones, iPads, and other devices. Also of note, it would appear that the popularity of nature documentaries is on the rise. David Attenborough's series from late 2016, *Planet Earth II*, reportedly drew in a record number of television viewers.[44] This is no doubt in part due to significant developments in technology, in both filming and viewing abilities; viewers feel closer to the action than ever.

Last, although there are very few in the UK due to lack of space and other barriers, it is apparent that there may be more educational value in visiting a (genuine) animal sanctuary than a zoo, on the expectation that the animals are provided with as close to a natural environment as practicably possible, rather than being housed in enclosures largely designed with the viewing public in mind. Although this is a complex discussion, a genuine sanctuary would be set up with a focus on the animals' needs, with appropriate restrictions on public access.

CONCLUSIONS

A review of the principal legislation surrounding zoos in the UK finds it to be inadequate, with minimal impetus or resources for enforcement. Within the current legal framework there is ample scope for inconsistency in how inspections are carried out and licenses are granted and renewed, while there is no centralized register of licensed zoos and limited guidance or training available. Accordingly, the law has not been significantly tested and scrutinized. Development is also difficult while there are no centrally held records of any cases brought under the principal legislation. Work to improve enforcement is left to organizations such as the Born Free Foundation. In addition to independent zoo visits and the guidance it provides to assist facilities in working within the existing legal framework, the foundation's work involves Freedom of Information Act requests to uncover inspection reports. While implementation and enforcement of the existing legislation, at both the EU and national levels, are crucial as a minimum, clearer guidance and development are desperately needed to assist this process.

REFERENCES

Animal Welfare Act 2006. https://www.legislation.gov.uk/ukpga/2006/45/enacted.

Born Free Foundation. *The EU Zoo Inquiry 2011: An Evaluation of the Implementation and Enforcement of the EC Directive 1999/22, Relating to the Keeping of Wild Animals in Zoos: England.* November 2011. Accessed October 1, 2018. https://www.bornfree.org.uk/storage/media/content/files/Publications/ENGLAND.pdf

Council of the European Union. "Council Directive 1999/22/EC of 29 March 1999 Relating to the Keeping of Wild Animals in Zoos." *Official Journal of the European Communities, L* 94 (1999). http://eur-lex.europa.eu/LexUriServ/LexUriServ.do?uri=OJ:L:1999:094:0024:0026:EN:PDF.

Department for Environment, Food and Rural Affairs. "Inspection Report." Accessed October 1, 2018. https://www.gov.uk/government/uploads/system/uploads/attachment_data/file/408848/zoo2-inspection-report-form.pdf.

———. *Secretary of State's Standards of Modern Zoo Practice*. 2012. https://assets.publishing.service.gov.uk/government/uploads/system/uploads/attachment_data/file/69596/standards-of-zoo-practice.pdf.

———. *Zoos Expert Committee Handbook.* November 2012. https://www.gov.uk/government/uploads/system/uploads/attachment_data/file/69611/pb13815-zoos-expert-committee-handbook1.pdf.

Department for Environment, Food and Rural Affairs, Animal and Plant Health Agency, and Natural England. "Guidance: Keeping Zoo Animals." May 28, 2015. Last updated September 9, 2015. https://www.gov.uk/guidance/keeping-zoo-animals.

Furness, Hannah. "David Attenborough's *Planet Earth II* Becomes Most-Watched Nature Show." *Telegraph*, November 14, 2016, http://www.telegraph.co.uk/news/2016/11/14/david-attenboroughs-planet-earth-ii-becomes-most-watched-nature/.

Howard, Jules. "Zoos Shouldn't Be Jails—Let's Reimagine Them and Enjoy Animals in the Wild." *Guardian,* March 1, 2017, https://www.theguardian.com/commentisfree/2017/mar/01/zoos-jails-reimagine-animals-wid-wildlife-vr.

Malamud, Randy. "The Ethics of Zoos." In *The Global Guide to Animal Protection*, edited by Andrew Linzey, 62–63. Urbana: University of Illinois Press, 2013.

Roberts, Rachel. "Cumbria Zoo Could Lose License after Nearly 500 Animals Die in Four Years and Tiger Mauls a Keeper to Death." *Independent*, March 1, 2017. https://www.independent.co.uk/news/uk/home-news/cumbria-zoo-lose-licence-south-lakes-safari-486-animals-die-four-years-tiget-mauls-keeper-death-2014-a7605761.html.

Tyson, Liz. "Making It Up as They Go Along: Marius and the Zoo Industry's Inconsistent Approach to Self-Regulation." *Journal of Animal Welfare Law* (Spring 2014): 5–7. http://alaw.org.uk/wp-content/uploads/alaw-journal-spring-2014.pdf.

World Association of Zoos and Aquariums. *A Global Evaluation of Biodiversity Literacy in Zoo and Aquarium Visitors*. 2014. http://www.waza.org/files/webcontent/1.public_site/5.conservation/un_decade_biodiversity/WAZA%20Visitor%20Survey%20Report.pdf.

Zhang, Charmmy. "Chinese Zoo Uses Virtual Reality to Allow Visitors to 'Interact' with Animals." *China Society*, January 2, 2018. https://www.scmp.com/news/china/society/article/2126494/chinese-zoo-uses-virtual-reality-allow-visitors-interact-animals.

Zoo Licensing Act 1981. https://www.legislation.gov.uk/ukpga/1981/37.

Zoological Society of London. "10 Things You May Not Know about ZSL London Zoo." April 27, 2018. https://www.zsl.org/blogs/zsl-london-zoo/10-things-you-may-not-know-about-zsl-london-zoo.

NOTES

1. "10 Things You May Not Know about ZSL London Zoo," Zoological Society of London, April 27, 2018, https://www.zsl.org/blogs/zsl-london-zoo/10-things-you-may-not-know-about-zsl-london-zoo.

2. Born Free Foundation, *The EU Zoo Inquiry 2011: An Evaluation of the Implementation and Enforcement of the EC Directive 1999/22, Relating to the Keeping of Wild Animals in Zoos: England*, November 2011, accessed October 1, 2018, https://www.bornfree.org.uk/storage/media/content/files/Publications/ENGLAND.pdf, 14.

3. Animal Welfare Act 2006, sec. 2, https://www.legislation.gov.uk/ukpga/2006/45/enacted.

4. Animal Welfare Act 2006, sec. 4.
5. Animal Welfare Act 2006, sec. 9.
6. Zoo Licensing Act 1981, sec. 1(2), https://www.legislation.gov.uk/ukpga/1981/37.
7. Zoo Licensing Act 1981, sec. 21.
8. Zoo Licensing Act 1981, sec. 1(2).
9. Zoo Licensing Act 1981, sec. 1A(a).
10. Born Free Foundation, *EU Zoo Inquiry 2011*, 6.
11. Zoo Licensing Act 1981, sec. 1A(b).
12. Zoo Licensing Act 1981, sec. 1A(c).
13. Zoo Licensing Act 1981, sec. 1A(c)(i).
14. Zoo Licensing Act 1981, sec. 1A(c)(ii).
15. Zoo Licensing Act 1981, sec. 2A.
16. Zoo Licensing Act 1981, sec. 10(14).
17. Department for Environment, Food and Rural Affairs, Animal and Plant Health Agency, and Natural England, "Guidance: Keeping Zoo Animals," May 28, 2015, last updated September 9, 2015, https://www.gov.uk/guidance/keeping-zoo-animals.
18. Council of the European Union, "Council Directive 1999/22/EC of 29 March 1999 Relating to the Keeping of Wild Animals in Zoos," *Official Journal of the European Communities, L* 94 (1999), http://eur-lex.europa.eu/LexUriServ/LexUriServ.do?uri=OJ:L:1999:094:0024:0026:EN:PDF.
19. Council of the European Union, "Council Directive 1999/22/EC."
20. Zoo Licensing Act 1981, sec. 11.
21. Zoo Licensing Act 1981, sec. 16.
22. Zoo Licensing Act 1981, sec. 19.
23. See Rachel Roberts, "Cumbria Zoo Could Lose License after Nearly 500 Animals Die in Four Years and Tiger Mauls a Keeper to Death," *Independent*, March 1, 2017, https://www.independent.co.uk/news/uk/home-news/cumbria-zoo-lose-licence-south-lakes-safari-486-animals-die-four-years-tiget-mauls-keeper-death-2014-a7605761.html.
24. Department for Environment, Food and Rural Affairs (Defra), *Secretary of State's Standards of Modern Zoo Practice*, 2012, https://assets.publishing.service.gov.uk/government/uploads/system/uploads/attachment_data/file/69596/standards-of-zoo-practice.pdf.
25. Liz Tyson, "Making It Up as They Go Along: Marius and the Zoo Industry's Inconsistent Approach to Self-Regulation," *Journal of Animal Welfare Law* (Spring 2014): 5, http://alaw.org.uk/wp-content/uploads/alaw-journal-spring-2014.pdf.
26. Tyson, "Making It Up," 5.
27. Zoo Licensing Act 1981, sec. 1A(b).
28. Defra, *Secretary of State's Standards*, 14–15.
29. Defra, *Zoos Expert Committee Handbook*, November 2012, https://www.gov.uk/government/uploads/system/uploads/attachment_data/file/69611/pb13815-zoos-expert-committee-handbook1.pdf, 23.
30. Defra, *Zoos Expert Committee Handbook*, 26.
31. Defra, *Zoos Expert Committee Handbook*, 91.

32. Defra, "Inspection Report," accessed October 1, 2018, https://www.gov.uk/government/uploads/system/uploads/attachment_data/file/408848/zoo2-inspection-report-form.pdf, 7.

33. Defra, "Inspection Report," accessed October 1, 2018, https://www.gov.uk/government/uploads/system/uploads/attachment_data/file/408848/zoo2-inspection-report-form.pdf, 7.

34. Defra, *Zoos Expert Committee Handbook*, 43.

35. Defra, *Zoos Expert Committee Handbook*, 51.

36. World Association of Zoos and Aquariums, *A Global Evaluation of Biodiversity Literacy in Zoo and Aquarium Visitors*, 2014, http://www.waza.org/files/webcontent/1.public_site/5.conservation/un_decade_biodiversity/WAZA%20Visitor%20Survey%20Report.pdf.

37. Born Free Foundation, *EU Zoo Inquiry 2011*, 26.

38. Defra, *Zoos Expert Committee Handbook*, 74.

39. Randy Malamud, "The Ethics of Zoos," in *The Global Guide to Animal Protection*, ed. Andrew Linzey (Urbana: University of Illinois Press, 2013), 62–63.

40. Defra, *Zoos Expert Committee Handbook*, 41.

41. See https://edu.google.co.uk/expeditions/ar/#about.

42. Charmmy Zhang, "Chinese Zoo Uses Virtual Reality to Allow Visitors to 'Interact' with Animals," *China Society*, January 2, 2018, https://www.scmp.com/news/china/society/article/2126494/chinese-zoo-uses-virtual-reality-allow-visitors-interact-animals.

43. Jules Howard, "Zoos Shouldn't Be Jails—Let's Reimagine Them and Enjoy Animals in the Wild," *Guardian*, March 1, 2017, https://www.theguardian.com/commentisfree/2017/mar/01/zoos-jails-reimagine-animals-wild-wildlife-vr.

44. See Hannah Furness, "David Attenborough's *Planet Earth II* Becomes Most-Watched Nature Show," *Telegraph*, November 14, 2016, http://www.telegraph.co.uk/news/2016/11/14/david-attenboroughs-planet-earth-ii-becomes-most-watched-nature/.

Chapter 12

Our Costly Obsession

Animal Welfare, Plastic Pollution, and New Directions for Change

By Mariah Rayfield Beck

Over 300 million tons of plastic are produced annually, and that number continues to grow every year. About half of all plastic produced is "disposable," or utilized and disposed of within one year of acquirement.[1,2] Since the beginning of mainstream plastics in the 1940s, plastic materials have been steadily integrated into nearly every aspect of life around the world. Plastics helped facilitate major societal and technological advancements over the last eighty years, such as the development of the film industry and new medical implant technology.[3] However, we have reached a point in time when plastic is being overused as a cheap grab-and-go material for nonessential purposes. Current waste-management protocols are ill-equipped to handle our increasing load of plastic waste, and as a result, plastic pollution can now be found in every corner of the animal kingdom. It has been discovered in the deepest point of the ocean, the Mariana Trench, and at the farthest reaches of land.[4] As plastic pollution increases, free-living animals are forced into close contact with plastic materials, resulting in dangerous obstructions, entanglements, and chemical toxicities that greatly reduce the animals' quality of life. These costly interactions constitute a serious and urgent animal welfare issue, as proven using the framework of the five freedoms.[5] Many laws, conventions, and agreements have been developed to address the issue of plastic pollution at a multitude of levels—local, state, regional, national, and even international. However, the problem is worsening. The relative inefficacy of current legislative motions can be addressed by a variety of new directions for legislation and, most important, by a serious paradigm shift in every individual and our collective society—from a linear economy to a circular economy and mindset.

PLASTIC AS A WELFARE ISSUE FOR FREE-ROAMING ANIMALS

In order to clearly define plastic pollution as a serious issue for animal welfare, the problem will be contextualized using the framework of the five freedoms, adjusted to apply more directly to free-living animal communities as follows:

1. Freedom from thirst, hunger, and malnutrition caused by humans.
2. Freedom from discomfort due to environmental disruption caused by humans.
3. Freedom from fear and distress caused by humans.
4. Freedom from pain, injury, and disease caused by humans.
5. Freedom to express normal behavior for the animal's species, regardless of whether the human use of or impact on the animal is for food, for sport hunting, or from destruction of habitat.[6]

1. Freedom from Thirst, Hunger, and Malnutrition Caused by Humans

As plastics are ingested by free-ranging animals, they can accumulate in the animals' digestive tract. These material buildups often cause gastrointestinal obstructions that prevent the animal from eating and digesting food normally. Alternatively, animals can become seriously entangled in the plastic materials—thus reducing their ability to hunt and/or forage for food. Furthermore, many birds have been shown to selectively feed on plastics, choosing plastic pieces that share certain features with that species' typical prey. For example, birds who typically hunt red prey may be found with a heavy load of red plastics in their digestive tract.[7] In all of these situations, animals are prevented from attaining essential nutrients as a result of their interactions with plastic pollution.

2. Freedom from Discomfort Due to Environmental Disruption Caused by Humans

Climate change is currently the major point of concern regarding anthropogenic environmental disruption. Important ways that climate change may negatively impact marine health include melting ice caps, rising sea level, changing currents, increasing temperature, and ocean acidification. An important factor associated with climate change is the increasing concentration of greenhouse gases released into the earth's atmosphere. One significant example of a greenhouse gas contributing to climate change is carbon dioxide produced by the combustion of fossil fuels.[8]

The raw materials most often used to produce plastic are fossil fuels such as oil and natural gas. Currently, 4 to 8 percent of extracted oil is used to produce raw plastic.[9] PET is a very common plastic used for myriad products, including beverage bottles. It is estimated that at least one ounce of carbon dioxide is released into the atmosphere for every ounce of PET produced. Other studies estimate that as much as five ounces of carbon dioxide are released for every ounce of PET. If we are currently producing over 300 million tons of plastic every year, then the plastic industry is producing at least 300 million tons of carbon dioxide annually, not including the emissions involved in transportation, use, and disposal of the plastic items.[10] Although the greatest impact of plastic waste is most often considered to be direct physical effects on free-living animals, plastic pollution also significantly infringes on the five freedoms for their welfare by contributing to the broader issue of climate change through the use of fossil fuels and the production of carbon dioxide.

3. Freedom from Fear and Distress Caused by Humans

When the injuries incurred by plastics are not fatal, they can trigger extreme stress levels in impacted animals. Aquatic animals are often found swimming with masses of material trailing behind them—restricting adequate movement, making them more vulnerable to predators, and reducing the animals' ability to defend themselves.[11] The combined effects of injuries, disease, and environmental disruption and the behavioral impact of plastic pollution trigger severe stress responses in these animals.

4. Freedom from Pain, Injury, and Disease Caused by Humans

Injuries from plastic pollution often occur from ingestion or entanglement. In addition to causing gastrointestinal obstructions, plastic also can become lodged in the respiratory tract, leading to suffocation and death. Entanglements commonly occur around the neck, limbs, gills, wings, or trunk, and over two hundred species of marine animals are found entangled in debris every year.[12] These occurrences often immobilize animals and subject them to painful injuries such as wounds, amputations, or strangulations that can become infected or necrotic.[13]

Plastic debris also has been shown to harbor microbial life, some of which can be harmful bacteria that cause disease in exposed animals and organisms. A recent study suggests that coral in reefs exposed to plastic waste go from a 4 percent chance of disease to an 89 percent risk of contracting three of the top six diseases of concern for coral reefs.[14]

Other diseases can be induced by exposure to chemical ingredients that are added to raw plastics to encourage different characteristics, such as pliability, durability, or color. Hazardous chemicals such as phthalates, brominated flame retardants, BPA, formaldehyde, and other volatile organic compounds have been recorded as residues on plastic materials.[15] Many of these chemicals have been proven to increase the risk of cancer. They also can affect enzyme secretions and cause organ dysfunction in the liver, kidney, thyroid, and reproductive and gastrointestinal organs.[16] Many animals exposed to these chemicals experience decreased fertility and disrupted sex hormone production, which can greatly affect the animals' natural behaviors and ability to successfully reproduce. Most research regarding the effects of plastic toxicity does not account for the potential synergistic effects of toxins because they are extremely challenging to study, but the combined effects of interacting chemicals are predicted to cause diverse behavioral and physiological changes, as well as disease.[17]

5. Freedom to Express Normal Behavior for the Animal's Species

The impacts described previously are only a glimpse of the myriad ways that plastic pollution changes and restricts the lives of marine animals. Ingestion, entanglement, and toxicity all change the animals' behaviors in different ways. Nesting birds incorporate plastics into their nests, trapping nestlings and restricting their ability to progress to the next stages of life. Plastics carry disease-causing organisms and invasive species, affecting animals' ability to function normally in their ecosystem. Other plastics physically restrain animals, restricting their ability to feed, defend themselves, or successfully complete migratory movements. Physiologically, plastic toxicants can affect an animal's ability to reproduce effectively and to maintain adequate organ function. Plastic debris has the potential to impact the lives of marine animals in ways that definitively make the problem of global plastic pollution a serious issue of animal welfare.

CURRENT LEGISLATION AND NEW DIRECTIONS

Many legislative changes have been devised in an attempt to mitigate this problem and reduce the amount of plastic pollution entering the natural world. Legislative strategies and changes have been applied and encouraged at many levels—grassroots, local, regional, national, and international. As the "zero waste" trend sweeps through social media platforms, grassroots organizations dedicated to this issue are becoming more common across the globe. Local and regional bans are becoming increasingly common as well. Plastic bags, disposable containers, and straws all have been banned in places such as California, Rwanda, and the United Kingdom.[18] International developments, such as the Honolulu strategy developed by the National Oceanic and Atmospheric Association and United Nations Environmental Program (UNEP), UNEP's Clean Seas campaign, and agreements made in Rio de Janeiro and Nairobi concerning the global crisis of marine plastic pollution, lack obligatory commitments and have fallen short of hopeful expectations.[19] Despite all of these legislative motions, none have yet caused major reductions in plastic production to significantly reduce and mitigate the negative impacts of plastic on marine animals.

The question then remains—what must change in order for legislation to make a discernible impact on the urgent and growing issue of plastic pollution? Although they are useful and effective on many levels, local and regional policies cannot effect change at a pace that is fast enough to effectively mitigate the worsening state of this issue. A powerful and effective international agreement would complement the regional bans to ensure effective mediation of this issue. Moving forward, an updated international agreement must incorporate key attributes to increase efficacy. Foremost, this agreement must require assertive commitments from all involved parties, as opposed to nonbinding agreements. The agreement should not only include larger ideological goals but also focus on discrete waste reduction targets that can be operationalized and implemented. Countries with diverse levels of resources and infrastructure should be encouraged to participate in the binding commitment through incentives and support for those countries.

There have been many other suggestions for designing a more efficacious international agreement to combat plastic pollution. For example, reclassifying plastic waste as hazardous or as a priority pollutant may encourage improved waste-management practices. Extended producer responsibility programs that require businesses to account for the environmental costs of their products could provide resources to establish a global fund. The fund could then be used to supply global programs and to allow states and countries with fewer resources to commit to the international agreement.[20]

Incentive programs also could be helpful at multiple levels. Fishers could be motivated to dispose responsibly of their own fishing gear and to collect stray fishing gear they find while at sea. Businesses could be encouraged to produce more sustainable, durable, and reusable items made from reusable or recyclable materials to minimize waste and contribute to a larger ideological and practical shift toward a circular economy.

The linear economy model is currently the most common economic paradigm subscribed to in our society. A linear economy embodies the idea of "take, make, and dispose." In this system, resources are extracted, processed, and manufactured into commercial goods. Then they are used and disposed of, mostly via landfill or incineration. A major economic and social paradigm shift toward a circular approach must be pursued if we are to establish a new international agreement that has the power to produce substantial change for the welfare of free-living animals around the globe.

Circular economies focus on the ideology that materials can exist in a continual circle of life, minimizing material disposal and resource extraction. Within the concept of a circular economy, two models exist—one that focuses on reusing items through repair and quality of care and another that focuses on recycling old goods, to use the component materials to manufacture new goods.[21]

Performance economies take this idea one step further by encouraging the selling of services or promoting the use of products through renting, leasing, or borrowing. In this way, fewer goods are made, and more are shared. The ownership of the goods remains with the manufacturer, who now profits from the sufficiency of goods, rather than the production of new goods. Overall, this shift supports the replacement of "production with sufficiency," encouraging stakeholders to "reuse what [they] can, recycle what cannot be reused, repair what is broken, [and] remanufacture what cannot be repaired."[22]

Several groups are already taking action to assist this transition. Companies that offer lifetime guarantees with unlimited repairs, such as Cotopaxi and Osprey®, are supporting the circular economy ideology. Newly popular online stores, such as Life Without Plastic and Poshmark, are increasing accessibility to secondhand purchasing and low-impact lifestyles with limited plastic use. Car- and bike-sharing programs, such as Citi Bike in New York City and Cycle Hire in London, are examples of performance-based economic models in action. Since the 1990s, companies such as Caterpillar and Xerox have been offering remanufacturing services for their goods, and newer companies like Staples and Apple currently offer programs for reusing and recycling their electronic products.[23]

New legislation must further incentivize nations, companies, and individuals to take discernible steps and actions. One example is a program that incentivizes fishers to collect stray fishing gear by allowing them to sell that material to companies that are using plastic waste to manufacture recycled plastic for reusable goods. Another important change would shift the responsibility to manufacturers by implementing producer responsibility programs and value-added taxes for activities that harvest additional raw materials. Legislation should be promoted that rewards stakeholders for participating in and promoting programs that support circular mindsets, such as reuse, repair, and remanufacture programs.[24]

In order to make a substantial impact on the urgent animal welfare issue of plastic pollution and to make progress toward an efficacious international commitment, governments and communities must create and support legislation that contributes to this shift from a linear economy toward a circular and performance-based model. This important paradigm shift will minimize natural resource extraction and disposal of plastics, discouraging the use of plastics as a single-use, short-term material. Together, these changes will make way for an international commitment that maximizes our ability as a global community to mitigate the effects of plastic pollution currently affecting the world's animal communities.

CONCLUSION

Developing a legislative solution that incorporates and supports all of these important ideals and implementable programs will be a challenging and time-consuming endeavor. It is of the utmost urgency that we mitigate the problem of plastic pollution because it continues to devastate animal communities every day by degrading their quality of life and infringing on their right to adequate welfare. We truly do not have time to spare. Just as human beings, a single species, have created the monumental problem of plastic pollution, it is humans who also must take action to develop solutions and expedite legislative changes that can lead to the implementation of significant, positive change. As citizens of the global community, we all must take this responsibility seriously. Every day, we have the opportunity to make choices that protect the ocean and the welfare of all the animals dwelling within it. Individuals and companies can choose to produce or purchase items without plastic. We can make conscious choices as individual consumers to support important and urgent societal change. We can choose to rent and borrow, buy secondhand, participate in cleanups, talk about the problem, or say no to straws and bags. Empowerment is a gift that can vitalize campaigns and push legislation toward efficacious change. As individuals and community members, we are each given the opportunity and challenge to take control of the direction of our species. We must act on behalf of the ocean and the welfare of animal populations everywhere because the issue of plastic pollution is not only an issue of marine animal welfare—it is an issue of global welfare.

REFERENCES

Borrelle, Stephanie B., Chelsea M. Rochman, Max Liboiron, Alexander L. Bond, Amy Lusher, Hillary Bradshaw, and Jennifer F. Provencher. "Why We Need an International Agreement on Marine Plastic Pollution." *Proceedings of the National Academy of Sciences of the United States of America* 114, no. 38 (2017): 9994–97.

Derraik, José G. "The Pollution of the Marine Environment by Plastic Debris: A Review." *Marine Pollution Bulletin* 44, no. 9 (2002): 842–52.

Freinkel, Susan. "A Brief History of Plastic's Conquest of the World." *Scientific American*, May 29, 2011.

Gibbens, Sarah. "Plastic Bag Found at the Bottom of World's Deepest Ocean Trench." *National Geographic*, May 11, 2018.

Gleick, Peter H., and Heather S. Cooley. "Energy Implications of Bottled Water." *Environmental Research Letters* 4 (2009): 1–6.

Hamblin, Abby. "New York Plastic Bag Ban? Here's What Happened after California's Ban." *San Diego Union-Tribune*, April 23, 2018, http://www.sandiegouniontribune.com /opinion/sd-new-york-plastic-bag-ban-california-20180423-htmlstory.html.

Haward, Marcus. "Plastic Pollution of the World's Seas and Oceans as a Contemporary Challenge in Ocean Governance." *Nature Communications* 9, no. 667 (2018): 1–3.

Lamb, Joleah B., Bette L. Willis, Evan A. Florenza, Courtney S. Couch, Robert Howard, Douglas N. Rader, James D. True, et al. "Plastic Waste Associated with Disease on Coral Reefs." *Science* 359 (2018): 460–62.

Morét-Ferguson, Skye, Kara Lavender Law, Giora Proskurowski, Ellen K. Murphy, Emily E. Peacock, and Christopher M. Reddy. "The Size, Mass, and Composition of Plastic Debris in the Western North Atlantic Ocean." *Marine Pollution Bulletin* 60, no. 10 (2010): 1873–78.

Nace, Trevor. "UK to Ban All Plastic Straws, Cotton Swabs, and Single-Use Plastics." *Forbes*, April 25, 2018. https://www.forbes.com/sites/trevornace/2018/04/25/uk-to-ban-all-plastic-straws-q-tips-and-single-use-plastics/#4d7adec51138.

National Oceanic and Atmospheric Association. "Entanglement of Marine Species in Marine Debris with an Emphasis on Species in the United States." *Marine Debris Program Report* (April 2014).

North, Emily J., and Rolf U. Halden. "Plastics and Environmental Health: The Road Ahead." *Reviews on Environmental Health* 28, no. 1 (2013): 1–8.

Paquet, Paul C., and Chris T. Darimont. "Wildlife Conservation and Animal Welfare: Two Sides of the Same Coin?" *Animal Welfare* 19 (2010): 177–90.

Pilgrim, Sophie. "Smugglers Work on the Dark Side of Rwanda's Plastic Bag Ban." *Aljazeera America*, February 25, 2016. http://america.aljazeera.com/articles/2016/2/25/rwanda-plastic-bag-ban.html.

Rochman, Chelsea M. "The Complex Mixture, Fate and Toxicity of Chemicals Associated with Plastic Debris in the Marine Environment." In *Marine*

Anthropogenic Litter, edited by Melanie Bergmann, Lars Gutow, and Michael Klages, 117–40. Cham, Switzerland: Springer, 2015.

Rochman, Chelsea, Eunha Hoh, Tomofumi Kurobe, and Swee J. Teh. "Ingested Plastic Transfers Hazardous Chemicals to Fish and Induces Hepatic Stress." *Scientific Reports* 3 (2013): 1–7.

Solomon, Susan, Gian-Kasper Plattner, Reto Knutti, and Pierre Friedlingstein. "Irreversible Climate Change Due to Carbon Dioxide Emissions." *Proceedings of the National Academy of Sciences of the United States* 106, no. 6 (2009): 1704–9.

Stahel, Walter R. "Circular Economy." *Nature* 531 (2016): 435–38.

Staley, Samantha. "The Link between Plastic Use and Climate Change: Nitty-Gritty." *Sage Stanford Alumni Magazine*, November 2009. https://alumni.stanford.edu/get/page/magazine/article/?article_id=30619.

Wilcox, Chris, Erik Van Sebille, and Britta Demise Hardesty. "Threat of Plastic Pollution to Seabirds is Global, Pervasive, and Increasing." *Proceedings of the National Academy of Sciences* 112, no. 38 (2015): 11899–904.

NOTES

1. I want to thank the Cornell University College of Veterinary Medicine and the Oxford Centre for Animal Ethics for supporting my academic endeavors. Thank you to all of the family, friends, and colleagues who have provided feedback for me. A special thank-you to all of my past students and audience members for their invaluable feedback, which constantly guides my journey as an educator. Finally, an immense thank you to the ocean for all it provides.

2. Emily J. North and Rolf U. Halden, "Plastics and Environmental Health: The Road Ahead," *Reviews on Environmental Health* 28, no. 1 (2013): 1–8.

3. Susan Freinkel, "A Brief History of Plastic's Conquest of the World," *Scientific American*, May 29, 2011.

4. Sarah Gibbens, "Plastic Bag Found at the Bottom of World's Deepest Ocean Trench," *National Geographic*, May 11, 2018.

5. Paul C. Paquet and Chris T. Darimont, "Wildlife Conservation and Animal Welfare: Two Sides of the Same Coin?," *Animal Welfare* 19 (2010): 177–90.

6. Paquet and Darimont, "Wildlife Conservation and Animal Welfare."

7. José G. Derraik, "The Pollution of the Marine Environment by Plastic Debris: A Review," *Marine Pollution Bulletin* 44, no. 9 (2002): 842–52; Skye Morét-Ferguson et al., "The Size, Mass, and Composition of Plastic Debris in the Western North Atlantic Ocean," *Marine Pollution Bulletin* 60, no. 10 (2010): 1873–78; Chelsea M. Rochman, "The Complex Mixture, Fate and Toxicity of Chemicals Associated with Plastic Debris in the Marine Environment," in *Marine Anthropogenic Litter*, ed. Melanie Bergmann, Lars Gutow, and Michael Klages (Cham, Switzerland: Springer, 2015), 117–40.

8. Susan Solomon et al., "Irreversible Climate Change Due to Carbon Dioxide Emissions," *Proceedings of the National Academy of Sciences of the United States* 106, no. 6 (2009): 1704–9.

9. Stephanie B. Borrelle et al., "Why We Need an International Agreement on Marine Plastic Pollution," *Proceedings of the National Academy of Sciences of the United States of America* 114, no. 38 (2017): 9994–97.

10. Peter H. Gleick and Heather S. Cooley, "Energy Implications of Bottled Water," *Environmental Research Letters* 4 (2009): 1–6; Samantha Staley, "The Link between Plastic Use and Climate Change: Nitty-Gritty," *Sage Stanford Alumni Magazine*, November 2009, https://alumni.stanford.edu/get/page/magazine/article/?article_id=30619.

11. Derraik, "Pollution of the Marine Environment." 846.

12. National Oceanic and Atmospheric Association, "Entanglement of Marine Species in Marine Debris with an Emphasis on Species in the United States," *Marine Debris Program Report* (April 2014).

13. Derraik, "Pollution of the Marine Environment"; Morét-Ferguson et al., "Size, Mass, and Composition of Plastic Debris."

14. Joleah B. Lamb et al., "Plastic Waste Associated with Disease on Coral Reefs," *Science* 359 (2018): 460–62.

15. Rochman, "Complex Mixture, Fate and Toxicity."

16. Chelsea M. Rochman et al., "Ingested Plastic Transfers Hazardous Chemicals to Fish and Induces Hepatic Stress," *Scientific Reports* 3 (2013).

17. Rochman, "Complex Mixture, Fate and Toxicity."

18. Sophie Pilgrim, "Smugglers Work on the Dark Side of Rwanda's Plastic Bag Ban," *Aljazeera America*, February 25, 2016; Trevor Nace, "UK to Ban All Plastic Straws, Cotton Swabs, and Single-Use Plastics," *Forbes*, April 25, 2018, https://www.forbes.com/sites/trevornace/2018/04/25/uk-to-ban-all-plastic-straws-q-tips-and-single-use-plastics/#4d7adec51138; Abby Hamblin, "New York Plastic Bag Ban? Here's What Happened after California's Ban," *San Diego Union-Tribune*, April 23, 2018, http://www.sandiegouniontribune.com/opinion/sd-new-york-plastic-bag-ban-california-20180423-htmlstory.html.

19. Marcus Haward, "Plastic Pollution of the World's Seas and Oceans as a Contemporary Challenge in Ocean Governance," *Nature Communications* 9, no. 667 (2018): 1–3; Borrelle et al., "Why We Need an International Agreement."

20. Borrelle et al., "Why We Need an International Agreement."

21. Walter R. Stahel, "Circular Economy," *Nature* 531 (2016): 435–38.

22. Stahel, "Circular Economy," 435.

23. Stahel, "Circular Economy," 436.

24. Stahel, "Circular Economy," 438.

Chapter 13

Why Anti-Cruelty Laws Are Not Enough

By Matthew J. Webber

Historically, there has been a need for laws that truly protect the most vulnerable in our societies, and not least among these are nonhuman animals. There are currently anti-cruelty laws that seek to do just this; however, such laws prove insufficient in addressing the full breadth of mistreatment and abuse. Cruel acts that take place in the name of science, technology, and food production remain unaddressed and unacknowledged. In endeavoring to cease the majority of abuses inflicted upon nonhuman animals, one must look beyond current anti-cruelty laws alone.

In this chapter, I shall address these concerns by first describing the current state of anti-cruelty laws and what such laws cover. Second, I will identify several areas in which the laws do not apply due to exemptions that allow for cruel and inhumane treatment of nonhuman animals. Next, I will argue that exposing these exemptions and educating the public are both necessary to ensure that the response is proactive and not reactionary, as has too often been the case. Finally, I will conclude by acknowledging the successful efforts thus far and what the next steps may be in the continued efforts to ensure that all cruelty inflicted on nonhuman animals is addressed, not just the forms that garner the greatest attention and sympathy.

CURRENT STATE OF ANIMAL CRUELTY LAWS

While some have sought to protect nonhuman animals from harm for the animals' own sake, others have found different motivation for the prevention of cruel and inhumane treatment of nonhuman animals, predicting that such cruelty would eventually extend to one's fellow humans. This argument has found advocates such as Thomas Aquinas, Locke, Schopenhauer, and Kant, to name a few. But this view is not relegated to the past; one need only skim current materials on anti-cruelty laws and the treatment of nonhuman animals to find the anthropocentric focus. As societal attitudes shifted over time, the human-centeredness of the laws decreased so that nonhuman animals found protection under anti-cruelty laws, not as protected individuals necessarily, but in many cases as property. Such nonhuman animals were utilized in agriculture, and thus protection was needed as a means of financial insurance, but protections later extended to companion animals also. Changes in law continue to be made so that cruelty toward nonhuman animals is no longer remedied simply by reimbursement for one's lost property. Neither is the primary concern today still the potential cruelty that may be exercised on one's fellow human.

In discussions of anti-cruelty laws, what often comes to mind are the most violent acts against nonhuman animals—beatings, stabbings, drownings, or blood sports in which nonhuman animals fight to the death. Such acts, however, constitute only a fraction of the cruelty inflicted on animals. The United Kingdom has been a leader on this front for many years, from Jeremy Bentham to the more recent outlawing of battery cages and sow stalls, but is this enough?[1] Within the United States, of which I am a citizen, various laws exist regarding the mistreatment of nonhuman animals with little to no uniformity across states. Some states are very explicit about the definition of cruel treatment and categorize neglect, including failure to provide sufficient food or water, as one form of abuse. More states are identifying the dangers of "animal hoarding," as well as seeking to establish the motive of the abuser as a factor in criminal cruelty. Other states, however, rely on ambiguous and vague language, leaving the final judgment up to legislators, who cite previous cases and precedent rather than what is fair to the abused.

Identifying what makes an act "cruel" is not simple. As even the novice in ethics knows, the definition of an act as cruel must be based on greater moral grounding than the mere attitude or "gut reaction" the act elicits. According to Arkow and Lockwood in their chapter "Definitions of Animals Cruelty, Abuse, and Neglect," anti-cruelty laws identify six elements establishing an act of cruelty:

1. the types of animals protected;
2. the types of acts prohibited or duties of care required;
3. the mental culpability required to meet a standard of liability;
4. the defenses to criminal liability;
5. certain activities exempted from the law; and
6. penalties for each offense.[2]

While these elements provide a base for statutes prohibiting cruelty toward nonhuman animals, they are far from all-encompassing. Ambiguities remain in the application of anti-cruelty laws based on the types of nonhuman animals covered by the laws, but also, via omission, those who will go unprotected. Moreover, relying on the ability to establish a motive, the intent of the individual committing the act, and his or her state of mind is problematic to say the least. Determination of whether an individual acted intentionally with cruel motives depends on the judge's and/or jury's definition or interpretation of the term "cruel." The issues of motive, whether or not nonhuman animals are protected by anti-cruelty laws, and what constitutes cruelty versus discipline, incentive, or utilization of one's property all pose problems within anti-cruelty legislation, leaving nonhuman animals to bear the cost.

A positive note is the introduction of the term "abuse" into anti-cruelty legislation. With such legislation adopting the language of child-abuse laws, "abuse" extends beyond the intentional act of cruelty toward a nonhuman animal and now includes acts of negligence and neglect. Whether the motivation of an abuser can be discerned no longer needs to hinder defining an act as cruel. Legislation protecting the most vulnerable humans may well protect vulnerable nonhumans too. Yet unlike human abuse victims, nonhuman animals cannot provide a statement as evidence when they suffer abuse. Instead, we must rely on reports of cruelty from human witnesses or the ability of veterinarians or law officers to identify forensic evidence of abuse. Thus, while there have been improvements to anti-cruelty laws, there remain pragmatic factors that continue to allow abuse to go unnoticed, unabated, and unpunished.

For a law to have any efficacy, not only must it be implemented, but violations of the law also must be addressed appropriately—"appropriately" being the key word. Many states have raised violations of anti-cruelty laws from misdemeanors to felony offenses.[3] However, the legal system allows for plea bargaining in which the guilty party may admit to a lesser charge, thus freeing up time and space in the already crowded courts. In addition, many cases of abuse rely on human agents to report the cruel acts, either as witnesses or through providing evidence of abuse for prosecution. Thus, as exceptions are made, abuse will continue, cruelty will go unpunished, and in the few instances where individuals are punished, many will assume justice has been done, allowing for the cruel exceptions to continue unabated. Yet instances of plea bargaining and deals to lessen an abuser's punishment, while a grave injustice, are not the most significant offense against nonhuman animals.[4] The most egregious violation against nonhuman animals is in cases when the eye of the law is blind to the pain and suffering endured because the creatures harmed are not identified as "animals."

NONHUMAN ANIMALS IN AGRICULTURE

Anti-cruelty laws exist, but so do exemptions to these laws, which allow for nonhuman animals to suffer in ways that would otherwise be illegal. Noting that intent plays a significant role in identifying an act as cruel, Bernard Rollin states that "only a tiny percentage of animal suffering is the result of deliberate, sadistic cruelty. Cruelty, as descriptive of psychological deviance, would not cover animal suffering that results from nonpathological pursuits such as industrial agriculture, safety testing of toxic substances on animals, and all other forms of research."[5] Complicating activism in the name of nonhuman animals is the fact that the harm done to nonhuman animals in these cases is believed to be for the greater good of society. Those who inflict pain are not criminals but are benefiting humanity. Rollin points out that such individuals "generally believe they are doing social good, providing cheap and plentiful food, or medical advances, or educational opportunities, and they are in fact traditionally so perceived socially."[6] Rollin estimates, "Of all the suffering that animals endure at human hands, only a tiny fraction, less than 1 percent, is the result of deliberate cruelty."[7]

Turning to one such exemption, we look to nonhuman agriculture. Setting aside the discussion about whether killing itself may be construed as "causing harm" to an individual—nonhuman animal or otherwise—the practice of raising nonhuman animals for eventual consumption does not ensure their lives are free from cruelty or pain. Anti-cruelty laws already in place to protect nonhuman animals apply only to those identified as "animals" under the law. This leaves many defined as "non-animal" without any protection from cruel treatment. According to the United States Department of Agriculture (USDA), the term

> "animal" means any live or dead dog, cat, monkey (nonhuman primate mammal), guinea pig, hamster, rabbit, or such other warm-blooded animal, as the Secretary may determine is being used, or is intended for use, for research, testing, experimentation, or exhibition purposes, or as a pet; but such term excludes (1) birds, rats of the genus Rattus, and mice of the genus Mus, bred for use in research, (2) horses not used for research purposes, and (3) other farm animals, such as, but not limited to livestock or poultry, used or intended for use as food or fiber, or livestock or poultry used or intended for use for improving animal nutrition, breeding, management, or production efficiency, or for improving the quality of food or fiber. With respect to a dog, the term means all dogs including those used for hunting, security, or breeding purposes.[8]

When the USDA defines beings as some category other than "animal," cruel treatment bears no penalty if only due to the lack of identifiable victim in the eyes of the law.

Perhaps the most disturbing exemption from the USDA's definition of "animals" is that of birds. Factory farms hold 99 percent of the chickens and turkeys who are raised and killed for food production, for whom there is no protection under the law regarding their lives or the manner in which they die.[9] One need only think of the treatment of birds in the production of foie gras, a practice in which a goose is restrained and force-fed via a metal tube. While sales and consumption of foie gras are illegal in certain states, it is still produced and advertised as a delicacy for the wealthy discerning palate. Should doubt arise as to whether a being belongs to the category "animal," the decision is left up to the secretary of agriculture, who is likely to side with the influential lobbyists who act at the behest of the meat industry.[10] As if to add further insult to injury, it is the USDA that inspects the means of "processing" as best it can, but it also relies on self-regulation to report violations or, in many cases, whistleblowers to report abuses.

The question worth asking is, why do laws protecting companion animals not also apply to other sentient nonhuman animals? There is increased understanding that nonhuman animals feel fear and stress, as evidenced by Temple Grandin's work bringing changes to the cattle industry. Similarly, many individuals in the meat industry insist that one can change the flavor of bacon by stressing a pig in the moments prior to slaughter. Since we recognize that these nonhuman animals possess emotions and feel stress, common sense would dictate that they too deserve protection under anti-cruelty laws already on the books.

As these acts continue unaddressed, however, one must admit that individuals somehow mentally disconnect the pain and suffering of nonhuman animals from their own consumption of animal products. It is precisely this disconnect that allows individuals to support laws prohibiting cruelty against nonhuman animals yet continue to eat nonhuman animals raised solely for the purpose of providing inexpensive meat. Additionally, even if the final moments of life for cattle, swine, fowl, or other nonhuman animals raised solely for meat consumption were free from abuse or injury, one must not overlook other acts of abuse and cruelty for which prohibitions do not apply to farmed animals. Isolation from one's mother, neglect, beating, and being denied interaction with other members of their species, not to mention hot-iron branding, are acts one could rightly consider abusive if not outright cruel.[11]

This is not just speciesism, distinguishing between human and nonhuman animals. Such mental gymnastics are evident even in the cultural regard for different species. Olympian Gus Kenworthy was celebrated for rescuing over ninety dogs from Korean dog-meat farms.[12] However, one seldom finds a story about an individual adopting a herd of cattle. In the end, anti-cruelty laws allow caring individuals to feel that something is being done to prevent cruelty toward nonhuman animals while they ignore the pain and suffering in which they themselves participate. While ignorance may be bliss for consumers, anti-cruelty laws fall well short of addressing the vast majority of nonhuman animal cruelty taking place.

NONHUMAN ANIMALS IN SCIENCE

Similar to the cruelty inflicted on nonhuman animals in the name of agriculture are the acts done in the name of science. Citing similarities in human and nonhuman animals, researchers test many drugs on nonhuman animal subjects to identify side effects or negative reactions. In order for certain drugs to be tested, however, a nonhuman animal must first exhibit the need for such medication. If the need for the drug does not occur naturally, the need is created. Thus, nonhuman animals are intentionally subjected to injuries, broken bones, and trauma, are injected with viruses or bacteria, and are induced to grow tumors foreign to their nature.[13] Worse, often these acts are performed with little or no analgesia. Were any of these acts to take place outside the confines of a laboratory, the perpetrator of the cruel acts would face prosecution regardless of the aforementioned legislative ambiguity.

The cruel acts inflicted on nonhuman animal test subjects in laboratories are not the only means by which suffering is caused. Even as the legal definition of cruelty has, in many cases, broadened to include neglect, within laboratories, food, water, and even the ability to move freely are withheld. Thus, while animals are subjected to tests due to similarities to humans in biology and physiology, other similarities between human and nonhuman animals, such as the desire to live pain-free, are ignored. Were one to hear the cries of a human after what appears to be a painful injury, one would likely seek a way to assuage the pain. But nonhuman cries of pain, wincing, or vomiting are ignored in the name of science.

The results of scientific testing on nonhuman animals have faced greater scrutiny thanks to the efforts of advocates for nonhuman animals,[14] but the institutionalized ideology that nonhuman animals are worthy test subjects for the benefit of humankind continues. Sadly, nonhuman animals continue to be subjected to painful tests that would be labeled as cruelty under the law were they inflicted in another setting or by anyone not adorned in a white lab coat.

ADDITIONAL REALMS OF CRUELTY

This chapter does not allow for examination of the full scope of cruelty suffered by nonhuman animals yet unaddressed by legislation, such as cosmetic testing, unnecessary veterinary practices such as the declawing of felines, or euthanasia performed out of convenience when an individual moves or their companion animal's fur does not match the new furniture. Nor have I addressed the cruelty done to nonhuman animals for entertainment purposes, whether in circuses, sideshow attractions, zoos, or the even more pernicious "crush films" for which prohibitive laws have been unsuccessful.

Neither does this chapter discuss culturally significant acts, such as hunting or bullfighting, that remain unaddressed by anti-cruelty laws. But it is interesting to note that when a cat or dog is shot or stabbed, the act is regarded as cruel, even when the dog or cat dies as a result. When one wants to shoot a nonhuman animal in the forest, preserve, or game park, all one needs to do is produce a government-issued license—many of which require no training or expertise in the weapon used—and one is able to stalk and kill those animals deemed to be "in season." Similarly, were one to repeatedly stab a nonhuman animal in any venue other than an arena, one could expect legal action, not celebration.

The breadth of cruelty inflicted upon nonhuman animals is greater than what is identified by many anti-cruelty laws. The treatment of nonhuman animals in their short lives prior to slaughter and the manner in which their lives end may remain cruel so long as the financial bottom line shows a profit. Similarly, although scientific institutions are unable to demonstrate the need for continued research in which nonhuman animals endure cruel means that produce few human ends, they remain unwilling to recognize this. In any other setting, poor husbandry and intentional harm to nonhuman animals would be deemed a violation of many anti-cruelty laws.

WHAT CAN BE DONE?

Already one can measure the progress taking place in the definitions and scope regarding cruelty inflicted upon nonhuman animals and legal precedent. When there is education of the public and exposure of the practices behind the production of the meat people consume, the testing taking place for the products they purchase, or the lack of results emerging from scientific testing, the respective industries are forced to reexamine their practices. One such example is the progress made in the diminishing use of confinement stalls to house pigs, commonly referred to as "sow stalls." With animal advocates long working to eliminate the use of sow stalls, as well as battery crates for egg-laying chickens and solitary crates for veal calves, some changes have come from within the industry, but at the behest of the consumer. In response to the social-ethical awareness of consumers, one of the largest pork producers in the world has eliminated the use of sow stalls. When consumers saw the manner in which the sows were confined and their inability to move freely or even turn around, many were moved to regard the cruelties inflicted on the pigs in the name of low-priced pork products to be far too great a price. In total, 78 percent of the public found sow stalls an unacceptable means of housing pigs, leading Smithfield Farms to eliminate the use of such cruel means in all of its US farms.[15]

Sadly, however, this is just one case. Countless other nonhuman animals endure overcrowded feedlots, unsanitary living quarters, confined spaces, and the withholding of medicine and treatment for easily curable ailments, all in the name of profit. While there are laws against the cruel and inhumane treatment of nonhuman animals on the books in many countries and states, animals raised for slaughter and consumption are excluded from these laws, subjecting them to cruel treatment prior to their unnatural deaths. Additionally, nonhuman animals undergo painful testing under the guise of scientific necessity.

There have been some significant changes in the realm of anti-cruelty laws in recent years that are worth mentioning. A vast majority of the recorded anti-cruelty crimes are reported by those uninvolved with regulatory institutions or policing agencies. Many violations of anti-cruelty laws are reported by neighbors or concerned citizens.[16] However, this reliance on eyewitness reporting has led to greater secrecy within institutions. Rather than increasing the scope of the anti-cruelty laws to include the cruel practices of factory farms or biomedical testing, lawmakers in several instances have introduced new legislation to punish those who endeavor to gain evidence against the aforementioned institutions. With proponents of such laws citing "extreme" anti-cruelty advocates, ecoterrorism legislation has been utilized to silence peaceful protests.[17] Those who obtain video evidence of the cruelty inflicted in meat production and scientific or cosmetic testing, as well as whistleblowers who dare expose the practices of their employers' acts of abuse, may themselves be found guilty of violating so-called ag-gag laws.

Perhaps what is needed is not additional laws or regulations, but simply consistent implementation of the laws prohibiting cruelty inflicted on nonhuman animals across all spectrums of human–nonhuman animal interaction, no matter the reason for the cruelty. Should a painful treatment be necessary, may it be to treat an injury that has occurred not as means to a human end or to test potential treatments for the sake of others. And if this painful treatment is necessary, may it be for the sake of the one who is injured or sick, not for the potential good of the one inflicting the pain or doing the testing. Should the day come when humans no longer eat the flesh of nonhuman animals, I will welcome that day, but until then, may those who are raised for eventual slaughter not be forced to endure greater pain for the sake of financial gain. All of these forms of cruelty already would warrant legal action were the cruelty not enacted by someone wearing a white lab coat or a Stetson.

Without a paradigm shift of Copernican scale, cruelty toward the most vulnerable in our world—nonhuman animals—will continue. Under current anti-cruelty laws, nonhuman animals are treated as property or commodities rather than as ends in and of themselves. In a recent article in the *Journal of Animal Ethics*,[18] Kathy Archibald calls for science to reexamine the use of nonhuman animals in experiments and testing, citing the lack of sufficient results and the danger posed to humans even when drugs appear safe in nonhuman animals. This argument, however, is built upon the facade of anthropocentricism, since this impetus for change lies in the human cost such experiments incur. One cannot help but speculate that if the results from testing on nonhuman animals were producing results that benefit human beings, Archibald and those in agreement would champion the utility of such testing, ignoring the cost. The so-called human cost to the practices that inflict pain upon nonhuman animals is nothing less than ghastly utilitarian calculus, giving little concern to the ones ultimately paying the price—nonhuman animals.

CONCLUSION

Perhaps this has been an exercise in common sense, simply recounting that which is already well known. If so, one may ask why nothing has been done to address the cruelty that takes place despite the current anti-cruelty laws. How does one address such a dearth in legal precedent? One answer is by educating the public that the acts defined by law as "animal cruelty" make up only a fraction of the abuses inflicted upon animals. That such abuses continue is evidence that the masses who favor humane treatment of animals remain unaware of what takes place every day in the meat, pharmaceutical, and cosmetics industries, where nonhuman animals are made to endure acts of cruelty. Additionally, the public must understand the negligible penalties for breaking anti-cruelty laws that do exist and also how seldom these penalties are actually implemented. Moreover, showing people how anti-cruelty laws fail to apply to the vast majority of the abuses taking place in various industries will expose the systemic flaw in jurisprudence.

The public must be made aware of how individual choices and feedback can have a direct impact on those who can bring about change. Many people believe that anti-cruelty laws are effective, leaving individuals unaware of much of the continued abuse that results from their purchases or lifestyles. From sow stalls to shock collars, from certified organic products to the manner in which nonhuman animals are treated in their short lives, the public has a responsibility to ensure their preferences are made known to those with the power to change legislation. Ethical changes in legislation require practical means. It is only through such means that there is any hope of making the necessary advances in establishing legal rights for our other-than-human animal companions in Creation. We must look beyond anti-cruelty laws to educate the public and remind individuals what is truly at stake—lives worthy of our care.

REFERENCES

Animal Welfare Act. 7 USC §§ 2131–2159. Accessed on February 6, 2022.

Archibald, Kathy. "Animal Research Is an Ethical Issue for Humans as Well as for Animals." *Journal of Animal Ethics* 8, no. 1 (2018): 1–11.

Arkow, Phil, and Randall Lockwood. "Definitions of Animals Cruelty, Abuse, and Neglect." In *Animal Cruelty: A Multidisciplinary Approach to Understanding*, edited by Mary P. Brewster and Cassandra L. Reyes, 3–23. Durham, NC: Carolina Academic Press, 2016.

Linzey, Andrew, and Clair Linzey, eds. *The Ethical Case against Animal Experiments*. Urbana: University of Illinois Press, 2018.

Lynn, S. J. "Olympian Gus Kenworthy Rescues 90 Dogs from Korean Dog Meat Farm." *Sporting News*, February 27, 2018. Accessed on February 6, 2022. http://www.sportingnews.com/athletics/news/olympian-gus-kenworthy-rescues-90-dogs-korean-dog-meat-farm/17inn1m5hlb6n19pm8az2vn142.

Navarro, John C., Jacqueline L. Schneider, and Egan Green, "Animal Cruelty for Sport and Profit" in *Animal Cruelty: A Multidisciplinary Approach to Understanding*, edited by Mary P. Brewster and Cassandra L. Reyes, 159–97. Durham, NC: Carolina Academic Press, 2016.

Rollin, Bernard. *Animal Rights and Human Morality*. Amherst, NY: Prometheus Books, 2006.

———. *A New Basis for Animal Ethics: Telos and Common Sense*. Columbia: University of Missouri Press, 2016.

US Department of Agriculture. *Animal Welfare Inspection Guide*. Accessed on February 6, 2022. https://www.aphis.usda.gov/animal_welfare/downloads/Animal-Care-Inspection-Guide.pdf.

NOTES

1. John C. Navarro, Jacqueline L. Schneider, and Egan Green, "Animal Cruelty for Sport and Profit" in Mary P. Brewster and Cassandra L. Reyes, eds., *Animal Cruelty:*

A Multidisciplinary Approach to Understanding (Durham, NC: Carolina Academic Press, 2016), 165.

2. Phil Arkow and Randall Lockwood, "Definitions of Animals Cruelty, Abuse, and Neglect," in *Animal Cruelty: A Multidisciplinary Approach to Understanding*, ed. Mary P. Brewster and Cassandra L. Reyes (Durham, NC: Carolina Academic Press, 2016), 5.

3. Brewster and Reyes, *Animal Cruelty*, 404. As of 2014, all fifty states in the United States have laws in which cruelty toward nonhuman animals is deemed a felony.

4. Bernard Rollin, *Animal Rights and Human Morality* (Amherst, NY: Prometheus Books, 2006), 160.

5. Bernard Rollin, *A New Basis for Animal Ethics: Telos and Common Sense* (Columbia: University of Missouri Press, 2016), 9.

6. Rollin, *A New Basis*, 9–10.

7. Rollin, *A New Basis*, 10.

8. Animal Welfare Act, 7 U.S.C. § 2132 (g); US Department of Agriculture, *Animal Welfare Inspection Guide*, https://www.aphis.usda.gov/animal_welfare/downloads/Animal-Care-Inspection-Guide.pdf.

9. Brewster and Reyes, *Animal Cruelty*, 162.

10. Rollin, *Animal Rights and Human Morality*, 161.

11. Rollin, *A New Basis*, 11.

12. S. J. Lynn, "Olympian Gus Kenworthy Rescues 90 Dogs from Korean Dog Meat Farm," *Sporting News*, February 27, 2018, http://www.sportingnews.com/athletics/news/olympian-gus-kenworthy-rescues-90-dogs-korean-dog-meat-farm/17inn1m5hlb6n19pm8az2vn142.

13. Andrew Linzey and Clair Linzey, eds., *The Ethical Case against Animal Experiments* (Urbana: University of Illinois Press, 2018), 15–19.

14. See, for instance, Linzey and Linzey, *Ethical Case against Animal Experiments*.

15. Rollin, *A New Basis*, 105–6.

16. Brewster and Reyes, *Animal Cruelty*, 143.

17. Brewster and Reyes, *Animal Cruelty*, 398

18. Kathy Archibald, "Animal Research Is an Ethical Issue for Humans as Well as for Animals," *Journal of Animal Ethics* 8, no. 1 (2018): 1–11.

PART III

Case Studies

Chapter 14

The European Union

Make Animal Law Work: The Direct Effect Principle in EU Law as an Instrument for Improving Animal Welfare

By Lena Hehemann

Growing public concern regarding animal welfare and little effective application of animal law demand improved legislation in regard to the human use of animals. The European Union adopted a series of legislative acts on the protection of animals being used for different purposes.[1] Regrettably, a great amount of legislation in this area is only partially effective, especially in terms of enforcement and faulty legislation. To a certain extent, this results from the nature of the legislative act. Most of these acts are laid down in the form of directives, which need to be transposed into national law to be applicable (cf. Article 288 of the Treaty on the Functioning of the European Union [TFEU]).[2] The directives impose levels of minimum harmonization, leaving considerable leeway to the member states in regard to the transposition and enforcement, which results in different levels of protection within the EU.

Enforcement of animal welfare legislation is furthermore primarily a "vertical" process between the member state and the individual. Private individuals' options to enforce animal welfare legislation on a national level themselves are rather limited, given that the established case law of the Court of Justice of the European Union (CJEU) does not allow the application of the doctrine of direct effect if the provision in question imposes obligations on an individual (horizontal direct effect).[3] In other words, private parties are not allowed to use provisions set in a directive against another individual in a national court, for example if an animal welfare provision is not applied properly. However, the principle of direct effect may still constitute an instrument for improving animal welfare as long as the horizontal effect is incidental or a "side effect" (the so-called "*Wells* approach"[4]).[5]

This chapter analyzes the impact of the doctrine of (horizontal) direct effect as an instrument to effectively enforce animal welfare legislation. For this purpose, the author provides an overview of the existing possibilities and developments, looking at Article 36(2) of Directive 2010/63 on the protection of animals used for scientific purposes,[6] which obliges the member states to ensure that a project evaluation of an animal experiment is conducted prior to its authorization. The CJEU's decision in *Wells* will provide the necessary tools in this regard.

The structure of this chapter will be as follows: First, the chapter provides a brief overview of the direct effect principle and its meaning in EU law. Based on this analysis, the author deploys the doctrine of Article 36(2) of Directive 2010/63. In particular, two aspects arise: first, whether the project evaluation criterion may give rise to direct effect is scrutinized; second, the author discusses whether the provision in question imposes an obligation to an individual and whether this effect is "incidental" (cf. *Wells*). Last, the chapter sets out evidence that the direct effect doctrine improves the enforcement of animal welfare legislation in certain cases. It ends with an appeal to use all available options in EU law to enforce animal welfare legislation effectively.

PRIVATE ENFORCEMENT OF EU LAW

General Remarks

In general, the direct effect principle applies to all binding EU law, including all primary and secondary law.[7] Its purpose lies in the judicial enforcement of provisions of EU law by an individual within the member state. Article 288 TFEU defines different types of EU instruments in this regard: First, the EU legislature can adopt regulations that shall be binding in their entirety and directly applicable in the member states. They apply to all legal persons in the EU rather than a particular individual. Because these regulations aim at an absolute harmonization of the different national legal systems, there is no need of an additional transposition into national law. Second, next to regulations, directives are the main instrument for adopting legislation within the EU. Directives require a national implementation in order to be judicially enforceable by an individual. They need to be transposed into national law, leaving the national legislators with a choice as to form and method. Directives cannot apply directly but may give rise to direct effect.

The Direct Effect of Directives

In its early jurisdiction, the CJEU developed the principle of direct effect for directives.[8] Although, in general, a directive needs to be implemented in national law within a certain time frame in order to be applicable, it is an established rule that provisions of unimplemented directives can have (vertical) direct effect.[9] Thus, if the national legislature is unable or unwilling to transpose the directive into national law (sufficiently), an individual can nevertheless invoke and rely on the provision before a national or EU court. The provision, therefore, becomes applicable for the national court or the administrator.[10]

Conditions

The CJEU sets out four conditions relating to the direct effect of directives. The requirements are to be demonstrated cumulatively for a provision to have direct effect.[11]

First, the member state in question must have failed to transpose the provision in time and/or correctly. Thus, the mere transposition of a directive does not prevent the directive from having direct effect when a "faulty transposition" fails to ensure that the provision can be applied properly.[12] Second, the provision in question needs to be unconditional, which means it is not dependent on any other provision. It is capable of being applied directly by a national court.[13] Furthermore, the provision in question needs to be sufficiently clear and precise. It must, therefore, be self-contained and impose a clear obligation on the member state or its institutions.[14] Finally, the provision must have a vertical direct effect, meaning the direct effect can be pled only against the state (or a public body). A directive is not capable of having a horizontal direct effect, which is the case if it imposes an obligation on an individual.[15] In other words, the direct effect does not allow the provision in question to be used as a legal basis for enforcing a right against another private party before a national court.

Incidental Horizontal Direct Effect

Although the CJEU does not acknowledge a horizontal direct effect of directives, this does not exclude "side or incidental horizontal effects" of vertical actions.[16] The CJEU's more recent case law indicates that an obligation resulting merely as a "side effect" or "reflexive" negative effect does not conflict with the doctrine of (horizontal) direct effect, as the repercussion on the individual arises from an accompanying procedural obligation of the state (e.g., contribution of certain requirements within a licensing procedure).[17] For instance, a third party may question a competent authority's decision regarding the granting of a permit, after which the permit holder (a second private party) could lose his or her permit. Despite the "horizontal" effects caused by the invoking of vertical direct effect in these cases, the CJEU has accepted this usage of vertical direct effect,[18] as long as the national legislator previously set out the modalities of the individual procedure and the requirements that apply. The "obligation" imposed on the individual arises incidentally because of the national procedure; the provisions of the directive itself do not impose these obligations. Thus, it is considered a "mere adverse repercussion."[19] Consequently, the court distances itself slightly from the rather strict no-horizontal-direct-effect rule; it evolves toward a more distinguished approach. Nevertheless, the court does not deviate from its position that direct effect can in general not be applied horizontally (e.g., licensing obligations as such). Finally, it acknowledges that unimplemented directives can give rise to a horizontal direct effect in cases where a provision has an "incidental effect" on private persons, which is great progress for EU law effectiveness.[20] The key distinction made here is that the incidental or adverse effect does not stem from the directive as such but from the failings of the authorities to fulfill their obligations laid down in the directive. To determine the potential "mere adverse repercussion," the court analyzes and evaluates each individual case; there is no general approach as to when the "mere adverse repercussion" on a (third) individual can be assumed.[21]

THE PROJECT EVALUATION OF ARTICLE 36(2) OF DIRECTIVE 2010/63

Directive 2010/63, revising Directive 86/609/EEC, on the protection of animals used for scientific purposes, was adopted on September 22, 2010. The member states had until December 31, 2012, to transpose the provisions into domestic law. The directive constitutes the major legislative act in regard to the protection of animals used in laboratories within the European Union.[22] In addition to a variety of requirements concerning housing, feeding, and performance of experiments, Directive 2010/63 demands that an authorization be issued by the competent national authority prior to each animal experiment (Art. 36).[23] According to Article 36(2) of Directive 2010/63, this authorization shall be issued only if a favorable project evaluation by the competent authority has been received. The requirements to be met by the project evaluation are set out in detail in Article 38 of the directive; in its essence a positive project evaluation requires the benefit of the specific experiment to outweigh the harm suffered by the animal being used. In some EU member states the transposition of Article 36(2) has been much criticized. In Germany,[24] for example, the national procedure allegedly does not meet the required criteria since it lacks the requirement of an exhaustive and independent evaluation of the experiment in question by the competent authority. It barely introduces a "plausibility check" of the project evaluation submitted by the applicant. Given that only the performance of an exhaustive harm–benefit analysis can ensure a high level of animal welfare within the licensing procedure, the transpositions at hand may be "faulty" and therefore open the scope of the direct effect doctrine. Building on the previous remarks, the following sections assess whether the doctrine of direct effect applies to the project evaluation criterion.

The Project Evaluation . . .

In order to give rise to direct effect, the provision in question—in this case, Article 36, paragraph 2—needs to be unconditional, clear, and precise and have only vertical effect. Only if these requirements are fulfilled may an individual make a claim for the performance of an exhaustive project evaluation by the national authority before a national or EU court. Thus, the following section focuses on the interpretation of the provision to show its direct effect.

Textual Interpretation

The wording of Article 36(2) of Directive 2010/63 indicates that the competent authority should perform the project evaluation itself ("projects are not carried out unless a favourable project evaluation by the competent authority has been received"). However, the considerably vague wording leaves some leeway regarding how detailed an evaluation the authority conducts. It is particularly unclear whether the authority must perform an exhaustive analysis of the project in question or only check for its coherence and plausibility with the criteria enshrined in Article 38 of Directive 2010/63. The latter case essentially requires the applicants to perform the project evaluation themselves and provide a recommendation to the authority.[25] Neither the German ("ein Projekt [wird] nur dann durchgeführt . . . , wenn es eine postive Projektbeurteilung durch die zuständige Behörde erhalten hat") nor the French ("les projets ne soient as exécutés sans autorisation préalable de l'autorité competence") translation contributes to the clarification of the authority's competences.

Teleological Interpretation

Since the textual analysis provides an ambiguous answer to the question of the competences, the provision's inherent purpose and intent shall be determined. Especially the recitals provide further insights in this regard; they make a substantial contribution to the interpretation and application of a directive, even though they are nonbinding.[26] Recital 38 of Directive 2010/63 offers an initial indication of each authority's competences (and obligations): The authority in charge is obliged (and authorized) to carry out its own (scientific) investigations with respect to the project evaluation and the expected scientific benefits of the requested experiment. The union legislator acknowledges a comprehensive and neutral assessment of a project involving the use of animals as the "heart" of the project authorization.[27] Recital 39, which deems the project evaluation to form a necessary part of the authorization procedure, points in the same direction: Accordingly, "it is essential, both on moral and scientific grounds, to ensure that each use of an animal is carefully evaluated as to the scientific or educational validity, usefulness and relevance of the expected result of that use. The likely harm to the animal should be balanced against the expected benefits of the project." An independent body shall carry out this impartial project evaluation in order to allow for a proper assessment.[28] The applicants naturally have a substantial interest in their applications' approval; thus, they are to be excluded from the evaluation. Nevertheless, they take part insofar as they provide sufficient elements that are necessary for the conduction of the comprehensive project evaluation. Recital 39, therefore, does not lay down an obligation for an impartial and independent project evaluation but rather makes a "recommendation," given that its wording is rather soft: the project evaluation "should" be carried out impartially as part of the approval procedure for animal experiments.

Therefore, it seems that the inherent purpose of Article 36(2) of Directive 2010/63 is to direct the responsible authority to conduct a comprehensive, impartial, and independent project evaluation (collectively with all other project requirements).[29]

Systematic Interpretation

The obligation of the competent authority to carry out a comprehensive project evaluation of the planned project also can be derived (directly and indirectly) from a number of other provisions. Especially three shall be addressed.

Article 37 of Directive 2010/63 specifies the documents to be submitted by the applicant in his or her application. According to Article 37(1), the application must contain (a) "the project proposal," (b) "a non-technical project summary," and (c) certain details on the project, the selected animal species, and the expected benefit (Annex VI, Dir. 2010/63). Given the importance of the project evaluation, it shall be assumed that if the applicants, and not the authority, were to carry out the evaluation, the project evaluation would have to be attached by the applicant so that the authority could check its coherence and plausibility. The applicants thus would provide the necessary details to perform the evaluation but would not provide the evaluation themselves.[30]

Moreover, Article 38(3) of the directive authorizes (and obliges) "the competent authority carrying out the project evaluation" to consider external expertise in certain areas during the evaluation. The call for consultation of external experts by the authority indicates that the authority itself should perform a proper and comprehensive evaluation. Apart from that, the wording of the cited article speaks for a comprehensive project evaluation by the competent authority ("the authority responsible for carrying out the project evaluation").

Finally, Article 38(4) of Directive 2010/63 requires that the project evaluation be carried out in an "impartial manner and may integrate the opinion of independent parties." This impartiality can be guaranteed only if the authority carries out a comprehensive project assessment itself.

From this systematic examination, it becomes clear that a favorable project evaluation required by Article 36(2) can only be conducted and issued by the competent authority.

. . . and Its Incidental Direct Effect

To give rise to direct effect, a provision must not impose obligations on an individual (horizontal direct effect). An exception applies if the individual's obligation does not arise directly from the EU directive but results from national law ("mere adverse repercussion"). Article 36(2) of Directive 2010/63 imposes obligations on the applicants insofar as they are obliged to ensure the project is granted a favorable project evaluation as a requirement for receiving an authorization to perform an animal experiment, which may prolong the administrative procedure and pose a risk of denial of authorization. However, national law defines the individual administrative procedure. Therefore, the applicant's burden or repercussion results from the national administrative law and thus is an "incidental direct effect."[31]

This results mainly from the CJEU's jurisdiction in *Wells*.[32] There, the CJEU disclaimed a direct link between the member states' obligations to conduct an environmental impact assessment (EIA) in accordance with the EIA Directive and the individual's obligations to participate in this assessment, with the argument that the EIA Directive requires a national administrative procedure.[33] This procedure, then, imposes obligations on the individual: The individual is obliged to fulfill certain conditions in order to provide for a favorable EIA and receive an authorization, whereas the national law sets out the different requirements to be met in this context. Thus, the obligations arise due to an additional administrative procedure and are therefore considered an "incidental direct effect."[34]

The *Wells* approach applies to Article 36(2) of Directive 2010/63 too: the favorable project evaluation constitutes a prerequisite for the authorization of an animal experiment, and the requirements regarding the latter are further defined and grounded in national procedural law. Article 36(2) itself does not yet create or impose any obligations on private individuals; a further "practical implementation" within the nationally structured approval procedure is required. Consequently, the obligation arises from the administrative procedure; it constitutes a "mere adverse repercussion." Against this background, there is in any case no direct link between the provision of Directive 2010/63 and the obligations of the individual. Article 36(2) of the directive, finally, gives rise to direct effect.

INTERIM CONCLUSION: PRIVATE ENFORCEMENT OF ARTICLE 36(2) OF DIRECTIVE 2010/63

As aforementioned, Article 36(2) gives rise to direct effect. It therefore allows an individual to rely on the article before a national court if he or she believes that the competent authority did not conduct the project evaluation—the most important animal welfare tool in Directive 2010/63—properly. In other words, an individual can enforce the comprehensive, impartial, and scientific as well as ethical assessment of the benefits and harms of the experiment in question, even though this may lead to an adverse repercussion for another individual.

"INCIDENTAL HORIZONTAL DIRECT EFFECT" AS AN ANIMAL WELFARE TOOL

Last, this chapter analyzes whether the "*Wells* approach" of direct effect of authorization procedures may improve animal welfare. The following section sets out reasons that a trend is emerging toward more direct effect of animal legislation when authorization requirements are involved.

The majority of animal welfare legislation provides for administrative procedures that need national drafting. As shown earlier, by prescribing a project evaluation, Directive 2010/63 defines an authorization requirement, whose exact design is further described in national procedural law; other directives on animal uses set similar requirements. The effectiveness of these directives can be diminished by "faulty" transposition in national law. If direct effect is involved, an EU provision sets national law aside if the latter conflicts with a directive.[35] This alteration remedies a procedural error on the side of the member state regarding the implementation of an EU directive on animal welfare. However, a provision cannot give rise to a horizontal direct effect. With *Wells*, the CJEU has offered a way out of this plight: the acknowledgment of a "mere adverse repercussion" or an "incidental horizontal direct effect" of a provision that addresses the public body allows an individual to enforce the animal welfare provision in question if a member state fails to provide for protection. This is even the case if the implementation imposes obligations on an individual. The *Wells* approach, therefore, supports the enforcement and application of animal welfare legislation. However, the CJEU emphasizes that a case-by-case analysis is required to determine whether a provision gives rise to direct effect. Regardless of the required demands on incidental direct effect set out by the court, the jurisdiction has not offered a comprehensive schema in this respect, which is due to the few cases decided in this regard. Furthermore, it is often unclear whether the provisions aiming at the protection of animals confer individual rights.[36] This leads to legal uncertainty for the national authorities as well as the individual seeking to enforce the provision directly.

With respect to these difficulties, when it comes to direct effect, it is essential that the EU takes a stand and shapes its animal welfare legislation in a way that applies directly to the member states (e.g., adoption of regulations) or by adopting directives whose wording allows for a direct effect in regard to the approach developed in *Wells*.

CONCLUSION

Because the enforcement of animal welfare legislation is predominantly in the hands of the member states, the premise on which this discussion has been based is that private enforcement of the EU's animal welfare legislation could be a positive development for animal protection within the EU. In this regard, the member states' unwillingness to transpose and enforce the (few) unional legislative acts—apart from the CJEU's consistent denial of a horizontal direct effect—constitutes the main obstacle to effective and direct applicability and enforcement of animal welfare provisions. However, the CJEU's judgement regarding the incidental horizontal direct effect supports the applicability of the direct effect doctrine for animal welfare legislation after all. Therefore, this chapter ends with an appeal to use all available options to enforce animal welfare legislation, including the theoretical principle of direct effect.

REFERENCES

Arnull, Anthony, and Damian Chalmers, eds. *The Oxford Handbook of European Union Law*. Oxford: Oxford University Press, 2015.

Bobek, Michael. "The Effects of EU Law in the National Legal Systems." In *European Union Law*, 2nd ed., edited by Catherine Barnard and Steve Peers, 143–76. Oxford: Oxford University Press, 2017.

Craig, Paul. "The Legal Effect of Directives: Policy, Rules and Exceptions." *European Law Review*, no. 3 (2009).

Craig, Paul P., and Gráinne de Búrca. *EU Law: Text, Cases, and Materials*. 6th ed. Oxford: Oxford University Press, 2015.

Dougan, Michael. "The 'Disguised' Vertical Direct Effect of Directives?" *Cambridge Law Journal* 59, no. 3 (2000): 586–612.

———. "When Worlds Collide! Competing Visions of the Relationship between Direct Effect and Supremacy." *Common Market Law Review* 44 (2007): 931–63.

Graf von Kielmannsegg, Sebastian. "Tücken im Dreieck—Die individualbelastende Richtlinienwirkung im Unionsrecht." *Europarecht* (2014): 30–60.

Hehemann, Lena. *Die Genehmigung von Tierversuchen im Spannungsfeld von Tierschutz und Forschungsfreiheit*. Zurich: Schulthess, 2019.

Hirt, Almuth, Christoph Maisack, and Johanna Moritz. *Tierschutzgesetz: Kommentar*. 3rd ed. Munich: Franz Vahlen, 2016.

Holder, Jane. "A Dead End for Direct Effect? Prospects for Enforcement of European Community Environmental Law by Individuals." *Journal of Environmental Law* 8, no. 2 (1996): 313–35.

Jarass, Hans, and Sasa Beljin. "Grenzen der Privatbelastung durch unmittelbar wirkende Richtlinien." *Europarecht* (2004): 714–38.

Leczykiewicz, Dorota. "Effectiveness of EU Law before National Courts: Direct Effect, Effective Judicial Protection, and State Liability." In *The Oxford Handbook of European Union Law*, edited by Anthony Arnull and Damian Chalmers, 212–48. Oxford: Oxford University Press, 2015.

Squintani, Lorenzo, and Hans H. B. Vedder. "Case Note—Towards Inverse Direct Effect? A Silent Development of a Core European Law Doctrine." *RECIEL* 23, no. 1 (2014): 144–49.

van Zeben, Josephine A. W. "The Untapped Potential of Horizontal Private Enforcement within EC Environmental Law." Amsterdam Center for Law and Economics working paper, 2008–09. Accessed June 19, 2018. http://www.acle.nl.

Wennerås, Pål. *The Enforcement of EC Environmental Law*. Oxford: Oxford University Press, 2007.

NOTES

1. See European Parliament, *Animal Welfare in the European Union*, PE 583.114 (2017), 24.

2. Art. 288 TFEU: "A directive shall be binding, as to the result to be achieved, upon each Member State to which it is addressed, but shall leave to the national authorities the choice of forms and methods"; see in general Paul Craig and Gráinne de Búrca, *EU Law: Text, Cases, and Materials*, 6th ed. (Oxford: Oxford University Press, 2015), 107–10.

3. The relevant case law will be cited below in the section concerning the direct effect of directives.

4. Case C-201/02, *Wells*, [2004] ECR I-723.

5. Similar attempts have been made in relation to EU environmental law; since animal welfare can in certain aspects be considered an aspect of environmental law, the following sections do not seek to discuss the relevant case law of the CJEU but refer to the different analyses in Lorenzo Squintani and Hans H. B. Vedder, "Case Note—Towards Inverse Direct Effect? A Silent Development of a Core European Law Doctrine," *RECIEL* 23, no. 1 (2014): 144; Paul Craig, "The Legal Effect of Directives: Policy, Rules and Exceptions," *European Law Review*, no. 3 (2009); Josephine A. W. van Zeben, "The Untapped Potential of Horizontal Private Enforcement within EC Environmental Law, Amsterdam Center for Law and Economics working paper (2008–09), 247; Jane Holder, "A Dead End for Direct Effect? Prospects for Enforcement of European Community Environmental Law by Individuals," *Journal of Environmental Law* 8, no. 2 (1996): 313.

6. *Official Journal of the European Union, L* 276 (2010): 33.

7. The direct effect of primary law will not be further discussed here. See instead only Michael Bobek, "The Effects of EU Law in the National Legal Systems," in *European Union Law*, 2nd ed., ed. Catherine Barnard and Steve Peers (Oxford: Oxford University Press, 2017), 143–76.

8. See Case 26/62, *Van Gend & Loos*, [1963] ECR 1 at 12; Case 152/84, *Marshall*, [1986] ECR I 723; Case 153/84, [1986] ECR 737; Case C-106/89, [1990] ECR I-4135; Case C-91–92, *Faccini Dori*, [1994] ECR I 3325.

9. Michael Dougan, "The 'Disguised' Vertical Direct Effect of Directives?," *Cambridge Law Journal* 59, no. 3 (2000): 586.

10. Bobek, "Effects of EU Law," 146; Dorota Leczykiewicz, "Effectiveness of EU Law before National Courts: Direct Effect, Effective Judicial Protection, and State Liability," in *The Oxford Handbook of European Union Law*, ed. Anthony Arnull and Damian Chalmers (Oxford: Oxford University Press, 2015), 213; Craig and de Búrca, *EU Law*, 204–9.

11. Joined cases C-397/01 and C-403/01, *Pfeiffer*, [2004] ECR I-8835; Case C-268/06, *Impact*, [2008] ECR I-2483.

12. Craig and de Búrca, *EU Law*, 200.

13. Case C-72/95, *Kraaijeveld*, [1996] ECR I-5403; Case C-236/92, *Lombardia*, [1994] ECR I-483.

14. Craig, "The Legal Effect."

15. Case 152/84, *Marshall*; Case C-91/92, *Faccini Dori*; see in this regard Leczykiewicz, "Effectiveness of EU Law"; Dougan, "The 'Disguised' Vertical Direct Effect," 587.

16. Cf. Case C-201/02, *Wells*; van Zeben, "The Untapped Potential," 247.

17. Leczykiewicz, "Effectiveness of EU Law," 239; Hans Jarass and Sasa Beljin, "Grenzen der Privatbelastung durch unmittelbar wirkende Richtlinien," *Europarecht* (2004): 714; Craig and de Búrca, *EU Law*, 216.

18. See Case C-201/02, *Wells*.

19. Case C-201/02, *Wells*, note 57; Leczykiewicz, "Effectiveness of EU Law"; van Zeben, "The Untapped Potential," 247.

20. Case C-194/94, *CIA*, [1996] ECR I-2201; Case C-443/98, *Unilever Italia*, [2000] ECR I-7535; Case C-201/02, *Wells*. For a critical view of the incidental effect, see Craig and de Búrca, *EU Law*, 216; Michael Dougan, "When Worlds Collide! Competing Visions of the Relationship between Direct Effect and Supremacy," *Common Market Law Review* 44 (2007): 931–63.

21. When asked whether a provision gives rise to (incidental horizontal) direct effect, the CJEU avoids taking a stand but rather interprets the provision in question in conformity with the directive. However, this increasingly blurs the distinction between the compliant interpretation and direct effect. See also Sebastian Graf von Kielmannsegg, "Tücken im Dreieck—Die individualbelastende Richtlinienwirkung im Unionsrecht," *Europarecht* (2014): 30–60.

22. The specific content of Dir. 2010/63 is of no further relevance.

23. For more information on the authorization process laid down in Dir. 2010/63 see also Lena Hehemann, *Die Genehmigung von Tierversuchen im Spannungsfeld zwischen Tierschutz und Forschungsfreiheit* (Zurich: Schulthess, 2019).

24. Almuth Hirt, Christoph Maisack, and Johanna Moritz, *Tierschutzgesetz Kommentar*, 3rd ed. (Munich: Franz Vahlen, 2016), § 8 TierSchG.

25. A similar approach is followed by Hirt, Maisack, and Moritz, *Tierschutzgesetz*, § 8 TierSchG.

26. Hehemann, *Die Genehmigung von Tierversuchen*, 57–69, providing further references.

27. Recital 38, Dir. 2010/63.

28. See Working document of the European Commission on inspections and enforcement to fulfill the requirements under Dir. 2010/63, Brussels, October 9–10, 2014, 13ff.

29. Hirt, Maisack, and Moritz, *Tierschutzgesetz*, *Tierschutzgesetz*, § 8 TierSchG para. 11.

30. See also Hirt, Maisack, and Moritz, *Tierschutzgesetz*, *Tierschutzgesetz*, § 8 TierSchG para. 11.

31. Jarass and Beljin, "Grenzen der Privatbelastung," 714, 733; Craig and de Búrca, *EU Law*, 216; Craig, "The Legal Effect."

32. Case C-201/02 *Wells*, para. 58.

33. Case C-201/02 *Wells*, para. 61; for similar judgements, see Case C-213–03, *Pêcheurs de l'étange de Berre*, [2004] ECR I-7357, para. 42; Case C-431/92, *Commission v. Germany*, [1995] ECR I-2189, para. 26; Case C-365/97, *Commission v. Italy*, [1999] ECR I-7773 (San Rocco), para. 63. See only Pål Wennerås, *The Enforcement of EC Environmental Law* (Oxford: Oxford University Press, 2007).

34. Van Zeben, "The Untapped Potential," 260; Jarass and Beljin, "Grenzen der Privatbelastung," 714.

35. Craig and de Búrca, *EU Law*, 200.

36. Holder, "A Dead End for Direct Effect?," 326.

Chapter 15

US and New Zealand

Farmed Animals and the Rule of Law

By Danielle Duffield

The rule of law is a revered ideal. Described by Justice Fraser, chief justice of the Alberta Court of Appeals, as one of the "crucibles within which all other laws are measured,"[1] and with traditions that date back to Athenian democracy, the rule of law has come to symbolize good governance, effective justice, and the expansion of rights and liberties around the globe.[2] Although the exact meaning and content of the rule of law remain subject to scholarly debate and elucidation, there is one thing on which almost all commentators agree: the rule of law matters.

With the election of Donald Trump as president of the United States in November 2016, and public outrage over his criticisms of institutions designed to serve as checks on executive power,[3] renewed and bipartisan interest in the ideals of the rule of law has sparked within the international community in recent years. Yet the regulation of one group of legal subjects has remained conspicuously absent from all such discussions: animals.

This chapter seeks to begin to remedy this omission by examining farmed animal welfare legislation in two common-law jurisdictions, the United States and New Zealand, from a rule-of-law perspective. First, this discussion will consider the most acute problem with animal welfare legislation in both jurisdictions: the law provides for different standards of treatment for different animals based on arbitrary considerations. This chapter will analyze this problem through the lens of the rule of law, focusing on the legislation's inconsistency with the rule of law's requirement that law be free from arbitrariness. Second, the chapter will examine enforcement difficulties experienced in both jurisdictions in terms of the requirements of the rule of law. In exploring these questions, the chapter will address the overarching question of whether the rule of law ought to apply to nonhuman subjects of the law. Finally, the chapter will consider the strategic advantages of framing the debate about animal law reform from the perspective of the rule of law as opposed to animal welfare.

THE NATURE AND CONTENT OF THE RULE OF LAW

Before we begin to address the compatibility of farmed animal law with the rule of law, it is important to highlight the need for caution. Acclaimed political theorist Judith Shklar has warned that the phrase "the rule of law" has been subject to much "ideological abuse and general over-use"—and that this has risked the concept becoming almost meaningless.[4] New York University law professor Jeremy Waldron has echoed Shklar's concern, suggesting that the utterance of the "rule of law" can sometimes mean little more than "Hooray for our side!"[5] Even Brian Tamanaha—one of the world's most acclaimed scholars on the rule of law—has expressed concern that the rule of law might devolve to an empty phrase "so lacking in meaning that it can be proclaimed with impunity by malevolent governments."[6]

While it is important to be cognizant of this problem, this misuse of rule-of-law arguments does not render the concept devoid of utility. Other politically loaded terms such as "democracy," "rights," and "efficiency" also are subject to widespread ideological abuse; but just as we don't abandon these concepts solely on this basis, we ought not to deem the rule of law meaningless for this reason either. The value of the rule of law is evident in the work of organizations such as the World Justice Project, which has made major advances around the world in improving access to civil and criminal justice, fundamental rights, the provision of institutional checks and balances, and other important democratic reforms by measuring and promoting the rule of law. The concept is the foundational doctrine of the constitutions of many of the world's democracies,[7] and as such, it resonates with audiences around the globe.

HISTORICAL ORIGINS OF THE RULE OF LAW

In his book *On the Rule of Law*, Brian Tamanaha explores the historical origins of the rule of law in classical Greek thought.[8] He explains how, after Plato's teacher Socrates was put to death by Athenian democracy, Plato and Aristotle became especially concerned about the potential for tyranny in a populist democracy.[9] Thus, they underscored the need for law to represent a permanent and unchanging order. Tamanaha writes that "the faith they expressed in the rule of law was in contemplation of its stability and restraining effect."[10] Plato and Aristotle emphasized that law should further the good of the community and enhance the development of moral virtue of all citizens, with Plato claiming that "the laws which are not established for the good of the whole state are bogus law."[11] Both Plato and Aristotle emphasized the need for government officials to be subject to the law and considered that if law was based on *reason*, it would serve as an internal check against potential abuse by those in power.[12] Tamanaha observes that at the height of Athenian governance, citizens had equality before the law; laws were framed in general terms, not against any individual; and the council, magistrates, and legislative assemblies were bound by the law.

In addition to historical origins in classical Greek thought, rule-of-law traditions include contributions from the Roman thinker Cicero, who wrote of the need for laws to be just, to be for the good of the community, and to preserve the happiness of the community's citizens;[13] the Magna Carta document promulgated in medieval England, which imposed restraints on the exercise of sovereign power;[14] and Germanic customary law, which required that law be oriented to the interest of the community.[15]

THE RULE OF LAW TODAY

In the sixth Sir David Williams lecture in 2006, acclaimed English jurist Lord Bingham, former lord chief justice of the House of Lords, famously distilled the rule of law into eight principles:[16]

1. The law must be accessible and, so far as possible, intelligible, clear and predictable.
2. Questions of legal right and liability should ordinarily be resolved by application of the law and not the exercise of discretion.
3. The laws of the land should apply equally to all, save to the extent that objective differences justify differentiation.
4. Ministers and public officers at all levels must exercise the powers conferred on them in good faith, fairly, for the purpose for which the powers were conferred, without exceeding the limits of such powers and not unreasonably.
5. The law must afford adequate protection of fundamental human rights.
6. Means must be provided for resolving, without prohibitive cost or inordinate delay, bona fide civil disputes which the parties themselves are unable to resolve.
7. Adjudicative procedures provided by the state should be fair.

8. The rule of law requires compliance by the state with its obligations in international law as in national law.

These principles are often interpreted through a human-centric lens. For example, in his paper "Assessing the Strength of the Rule of Law in New Zealand," the Honorable Matthew Palmer, now a judge of the High Court of New Zealand, claims that "all law is, of course, a human construct—formulated by humans, applied by humans, to humans."[17] It is apparent that in making this statement, Justice Palmer was not intending to express a judgment as to whether or not the rule of law applies to animals, but rather sought to emphasize that law is "inherently an interpretative exercise" by a community of human actors.[18] However, an examination of the history and purpose of the rule of law suggests that its underlying principles ought to extend to animals too.

First, the rule of law is essentially concerned with the fair treatment—both procedurally and substantively—of *legal subjects*. In his book *The Rule of Law in the Real World*, Paul Gowder, a professor of law at the University of Iowa, argues that "the rule of law is morally valuable because it is required for the state to treat subjects of law as equals."[19] Gowder defines "legal subjects" (whom he also describes as "individuals" or "citizens") to mean all of those whom the state claims the *authority to command*. He explains that the category is "not limited to those who count as members of the political community ('citizens,' in the conventional sense) and includes, for example, aliens stopped at the border, transients incidentally in the territory, and those whom the state has disenfranchised or enslaved."[20] Thus, although animals are not citizens in the conventional sense, they arguably fit well within the scope of this definition as those that the state claims the authority to command.

This makes sense. At its heart, the rule of law is about protecting legal subjects from tyranny, not just from governments but from any parties who may hold the power to sway law to their advantage.[21] Given that animals, as subjects commanded by the state, are exposed to such risks in the same way humans are, it would seem plainly contrary to the underlying purpose of the rule of law to exclude them arbitrarily.

An example of a judicial opinion that examines animal interests from a rule-of-law perspective is the dissenting opinion of Chief Justice Fraser of the Alberta Court of Appeal in *Reece v. Edmonton*.[22] In this case, animal advocates sought a declaration that the city of Edmonton was in violation of provincial regulatory legislation governing the care of animals in relation to its solitary confinement of a thirty-six-year-old Asian elephant residing at the Edmonton Valley Zoo. In her dissenting opinion, as Maneesha Deckha has argued,[23] Chief Justice Fraser views the importance of protecting animal interests against harm at the hands of government actors as a rule-of-law matter. She states, "The significance is this. The rule of law, which forms part of the bedrock of our democracy, requires that all government action comply with the law. No one in Canada is above the law. And that includes government itself."[24] Thus, the fact that the rule-of-law interests that the plaintiffs sought to uphold were those of animals did not render the doctrine inapplicable. Rather, because the law recognizes that humans have a moral and ethical obligation to treat animals humanely, Justice Fraser considered the rule of law to be applicable.[25]

The reality is that animals were traditionally ignored in rule-of-law scholarship not because they logically fall outside of its ambit, but for an obvious historical reason. At the time rule-of-law concepts were developed, and indeed for most of history, animals simply weren't legal subjects; there was no law that protected them. Thus, there was no need to consider the compliance of animal welfare laws from a rule-of-law perspective. It wasn't until the adoption of world's first comprehensive anti-cruelty statute, the Cruel Treatment of Cattle Act ("Martin's Act") in England in 1822, which outlawed cruelty to cattle, horses, and sheep, that animals finally came within the scope of the law and, hence, within the scope of the rule of law.[26]

Indeed, Justice Palmer himself describes the ideal of the rule of law as striving to remove the *influence of particular human actors*.[27] He claims that the rule of law seeks to further justice by "invoking a Rawlsian veil of ignorance of one's particular interests in relation to its content."[28] He considers that the rule of law implies some distinctly separate or objective meaning to law that is independent of human interests: "it is law itself . . . that rules and that should rule."[29] There is nothing in this construction of the doctrine that excludes animal subjects any more than it excludes certain human subjects.

THE GENERALITY REQUIREMENT: LAW MUST NOT BE ARBITRARY

Freedom from arbitrariness is a central element of the rule of law. Lord Bingham suggests that this idea—that the laws of the land should apply equally to all, save to the extent that objective differences justify differentiation—is unlikely to "strike a modern audience as doubtful."[30] He goes on to say,

> While some special legislative provision can properly be made for some categories of people such as children, prisoners and the mentally ill, based on the peculiar characteristics of such categories, we would regard legislation directed to those with red hair (to adopt Warrington L. J.'s long-lived example) as incompatible with the rule of law . . .

> In much more recent times our law not only tolerated but imposed disabilities not rationally based on their religious beliefs on Roman Catholics, Dissenters and Jews, and disabilities not rationally connected with any aspect of their gender on women.[31]

This notion that the law must apply equally to all, save to the extent that objective differences justify differentiation, also known as the principle of generality, is widely accepted among rule-of-law scholars as fundamental. For example, while Justice Palmer offers a different conception of the rule of law from Lord Bingham, he nevertheless adopts a definition that "centers on certainty and the freedom from arbitrariness in the law."[32] Similarly, Geoffrey Walker distills the rule of law into twelve principles, including that laws be of general application to all subjects and apply equally to all.[33] Walker explains how this principle militates against the making of laws that discriminate against sections of society.[34]

Paul Gowder argues that the generality principle is "morally valuable because it is required for the state to treat subjects of law as equals."[35] In order for the state to comply with the principle of generality, government officials must use the state's coercive power only in accordance with laws that do not draw irrelevant distinctions between individuals.[36] This, he explains, is the "similarity conception of generality," which aims to police the extent to which the law classifies citizens into different groups in order to ensure that it treats like cases (and citizens) alike.[37]

APPLICABILITY OF GENERALITY PRINCIPLE TO FARMED ANIMAL WELFARE LEGISLATION

The rule of law's requirement that law be free from arbitrariness—that it apply equally to all, except to the extent that objective differences justify differentiation—raises important questions about the compatibility of animal welfare legislation with rule-of-law doctrine. The most widespread and acute problem with animal welfare legislation in many jurisdictions is that it provides for different standards of treatment for different animals based on what only can be regarded, on any rational view, as arbitrary considerations. This problem is often characterized as "speciesism"[38]—and it is a problem that is entrenched in the law. Although most countries enact legislation that prohibits animal cruelty, many jurisdictions exempt farmed animals from these laws, despite these animals constituting the vast majority of the world's domesticated animal population. These legislative carve-outs for farmed animals are explored in the following sections with reference to the legal frameworks for farmed animal welfare in the United States and New Zealand.

EXEMPTIONS FOR FARMED ANIMALS IN ANIMAL WELFARE LEGISLATION IN THE UNITED STATES

Transport and Slaughter

The legal regime governing animal welfare in the United States provides a striking example of sweeping exemptions that are not founded on rational considerations. There are two federal laws that directly regulate animal welfare—yet both exclude the vast majority of farmed animals from the protections afforded by the legislation. These exemptions have been discussed extensively by scholars elsewhere and are set out briefly here only for the purpose of examining the consistency of these exemptions with rule-of-law doctrine.

The Twenty-Eight Hour Law

The Twenty-Eight Hour Law, first enacted in 1873, regulates the transport of so-called "livestock" across US states. The rule requires that animals be provided with food, water, and five hours of rest after twenty-eight hours of consecutive travel.[39] Originally, the USDA insisted that the law did not apply to trucks, despite the fact that over 90 percent of farmed-animal transport in the United States is by truck; however, the USDA reversed its position on this issue in 2006 in response to a petition by the Humane Society of the United States.[40] Nevertheless, the act as it currently stands is extremely limited in its scope because the USDA maintains that it excludes chickens, turkeys, and other birds from coverage—despite these animals making up the vast majority of land animals transported and killed for food in the United States.[41] Furthermore, the USDA also takes the position that the act excludes fish.[42]

The Humane Methods of Slaughter Act

The Humane Methods of Slaughter Act purports to protect farmed animals from inhumane slaughter.[43] The act requires either that animals be rendered insensible to pain before they are slaughtered or that they be slaughtered under religious standards where they are not rendered insensible to pain. However, despite the fact that chickens and turkeys represent more than 98 percent of slaughtered land animals in the United States, the USDA has refused to promulgate regulations that would protect poultry from inhumane slaughter.[44] Instead, the USDA takes the position that the act does not give it authority to protect birds.[45] Similarly, the USDA has not promulgated any regulations under the act that provide for the humane slaughter of fish.[46]

Life on the Farm

Even more significant than the absence of protection for most farmed animals from cruel slaughter is the lack of protections for these animals during their lives on (mostly factory) farms. Despite the fact that 98 percent of all domesticated animals in the United States are farmed animals,[47] there are no federal laws governing the conditions in which they are raised.[48] As Cheryl Leahy puts it, there are "no federal statutes or regulations governing the way that animals are treated from the time they are born or hatched to the time they are sent off to be slaughtered."[49]

Unfortunately, state laws in most states are also of little avail. This is because most state anti-cruelty laws either exempt "commonly accepted" agricultural practices[50] or expressly exclude farmed animals from the scope of the legislation.[51] As Cheryl Leahy observes, the implications of these carve-outs are wide-reaching since routine industry practices will not be considered cruel under the law regardless of how much suffering they entail.[52] Leahy also notes how the definitions and wording of the substantive offenses further limit the scope for applying the offenses to factory farming practices.[53]

EXEMPTIONS FOR FARMED ANIMALS IN NEW ZEALAND ANIMAL WELFARE LEGISLATION

At first glance, New Zealand's regulatory regime for animal welfare looks very different from that of the United States. Whereas poultry and fish are excluded from federal legislation in the United States, New Zealand's Animal Welfare Act 1999 has a wide definition of "animal," encompassing all mammals, birds, reptiles, amphibians, fish, octopuses, squids, crabs, lobsters, and crayfish.[54] The long title of the act also acknowledges that all animals are sentient.[55]

The act also appears sweeping in the protections it provides to *all* animals. The act prohibits the ill-treatment of animals[56] and provides that animals must be provided with the "five freedoms"—one of which is the opportunity to display normal patterns of behavior.[57] Further, the Code of Welfare: Commercial Slaughter 2018 requires that all land animals be stunned so that they are immediately rendered insensible and that they be maintained in that state until death supervenes.[58] Thus, on its face, New Zealand's regulatory regime for animal welfare appears to protect farmed animals from inhumane treatment both on the farm and at slaughter.

Yet New Zealand's animal welfare regime suffers from a similar, albeit more covert, problem to the US regime: although the Animal Welfare Act 1999 prohibits the ill-treatment of (ostensibly all) animals and provides that animals must have the opportunity to display normal patterns of behavior, industry-specific "codes of welfare" promulgated under the act frequently permit factory farming practices that do not allow the animals to express normal patterns of behavior. This is despite the fact that the act requires that minimum standards in codes be the minimum necessary to ensure that the purposes of the act are met.[59] Because compliance with a code of welfare is a defense to a prosecution for ill-treatment or the failure to meet the behavioral needs of animals under the act,[60] the standards contained in codes of welfare render the protections afforded in the Animal Welfare Act 1999 meaningless for many animals.

Take farrowing crates, for example. The Animal Welfare (Pigs) Code of Welfare 2010 permitted pig farmers to confine mother pigs for five days before farrowing and for four weeks afterward.[61] In these crates, the mother pigs cannot turn around, and contact with their piglets is restricted.[62] New Zealand's National Animal Welfare Advisory Committee (NAWAC),[63] a governmental committee that is responsible for developing codes of welfare,[64] acknowledged that farrowing crates do not provide for "every behavioral need of the sows" but continued to permit their use."[65] It was only following a successful judicial review in 2020 brought by the New Zealand Animal Law Association and SAFE,[66] two animal welfare charities, that the Ministry for Primary Industries promulgated regulations for phasing out the use of farrowing crates by 2025.[67] Other practices inconsistent with the requirement that animals be permitted the opportunity to express normal patterns of behavior, such as colony cages for egg-laying hens and densely packed barns for chickens raised for meat, remain in place without any phaseout period.[68]

The act also contains an exemption clause that can operate to limit the central protections afforded by the act. Previously, a section of the act allowed codes, in "exceptional circumstances," to have minimum standards that do not fully comply with the obligations of the act.[69] However, the section was given an exceptionally wide interpretation by NAWAC and was routinely used to justify intensive confinement systems such as battery cages and sow stalls—not just in truly "exceptional circumstances."[70]

A 2015 amendment removed this loophole. However, a new exemption clause, section 183A, was enacted to replace it. The new provision allows the Ministry for Primary Industries to promulgate regulations that do not comply with the obligations of the act, including the requirement that animals be able to express natural patterns of behavior, if "any adverse effects of a change from current practices to new practices have been considered and there are no feasible or practical alternatives currently available," or if "not to do so would result in an unreasonable impact on a particular industry sector within New Zealand, a sector of the public, or New Zealand's wider economy." The provision permits noncompliant regulations to operate for up to ten years, with one right of renewal up to five years.

The prevalence of minimum standards in codes of welfare that do not fully meet the requirements of the act and the exemption clause provided by section 183A significantly limit the reach of the ostensibly progressive protections provided for New Zealand's animals. It is apparent that New Zealand's Animal Welfare Act, while providing extensive protections for non-farmed animals, may not ensure even the most basic of welfare needs for many farmed animals.

COMPATIBILITY OF FARMED ANIMAL LEGISLATION WITH THE GENERALITY PRINCIPLE OF THE RULE OF LAW

At its core, this problem of sweeping carve-outs for farmed animals can, and should, be regarded as a problem of the rule of law: animal welfare laws do not apply "equally to all, save for objective differences justifying differentiation."[71] Indeed, it is posited that animal welfare legislation in both jurisdictions—perhaps more than any other area of law—is *characterized* by arbitrariness.

Consider the exclusion for chickens in the US Humane Methods of Slaughter Act. As Bruce Friedrich and Nicholas Kristof have cogently argued, this exemption is wholly lacking in any scientific basis.[72] Rather, the science on the sentience of birds is patently clear: they feel pain just as mammals do. They are "cognitively, behaviorally, and emotionally at least as complex."[73] Friedrich notes how in numerous tests of cognitive and behavioral sophistication, chickens outperform not only cats and dogs but also four-year-old human children.[74] Yet the legislative regime fails to provide the most elementary protection any state could give its subjects: freedom from a cruel death.

Insofar as the New Zealand Animal Welfare Act is concerned, the act recognizes that *all* animals are sentient—not just companion animals. Yet the law fails to comply with the principle of generality and instead operates in a way that means that the act's most important protection—of animals' ability to express normal patterns of behavior—is not provided to many farmed animals.

Thus, in both jurisdictions, the law is not treating "like cases alike."[75] Rather, the legal regimes are tolerating what Lord Bingham would describe as "disabilities" that are not rationally connected to any aspect of the animals' species, in the same way law has recently tolerated disabilities "not rationally based on their religious beliefs on Roman Catholics, Dissenters, and Jews, and disabilities not rationally connected with any aspect of their gender on women."

Of course, some might argue that exemptions for farmed animals are fairly related to the objective of the regulation,[76] or that farmed animals are, on the basis of their particular characteristics, more akin to one of the special categories alluded to by Lord Bingham, such as children, prisoners, and the mentally ill.

Yet scholarship on the principle of generality suggests that such arguments are weak. For example, Paul Gowder defines a distinction as irrelevant if it is "not justifiable by public reasons to *all* concerned."[77] Similarly, Friedrich Hayek comments how general law can single out particular classes so long as the distinction made is *equally justifiable to those within and outside of the classes to which it applies*.[78] Clearly, exemptions for farmed animals based on people's desire to consume the animals' meat or products produced by the animals at the lowest cost may be justifiable to those outside the class to which the exemptions apply, but could not reasonably be considered justified to the classes subject to the exemptions—that is, to farmed animals themselves. Such exemptions therefore cannot reasonably be said to satisfy the "public reasons" test required for any exceptions to the principle of generality.

Indeed, the differences between pigs and dogs are hardly analogous to the differences between the categories that might justify differential treatment identified by Lord Bingham. Lord Bingham considered that children may have peculiar characteristics that justify different treatment from adults, and mentally ill adults may have peculiar characteristics that justify different treatment compared with mentally well adults.[79] But there are no such analogous differences (cognitively, behaviorally, or otherwise) between farmed animals and non-farmed animals that would justify disparate treatment in law. Rather, the difference between dogs and pigs, or even chickens and dogs, is more akin to the difference between a human subject with blond hair and a human subject with red hair, to invoke the example given by Lord Bingham again. In both cases, basing a difference in legal entitlements on such immaterial differences cannot be justified by the "public reasons" exception to the generality principle.

Importantly, the exemptions made for farmed animals in both jurisdictions are not just arbitrary but also have fatal consequences: they effectively place the vast majority of animals outside the key protections of the law. As David Wolfson has postulated, we would—rightly—regard a society in which the rule of law applied to only 2 percent of the population as lawless.[80] Consequently, as long as these sweeping exemptions for farmed animals continue to operate, the entire discipline of animal law—for all its rising prominence and scholarship—will remain, to an extent, "functionally irrelevant."[81]

REQUIREMENT THAT LAW BE APPROPRIATELY ENFORCED

Another critical element of the rule of law is enforcement. This element underpins Lord Bingham's principle that questions of legal right and liability be ordinarily resolved by application of the law and not the exercise of discretion.

In his paper "The Rule of Law and Enforcement," Justice Spigelman, former chief justice of the Supreme Court of New South Wales in Australia, emphasizes the importance of enforcement to the rule of law. He notes that laws must be enforced in a rational and fair manner if the reasonable expectations of citizens are to be realized.[82] Justice Spigelman comments,

> It is an obvious, even trite, observation to say that there can be no rule by law and, therefore, no rule of law, unless the laws are enforced in the sense of being reasonably, fairly and consistently applied to determine the actual outcome of disputes about rights and duties. . . . Without a substantial level of enforcement, the rule of law is simply devoid of meaningful content.[83]

Many other scholars underscore the importance of enforcement to the rule of law.[84] For example, in his article assessing environmental law from a rule-of-law perspective, John Cruden echoes the sentiment of Justice Spigelman in claiming that at the heart of the rule of law is enforcement, for a nation can have the best environmental laws, but such laws are "rendered meaningless" without adequate enforcement.[85]

The requirement of sufficient enforcement represents a further respect in which animal welfare legislation in both the United States and New Zealand is failing to meet rule-of-law standards.

ENFORCEMENT IN THE UNITED STATES

The limited federal farmed animal welfare legislation in the United States suffers from severe under-enforcement. Consider the Twenty-Eight Hour Law, for example. In 2011, the USDA passed a Food Safety and Inspection Service directive that requires inspection program personnel ("IPP") to inquire with establishment management regarding whether the truck driver stopped within the preceding twenty-eight hours to provide the animals rest, food, and water if the animals, upon entrance to a slaughterhouse on a transport vehicle, appear exhausted or dehydrated.[86] If the truck driver or establishment refuses to provide the information, or if the IPP believe the condition of the animals may be the result of a breach of the act, IPP are instructed to contact the Animal and Plant Health Inspection Service so that it can initiate an investigation.[87]

However, the directive is deficient in that it fails to require reporting of suspected violations of the act involving animals shipped for breeding and feeding purposes.[88] Furthermore, the treatment of animals who do not reach the threshold of appearing "dehydrated or exhausted" is not investigated.[89] Given these deficiencies, it is unlikely that the directive is strong enough to prevent the kinds of routine violations of the 28-Hour Law that were exposed in a 2005 investigation by Compassion over Killing.[90]

Similarly, the Humane Methods of Slaughter Act suffers from chronic under-enforcement. Many of these difficulties are examined by Bruce Friedrich in his article "When Regulators Refuse to Regulate: Pervasive USDA Underenforcement of the Humane Slaughter Act."[91] Friedrich highlights various examples of egregious cruelty at slaughterhouses and the evidence to suggest that such violations of the act are commonplace in American slaughterhouses.[92] He notes that the Government Accountability Office and the USDA's Office of the Inspector General have evaluated the USDA Food Safety and Inspection Service's humane slaughter oversight repeatedly since 2004, and both agencies have consistently documented significant under-enforcement of the law.[93] Furthermore, both agencies have repeatedly highlighted how many inspectors do not understand their most basic duties.[94] Friedrich concludes that the under-enforcement is so bad that the USDA inspectors "are not protecting animals from even sadistic cruelty."[95]

ENFORCEMENT IN NEW ZEALAND

Insofar as New Zealand's farmed animals are concerned, currently the government has a memorandum of understanding with the Royal New Zealand Society for the Prevention of Cruelty to Animals (RNZSPCA) whereby the RNZSPCA will investigate complaints concerning companion animal welfare and small farms, whereas the government's Ministry for Primary Industries is responsible for investigating complaints relating to larger farms (which make up the vast majority of farms in New Zealand).[96] Yet enforcement of farmed animal welfare is significantly underfunded, with the Ministry for Primary Industries employing only twenty-two full-time inspectors for over 150 million farmed animals nationwide.[97]

Unsurprisingly, with each full-time inspector being effectively responsible for enforcing the welfare of more than six million farmed animals—spanning vast geographical terrain—it is likely that the overwhelming majority of cruelty to farmed animals goes undetected, with the Ministry for Primary Industries undertaking only a handful of farmed animal welfare prosecutions each year. It is thus unsurprising that many of the most egregious known instances of farmed animal cruelty, such as the abuse of dairy cows at a Waikato slaughterhouse in 2015, have come to light not through careful investigative efforts of the Ministry for Primary Industries but rather from undercover footage filmed by animal rights activists.[98]

The Ministry for Primary Industries' inadequate enforcement of farmed animal welfare is reflective of a wider defective enforcement regime for animal welfare. Investigations of breaches of the Animal Welfare Act concerning companion animals and smaller farms are left entirely to the RNZSPCA, which funds enforcement largely from private donations, with only 25 percent of its enforcement budget coming from the New Zealand government.[99] Relying on a private charity to enforce the criminal law in this manner severely undermines the detection, investigation, and prosecution of breaches of the act.[100] As Elizabeth Ellis has argued in relation to the similar enforcement regime in Australia, the enforcement of a criminal statute by an inadequately resourced charity is entirely inconsistent with good governance and the rule of law.[101]

All legislation requires enforcement if its objective is to be sufficiently realized—this is why enforcement is so critical from a rule-of-law perspective. But there are many reasons why enforcement is particularly crucial in the context of farmed animal welfare: the fact that animals are unable to report abuse themselves and therefore rely on humans to report the abuse; the commercial context in which animal agriculture occurs, which means that farmers often may have an economic incentive to neglect the animals' well-being;[102] and the fact that the abuse generally occurs away from the public eye, inside factory farms, slaughterhouses, and trucks, which generally precludes such abuse from being detected by members of the public. Together, these factors necessitate robust enforcement, including thorough routine inspections; yet no such routine, preventative enforcement occurs in either jurisdiction. Instead, enforcement is sparse and reactionary, resulting in the object of the laws remaining unrealized.

STRATEGIC ADVANTAGES OF APPROACHING ANIMAL LAW FROM A RULE-OF-LAW PERSPECTIVE

Characterizing a central problem with animal law as arbitrariness sounds a lot like the criticism that animal law is "speciesist." Speciesism is an idea initially coined by Richard Ryder but developed and popularized by Peter Singer in his book *Animal Liberation*.[103] Singer defines speciesism as "a prejudice or attitude of bias toward the interests of members of one's own species and against those of members of other species," in a manner akin to racism or sexism.[104]

Given this overlap between the two concepts, why not just speak of speciesism? What value do rule-of-law arguments about the generality principle provide over and above speciesism?

Conceptually, there is arguably no material difference between the underlying rationale of this tenet of the rule of law and the underlying rationale of a conception of equality that shuns speciesism. In both cases, the problem pivots on unfair treatment of certain groups on the basis of arbitrary distinctions.

However, strategically, there are many reasons animal advocates might want to criticize animal welfare laws on the basis of their lack of compliance with the rule of law as opposed to their speciesist premises. First, it is about speaking the language of the legal system. Noncompliance with the rule of law reflects a legal problem; speciesism reflects a moral problem. Thus, the former problem is likely to be of much greater interest to lawyers, legislators, judges, and legal scholars than any appeal to anti-speciesism.

Second, the rule of law is a far more palatable concept to the *general public* than speciesism is—the latter remaining a controversial and at times inflammatory term. The reality is that many people are not familiar with the concept of speciesism, and among those who are, many either misunderstand or reject it. By way of contrast, as Paul Gowder writes, "everyone seems to care about the rule of law."[105] That is, even if their understanding of what exactly it entails is somewhat vague, most people (or at least many) are familiar with, and believe in, the rule of law. Indeed, one need not care about animal welfare at all to believe that laws should be free from arbitrariness and, moreover, that once enacted, laws should be appropriately enforced.

In this regard, there are many unrealized possibilities. Many scholars emphasize the need for animal advocates to collaborate with other public interest groups concerned about the negative effects that animal agriculture has on disadvantaged humans, including immigrants, low-paid workers, women, and communities of color.[106] The growing community of citizens and legal advocates concerned about the rule of law represents a further movement with which animal advocates could seek to collaborate.

The organizations that concern themselves with the promotion of the rule of law, and thus with which animal advocates could potentially collaborate, are numerous and varied. They include, among others, the World Justice Project, the United Nations, the World Bank, the American Bar Association, and the Open Society Foundations.[107] Many of these organizations host frequent conferences and events around the world dedicated to strengthening and promoting the rule of law, in which animal advocates could seek to participate.[108]

Indeed, failure to collaborate in this way at a time when the rule of law is enjoying such heightened intellectual attention from legal scholars and the wider public would be a missed opportunity. The increased focus on rule-of-law issues is present not just in news media, bar associations, and international organizations, but also in law schools and legal institutions. For example, Harvard Law School now offers courses on the rule of law and has a rule-of-law student group.[109] Thus, with the great present awareness that basic democratic and rule-of-law conventions can be easily eroded, this is an opportune time to invite reflection on one area of the law where such norms have never been present to begin with.

In fact, it is noteworthy that New Zealand has one of the highest rankings in the world in the World Justice Project's rule of law index, ranking at number 7 globally.[110] The United States also ranks relatively highly, at number 21 globally.[111] This is not surprising: both countries are advanced democracies that purport to champion the rule of law. Yet insofar as animal welfare laws are concerned, it is no exaggeration to say that both countries better resemble countries with very weak rule-of-law rankings. This, in itself, ought to compel rule-of-law scholars and activists to put animal law at the forefront of their concerns.

Ultimately, this strategy is about shifting the focus of the debate from a problem with animal welfare to a problem of democracy—and the baseline expectations we have of laws. By reframing the debate in this manner, animal advocates can expand the circle of individuals concerned about and willing to support animal law reform and efforts to ensure such laws are appropriately enforced. Furthermore, by collaborating with the community of rule-of-law activists and scholars, animal advocates may be able to learn which strategies employed to improve the rule of law as it governs human subjects may be of utility in improving problems with animal welfare legislation.

CONCLUSION

The legal regimes governing animal welfare in the United States and New Zealand are broken. They are failing to meet basic rule-of-law standards by virtue of their sweeping exemptions for farmed animals, which are based on patently arbitrary grounds. Moreover, poor enforcement of the legislation in both jurisdictions fundamentally undermines the rule of law by rendering the limited statutory protections that are provided largely illusory. Given the heightened international attention that rule-of-law principles are enjoying in the aftermath of the Trump era, animal advocates ought to consider invoking rule-of-law arguments and collaborating with rule-of-law advocates in their calls for legislative reform and better enforcement. This is, after all, an urgent project: until the legislative exclusions for farmed animals are removed and the laws are appropriately enforced, the United States and New Zealand will remain lawless societies—for many animals, at least.

REFERENCES

Animal Legal Defense Fund. "Farmed Animals and the Law." http://aldf.org/resources/advocating-for-animals/farmed-animals-and-the-law.

Bingham, Lord. "The Rule of Law." *Cambridge Law Journal* 66 (2007): 67–85.

Bingham, Tom. *The Rule of Law*. London: Penguin Books, 2010.

Brindle, Kate. "Farmed Animals in Transport: An Analysis of the Twenty-Eight Hour Law and Recommendations for Greater Animal Welfare." Michigan State College of Law Student Scholarship, 2016.

Burrows, Matt. "SPCA List of Shame 2021: New Zealand's ten worst animal cruelty cases of the last year exposed," 2021. https://www.newshub.co.nz/home/new-zealand/2021/02/spca-list-of-shame-2021-new-zealand-s-ten-worst-animal-cruelty-cases-of-the-last-year-exposed.html.

Cassuto, David. "What Use Animal Law?" *Animal Blawg*, March 26, 2009. https://animalblawg.wordpress.com/2009/03/26/what-use-animal-law/.

Compassion over Killing. "Farm Animal Transport Cruelty Investigation." http://cok.net/inv/farm-animal-transport/.

Coumbe, Gillian. "Beyond Charlotte's Web—The Blight of Factory Farming: An Argument for Law Reform." Presentation at the Auckland Women Lawyers' Association seminar "Female of the Species: Women in Animal Law," Auckland, March 5, 2015.

Cowdery, Nicholas, and Adrian Lipscomb. "The Just Rule of Law." *Southern Cross University Law Review* 4 (2000): 1–16.

Cruden, John. "The Work of the Department of Justice Environment and Natural Resources Division: Promoting Environmental Rule of Law and the Advancement of Sustainable Development Goals." *South Carolina Journal of International Law and Business* 12, no. 2 (2016).

Deckha, Maneesha. "Initiating a Non-Anthropocentric Jurisprudence: The Rule of Law and Animal Vulnerability under a Property Paradigm." *Alberta Law Review* 50 (2013).

Democracy Web. "Rule of Law: History." http://democracyweb.org/rule-of-law-history.

Duffield, Danielle. "The Enforcement of Animal Welfare Offences and the Viability of an Infringement Regime as a Strategy for Reform." *New Zealand Universities Law Review* 25 (2013).

———. "Reputation, Regulatory Capture and Reform: The Case of New Zealand's Bobby Calves." *Animal Law* 26, no. 2 (2020).

Duffield, Danielle, and M. B. Rodriguez Ferrere. "*New Zealand Animal Law Association v Attorney General*: New Zealand's Most Significant Animal Law

Case in a Generation." *New Zealand Universities Law Review* 29, no. 3 (June 2021).

Ellis, Elizabeth. "Making Sausages & Law: The Failure of Animal Welfare Laws to Protect Both Animals and the Fundamental Tenets of Australia's Legal System." *Australian Animal Protection Law Journal* 4 (2010).

Ferrere, Marcelo Rodriguez, Mike King, and Levi Mros Larsen. *Animal Welfare in New Zealand: Oversight, Compliance, and Enforcement*. 2019.

Final Report on Complaint about Animal Welfare (Layer Hens) Code of Welfare 2005. Report of the Regulations Review Committee, May 2006. https://www.parliament.nz/resource/mi-NZ/48DBSCH_SCR3418_1/e12726b855181ef2b22a8013097f519fc3870b17.

Frasch, Pamela, Katherine Hessler, Sarah Kutil, and Sonia Waisman, eds. *Animal Law in a Nutshell*. St. Paul, MN: Thomson Reuters, 2011.

Friedrich, Bruce. "Still in the Jungle: Poultry Slaughter and the USDA." *New York University Environmental Law Journal* 23 (2015).

———. "When Regulators Refuse to Regulate: Pervasive USDA Underenforcement of the Humane Slaughter Act." *Georgetown Law Journal* 104 (2015).

Fuchs, Michael H. "An Open Door to Anarchy." *US News & World Report*, August 31, 2017. https://www.usnews.com/opinion/world-report/articles/2017-08-31/donald-trumps-assault-on-rule-of-law-is-our-biggest-threat.

Goodfellow, Jed. "Animal Welfare Law Enforcement: To Punish or Persuade." In *Animal Law in Australasia*, 2nd ed., edited by Peter Sankoff, Steven White, and Celeste Black. Sydney: Federated Press, 2013.

Gowder, Paul. *The Rule of Law in the Real World*. New York: Cambridge University Press, 2016.

Kristof, Nicholas. "Are Chicks Brighter than Babies?" *New York Times*, October 19, 2013. http://www.nytimes.com/2013/10/20/opinion/sunday/are-chicks-brighter-than-babies.html.

Leahy, Cheryl. "Large-Scale Farmed Animal Abuse and Neglect: Law and Its Enforcement." *Journal of Animal Law and Ethics* 4 (2011).

Levenda, Kelly. "Legislation to Protect the Welfare of Fish." *Animal Law Review* 20 (2013): 119–44.

Lovvorn, Jonathan. "Climate Change Beyond Environmentalism Part II: New Options for Near-Term Climate Mitigation in a Post-Regulatory Era." *Georgetown International Environmental Law Review* 30 (2018).

Menzies, James. "USDA Clarifies 28-Hour Law for Livestock Transporters." *Truck News*, November 1, 2006. https://www.trucknews.com/features/usda-clarifies-28-hour-law-for-livestock-transporters/.

Palmer, Matthew. "Assessing the Strength of the Rule of Law in New Zealand." Paper presented to the New Zealand Centre for Public Law Conference, "Unearthing New Zealand's Constitutional Traditions," Wellington, New Zealand, August 2013.

Schmidt, Kari, Danielle Duffield, Marcelo Rodriguez Ferrere, and Andrew Knight. *Farmed Animal Welfare Law in New Zealand: Investigating the Gap between the Animal Welfare Act 1999 and Its Delegated Legislation*. New Zealand Animal

Law Association, February 2021. https://nzala.org/w/wp-content/uploads/2021/02/NZALA_Farmed_Animal_Report.pdf.

Shklar, Judith N. "Political Theory and the Rule of Law." In *The Rule of Law: Ideal or Ideology*, edited by Allan C. Hutcheson and Patrick Monahan. Toronto: Carswell, 1987.

Singer, Peter. *Animal Liberation: A New Ethics for Our Treatment of Animals*. New York: Random House, 1975.

Spigelman, James. "The Rule of Law and Enforcement." *UNSW Law Journal* 26 (2003): 200.

Strongman, Susan. "Animal Welfare and the Law." *Wireless* (New Zealand), June 30, 2017. http://thewireless.co.nz/articles/animal-welfare-and-the-law.

Waisman, Sonia S., Pamela D. Frasch, and Bruce A. Wagman, eds. *Animal Law: Cases and Materials*. 5th ed. Durham, NC: Carolina Academic Press, 2014.

Waldron, Jeremy. "Is the Rule of Law an Essentially Contested Concept (in Florida)?" *Law & Philosophy* 21 (2002): 139.

Wells, N. *Animal Law in New Zealand*. Wellington, New Zealand: Brookers, 2011.

Wolfson, David, and Mariann Sullivan. "Foxes in the Hen House—Animals, Agribusiness, and the Law: A Modern American Fable." In *Animal Rights: Current Debates and New Directions*, edited by Cass R. Sunstein and Martha C. Nussbaum. Oxford: Oxford University Press, 2004.

World Justice Project. *World Justice Project Rule of Law Index 2020*.

NOTES

1. *Reece v. Edmonton (City)*, 2011 ABCA 238, at footnote 6.

2. *Democracy Web*, "Rule of Law: History," http://democracyweb.org/rule-of-law-history (accessed 21 February 2022).

3. See, for example, Michael H. Fuchs, "An Open Door to Anarchy," *US News & World Report*, August 31, 2017, https://www.usnews.com/opinion/world-report/articles/2017-08-31/donald-trumps-assault-on-rule-of-law-is-our-biggest-threat.

4. Judith N. Shklar, "Political Theory and the Rule of Law," in *The Rule of Law: Ideal or Ideology*, ed. Allan C. Hutcheson and Patrick Monahan (Toronto: Carswell, 1987), 1.

5. Jeremy Waldron, "Is the Rule of Law an Essentially Contested Concept (in Florida)?," *Law & Philosophy* 21 (2002): 139.

6. Brian Z. Tamanaha, *On the Rule of Law: History, Politics, Theory* (Cambridge: Cambridge University Press, 2004), 114.

7. For example, New Zealand High Court Judge Matthew Palmer makes this comment in relation to New Zealand. See Matthew Palmer, "Assessing the Strength of the Rule of Law in New Zealand" (paper presented to the New Zealand Centre for Public Law Conference on "Unearthing New Zealand's Constitutional Traditions," Wellington, August 2013), 1.

8. Tamanaha, *On the Rule of Law*, 7.

9. Tamanaha, *On the Rule of Law*, 8.

10. Tamanaha, *On the Rule of Law*, 8.
11. Tamanaha, *On the Rule of Law*, 9.
12. Tamanaha, *On the Rule of Law*, 9.
13. Tamanaha, *On the Rule of Law*, 11.
14. Tamanaha, *On the Rule of Law*, 15.
15. Tamanaha, *On the Rule of Law*, 24.
16. Tom Bingham, *The Rule of Law* (London: Penguin Books, 2010), 37.
17. Palmer, "Assessing the Strength," 7.
18. Palmer, "Assessing the Strength," 7.
19. Paul Gowder, *The Rule of Law in the Real World* (New York: Cambridge University Press, 2016), 7.
20. Gowder, *Rule of Law*, 11.
21. For example, Tamanaha writes of how in Ancient Greece, the rule of law aimed to protect against populist tyranny, which could be as tyrannical as absolute monarchies. Tamanaha, *On the Rule of Law*, 8.
22. *Reece v. Edmonton (City)*, 2011 ABCA 238.
23. This article represents one of the few pieces of legal scholarship that invokes rule-of-law scholarship in the context of animal law and its enforcement. See Maneesha Deckha, "Initiating a Non-Anthropocentric Jurisprudence: The Rule of Law and Animal Vulnerability under a Property Paradigm," *Alberta Law Review* 50 (2013): 797–98.
24. *Reece*, 2011 ABCA 238, at [41].
25. See *Reece*, 2011 ABCA 238, at [42].
26. Cruel Treatment of Cattle Act 1822 (UK), 2 Geo IV c. 71. See N. Wells, *Animal Law in New Zealand* (Wellington, New Zealand: Brookers, 2011), 50.
27. Palmer, "Assessing the Strength," 7.
28. Palmer, "Assessing the Strength," 7.
29. Palmer, "Assessing the Strength," 6.
30. Lord Bingham, "The Rule of Law," *Cambridge Law Journal* 66 (2007): 73.
31. Bingham, "Rule of Law," 73.
32. Palmer, "Assessing the Strength," 6.
33. Cited in Nicholas Cowdery and Adrian Lipscomb, "The Just Rule of Law," *Southern Cross University Law Review* 4 (2000): 12.
34. Cowdery and Lipscomb, "Just Rule of Law," 12.
35. Gowder, *Rule of Law*, 7.
36. Gowder, *Rule of Law*, 28.
37. Gowder, *Rule of Law*, 31.
38. The concept of speciesism, and its overlap with rule of law principles, is discussed in more detail as this essay continues.
39. Transportation of Animals, 49 U.S.C. § 80502.
40. Sonia S. Waisman, Pamela D. Frasch, and Bruce A. Wagman, eds., *Animal Law: Cases and Materials*, 5th ed. (Durham, NC: Carolina Academic Press, 2014), 378. Also see James Menzies, "USDA Clarifies 28-Hour Law for Livestock Transporters," *Truck News*, November 1, 2006, https://www.trucknews.com/features/usda-clarifies-28-hour-law-for-livestock-transporters/.

41. The Supreme Court of New York agreed with the USDA's interpretation in *Clay v. New York Cent R.R. Co.*, 231 N.Y.S. 424, 424 (N.Y. App. Div. 1928), cited in Waisman et al., *Animal Law*, 378.

42. Letter from W. Ron DeHaven, Administrator, U.S. Dept. of Agriculture, Animal & Plant Health Inspection Service, to Peter A. Brandt, Attorney, Humane Society of the U.S., Response to Petition for Rulemaking 1 (September 22, 2006), cited in Kelly Levenda, "Legislation to Protect the Welfare of Fish," *Animal Law Review* 20 (2013), 129.

43. 7 U.S.C. § 1901 et seq. The Federal Meat Inspection Act, 21 U.S.C. § 601 et seq., also requires that all slaughterhouses comply with the standards for humane handling and slaughter of animals set out in the Humane Methods of Slaughter Act of 1958.

44. See Bruce Friedrich, "Still in the Jungle: Poultry Slaughter and the USDA," *New York University Environmental Law Journal* 23 (2015): 245. Also see USDA, "Humane Methods of Slaughter Act," https://www.nal.usda.gov/awic/humane-methods-slaughter-act.

45. Friedrich, "Still in the Jungle," 245.

46. Levenda, "Legislation to Protect."

47. David Wolfson and Mariann Sullivan, "Foxes in the Hen House—Animals, Agribusiness, and the Law: A Modern American Fable," in *Animal Rights: Current Debates and New Directions*, ed. Cass R. Sunstein and Martha C. Nussbaum (Oxford: Oxford University Press, 2004), 206.

48. See Cheryl Leahy, "Large-Scale Farmed Animal Abuse and Neglect: Law and Its Enforcement," *Journal of Animal Law and Ethics* 4 (2011): 63.

49. Leahy, "Large-Scale Farmed Animal Abuse," 75.

50. For a discussion of these exemptions, see Pamela Frasch et al., eds., *Animal Law in a Nutshell* (St. Paul, MN: Thomson Reuters, 2011), 290. Also see Animal Legal Defense Fund, "Farmed Animals and the Law," http://aldf.org/resources/advocating-for-animals/farmed-animals-and-the-law/.

51. See, for example, Ohio Rev. Code Ann. § 959.131, which defines "companion animal" to exclude "livestock" or "wild" animals. Only a few states, such as California and New York, have anti-cruelty statutes that appear to include farmed animals within the scope of the statutes. See Frasch et al., *Animal Law in a Nutshell*, 290.

52. Leahy, "Large-Scale Farmed Animal Abuse," 77–78.

53. Leahy, "Large-Scale Farmed Animal Abuse," 78. For completeness, it is worth noting that the Animal Welfare Act, 7 U.S.C.A. §§ 2131–2159, which regulates animals used for research, experimental, or exhibition purposes or for holding them for sale as "pets," expressly excludes animals used for food from its coverage.

54. Animal Welfare Act 1999 (NZ), sec. 2.

55. Animal Welfare Act 1999 (NZ), long title.

56. Animal Welfare Act 1999 (NZ), sec. 29(a).

57. Animal Welfare Act 1999 (NZ), secs. 4 and 10.

58. Animal Welfare (Commercial Slaughter) Code of Welfare 2018, Minimum Standards 6, 12, and 15. An exception is made for shechita slaughter of chickens.

59. See Animal Welfare Act 1999 (NZ), at sec. 73(1).

60. Secs. 13(2)(c) and 30(2)(c).

61. The Animal Welfare (Pigs) Code of Welfare 2010, Minimum Standard 10.

62. See *New Zealand Animal Law Association v. Attorney-General* [2020] NZHC 3009 at [36].

63. See Ministry for Primary Industries, "National Animal Welfare Advisory Committee," https://www.mpi.govt.nz/protection-and-response/animal-welfare/overview/national-animal-welfare-advisory-committee/.

64. See Ministry for Primary Industries, "NAWAC Members," https://www.mpi.govt.nz/protection-and-response/animal-welfare/overview/national-animal-welfare-advisory-committee/nawac-members/.

65. See *New Zealand Animal Law Association v. Attorney-General* [2020] NZHC 3009 at [54].

66. *New Zealand Animal Law Association v. Attorney-General* [2020] NZHC 3009.

67. See Animal Welfare (Care and Procedures) Amendment Regulations (No. 2) 2020.

68. See Kari Schmidt et al., *Farmed Animal Welfare Law in New Zealand: Investigating the Gap between the Animal Welfare Act 1999 and Its Delegated Legislation*, New Zealand Animal Law Association, February 2021, https://nzala.org/w/wp-content/uploads/2021/02/NZALA_Farmed_Animal_Report.pdf; Gillian Coumbe, "Beyond Charlotte's Web—The Blight of Factory Farming: An Argument for Law Reform" (presentation at the Auckland Women Lawyers' Association seminar "Female of the Species: Women in Animal Law," Auckland, March 5, 2015) [13]; Danielle Duffield and M. B. Rodriguez Ferrere, "*New Zealand Animal Law Association v Attorney General*: New Zealand's Most Significant Animal Law Case in a Generation," *New Zealand Universities Law Review* 29, no. 3 (June 2021): 243.

69. Animal Welfare Act 1999 (NZ) as at March 26, 2015, sec. 73(3).

70. See *Final Report on Complaint about Animal Welfare (Layer Hens) Code of Welfare 2005* (Report of the Regulations Review Committee, May 2006), https://www.parliament.nz/resource/mi-NZ/48DBSCH_SCR3418_1/e12726b855181ef2b22a8013097f519fc3870b17. See also Duffield and Rodriguez Ferrere, "New Zealand's Most Significant Animal Law Case," 238.

71. Palmer, "Assessing the Strength," 5.

72. See Friedrich, "Still in the Jungle," 251; and Nicholas Kristof, "Are Chicks Brighter than Babies?," *New York Times*, October 19, 2013, http://www.nytimes.com/2013/10/20/opinion/sunday/are-chicks-brighter-than-babies.html.

73. Friedrich, "Still in the Jungle," 251.

74. Friedrich, "Still in the Jungle," 251.

75. Gowder, *Rule of Law*, 31.

76. Lord Bingham stated, "There is, I think, profound truth in the observation of Justice Jackson in the Supreme Court of the United States in 1949: regard it as a salutary doctrine that cities, states and the Federal Government must exercise their powers so as not to discriminate between their inhabitants except upon some reasonable differentiation fairly related to the object of regulation." Bingham, "Rule of Law," 75.

77. Gowder, *Rule of Law*, 7.

78. Cited in Gowder, *Rule of Law*, 29.

79. See Bingham, "Rule of Law," 73.

80. See David Cassuto, "What Use Animal Law?," *Animal Blawg*, March 26, 2009, https://animalblawg.wordpress.com/2009/03/26/what-use-animal-law/.

81. See Cassuto, "What Use Animal Law?"

82. James Spigelman, "The Rule of Law and Enforcement," *UNSW Law Journal* 26 (2003): 203.

83. Spigelman, "Rule of Law and Enforcement," 202.

84. For example, Nicholas Cowdery comments that there must be institutions and procedures that are capable of expeditiously enforcing the law. See Cowdery and Lipscomb, "Just Rule of Law," 12.

85. John Cruden, "The Work of the Department of Justice Environment and Natural Resources Division: Promoting Environmental Rule of Law and the Advancement of Sustainable Development Goals," *South Carolina Journal of International Law and Business* 12, no. 2 (2016): 153.

86. Kate Brindle, "Farmed Animals in Transport: An Analysis of the Twenty-Eight Hour Law and Recommendations for Greater Animal Welfare" (Michigan State College of Law Student Scholarship, 2016), 7.

87. Brindle, "Farmed Animals in Transport," 7.

88. Brindle, "Farmed Animals in Transport," 8.

89. Brindle, "Farmed Animals in Transport," 8.

90. See Compassion over Killing, "Farm Animal Transport Cruelty Investigation," http://cok.net/inv/farm-animal-transport/.

91. Bruce Friedrich, "When Regulators Refuse to Regulate: Pervasive USDA Underenforcement of the Humane Slaughter Act," *Georgetown Law Journal* 104 (2015): 197.

92. Friedrich, "When Regulators Refuse to Regulate," 205–7.

93. Friedrich, "When Regulators Refuse to Regulate," 204.

94. Friedrich, "When Regulators Refuse to Regulate," 204.

95. Friedrich, "When Regulators Refuse to Regulate," 207.

96. Julie Collins Audit Report: Delivery of Animal Welfare Services by the Waikato Branch of the RNZSPCA (Ministry of Agriculture, Biosecurity, December 14, 2004), 1.2.4.

97. See Marcelo Rodriguez Ferrere, Mike King, and Levi Mros Larsen, *Animal Welfare in New Zealand: Oversight, Compliance, and Enforcement* (University of Otago, 2019): 11, https://ourarchive.otago.ac.nz/handle/10523/9276; and Danielle Duffield, "Reputation, Regulatory Capture and Reform: The Case of New Zealand's Bobby Calves," *Animal Law* 26, no. 2 (2020): 20.

98. See *Erickson v Ministry for Primary Industries*, [2017] NZCA 271.

99. See Matt Burrows "SPCA List of Shame 2021: New Zealand's ten worst animal cruelty cases of the last year exposed" *Newshub* (23 February 2021), https://www.newshub.co.nz/home/new-zealand/2021/02/spca-list-of-shame-2021-new-zealand-s-ten-worst-animal-cruelty-cases-of-the-last-year-exposed.html.

100. See Danielle Duffield, "The Enforcement of Animal Welfare Offences and the Viability of an Infringement Regime as a Strategy for Reform," *New Zealand Universities Law Review* 25 (2013): 897.

101. Ellis comments on how the Australian government provides only a very small level of funding to the Australian RSPCA and how this significantly limits the number of animal cruelty cases that are prosecuted. See Elizabeth Ellis, "Making Sausages & Law: The Failure of Animal Welfare Laws to Protect Both Animals and the Fundamental Tenets of Australia's Legal System," *Australian Animal Protection Law Journal* 4 (2010): 24.

102. See Jed Goodfellow, "Animal Welfare Law Enforcement: To Punish or Persuade," in *Animal Law in Australasia*, 2nd ed., ed. Peter Sankoff, Steven White, and Celeste Black (Sydney: Federated Press, 2013), 199–202.

103. Peter Singer, *Animal Liberation: A New Ethics for Our Treatment of Animals* (New York: Random House, 1975).

104. Singer, *Animal Liberation*, 7.

105. Gowder, *Rule of Law*, 1.

106. For example, Jonathan Lovvorn argues that animal advocates ought to collaborate with environmentalists and other public interest groups on climate change advocacy strategies targeting consumers, corporations, and courts, given that animals and disadvantaged humans will be most harmed by the negative effects of climate change. See Jonathan Lovvorn, "Climate Change Beyond Environmentalism Part II: New Options for Near-Term Climate Mitigation in a Post-Regulatory Era," *Georgetown International Environmental Law Review* 30 (2018).

107. Gowder, *Rule of Law*, 2.

108. See, for example, World Justice Project, "Events," https://worldjusticeproject.org/our-work/engagement/events.

109. See "HLS Rule of Law," https://orgs.law.harvard.edu/ruleoflaw/.

110. See World Justice Project, *World Justice Project Rule of Law Index 2020*, at 16.

111. World Justice Project, *Rule of Law Index 2020*, at 16.

Chapter 16

Africa: Crimes against Nonhumanity? The Case of the African Elephant

By Ruaidhrí D. Wilson

In recent years, a growing movement has argued that certain cognitively complex nonhuman animals should be recognized as individual legal "persons," as opposed to "things." Legal arguments for nonhuman personhood have been put forward on behalf of individual great apes, cetaceans, and elephants held in captivity. However, the logical moral and ethical implications of accepting such arguments, particularly with regard to free-living animal populations of cognitively complex species, have so far not been widely considered. If the individual members of a certain species have personhood, this raises the question of whether collectively such a species should be considered a people. Given the threatened nature of many of the candidates for nonhuman personhood, the implications of this are interesting and potentially extremely far-reaching, particularly when considering how we should conceptualize acts of collective violence against them.

The first part of this chapter summarizes the case for rights for nonhuman persons. The second part explores how acts of collective violence against nonhuman persons should be conceptualized in light of this. Taking the case of the African elephant as an example, this discussion gives special consideration to the unique and interconnected nature of individual elephants, their personhood, and the systematic nature of the violence against elephants. Existing conceptual frameworks of ecocide or specicide do not capture the collective suffering of elephants. This chapter proposes instead that the destruction of elephant populations be viewed as a crime against nonhumanity.

NONHUMAN PERSONHOOD

Conceptual Moral Framework

This discussion begins with the simple utilitarian premise that pain and suffering are bad, and therefore prevention or reduction of pain and suffering is good. The most relevant question is not "Are nonhumans rational or intelligent?" but "Can they suffer?" The philosopher Peter Singer argues that all animals are equal, and their interests should be given equal consideration.[1] This position is readily misinterpreted, and it is important to be clear that equal consideration of interests is not the same as equal interests. Singer is suggesting not that nonhumans and humans are the same, but rather that *pain is pain* irrespective of who is experiencing it. The reason it may be acceptable to treat different species differently is not because their pain does not matter but rather because not all animals have the same *capacity* for pain.

Steven Wise, of the Nonhuman Rights Project (NhRP), takes a narrower approach in which he concedes that because it is the role of the moral philosopher to determine what is right, Singer represents an ideal. However, as a lawyer Wise aims to work within existing legal frameworks, placing the emphasis on whether nonhumans have autonomy, a property that is recognized by common law judges, rather than on their capacity to suffer.[2] In practice these two positions are broadly aligned since autonomy and self-awareness may bring with them a greater capacity for suffering.

What Is a Person?

What is it to be a human? Or more importantly for this discussion, what is it about humans that makes them persons?

There is no universal agreement on when humans either attain or relinquish personhood. The Catholic Church, among other schools of Christian thought, holds that personhood begins from the moment of conception. Many Islamic scholars have contended that "ensoulment," and with it personhood, occurs at four months' gestation.[3] Various milestones in embryonic and fetal development also have been proposed, such as the development of the heart, movement, and brain activity.[4] In English law as well as US law, fetuses are not recognized as persons until the moment of birth; nonetheless, there are still limitations on abortions and gray areas as to whether a fetus can be a victim of a crime such as murder.[5] Equally, legal gray areas associated with implicit personhood can be found at the other end of human life, such as when a human enters a coma or a persistent vegetative state. Depending on the nature of the condition and the jurisdiction, the decision to either continue or end life support may be made by a medical professional or require a decision from the courts.[6] What is constant in all of these places, times, cultures, and stages of life is that the boundaries of personhood are ultimately arbitrary. In turn this means that in certain circumstances humans who exhibit few or even none of the characteristics we associate with personhood are nonetheless recognized as persons, while nonhumans who do exhibit such traits are still excluded.

A trait often cited as relevant to human personhood is "intelligence."[7] This is seemingly reasonable enough. Intelligence is, after all, something that can broadly be measured, if not exactly quantified. The arts, written language, industrialization, life-extending biomedicine, and the exploration of our solar system—all are testimony to the unique brilliance of humanity. However, with regard to rights, all are equally irrelevant. Under the Universal Declaration of Human Rights, *all* humans—whatever their abilities—are, in principle, afforded the same fundamental rights.[8] Once we accept that the achievements we associate with intelligence do not in themselves bring entitlement, then we must apply this consistently. As Singer succinctly puts it, "if possessing a higher degree of intelligence does not entitle one human to use another for his or her own ends, how can it entitle humans to exploit non-humans?"[9]

Nonetheless, what is broadly termed "intelligence" may be connected with other attributes that are indeed relevant to the concept of personhood. Intelligence gives us our sense of self, gives us awareness of our own existence and mortality, and enables the complex social structures of human society and the ability of people to form strong social bonds. The origins of human behavior can be understood within the context of evolutionary biology, and therefore it would be expected that these attributes existed in some proto-form in our earlier ancestors. This is something that the fossil record has corroborated—our own evolutionary ancestors lived in social groups, collaborated, and developed tools for at least the last two million years.[10] It is no great leap of logic to then consider whether such characteristics might also exist in some form amid our near-relatives or, through a process of convergent evolution, in other intelligent, social, and emotional species. Indeed, there is an ever-growing body of zoological knowledge demonstrating that many behaviors—symbolic communication, tool use, reciprocal altruism—once thought to be uniquely human are not. Furthermore, almost no behaviors that are uniquely human are universal to all humans.

Why Do Humans Get Rights? (And Why Don't Nonhumans?)

This issue of rights is inextricably tied to personhood, given that only legal persons hold rights, and ideas around rights are rooted in the evolution of morality and ethics. Broadly, human rights exist as a result of a general recognition (rooted in a capacity for empathy) that humans have the capacity to suffer. Ethics has developed beyond this recognition into a system of rules and practices aimed at ensuring protection, consistency, and mutual benefit.[11] Legal rights are effectively a further codification of this behavior. However, this does not explain why in many contemporary legal systems rights are universal to all humans and yet exclusive of all other beings.

Wise has argued that effectively, humans get rights because they are human. He cites the example of a human baby born with only a brain stem, with no consciousness, no sentience, and no possibility of developing either. Yet, Wise notes, most of us would be horrified by the notion that it would be morally acceptable to harm this baby. Thus, in legal terms it may be useful that anything with human form should get rights, and in moral terms this precautionary approach is sensible (and enshrined in medical science through the principle of *Primum non nocere*). However, Wise contends that affording rights simply on the basis of form is irrational, commenting, "Why is a human individual with no cognitive abilities whatsoever a legal person with rights, while cognitively complex beings such as Tommy [a chimpanzee], or a dolphin, or an orca are things with no rights at all?"[12]

If this is indeed inconsistent and irrational, then how *should* differentiation between species be looked at? In many cases there is a straightforward and clear-cut division—humans have a central nervous system; oysters do not have such a system or even a brain, and consequently, as far as we are able to tell, oysters do not experience pain, and even Singer excludes them from moral concern.[13] But the capacity to experience physical or emotional pain varies among species. Fish appear to experience physical pain, and studies on zebra fish have shown that they will seek analgesic treatment if subjected to a painful stimulus.[14] However, distress and suffering may not always be physical, and for complex social animals the possibility for emotional harm also must be considered. Herd mammals such as cows show clear signs of distress when separated from their social group, which is standard practice for weaning calves.[15] These interlinked social structures add a layer of complexity when it comes to considering suffering. In assessments of the harm resulting from trauma to one individual animal, the emotional impact on the whole group must be considered. Highly social, interconnected, and empathic persons are not interchangeable. To kill one is to kill someone unique, and something unique is lost for the others who remain.

Further complexity emerges when we consider beings who may be self-aware because this holds profound implications in terms of personhood and, in turn, rights. Chan and Harris cite a philosophical tradition dating back to John Locke that places self-awareness at the center of personhood. If a being is aware of their own existence, they can place a value on that existence, and accordingly, to deprive them of that is to deprive them of something of value.[16] Since careful empirical research has revealed that great apes, cetaceans, corvids, parrots, and elephants appear to have a degree of self-awareness, episodic memory, and a capacity to consider the future, their personhood becomes a practical and not hypothetical question.

Can Animals Be People Too?

We have seen here that those aspects of intelligence and cognition that underpin a capacity for self-awareness and an interest in one's own existence are relevant to the question of personhood. In 2014 members of Argentina's Association of Professional Lawyers for Animal Rights (AFADA) successfully argued that on account of her probable cognitive capabilities, an orangutan named Sandra should be legally considered not an object but rather a "non-human person."[17] The case was a legal first and could set a precedent for the extension of rights not only for other great apes, but also for other sentient animals with advanced cognitive capabilities.

This demonstrates an evenhanded allocation of rights with qualifying criteria based not on form but on nature. If a being exhibits key characteristics of personhood—advanced cognitive capabilities, complex interconnected social structures, and above all autonomy and a sense of self, are not they too worthy of protection? Logically, the answer to this question, at least in principle, must be yes, they are, and practically, the question has been taken up by the NhRP, which has focused its efforts in the United States to try to obtain bodily liberty for a series of chimpanzees.

Legal technicalities often have prevented the merits of NhRP cases from being fully examined in court. However, in 2015, the NhRP filed for a writ of habeas corpus on behalf of Tommy, a circus chimpanzee housed alone in a warehouse, claiming Tommy was autonomous, intelligent, and self-aware. The New York State Appellate Court did not recognize Tommy as a person. The court found that "so far as legal theory is concerned, a person is any being whom the law regards as capable of rights and duties. Unlike human beings, chimpanzees cannot bear any legal duties, submit to [human] societal responsibilities or be held accountable for their actions."[18]

Even the most cursory examination of how and when human rights are afforded shows that the argument that they are always contingent on duties is fundamentally flawed. Many humans—including infants and those affected by a serious traumatic brain injury or degenerative neurological condition—do not have the capabilities to bear any legal duties. The court attempted to address this by stating that "collectively" humans are uniquely able to bear duties. Subsequently, Wise has noted that to afford rights to all members of a collective based on the abilities of some individuals is circular reasoning and asks why the grouping should be of humans and not of, say, great apes.[19]

The definition of a person that the court cited in its decision was taken from *Black's Dictionary of Law*. However, given the obviously problematic nature of having personhood linked to rights *and* duties, the NhRP investigated further and found that the definition was based on a single source—the tenth edition of Sir John Salmond's *Jurisprudence*, published in 1947. Upon viewing the original text defining personhood, the NhRP found that it in fact read "rights *or* duties." When informed, *Black's Dictionary of Law* subsequently issued a correction.[20] Although the NhRP was subsequently denied leave to appeal, once again on a technicality, New York Court of Appeals judge Eugene M. Fahey concluded, "While it may be arguable that a chimpanzee is not a 'person,' there is no doubt that it is not merely a thing."[21]

Yet if nonhumans are deserving of personhood and with it at least the most basic of rights—bodily liberty, freedom from torture, and the right to life—this raises profound moral questions about humanity's treatment of these species, no more so than in the case of the African elephant.

Cognitive and Emotional Capabilities of Elephants

Elephants have extraordinary cognitive and emotional lives. It is an old adage that an elephant never forgets, and their extraordinary ability to recall migratory routes, recognize individuals, and find specific watering holes or feeding sites in different years is well documented. Neurological study has shown that in an African elephant the hippocampus accounts for 0.7 percent of the total brain mass, making the region proportionally larger than in humans, where the hippocampus accounts for 0.5 percent.[22] The hippocampus is associated with long-term memory, especially spatial memory. One exciting area of research concerns the nature of spindle neurons, also known as von Economo neurons. The neurons are relatively large and have only a single dendrite—the part of the neuron that receives signals—whereas other types of neuron have many dendrites. The purpose of this structure may be to allow the rapid communication of information across a relatively large brain. A high number of such neurons are found in the human brain, but they also have been found in other species—including great apes, a number of cetaceans including orca whales, and elephants.[23] Despite these three groups having diverged tens of millions of years ago, elements of the neurological structures of these animals show some remarkable commonality with each other. Spindle neurons are associated with spatial awareness—something elephants, and indeed many cetaceans, show an extraordinary sense of, as demonstrated by their impressive navigational abilities. These neurons are also found in the dorsolateral prefrontal cortex of both the human and elephant brain, an area that is thought to play a crucial role in executive functions, including working memory, planning, inhibition, and abstract reasoning. Most significantly for this discussion, they are found in the anterior cingulate cortex of elephant species, an area of the brain that plays a central role in emotion and self-awareness.[24]

Historically, our understanding of elephant communication has been hampered because their infrasonic vocalizations are outside the range of human hearing. But recent spectrographic analysis has enabled an unprecedented insight into the complexities of elephant communications, showing many language-like structures, including specific alarm calls for different threats, such as bees or humans.[25]

Outside of controlled study, the elephant's sense of self seemingly manifests in more complex behaviors. Perhaps most remarkably, elephants appear to have a sense of death that is in many ways comparable to our own. Cynthia Moss recorded multiple such instances during her extensive fourteen-year study of elephants in Amboseli National Park. Following a death within a family group, the members of the group exhibit mourning-like behavior—often standing vigil over the bodies of their dead as well as covering the body with earth and branches.[26] Iain Douglas-Hamilton, one of the first Western scientists to extensively study elephant behavior, though initially skeptical, was left in little doubt that elephants experience something similar to grief.[27] To suggest as much about a nonhuman is to commit one of the cardinal sins of ethology—anthropomorphism, the projection of human characteristics onto animals. Yet Frans de Waal counters that to ignore such similarities is "anthropodenial," which he describes as "a blindness to the humanlike characteristics of other animals, or the animal-like characteristics of ourselves."[28] The question this raises is whether anthropomorphism is really the most likely explanation, or rather, are the behaviors observed by scientists such as Douglas-Hamilton and Moss signs of real emotions? An elephant's experience of joy and sadness may not be the same as our own, but just the fact that we cannot explain nonhuman emotion does not mean that the emotion does not exist. Indeed, we cannot fully explain, let alone quantify, human emotion, yet its existence is not in question.

The assertion that there is a clear and total separation between humans and other species is fundamentally incompatible with an acceptance of evolution. If a being is self-aware, killing her, even in a "humane" fashion, does not just end her life but also destroys her plans for the future. If a being understands his life, ending that life represents a loss to that being. For beings with interconnected emotional lives, killing one inflicts harm on those who remain. Such is the complex and social nature of this emotional suffering that an individual cannot be killed without harm being done. Recognizing this raises disturbing questions. Specifically, if every elephant already killed was an individual, now that so few remain, how should we understand such a massive act of collective violence against elephants as a whole?

THE CASE OF THE AFRICAN ELEPHANT

A History of Violence

African elephants are facing a crisis. Demand for ivory has resulted in poachers killing elephants at rates that could push the species to extinction in their natural habitats. This destruction has been a long time coming—in prehistoric ages, as humans spread, mammoths and prehistoric elephants disappeared from Eurasia and North America.[29] The North African elephant, *Loxodonta africana pharaoensis*, disappeared around the sixth century CE, and the Syrian Asian elephant disappeared from the Levant around 100 BCE.[30] For a time, large sub-Saharan African elephant populations remained relatively undisturbed during periods where human activity was at subsistence levels.[31] Nor did domesticated animals raised for food necessarily come into conflict with free-roaming animals. Though in areas of what is now Kenya, Maasai warriors would sometimes prove their bravery though hunting elephants or other potentially dangerous animals, being pastoralists, the Maasai still largely co-grazed their cattle with relatively little conflict.[32] However, from the sixteenth century, traditional ways of life across sub-Saharan Africa would come under threat from foreign interests pursued through violence.

In the sixteenth century, Portuguese merchants began trading large quantities of ivory in West Africa via local intermediaries. European involvement in the ivory trade became more direct with the establishment of the Dutch Cape Colony in the seventeenth century, such that by the 1830s, the once abundant elephants were so rare in Cape Province that the now British administration placed a prohibition on hunting them.[33] In eighteenth-century East Africa, the trades in slaves and ivory grew together. As hunting destroyed coastal elephant populations, an "Ivory Frontier" opened up, with traders pushing inland. As distances for transportation to the coast grew, so did the demand for labor to bear the heavy tusks; the traders thus were quick to exploit slave labor, selling the enslaved laborers on to Arab and European costal traders.[34]

Over the course of the nineteenth century, aggressive European expansionism and colonization during the "Scramble for Africa" would prove disastrous for many of Africa's free-roaming animal species. Traditional subsistence and pastoralist societies were pushed aside, habitats destroyed through logging and agriculture, and large animals hunted for sport on an unprecedented scale. For a time, diseases limited European settlement and animal agriculture.[35] While this provided respite for some recovery in elephant numbers, over the course of the twentieth century, populations continued to fall. In the ten years prior to the 1989 ivory ban, a decade dubbed the "Ivory Wars," the number of elephants halved from 1.2 million to 600,000.[36] Since then, some populations have stabilized, with numbers increasing in some areas, but the overall trend is one of continued decline—there are now just an estimated 470,000 elephants left.[37] Given that at the start of the nineteenth century, there were an estimated 20.5 million elephants in Africa, this represents a decline in excess of 97 percent.[38] Surviving populations are fragmented, with their ancient migratory routes divided and their historic ranges confined. The signs of collective psychological trauma have started to show.

In the early 1990s a disturbing phenomenon was documented in the Hluhluwe-Umfolozi Game Reserve—rhinoceroses were being found dead with traumatic injuries. Due to their size and strength, adult rhinoceroses have no predators besides humans, and there was only one possible perpetrator. Young male bull elephants were attacking, killing, and seemingly sexually assaulting rhinos on an apparently random basis without provocation.[39] This behavior was extremely abnormal. Elephants, being large social herbivores, are not naturally aggressive.[40]

The bull elephants at Hluhluwe-Umfolozi were young orphans who had been taken from families destroyed in "culling" programs. "Culling" teams would begin by killing the matriarch and older females, and without their guidance to mount an organized defense, the juveniles would panic. The calves, destined for sale to game reserves, foreign zoos, or circuses, would then be tied to the bodies of their mothers to prevent them from fleeing. Traumatized elephants, both male and female, exhibited other unusual behaviors, including abnormal startle responses, behaviors associated with depression, infant neglect, and post-traumatic stress disorder. Without the stable structure of elephant society, young males had not learned how to behave. Subjected to seemingly random and unprovoked violence at a young age, they had responded in kind. The importance of social structure and hierarchy, even among the seemingly loose association of juvenile and adult bulls, was reaffirmed when mature bulls were brought into the Hluhluwe-Umfolozi Reserve and the violence subsided.[41]

It has been argued that it is not just individuals or family groups who have been destroyed but elephants' society, collective knowledge, and way of life. After decades of poaching, "culling," and habitat loss, surviving elephant populations are suffering from species-wide trauma and chronic stress. This has profoundly disrupted the intricate web of familial and societal relations within elephant society and has pushed elephant culture to the point of collapse.[42] This in turn has manifested in both inter- and intra-species violence. In Addo Elephant National Park, in South Africa, up to 90 percent of male elephant deaths are now attributable to intra-species violence. In stark contrast, just four instances of one elephant killing another were recorded in over thirty years of study in Amboseli National Park, all of which were fights between bulls.[43] The surviving members of the species face a continued existential threat, and all of this was brought about by another species, our own.

Loxodonta africana v. Homo sapiens sapiens—The Case against Humanity

> What one generation finds ridiculous, the next accepts; and the third shudders when it looks back on what the first did.
>
> —Peter Singer[44]

If elephants are deserving of personhood, then collectively they are a nonhuman people, and there is a word for the destruction of an entire people: it is called a genocide.

Genocide, from the Greek *genos* (race, people) and Latin *caedere* (to kill), is a highly emotive term, and even the suggestion of applying it to nonhumans will be shocking or even offensive to many. Nonetheless, such a use is not without precedent; a number of parallels have been drawn between nonhuman suffering and the Holocaust. The Jewish author and Nobel laureate Isaac Bashevis Singer has made such a comparison, with the protagonist of one of his stories stating, "In relation to them [animals], all people are Nazis; for the animals, it is an eternal Treblinka."[45] The renowned South African writer J. M. Coetzee, another Nobel Prize winner, has drawn similar parallels.[46] The Israeli historian Yuval Noah Harari, while avoiding direct comparison, has called factory farming, in terms of aggregate suffering inflicted on sentient beings, one of "the worst crimes in history."[47] However, animal rights activist Roberta Kalechofsky rejects such comparisons, arguing, "Human beings do not hate animals . . . do not hunt them because they hate them. These were the motives for the Holocaust. Human beings have no ideological or theological conflict with animals."[48] This is an important point to consider, and it may be conceded that the killing of so many elephants has been driven largely not by hatred but by indifference to their suffering. Nonetheless, in legal terms the question is not so much one about hatred but rather is about intent. The UN Convention on the Prevention and Punishment of the Crime of Genocide, adopted in 1948, set out a legal definition of genocide for the first time. That definition, which has since been adopted by the 2002 Rome Statute of the International Criminal Court, as well as being incorporated into national criminal legislation, is as follows:

> any of the following acts committed with *intent* to destroy, in whole or in part, a national, ethnical, racial or religious group, as such:
>
> (a) Killing members of the group;
>
> (b) Causing serious bodily or mental harm to members of the group;

(c) Deliberately inflicting on the group conditions of life calculated to bring about its physical destruction in whole or in part;

(d) Imposing measures intended to prevent births within the group.[49]

In the case of the African elephant, this intent is largely lacking. Therefore, the elimination of elephants due to ivory poaching falls short of nonhuman genocide, although in theory the concept may be valid. "Culling" practices are clearly intended to destroy part of a species, but the expressed overall intent is the "management" of that species. So although these are acts of intentional killing, however cruel they may be, their expressed aim is not one of destruction but of preservation. Again, this does not merit use of the term nonhuman genocide. Whatever the intent, the suffering inflicted on African elephants is real and goes far beyond the suffering of the individuals. If not nonhuman genocide, is there another term that can adequately capture this?

The term specicide has been used, though not widely, to differentiate the deliberate intentional killing, or attempted killing, of all members of a species from a species' unintended extinction. However, this term primarily has been used to refer to the elimination of the malaria mosquito.[50] In this context the term has potentially positive connotations and consequently does not adequately reflect the specific nature of the harm done to elephant populations. Another term that has been used to refer to the destruction of the natural world is ecocide. Some interpretations focus on ecocide being a crime against future (human) generations, an anthropocentric view that ascribes value to ecosystems because they provide some utility for humans. Other interpretations focus on the ecosystem as having its own value, as in the philosophical vein of deep ecology. This school of thought, first espoused in its current form by the Norwegian philosopher Arne Naess, holds that all living things have an inherent worth.[51] There are working definitions of what ecocide law might look like, and in 2010 proposals were submitted by campaigners to the United Nations International Law Commission to amend the Rome Statute of the International Criminal Court to include ecocide.[52] Under the proposals, ecocide could be carried out with intent but also could be the result of negligence, and therefore, unlike with genocide laws, the question of intent is not relevant, only the consequences. For elephants and their ecosystem, those consequences have been profound. Elephants play a fundamental role in shaping and maintaining their surrounding ecosystems. Consequently, the destruction of African elephants may be an act of ecocide, but such an interpretation focuses on their value as part of a wider system and not their value as individuals. If we accept that elephants may have personhood, then the importance of *each and every* individual cannot be ignored in this way. As with specicide, ecocide remains an unsatisfactory term.

Perhaps existing laws are enough? Elephants, being a charismatic species, are not without allies. Many politicians and celebrities have spoken of the need to preserve them. The poaching of elephants is illegal, as is the international trade in ivory, and park rangers put their lives on the line every day to enforce these laws. However, none of these measures recognize elephants as individuals, which is an integral part of their nature. In moral terms the question cannot simply be one of welfare or conservation but should be one of rights. For the most part, questions of nonhuman rights so far have been raised regarding animals kept in captivity. However, the same moral and scientific arguments made in favor of nonhuman rights have profound implications for how we think about the plight of these species in their natural habitats. Recognizing the value of each and every individual leads to the following question: just as there are crimes against humanity, when many people are harmed in acts of collective violence, can there be, in the moral sense, such a thing as a crime against nonhumanity?

Again, the Rome Statute sets out the basis for crimes against humanity. The definition clearly refers to humans, and not persons, so even if nonhuman personhood were widely recognized in a legal sense, the statute would not apply. Nonetheless, if we are looking beyond the species barrier, the statute provides a useful basis for how laws on mass violence look and in turn may be used as a rap sheet for humanity to be scored against. Had an authority done to people what humans have done to elephants, they would be guilty of multiple counts of offenses under Article 7—including (a) murder, (b) extermination, (c) enslavement, and (d) deportation or forcible transfer of population.[53]

In determining how crimes against humanity are exceptional from other acts of violence, Antonio Cassese comments that "one ought to look at these atrocities or acts in their context and verify whether they may be regarded as part of an overall policy or a consistent pattern of an inhumanity, or whether they instead constitute isolated or sporadic acts of cruelty and wickedness."[54] While violence against humans and elephants is not the same, these criteria are still applicable in determining whether some form of collective violence has taken place.

Throughout the nineteenth and for much of the twentieth century, there were undoubtedly consistent patterns of violence. Ninety-eight percent of a population is not killed through sporadic acts of cruelty and wickedness. This was systematic, organized violence. However, since the 1989 ivory ban, the picture has been less clear. Government positions vary, though there are two main factions: one led by Kenya, which takes a hard anti-poaching, anti–ivory trade line, and one led by South Africa, which has indicated that it favors a controlled trade in ivory, though it abides by the current international restrictions. Nonetheless, de facto authorities still play a central role in orchestrating violence against elephants. Organized crime groups as well as militant organizations such as the Lord's Resistance Army (LRA) and Al-Shabaab are heavily involved in the ivory trade (it is perhaps not wholly a coincidence, given their disregard for the value of life, that both groups also have been accused of grave human rights violations, and leaders of the LRA have been charged with crimes against humanity by the International Criminal Court).[55]

So the situation we arrive at is this. A group of cognitively complex, social beings with interconnected emotional lives, each one an individual with a sense of self, have been systematically killed. Their characteristics are such that to deny them legal personhood would be inconsistent with how we treat members of our own species, even those members who do not possess or have lost fundamental human attributes. Yet if we recognize and grant that personhood to individuals, we must in turn confront the harm that has been inflicted on the collective. This is a scenario that deserves special moral consideration. There is no conceptual, or much less legal, framework at present that captures this kind of violence, and existing concepts such as specicide and ecocide are not sufficient. How we think about collective violence against our own species provides the best model. We recognize that such violence is somehow greater than the sum of its parts—a massacre is not just a series of murders. Thus, just as there are crimes against humanity, for animals with personhood it follows that in moral terms there also can be crimes against nonhumanity. Recognizing the capacity of the individual persons to suffer means we must recognize the capacity of the collective to suffer. A new term is required to describe this for species other than our own.

SUMMARY AND CONCLUSION

Western philosophy has been characterized by an expanding circle of moral concern. This expansion has been uneven and nonlinear, but moral progression can be seen. Rooted in altruistic behavior, there is something of an innate moral sense—some capacity for empathy—that, while undoubtedly flawed, drove the formation of institutions and processes to resolve disputes and ultimately the codification of right and wrong into law.

There are very few defining attributes unique to humans, and of those, almost none are universal to all humans. In aggregate, humans may be exceptional in some ways, but few of these differences are morally relevant. Crucially, we may well *not* be exceptional in our capacity to suffer. Nor are we necessarily unique in having personhood, something that is not defined by achievement or even intelligence. Personhood, though linked to complex cognitive processes, is characterized by autonomy and self-awareness, and above all, it is about having a sufficient sense of one's own existence such that being deprived of that existence would represent a loss. Furthermore, when considering the suffering of persons, it is essential to consider their unique and interconnected nature—individuals are not interchangeable, and the loss of one has an effect on the others.

It is logical that rights should be afforded on the basis of nature and not form—and cases arguing just this are now making their way into courtrooms. However, the recognition of personhood, even in just a small number of other species, raises profound questions about how we have treated nonhumans and how we should treat them.

Human action has inflicted immeasurable suffering on African elephants, and it may be time to recognize the collective harm that has been done. Just as mass violence against human persons may be a crime against humanity, so mass violence against nonhuman persons may be a crime against nonhumanity. This is a moral argument and not a legal recommendation, but the former must precede the latter. The purpose of affirming this is not to draw a direct equivalence between the two and say they are the same, but simply to highlight that suffering has taken place in such a way that the total impact is greater than the sum of its parts. We can look away or flat-out deny that we cause harm, or perhaps we can come up with a justification for why it is okay, arguing how our own needs are always greater, but if humanity has one redeeming characteristic, it is our capacity for empathy: to see pain, share it, and seek to stop or heal it. Elephants may not be like us, but they suffer like we do, and we are the ones inflicting that suffering. Consequently, we also are the ones who can end that suffering. Recognizing our responsibility is a first step.

REFERENCES

BBC News. "Court in Argentina Grants Basic Rights to Orangutan." December 21, 2014. http://www.bbc.com/news/world-latin-america-30571577.

Bradshaw, Gay A. *Elephants on the Edge: What Animals Teach Us about Humanity*. New Haven, CT: Yale University Press, 2009.

Butti, Camilla. "Total Number and Volume of Von Economo Neurons in the Cerebral Cortex of Cetaceans." *Journal of Comparative Neurology* 515 (March 2009): 243–59.

Campbell, Gwyn. *The Structure of Slavery in Indian Ocean Africa and Asia*. London: Frank Cass, 2003.

Cassese, Antonio, Paola Gaeta, and John R. W. D. Jones. *The Rome Statute of the International Criminal Court: A Commentary*. Oxford: Oxford University Press, 2002.

Chan, Sarah, and John Harris. "Human Animals and Nonhuman Persons." In *Oxford Handbook of Animal Ethics*, edited by Tom L. Beauchamp and R. G. Frey, 304–31. Oxford: Oxford University Press, 2011.

Choplin, Lauren. "*Black's Law Dictionary* to Correct Definition of 'Person' in Response to Nonhuman Rights Project Request." Nonhuman Rights Project, November 4, 2017. https://www.nonhumanrights.org/media-center/04-11-17-media-release-blacks-law/.

———. "NhRP Statement on NY Court of Appeals Decision in Chimpanzee Rights Cases." Nonhuman Rights Project, May 8, 2018. https://www.nonhumanrights.org/blog/nhrp-statement-fahey-opinion/.

Choudhury, A., et al. "*Elephas maximus*." *The IUCN Red List of Threatened Species*. 2008. Accessed November 20, 2018. http://dx.doi.org/10.2305/IUCN.UK.2008.RLTS.T7140A12828813.en.

Christy, Bryan. "Tracking Ivory." *National Geographic*, September 2015, 36–59.

de Waal, Frans. "Are We in Anthropodenial?" *Discover* 18 (July 1997): 50–53.

Douglas-Hamilton, Iain. *Among the Elephants*. London: Viking, 1975.

Hakeem, Atiya., Patrick R. Hof, Chet C. Sherwood, Robert C. Switzer III, L. E. L. Rasmussen, and John M. Allman. "Brain of the African Elephant (*Loxodonta africana*): Neuroanatomy from Magnetic Resonance Images." *Anatomical Record Part A: Discoveries in Molecular, Cellular, and Evolutionary Biology* 287 (October 2005): 1117–27.

Hakeem, Atiya, Chet C. Sherwood, Christopher J. Bonar, Camilla Butti, Patrick R. Hof, and John M. Allman. "Von Economo Neurons in the Elephant Brain." *Anatomical Record* 292 (December 2008): 242–48.

Harari, Yuval Noah. "Industrial Farming Is One of the Worst Crimes in History." *Guardian*, September 25, 2015, https://www.theguardian.com/books/2015/sep/25/industrial-farming-one-worst-crimes-history-ethical-question.

Human Rights Watch. *The Christmas Massacres: LRA Attacks on Civilians in Northern Congo*. Report, 2009.

Jennett, Bryan. "Should Cases of Permanent Vegetative State Still Go to Court?" *BMJ* 319, no. 7213 (September 1999): 796–97.

Jowit, Juliette. "British Campaigner Urges UN to Accept 'Ecocide' as International Crime." *Guardian*, September 9, 2010. https://www.theguardian.com/environment/2010/apr/09/ecocide-crime-genocide-un-environmental-damage.

Judson, Olivia. "A Bug's Death." *New York Times*, September 9, 2003, http://www.nytimes.com/2003/09/25/opinion/a-bug-s-death.html.

Kalechofsky, Roberta. *Animal Suffering and the Holocaust: The Problem with Comparisons*. Marblehead, MA: Micah Publications, 2003.

Miklavcic, John Janez, and Paul Flaman. "Personhood Status of the Human Zygote, Embryo, Fetus." *Linacre Quarterly* 84, no. 2 (May 2017): 130–44.

Mithen, Steven. *After the Ice: A Global Human History, 20,000–5000 BC*. Cambridge, MA: Harvard University Press, 2006.

Moss, Cynthia. *Elephant Memories: Thirteen Years in the Life of an Elephant Family*. New York: Fawcett Columbine, 1988.

Naess, Arne. "The Shallow and the Deep, Long-Range Ecology Movement: A Summary." *Inquiry* 16 (1973): 95–100.

Nonhuman Rights Project. "Client, Tommy (Chimpanzee)." 2018. https://www.nonhumanrights.org/client-tommy/.

Opoku, J. K., and E. Manu. "The Status of the Human Embryo: An Analysis from the Christian and Islamic Viewpoints." *European Journal of Biology and Medical Science Research* 3 (August 2015): 24–60.

Poyne, Jane. *J. M. Coetzee and the Idea of the Public Intellectual*. Athens: Ohio University Press, 2006.

Rome Statute of the International Criminal Court. July 17, 1998.

Schrag, Daniel P. "Geobiology of the Anthropocene." In *Fundamentals of Geobiology*, edited by Andrew H. Knoll, Don E. Canfield, and Kurt O. Konhauser, 425–36. Oxford: Wiley-Blackwell, 2012.

Seymour, John. *Childbirth and the Law*. Oxford: Oxford University Press, 2000.

Siebert, Charles. "Should a Chimp Be Able to Sue Its Owner?" *New York Times Magazine*, April 24, 2014. http://www.nytimes.com/2014/04/27/magazine/the-rights-of-man-and-beast.html.

Singer, Isaac Bashevis. *Collected Stories: Gimpel the Fool to the Letter Writer*. New York: Library of America, 2004.

Singer, Peter. *Animal Liberation*. New York: Random House, 1975.

———. *The Expanding Circle: Ethics, Evolution, and Moral Progress*. Princeton, NJ: Princeton University Press, 2011.

———. "The Great Ape Project." *BBC Wildlife Magazine* 11 (June 1993): 28–32.

Smil, Vaclav. *Harvesting the Biosphere: What We Have Taken from Nature*. Cambridge, MA: MIT Press, 2013.

Sneddon, Lynne U. "Pain in Aquatic Animals." *Journal of Experimental Biology* 218 (April 2015): 967–76.

Soltis, Joseph, Lucy E. King, Iain Douglas-Hamilton, Fritz Vollrath, and Anne Savage. "African Elephant Alarm Calls Distinguish between Threats from Humans and Bees." *PLoS ONE* 9 (February 2014): e89403.

UN General Assembly. Universal Declaration of Human Rights, Resolution 217A (III). Paris, December 1948.

Weary, Daniel M., Jennifer Jasper, and Maria J. Hötzel. "Understanding Weaning Distress." *Applied Animal Behaviour Science* 110 (March 2008): 24–41.

WildAid. *Ivory Demand*. Report, 2012.

Wise, Steven. *Drawing the Line: Science and the Case for Animal Rights*. Cambridge, MA: Perseus Books, 2003.

———. "Introduction to Animal Law Book." *Syracuse Law Review* 67 (2017): 7–30.

Wood, Bernard. "Fifty Years after *Homo habilis*." *Nature* 508 (April 2014): 31–33.

World Wildlife Fund. "African Elephants." Accessed October 23, 2018. http://wwf.panda.org/what_we_do/endangered_species/elephants/african_elephants.

NOTES

1. Peter Singer, *Animal Liberation* (New York: Random House, 1975), 1–5.

2. Steven Wise, *Drawing the Line: Science and the Case for Animal Rights* (Cambridge, MA: Perseus Books, 2003), 33–34.

3. J. K. Opoku and E. Manu, "The Status of the Human Embryo: An Analysis from the Christian and Islamic Viewpoints," *European Journal of Biology and Medical Science Research* 3 (August 2015): 24–60.

4. John Janez Miklavcic and Paul Flaman, "Personhood Status of the Human Zygote, Embryo, Fetus," *Linacre Quarterly* 84, no. 2 (May 2017): 133–36.

5. John Seymour, *Childbirth and the Law* (Oxford: Oxford University Press, 2000), 135–52.

6. Bryan Jennett, "Should Cases of Permanent Vegetative State Still Go to Court?," *BMJ* 319, no. 7213 (September 1999): 796–97.

7. Miklavcic and Flaman, "Personhood Status," 139.

8. UN General Assembly, Universal Declaration of Human Rights, Resolution 217A (III), Paris, December 1948.

9. Singer, *Animal Liberation*, 6.

10. Bernard Wood, "Fifty Years after *Homo habilis*," *Nature* 508 (April 2014): 31–33.

11. Peter Singer, *The Expanding Circle: Ethics, Evolution, and Moral Progress* (Princeton, NJ: Princeton University Press, 2011), 54–86.

12. Charles Siebert, "Should a Chimp Be Able to Sue Its Owner?," *New York Times Magazine*, April 24, 2014, http://www.nytimes.com/2014/04/27/magazine/the-rights-of-man-and-beast.html.

13. Singer, *Animal Liberation*, 188.

14. Lynne U. Sneddon, "Pain in Aquatic Animals," *Journal of Experimental Biology* 218 (April 2015): 967.

15. Daniel M. Weary, Jennifer Jasper, and Maria J. Hötzel, "Understanding Weaning Distress," *Applied Animal Behaviour Science* 110 (March 2008): 25.

16. Sarah Chan and John Harris, "Human Animals and Nonhuman Persons," *in Oxford Handbook of Animal Ethics*, ed. Tom L. Beauchamp and R. G. Frey (Oxford: Oxford University Press, 2011), 306–22.

17. *BBC News*, "Court in Argentina Grants Basic Rights to Orangutan," December 21, 2014, http://www.bbc.com/news/world-latin-america-30571577.

18. Nonhuman Rights Project, "Client, Tommy (Chimpanzee)," 2018, https://www.nonhumanrights.org/client-tommy/.

19. Steven Wise, "Introduction to Animal Law Book," *Syracuse Law Review* 67 (2017): 23.

20. Lauren Choplin, "*Black's Law Dictionary* to Correct Definition of 'Person' in Response to Nonhuman Rights Project Request," Nonhuman Rights Project, November 4, 2017, https://www.nonhumanrights.org/media-center/04-11-17-media-release-blacks-law/.

21. Lauren Choplin, "NhRP Statement on NY Court of Appeals Decision in Chimpanzee Rights Cases," Nonhuman Rights Project, May 8, 2018, https://www.nonhumanrights.org/blog/nhrp-statement-fahey-opinion/.

22. Atiya Y. Hakeem et al., "Brain of the African Elephant (*Loxodonta africana*): Neuroanatomy from Magnetic Resonance Images," *Anatomical Record Part A: Discoveries in Molecular, Cellular, and Evolutionary Biology* 287 (October 2005): 1119.

23. Camilla Butti, "Total Number and Volume of Von Economo Neurons in the Cerebral Cortex of Cetaceans," *Journal of Comparative Neurology* 515 (March 2009): 243.

24. Atiya Y. Hakeem et al., "Von Economo Neurons in the Elephant Brain," *Anatomical Record* 292 (December 2008): 242–48.

25. Joseph Soltis et al., "African Elephant Alarm Calls Distinguish between Threats from Humans and Bees," *PLoS ONE* 9 (February 2014): e89403.

26. Cynthia Moss, *Elephant Memories: Thirteen Years in the Life of an Elephant Family* (New York: Fawcett Columbine, 1988), 170, 270–71.

27. Iain Douglas-Hamilton, *Among the Elephants* (London: Viking, 1975), 273.

28. Frans de Waal, "Are We in Anthropodenial?," *Discover* 18 (July 1997): 50–53.

29. Steven Mithen, *After the Ice: A Global Human History, 20,000–5000 BC* (Cambridge, MA: Harvard University Press, 2006), 252–54.

30. A. Choudhury et al., "*Elephas maximus*," *The IUCN Red List of Threatened Species*, 2008, http://dx.doi.org/10.2305/IUCN.UK.2008.RLTS.T7140A12828813.en.

31. Daniel P. Schrag, "Geobiology of the Anthropocene," in *Fundamentals of Geobiology*, ed. Andrew H. Knoll, Don E. Canfield, Kurt O. Konhauser (Oxford: Wiley-Blackwell, 2012), 426–27.

32. Moss, *Elephant Memories*, 51.

33. Douglas-Hamilton, *Among the Elephants*, 249–50.

34. Gwyn Campbell, *The Structure of Slavery in Indian Ocean Africa and Asia* (London: Frank Cass, 2003), 182.

35. Douglas-Hamilton, *Among the Elephants*, 249–54.

36. WildAid, *Ivory Demand* (report), 2012, 1.

37. World Wildlife Fund, "African Elephants," accessed October 23, 2018, http://wwf.panda.org/what_we_do/endangered_species/elephants/african_elephants/.

38. Source data from Vaclav Smil, *Harvesting the Biosphere: What We Have Taken from Nature* (Cambridge, MA: MIT Press, 2013), 94.

39. Gay A. Bradshaw, *Elephants on the Edge: What Animals Teach Us about Humanity* (New Haven, CT: Yale University Press, 2009), 34–36.

40. Moss, *Elephant Memories*, 114–15.

41. Bradshaw, *Elephants on the Edge*, 81–87.

42. Bradshaw, *Elephants on the Edge*, 78–80.

43. Bradshaw, *Elephants on the Edge*, 34–35.

44. Peter Singer, "The Great Ape Project," *BBC Wildlife Magazine* 11 (June 1993): 32.

45. Isaac Bashevis Singer, *Collected Stories: Gimpel the Fool to the Letter Writer* (New York: Library of America, 2004), 750.

46. Jane Poyne, *J. M. Coetzee and the Idea of the Public Intellectual* (Athens: Ohio University Press, 2006), 197.

47. Yuval Noah Harari, "Industrial Farming Is One of the Worst Crimes in History," *Guardian*, September 25, 2015, https://www.theguardian.com/books/2015/sep/25/industrial-farming-one-worst-crimes-history-ethical-question.

48. Roberta Kalechofsky, *Animal Suffering and the Holocaust: The Problem with Comparisons* (Marblehead, MA: Micah Publications, 2003).

49. Rome Statute of the International Criminal Court, July 17, 1998, Article 6; emphasis added.

50. Olivia Judson, "A Bug's Death," *New York Times*, September 9, 2003, http://www.nytimes.com/2003/09/25/opinion/a-bug-s-death.html.

51. Arne Naess, "The Shallow and the Deep, Long-Range Ecology Movement: A Summary," *Inquiry* 16 (1973): 95–100.

52. Juliette Jowit, "British Campaigner Urges UN to Accept 'Ecocide' as International Crime," *Guardian*, September 9, 2010, https://www.theguardian.com/environment/2010/apr/09/ecocide-crime-genocide-un-environmental-damage.

53. Rome Statute of the International Criminal Court, Article 7.

54. Antonio Cassese, Paola Gaeta, and John R. W. D. Jones, *The Rome Statute of the International Criminal Court: A Commentary* (Oxford: Oxford University Press, 2002), 361.

55. Bryan Christy, "Tracking Ivory," *National Geographic*, September 2015, 36–59; Human Rights Watch, *The Christmas Massacres: LRA Attacks on Civilians in Northern Congo* (report), 2009, 14–15.

Chapter 17

India

Whither Bovinity? Hindu Dharma, the Indian State, and Conflicting Moral Perspectives over Cow Protection

By Kenneth Valpey

Shortly before India would gain independence from British rule in August 1947, Mahatma Gandhi, a vigorous champion for cow care and the ending of cow slaughter, expressed doubt about the efficacy of positive law to protect bovines: "Cow slaughter can never be stopped by law. Knowledge, education, and the spirit of kindliness towards [cows] alone can put an end to it."[1] In November 1949, less than two years after India mourned Gandhi's assassination, and despite his reservations about the efficacy of state law to realize one of his most cherished dreams, the Indian Constituent Assembly moved to include Article 48 in the Constitution of India as a Directive Principle of State Policy:

> That the State shall endeavour to organise agriculture and animal husbandry on modern and scientific lines and shall, in particular, take steps for preserving and improving the breeds, and prohibiting the slaughter, of cows and calves and other milch and draught cattle.[2]

Ian Copland may be correct in viewing the Constituent Assembly's approval of Article 48 as "less altruistic and more calculating, less like a humane intervention on behalf of suffering cows and more like a calculated strike against the nation's Muslim minority."[3] Yet we might also see other sides of this event. It also may be seen as an attempt to resolve a long-persisting conflict, albeit in favor of a largely Hindu understanding about the sanctity of bovines—particularly cows, both female and male. On a deeper level adoption of the article may be seen as a gesture toward enshrining care for animals in general in the highest level of India's law, with cows being emblematic of nonhumanity's ideal place comparable to, if not identical with, citizenship. That this constitutional article was a result of political maneuvering surely highlights its ineffectiveness to end a long history of political—and at times violent—conflict over the issue of cow protection. Indeed, it is a conflict that has gone hand in hand with India's struggle for independence and its emergence as a nation-state, and it persists amid India's current surge into modernization, globally connected industrialization, and accelerated increase of human population. The question arises, how might a deeper value and purpose in this legal measure be better served, for the benefit of all?

Given the ponderously divisive situation surrounding cow care in India, I wish to raise the question of whether and how an understanding of the ancient Indian notion of *dharma*—a Sanskrit term that in some contexts (but only some) may be translated as "law"—could help to better serve the interests of bovines and other animals in India than the present legal systems of India seem able to deliver. I argue that such a deeper comprehension of dharma, despite its usual association with religion (mainly though not exclusively Hinduism), if carefully applied to the country's secular legal system, could serve to reduce if not eliminate the communalist tensions that tend to be fueled by current Indian legal mechanisms meant to protect bovines. Such recourse to a deeper comprehension of dharma could generate practical means by which bovines' interests would be cared for throughout the animals' natural lives, and human citizens could better cooperate for their own well-being and the well-being of the land upon which all creatures depend.

I will begin this exploration with a brief discussion on basic relevant features of classical notions of dharma to see how the constitutional article in question might be understood in relation to dharma conceptualization. Next, I will introduce another Indian constitutional article, Article 51A, as relevant to this discussion, with its call for all citizens "to have compassion for all creatures," which I will then suggest would serve well as the explicit moral foundation for Article 48. Third, I will suggest how we may better understand the dynamics of dysfunctionality that characterize the political issue in question with the help of Jonathan Haidt's and his colleagues' identification of six "moral foundations" of political ideology. By regarding a secular government's priority as pursuing constant reaffirmation of all six moral foundations, we can get a sense of the bigger picture indicated in classical Indian notions of dharma. From this position it becomes possible to envision a contemporary program that could progressively lead toward the goal of not only bovine protection but also a broadly inclusive respect for and protection of other nonhuman animals in India.

DHARMA'S MULTIDIMENSIONALITY

It is commonplace, when discussing Hinduism, to acknowledge the great importance of the concept of dharma and, in the same breath, to either attempt to give multiple translations of the term or to despair of giving any satisfactory translation thereof.[4] Suffice for our purposes to note that the Sanskrit word *dharma* is thought to be derived from the verbal root **dhṛ*—"uphold, support, give foundation to"[5]—indicating the broadest sense of the word's semantic field. From here, an initial distinction between normative and descriptive usage of the term *dharma* will be helpful for our purpose. In current usage, most often, *dharma* is regarded as essentially normative in nature, due to the injunctive character of much sacred Hindu literature, especially that of the *Dharmashastra* genre. It is tempting to view such injunctive material as positive law in the present-day sense, although there are limits to such a comparison.[6] Dharmashastra works, such as the *Manusmriti*,[7] typically contain detailed injunctions and prohibitions, punishments for specific transgressions, atonements to be observed, and rites to be performed, addressing the broad sphere of human ethical and legal concerns. It is important for us to note that dharma injunctions and prohibitions tend to be place-, time-, and person-specific (*desha, kala, patra*). In this dimension of dharma, there is little in the way of categorical imperative: what may be wrong in one circumstance may be right, permitted, or enjoined in another. However, there is also an important category of normative dharma called *sadharana-dharma*—"general dharma"—that consists of directives intended for all human beings at all times and that, much more than injunctions for specific groups (*sva-dharma*), can be identified as injunctions toward the pursuit of morality and the cultivation of virtue.[8] I shall return to this topic shortly, in relation to a second passage in the Indian Constitution relevant to our topic, Article 51A, which enjoins care for nature and "compassion for living creatures."

Turning to descriptive dharma, it is helpful to see descriptive dharma as the basis for normative dharma. To recognize the essential quality, nature, or feature of an entity or type of entities (especially of living beings) is the descriptive aspect of dharma.[9] In this practice, description can be either general/inclusive or specific/exclusive. In Hindu traditions, specificity and exclusivity in descriptive dharma tend to characterize individual persons as each possessing a particular *sva-dharma*—"one's own dharma"—which in turn typically locates one within a specific social grouping to which specific duties pertain (to which normative dharma applies). In contrast, an example of general and inclusive description relevant to our topic would be to identify the dharma (in this context, "common feature") of *all* living beings—namely, that they are sentient selves, nontemporal entities, *atman*. The Bhagavad-Gita and other classical Sanskrit texts that are regarded as definitive for most Hindus emphasize that living beings in their essence are distinct from their temporal bodies, and as such—as *atman*—they are indestructible, though temporarily inhabiting particular bodies destined to die. Since this description is all-inclusive (inclusive of all living beings), the relevant type of normative injunction for moral behavior that acknowledges this feature would be of the general—*sadharana*—sort. Indeed, the inclusive normative injunction most applicable and much emphasized in classical dharma literature is the practice of "nonviolence" (*ahimsa*), the concerted effort by human beings to restrain and minimize the tendency to inflict suffering on living creatures and thus to cultivate a sense of compassion for all.

"IT SHALL BE THE DUTY OF EVERY CITIZEN"

The ideal or virtue of compassion is explicitly voiced in the Indian Constitution, in a context that suggests accord with the notion of *sadharana-dharma.* This is Article 51A (constituting the whole of Part IV-A, "Fundamental Duties").[10] This article consists of one general imperative with eleven specifications. The general imperative is the phrase "It shall be the duty of every citizen," and each succeeding specification consists of an infinitive verb (e.g., "to abide . . . "; "to cherish . . . "; "to uphold . . . "; "to defend . . . "). The seventh specification (g) states "to protect and improve the natural environment including forests, lakes, rivers and wild life, and to have compassion for living creatures."

The opening phrase, with its inclusion of "every citizen," is a clear echo of the *sadharana-dharma* principle of inclusion in a normative injunction (recognizing all citizens as moral agents); similarly, the exhortation to "have compassion for living creatures" echoes the inclusiveness of descriptive dharma's general identification of all creatures as having the same nontemporal nature as *atman* (thus recognizing all creatures as moral patients).

ARTICLE 48 AS DHARMA?

This tentative association of Article 51A with traditional *sadharana-dharma* raises the question of how Article 48 might be similarly understood in terms of dharma, by which I mean what Hindus in particular would regard as dharma. There is no doubt that the final phrase of the article, which urges the Indian states to prohibit the slaughter of bovines, would be regarded as conforming to normative dharma, especially by Hindus but also by others in India.[11] But the case is complicated by the fact that this constitutional directive to prohibit cow slaughter is embedded within a directive of a quite different—even opposite—discourse: namely, the organization of agriculture and animal husbandry "on modern and scientific lines." Although there need be nothing intrinsically discordant in bringing modern and scientific agricultural knowledge and practices to bear in the care for bovines and their protection from slaughter, the actual application of agricultural modernization in India today shows otherwise. The agricultural modernization now practiced in India with its connection to global markets has compounded the slaughter of bovines rather than facilitated its reduction.[12] Such modernization seems, rather, to go hand in hand with the rapid urbanization and globalization in India to which bovines—and small farmers subjected to spiraling debt—have become victims. Therefore, one has to question the purpose, value, and efficacy of this cow slaughter prohibition phrase as it is presently positioned in the Indian Constitution.

In light of our previous analysis of Article 51A(g) in classical dharma terms, it could well be that a simple yet significant organizational adjustment in the Constitution would be a positive step toward the desired goal. The cow slaughter clause could be shifted from its present agro-economics context to a position as an entailment of the "*sadharana-dharma*" category, the "duty of every citizen . . . to have compassion for living creatures." This would call attention to the noninstrumental character of bovines, thus upholding their sanctity as regarded by Hindus and highlighting their inviolability as sentient living beings—*atman*—recognized in the broader dharma tradition.

DYSFUNCTIONAL POLITICS TO MORAL FOUNDATIONS

One may object that such an adjustment to the Indian Constitution, although well-meant, would ignore the grim reality of current Indian politics, whereby the divisive "communalism" of religious difference holds grip over the (mal) treatment of bovines. The reality is that very large minorities in India—especially Muslims, but also Dalit ("lower caste") populations—care little for Hindu or other Indic notions of dharma. Or if one persists in using the term *dharma*, Muslims, Christians, Dalits, and others have their own dharmas in which bovines do not hold the sanctity they carry in Hindu and other Indic traditions. In fact, as a secular state (declared as such in the Indian Constitution's opening paragraph), India as a nation has been careful to avoid using the term *dharma* in the Constitution because of its identification with religion, or with specific religions. Rather, the adversarial character of modern democratic (or quasi-democratic) politics persists in the foreground of the cow protection issue. And in this political atmosphere, in which most of India's states and territories have indeed passed laws against cow slaughter, there persist cultures of institutional corruption, webs of legal loopholes, and economic pressures (on the level of the national government, for which the gain of foreign exchange from beef and leather is a high priority, as much as on the level of individual farmers who are without the means to maintain unproductive bovines).[13] Further aggravating the contentious landscape is the typically violent activity of vigilantes who police villages and highways against local cow slaughter and clandestine bovine export. Add to this the engrained corruption of police who accept bribes from all parties involved in bovine trafficking. Thus, is there any hope, from the side of state jurisprudence, for the tide to change in the interest of bovines in India?

Continuing in the spirit of seeking a dharmic perspective (in the sense of a broader perspective that holds to a sense of moral grounding) on the bovine issue in India, let us consider how a typology of "moral foundations" of political ideology developed by American social-psychologist Jonathan Haidt and his colleagues might illuminate our issue. On the basis of considerable empirical research, Haidt identifies five positive foundational moral themes that motivate and energize political discourse, each having an opposite or negative principle sought to be avoided or suppressed. The five positive/negative pairs are care/harm, fairness/cheating, loyalty/betrayal, authority/subversion, and sanctity/degradation. Haidt also adds a sixth as-yet less empirically confirmed foundation: liberty/oppression. According to Haidt's research, there is a definite correlation between how one identifies oneself politically and which of these moral foundations one will regard as important and worth defending. At the same time that one champions certain of these moral foundations, one will tend to maintain blindness to the importance of the other foundations, thus preventing one from being able to listen to and acknowledge the values held by one's political opponents.[14]

In relation to our issue of cow protection politics and the Indian Constitution, we may note that Hindus will tend to emphasize the *sanctity* of cows as a key element of dharma, one that they will link closely to the *authority* of the classical dharma literature (considered to be rooted in the ancient Vedas). In turn, they will regard these two foundations as closely tied with *loyalty* to the Indian nation. On the other hand, non-Hindus, for whom cow slaughter is not considered necessarily wrong or forbidden, the foundational moral principles invoked tend to be *fairness* and *liberty*: fairness demands that non-Hindus be given equal treatment before the law in terms of social and economic opportunity (such as would be expected by persons whose livelihoods depend on animal flesh or leather). Similarly, the moral foundation of liberty is regarded as entailing that non-Hindus have the freedom of dietary choice for themselves and their families. Thus, according to this analysis, champions of cow protection will tend to ignore the moral foundations of fairness and liberty (at least as conceived in this context by their opponents), and non-Hindus will be likely to ignore, or hold different perceptions of, the moral foundations of sanctity (of cows), authority (of dharma literature followed by Hindus), and loyalty (to a nation conceived of by many Hindus as being essentially a Hindu nation).

As for the first of Haidt's moral foundations—care—I would argue that this is the principle least considered and least effectively practiced in India with respect to cows, even by many who profess to champion cow protection and cow care. To be sure, the moral foundation of care can be said to be articulated in a general way in the Constitution, in Article 51A(g), by invocation of "compassion for living creatures." However, the disconnect between this and the Article 48 directive to prohibit cow slaughter may be seen as indicative of the deeper disconnect between care and prevention of slaughter that is widely evident in India today: abandoned cows in urban and semi-urban areas are left to their own resources, scavenging in refuse bins and thereby becoming disabled from consumption of inedible substances such as plastic bags. Less visible but much more disturbing is the massive scale on which foreign beef and leather industries implicate India as a major supplier.[15]

What seems to be needed to move the issue of cow protection beyond its present political impasse is prioritization of the moral foundation of *care*. This would turn the discourse of cow care away from the masculine-leaning "morality of rights" that dominates discussions of fairness and move instead to a more feminine-leaning "discourse of responsibility."[16] This could serve to foreground the simple point that if cows are not to be slaughtered, they require considerable care—genuine care, not token maintenance—throughout their natural lives. And for such care, extensive facilities, organization, and human labor need to be arranged. Further, making care a priority would mean making all arrangements necessary for widespread education on the value—for all members of human society—of cows and lifetime cow care. Essential for this education would be teaching by example, which, radical or bizarre as it might sound, means that leaders of society would do well to show by personal example the importance of care for cows.[17] Through such examples, everyone, whatever their religious or social identity, could develop appreciation for the benefit of cow care and could hence become inclined to give up cow slaughter.

CONCLUDING REFLECTIONS

Returning to Mahatma Gandhi's expression of skepticism about the effectiveness of law to protect cows, let us recall the positive suggestions he made in the same statement: "Cow slaughter can never be stopped by law. Knowledge, education, and the spirit of kindliness towards [cows] alone can put an end to it." How might the secular government of India accommodate in its legal framework ways and means for fostering the sort of "knowledge, education, and the spirit of kindliness toward [cows]" that Gandhi had in mind? In fact, almost twenty years prior to making this comment, Gandhi drafted a six-point suggestion for how the Indian state could practically foster cow care and protection from slaughter. His general argument was that "cow slaughter should be and can be made economically impossible" and that, conversely, proper management could bring about an economically viable program of cow care for all cows and their progeny throughout their natural lives.[18]

Over recent decades the means for implementing comprehensive cow protection in an economically viable way has, indeed, been a subject of considerable discussion and experimentation by individuals, institutions, and state governments in India. Yet it is important to keep in mind that the dharma tradition that enjoins special care for cows shows a concern that goes beyond economics. How might this greater-than-economic value be affirmed in legal terms? Recalling the association of cows with sanctity, which, in turn, we saw as a moral foundation of political ideology, let us venture to imagine India as a country wherein an experiment with animal *citizenship*—beginning with cow citizenship—could be implemented. Following the reasoning of Sue Donaldson and Will Kymlicka, granting citizenship to nonhuman domesticated animals would be a plausible solution toward resolving the impasse currently encountered in animal rights theory and the animal rights movement. Through such a move, the issue of cow protection, as a discourse in negative rights, could effectively shift to a discourse of positive relational duties, which would be another way of saying that the ethics of care's emphasis on responsibility would be given a legal dimension.[19]

Even if such imagining is too wishful in the face of current international nation-statehood, whereby anthropocentrism is the deeply entrenched mode of legal structures, we might dare to conceive that one or another of the Indian states—most of which already have nominal cow slaughter bans in place—could take such a bold step.[20] In due course, this experimental state or province could become a functioning model: with cow citizenship in place, on the level of individual farmers, the sense that cows are family members—a common sensibility in earlier times—could be recovered, and the inclination of farmers and other human citizens to care for their cows would flourish. Such bovine citizenship could be a window through which the traditional dharma vision that all sensate creatures are *atman* could unfold to become a widespread cultural reality. Why such an unfolding may begin with cows was hinted by Gandhi when he commented, "Man, through the cow, is enjoined to realize his identity with all that lives."[21] The dharma tradition, with its emphasis on the value or even necessity of cow care for sustaining human well-being in a well-ordered cosmos, would suggest the same.

Still, the notion surely lingers that dharma is, after all, a sectarian, religious notion, not to be acknowledged in the legal apparatus of India. Much could be said on this topic, but suffice to note, in the closing of this discussion, that in its original understanding dharma was arguably secular, in the sense that it was intended as the broadest possible way of conceptualizing and appropriately acting in relation to real-world order and conditions. As such, a basic function of dharma may be regarded as maintaining a vision for human society by which all six of the moral foundations of political ideology mentioned previously are properly honored and pursued.[22] Based on such a conception of dharma, with care for citizens (including nonhuman animal citizens) as the overarching principle of governance, the other principles would fall into place: fairness based on recognition of ultimate equality of all beings; the fostering of a sense of loyalty to the protectors of human and animal well-being, which would go hand in hand with a recognition of authority as dwelling with those who act as such protectors; a sense of sacredness rooted in the dharmic identification of all life as sacred; and finally, a fostering of the pursuit of liberty, based on the dharmic sense that true liberty is a state of realization of existence beyond the confines of temporality, a realization made possible by the pursuit of freedom from the exercise of violence against living creatures. If dharma were seen in this way, it could be assured that cow protection and cow care could be fostered in a spirit of transcending politics, whereby the dignity of being human would be confirmed in the active pursuit of care and protection for fellow creatures as citizens in an expanding moral community in the making of a truly inclusive nation.

REFERENCES

Constitution of India. January 26, 1950. Accessed August 28, 2018. http://www.refworld.org/docid/3ae6b5e20.html.

Copland, Ian. "Cows, Congress and the Constitution: Jawaharlal Nehru and the Making of Article 48." *South Asia: Journal of South Asian Studies* 40, no. 4 (2017). https://doi.org/10.1080/00856401.2017.1352646.

Dalmiya, Vrinda. *Caring to Know: Comparative Care Ethics, Feminist Epistemology, and the Mahābhārata.* New Delhi: Oxford University Press, 2016.

Davis, Donald R., Jr. "Hinduism as a Legal Tradition." *Journal of the American Academy of Religion* 75, no. 2 (June 2007): 241–67.

Donaldson, Sue, and Will Kymlicka. *Zoopolis: A Political Theory of Animal Rights.* Oxford: Oxford University Press, 2013.

Donovan, Josephine, and Carol J. Adams, eds. *The Feminist Care Tradition in Animal Ethics.* New York: Columbia University Press, 2007.

Gandhi, M. K. *The Collected Works of Mahatma Gandhi*. 98 vols. New Delhi: Publications Division Government of India, 1999.

———. *Young India: 1927–1928*. Quoted in *Gandhiji on Cow Protection*. Ministry of Information and Broadcasting, Government of India, June 1967.

Gandhi, Maneka. "India's Slaughterhouses: India Has Become a Large Slaughterhouse for Cows," 2012. Accessed January 26, 2022. https://bharatabharati.in/2012/08/12/india-has-become-a-large-slaughter-house-for-cows-maneka-gandhi.

Govindrajan, Radhika. *Animal Intimacies: Interspecies Relatedness in India's Central Himalayas.* Chicago: University of Chicago Press, 2018.

Haidt, Jonathan. *The Righteous Mind: Why Good People Are Divided by Politics and Religion.* New York: Pantheon Books, 2012.

Hiltebeitel, Alf. *Dharma: Its Early History in Law, Religion, and Narrative*. Oxford: Oxford University Press, 2011.

Landes, Maurice, Alex Melton, and Seanicaa Edwards. "From Where the Buffalo Roam: India's Beef Exports." LDPM-264–01. Washington, DC: United States Department of Agriculture, June 2016.

Monier-Williams, Monier. "Dharma." *A Sanskrit-English Dictionary*. 1899. Delhi: Motilal Banarsidass, 1995.

Narayanan, Yamini. "Dairy, Death and Dharma: The Devastation of Cow Protectionism in India." *Animal Liberation Currents*, June 18, 2017. Accessed August 29, 2018. https://www.animalliberationcurrents.com/dairy-death-dharma/.

Prabhu, R. K., and U. R. Rao, eds. *The Mind of Mahatma Gandhi.* Ahmedabad, India: Navajivan Trust, 1960. Accessed August 28, 2018. https://www.mkgandhi.org/momgandhi/main.htm.

Prasad, Rajendra. "Go-palan Sanatan Dharm Hai." *Kalyan: Go Ankh*, no. 1773 (1945). Gorakhpur, India: Gita Press, 2014 (*samvat* 2072).

Sutton, Nicholas. *Religious Doctrines in the Mahābhārata.* Delhi: Motilal Banarsidass.

Tendulkar, D. G., and Vithalbhai K. Jhaveru. *Mahatma: Life of Mohandas Karamchand Gandhi*. 8 vols. 1951. Bombay: Ministry of Information, 1960.

NOTES

1. *Harijan*, September 15, 1946, 310 (journal published 1933–1956), quoted in *The Mind of Mahatma Gandhi*, comp. and ed. R. K. Prabhu and U. R. Rao (Ahmedabad, India: Navajivan Trust, 1960), accessed August 28, 2018, https://www.mkgandhi.org/momgandhi/main.htm.

2. Article 48 of the Constitution of India, *Constituent Assembly Debates: Official Report*, vol. 11 (New Delhi: Lok Sabha Secretariat, 1950), 558, 584–85, quoted in Ian Copland, "Cows, Congress and the Constitution: Jawaharlal Nehru and the Making of Article 48," *South Asia: Journal of South Asian Studies* 40, no. 4 (2017), https://doi.org/10.1080/00856401.2017.1352646, 1.

3. Copland, "Cows, Congress and the Constitution," 2.

4. Some terms used to translate *dharma*: "virtue, morality, religion, religious merit, good works"; "usage, practice, customary observance or prescribed conduct, duty";

"nature, character, peculiar condition or essential quality, property." Also: "the law or doctrine of Buddhism"; "the ethical precepts of Buddhism." The meaning of the term is vastly expanded by a profusion of modifying terms—e.g., *dharma-tattva*, the real essence of the dharma. Monier Monier-Williams, "Dharma," *A Sanskrit-English Dictionary* (1899; Delhi: Motilal Banarsidass, 1995), 510–11.

5. Alf Hiltebeitel, *Dharma: Its Early History in Law, Religion, and Narrative* (Oxford: Oxford University Press, 2011), 54, quoting Joel Brereton, "*Dharman* in the *Ṛgveda*," *Journal of Indian Philosophy* 32, nos. 5–6: 449–89.

6. See Donald R. Davis Jr., "Hinduism as a Legal Tradition," *Journal of the American Academy of Religion* 75, no. 2 (June 2007): 241–67, for a discussion of dharma as law in Hinduism.

7. Sir William Jones gave his English translation of the *Manusmriti* the title *Institutes of Hindu Law: or, the Ordinances of Menu, according to the Gloss of Cullúca*, first published in 1796.

8. Nicholas Sutton, *Religious Doctrines in the Mahābhārata* (Delhi: Motilal Banarsidass, 2000), 303–4.

9. Hiltebeitel, *Dharma*, 125. Hiltebeitel notes that the very early Vedic usage of *dharman* as meaning the "nature" or "quality" that something possesses is also found in later, Buddhist literature.

10. Part IV-A, "Fundamental Duties," was not instituted until 1976, as the Constitution (Forty-second Amendment) Act. Previous to this, "Directive Principles of State Policy," which includes Article 48, constituted Part IV. Part IV, in turn, follows the Constitution's list of "Fundamental Rights" in Part III.

11. It is not uncommon to find expressions of connection between or equivalence of cow protection and *sanatana-dharma*, "everlasting-dharma," as in the Hindi phrase "cow protection is *sanatana-dharma*" (*go-palan sanatan dharm hai*). Rajendra Prasad, "Go-palan Sanatan Dharm Hai," *Kalyan: Go Ankh*, no. 1773 (1945; Gorakhpur, India: Gita Press, 2014 [*samvat* 2072]), 24.

12. For a biting and well-documented critique of present-day industry- and politics-driven Indian cow-protection discourse, see Yamini Narayanan, "Dairy, Death and Dharma: The Devastation of Cow Protectionism in India," *Animal Liberation Currents*, June 18, 2017, accessed August 29, 2018, https://www.animalliberationcurrents.com/dairy-death-dharma/. See also Maneka Gandhi, "India's Slaughterhouses: India Has Become a Large Slaughterhouse for cows," accessed August 29, 2018, http://affcap.org/ArticleDetail.aspx?Id=1023.

13. See Maneka Gandhi's article, "India's Slaughterhouses."

14. See especially chapters 7 and 8 of Jonathan Haidt, *The Righteous Mind: Why Good People Are Divided by Politics and Religion* (New York: Pantheon Books, 2012).

15. In 2014 India was identified as the largest beef exporter in the world. See Maurice Landes, Alex Melton, and Seanicaa Edwards, "From Where the Buffalo Roam: India's Beef Exports," LDPM-264–01 (Washington, DC: United States Department of Agriculture, June 2016), 1.

16. Josephine Donovan and Carol J. Adams, eds., *The Feminist Care Tradition in Animal Ethics* (New York: Columbia University Press, 2007), 2, citing Carol Gilligan, *In a Different Voice* (1982).

17. As Vrinda Dalmiya points out, caregivers are generally in socially and politically marginal positions; yet the ethics of care deeply challenges such politics, suggesting that the notion of leaders modeling caregiving need not be dismissed as preposterous. Vrinda Dalmiya, *Caring to Know: Comparative Care Ethics, Feminist Epistemology, and the Mahābhārata* (New Delhi: Oxford University Press, 2016), 46–47.

18. Gandhi's six-point suggestion for state support of cow protection is as follows:

> (1) The State should in the open market buy out every cattle offered for sale by outbidding every other buyer; (2) The State should run dairies in all principal towns ensuring a cheap supply of milk; (3) The State should run tanneries where the hides, bones, etc., of all dead cattle in its possession should be utilised, and should offer to buy again in the open market all private-owned dead cattle; (4) The State should keep model cattle-farms and instruct the people in the art of breeding and keeping cattle; (5) The state should make liberal provision for pasture land and import the best experts in the world for imparting a knowledge of the science of cattle to the people; and (6) There should be a separate department created for the purpose, and no profit should be made in the department, so that the people may receive the full benefit of every improvement that might be made in the different breeds of cattle and other matters pertaining to them.
>
> M. K. Gandhi, "The Cow in Mysore," in Mahatma Gandhi, *Young India 1927–1928.* Madras: S. Ganesan, 1935, 240–45.; quoted in N/A *A Review of 'Beef in Ancient India'* (Mathura, India: Shree Krishna Janmasthan Seva-Sansthan, 1983), 3.

19. In their argument for granting citizenship to domesticated animals, Donaldson and Kymlicka propose three categories of animals—namely, domesticated animals as citizens; opportunistic human-related animals as "denizens"; and free-living animals as having their own domains of sovereignty. Sue Donaldson and Will Kymlicka, *Zoopolis: A Political Theory of Animal Rights* (Oxford: Oxford University Press, 2013), 1–16.

20. Most of the Indian states have enacted laws that restrict or ban cow slaughter. For example, in 2007 the Bharatiya Janata Party, the controlling political party of Uttarakhand (in the Indian Himalayan region), enacted a law forbidding the slaughter of cows, bulls, and bullocks (oxen) of any age. Radhika Govindrajan, *Animal Intimacies: Interspecies Relatedness in India's Central Himalayas* (Chicago: University of Chicago Press, 2018), 62.

21. D. G. Tendulkar and Vithalbhai K. Jhaveru, *Mahatma: Life of Mohandas Karamchand Gandhi*, 2nd ed. (1951; Bombay: Ministry of Information, 1960), 2:51. Also, linking a similar point to dharma, Gandhi wrote, "We can realize our duty towards the animal world and discharge it by wisely pursuing our dharma of service to the cow. At the root of cow-protection is the realization of our dharma towards the sub-human species." And the immediate subsequent sentence is telling: "But our service to the cow is service only in name and all of us are therefore tending to forget our dharma." Speech at Goseva Sangh meeting, Nalwadi, September 30, 1941, in M. K.

Gandhi, *The Collected Works of Mahatma Gandhi* (New Delhi: Publications Division Government of India, 1999), 81:139–40.

22. See Dalmiya's discussion on "big-D dharma" as the harmonization of values. Dalmiya, *Caring to Know*, 58.

Chapter 18

United Kingdom and Ireland

Animal Law Compared

By Maureen O'Sullivan and Stephanie O'Flynn

This chapter sets out to compare and contrast the protection of animals under the law in the UK and Ireland. Both jurisdictions are common law jurisdictions primarily, although since independence, Ireland has diverged somewhat in that a written constitution was adopted,[1] and the elected head of state is the president of Ireland rather than a hereditary monarch. Like the British counterpart, this position is largely that of a figurehead only. Because the 1911 Protection of Animals Act[2] was in force prior to independence, at one point it was the governing legislation in what was then a single jurisdiction. Since Ireland's exit from the UK in 1922, the law has developed on somewhat divergent paths. A commonality in the UK and Ireland to the present day is that our policies lack an overarching principle and are consequential in that animals' permitted treatment will depend on the use to which they are put. Exceptions to compassionate management are explicable, if not justifiable, through perceived economic and other benefits such as the sport of particular practices such as hunting, fishing, and racing.

This work will first outline the 1911 act and then trace the development of the protection of animals in both the UK and Ireland, noting a changing zeitgeist in terms of what is deemed acceptable. It will focus especially on dogs due to this being a very topical issue. While the UK did carry out reform of its animal protection laws in 2006, Irish inertia meant that it did not follow suit until 2013. Of note is that single issues can gather pace at grassroots level and foment principle where this has lacked in the legislative framework or among the political class. For instance, popular campaigns questioning the inconsistency in the way people eat some animals with abundance while treating their companion animals as members of their family are creating something of a deontological groundswell. Concern is spreading among the populace about issues from puppy farming to the lives of cows and chickens as more people question, reduce, or even abandon their consumption and use of animals. Environmental awareness also informs this preoccupation. Where the legislature has been unashamedly utilitarian in the issue of fur farming, in Ireland a recent U-turn was achieved when the government realized that an independent member of Parliament's bill banning fur farming was set to be approved.[3] At the eleventh hour, the minister for agriculture, Michael Creed,[4] nixed her efforts in order to introduce the government's own legislation and thus endeavor to take the credit for the action. It appears that the government realized that the court of public opinion in many different countries and even among fashion houses had paved the way toward the banning of fur farming, and it duly followed suit.

A light also has been shone on the greyhound industry in a recent harrowing documentary by the Irish state broadcaster, RTÉ, which showed the industry's horrors and which has stoked public consciousness.[5] Nevertheless, significant subsidies have since been given to the industry in a budget that was passed shortly afterward,[6] although matters may change in due course as nationwide protests outside stadiums become a regular activity of grassroots groups opposed to the practice.[7] High-profile protestor Pauline McLynn, who played the role of Mrs. Doyle in the TV comedy show *Father Ted*, has said that "even the dogs on the street know it is wrong."[8] From our research it would appear that most of the protestors are women, while most of the racing supporters and dog "owners" are men.

A STEP BACK IN TIME TO 1911

Prior to the enactment of the Animal Welfare Act 2006 in the UK and the Animal Health and Welfare Act 2013 in Ireland, animal welfare law was largely reactive, and action could be taken only once an animal was deemed to have suffered unnecessarily. Under the Protection of Animals Act 1911, it was an offense to cause unnecessary physical or mental suffering to an animal, but enforcement action could be taken to protect an animal only after the animal had suffered.

The 1911 act made it an offense of cruelty to "cruelly beat, kick, ill-treat, over-ride, over-drive, over-load, torture, infuriate, or terrify any animal" or permit an animal to be so used, but this obviously raises a question as to whether one can beat and kick an animal in a manner that is not cruel. Similarly, what constitutes overuse? This would come down to an individual court to decide on a particular day in the absence of a more detailed legislative framework. The act then defines offenses further, prohibiting conveying or carrying any animal in a way that would cause them any unnecessary suffering or facilitating these actions. It prohibits causing or assisting in the fighting or baiting of any animal, and it also bans poisoning or administering (directly or indirectly) injurious drugs or substances to any animal. Similarly, it requires humane treatment in the carrying out of operations. One can see how weak this legislation was when one considers that animals regularly had bodily parts cut off or docked without anesthetic despite the legislative requirements.

In terms of the punishment meted out, any person found guilty of such an offense of cruelty would be liable to a fine of a maximum of twenty-five pounds and also could be imprisoned for up to six months, "with or without hard labour."[9]

REFORMING WAYS: THE UK ANIMAL WELFARE ACT 2006

A public consultation was begun in the UK in January 2002, and a variety of different interest groups, including many animal welfare campaigners, such as the RSPCA (Royal Society for the Prevention of Cruelty to Animals) were consulted. The subsequent legislation repealed and replaced the Protection of Animals Act 1911 and came into force in England and Wales in 2007.[10]

The Animal Welfare Act 2006 (AWA) was introduced to combat animal abuse. Its aim was to update the principles of the Protection of Animals Act 1911, making the law reflect twenty-first-century practice and the developments in veterinary science. The new act streamlined and modernized a number of existing laws and brought the law relating to non-farmed animals further into line with that already in place for farmed animals. The act covers matters such as the prevention of harm, promotion of welfare, licensing and registration, codes of practice, animals in distress, enforcement, and prosecution.

Scope of Protection

The AWA provides for the welfare of all "protected" animals. In order to enjoy the coverage of the act, an animal must fall within this definition. These criteria must be determined to be under one of the following three scenarios:

(a) of a kind commonly domesticated in the British Islands,
(b) under human control whether on a temporary or permanent basis, or
(c) not living in a wild state.[11]

The act consolidates and updates legislation that already existed to promote the welfare of vertebrate animals (other than those living free in nature), some of which dates from 1911.[12] It is considered the single most important piece of animal welfare legislation to have been enacted in England and Wales for nearly one hundred years and places a legal obligation on "owners" and keepers of animals to care for them appropriately.

The act's scope covers animals, and these are defined as vertebrates other than humans. Fetal or embryonic animals are excluded from protection, which leaves biotechnological experimentation uncovered by the legislation. The act does not extend to invertebrate animals within the meaning of AWA section 1(3)(a), so they are not currently protected by the animal welfare regime. The vast majority of the animal kingdom's members are invertebrates.[13] However, the state explicitly recognizes that there is scope to extend this part of the act to certain invertebrate species if the appropriate national authority is satisfied, based on scientific evidence, that the invertebrate species concerned can experience pain or suffering.[14]

This raises a question as to whether a precautionary approach should be utilized. Such a cautionary overview would not assume an inability to suffer unless this could be proven. However, this is not the current method of assessment, meaning that much suffering can occur. This seems to subvert humane treatment requirements. The Cartesian myth about animals being unfeeling automatons is alive and well in the legislation, it would appear, unless it is demonstrated otherwise.

Provisions of the Act

The act places an onus, under section 9, to act with a duty of care toward animals under one's control. People with control over animals must take reasonable steps to satisfy the welfare needs of their animals. Keepers of companion animals must provide for their animals' basic needs, such as suitable accommodation, adequate food and water, and veterinary care. This means that anyone responsible for animals must take reasonable steps to make sure their needs are met. Previously, this had applied only to farmed animals.

The duty is not universal to all animals, however. For example, the obligation to ensure an animal's welfare applies only to animals who are "owned" or for whom someone is otherwise responsible. Offenses relating to cruelty and fighting have a wider application.

These responsibilities toward animals are framed under the act on the basis of the Five Freedoms. Any person responsible for an animal must ensure that five specific needs of the animal are met. The first two relate to a suitable environment and diet. The animal must also be able to exhibit normal behavior patterns. The fourth provision requires that the animal be housed either with or apart from other animals, depending on whether the animal is a social or a solitary species. The final rule is that the animal be protected from pain, suffering, injury, and disease.

The new legislation makes it an offense not to provide for the needs of an animal, thereby making it possible for enforcement agencies to take steps to prevent animal suffering, rather than act only afterward. The act established a new enforcement framework allowing preventative action to be taken. Enforcement agencies can issue improvement notices and order the seizure or destruction of animals, in cases of emergencies, without the need to apply for a court order.

The offenses under the act are the causing of unnecessary suffering,[15] mutilation,[16] docking of dogs' tails,[17] administration of poisons,[18] and fighting.[19] People responsible for animals have a duty to ensure their welfare,[20] and the transfer of animals by way of sale or prize to persons aged under sixteen years without parental accompaniment is not permitted.[21]

The act placed a ban on the docking (cutting or removal) of animals' tails for cosmetic or aesthetic reasons, under section 6 with the exception of "working" dogs such as those in the police and armed forces. Exceptions apply for the purpose of medical treatment. Mutilations other than docking of dogs' tails are prohibited under section 5.

Levels of Suffering

One of the notable changes in the act has been the widening of the scope of the existing offense of causing unnecessary suffering. A definition of "suffering" is provided in section 62 of the act, and it includes both physical and mental suffering along with "related expressions."

An offense is committed if a person "responsible" for the animal involved knew, or ought reasonably to have known, that an act or a failure to act and failed to take reasonable steps to prevent unnecessary suffering, caused unnecessary suffering to a "protected animal."

Codes of Practice[22]

Codes of practice are used to promote the welfare of farmed animals, and this act extends their use to non-farmed animals.[23] Codes of practices that provide care guidelines for dogs, cats, rabbits, equines, and nonhuman primates have been introduced in order to highlight and explain the relevant legal requirements to keep these animals and to promote and give examples of good practice on how best to care for the animals in question. The codes are not legally binding and are only advisory. However, they can be used to help with prosecutions if welfare needs are not met and may be relied on in court to establish or negate liability. Codes of practice in respect of cats, dogs, equines, and privately kept nonhuman primates were published and updated and replaced.[24] A code of practice in relation to the welfare of so-called game birds "reared for sporting purposes" also came into force in 2011.[25]

Exemptions

The scope of the Animal Welfare Act 2006 is limited due to the explicit exclusion of scientific procedures lawfully done under the Animals (Scientific Procedures) Act 1986. Section 58 deals with scientific research and states that scientific procedures on animals are governed by the Animals (Scientific Procedures) Act 1986 (ASPA) which permits research to be carried out on animals. The protections set out in the AWA do not apply to anything lawfully done under the ASPA. For example, section 58(2) specifies that the powers of entry set out in the AWA do not apply in relation to places designated under sections 6 and 7 of the ASPA. The only exception to this is the power of entry to inspect farming premises. However, the power to inspect farm premises is permitted only in relation to animals who are reasonably believed to be bred or kept for farming purposes. Therefore, the power of entry does not apply to those animals on the premises who are being bred, kept, or used for experimental or scientific purposes.

The AWA also excludes any activity that takes place in the "normal course of fishing," although the act does not enlighten further as to what would be considered "abnormal." It applies to actions taken on the land and all inland waters and estuaries in England and Wales, but not the sea.[26]

The humane destruction of an animal is not prohibited.

Punishment

The penalties include disqualification orders, deprivation orders, custodial sentences, and fines.

The RSPCA can initiate prosecutions, as can the local authority or the police, for failure to uphold the welfare principles of the act. Fines of up to £5,000 or a maximum jail term of five years and a lifetime ban can be imposed since the Animal Welfare (Sentencing) Act 2021.[27] Of note is that the penalties for animal welfare cases in England were before the 2021 Act among the lowest in Europe.

For instance, in Ireland, there is a maximum penalty of €250,000 and a five-year prison sentence.[28] In Switzerland, animal cruelty can result in a prison term up to three years.[29] Other penalties and ancillary powers include improvement notices,[30] powers of entry involving animals in distress,[31] warrants,[32] deprivation orders concerning animals connected to an offense,[33] disqualification orders banning certain dealings with animals,[34] and seizure orders connected to disqualification.[35]

Under section 34 of the act, a convicted person may be disqualified for such period as a court think fit from "owning," keeping, or participating in keeping animals or being party to an arrangement entitling him/her to control or influence the way in which animals are kept. The disqualification order may apply to animals generally or be limited to specified kinds. For example, in a case where the animal who suffered abuse was a dog, the person involved may receive an order disqualifying the person from owning or possessing dogs for the next five years.

The power to introduce secondary legislation to promote the welfare of farmed animals has been extended to non-farmed animals. These regulations have the force of law and create additional offenses and penalties.[36] They came into effect on October 1, 2018, under several pieces of legislation.[37]

There is also a prohibition on organized animal fighting under section 8 of the act, which prohibits both the organization of and attendance at fights.

Recent Reform

The use of undomesticated animals in circuses has been the subject of reform in the UK. Such animals were permitted in circuses until recently; however, the UK government announced early in 2018 that "wild animal" circuses would be banned in 2020. The Welfare of Wild Animals in Travelling Circuses (England) Regulations 2012 remained in place until January 2020. These regulations were introduced as a temporary measure following a commitment by the government to ban the use of undomesticated animals in traveling circuses.[38] The regulations expired in January 2020. At the time of introducing these regulations, the government stated that it did not intend to renew them because it intended to ensure that a legislative ban was introduced by then. A ban commenced from January 2020.[39]

Additionally, a ban has been introduced prohibiting the sale of ivory, which is due to come into effect in 2022. The act has been described as "a landmark in our fight to protect wildlife and the environment."[40] The act will introduce a ban on trading in items containing elephant ivory, regardless of the items' age, within the UK. It further places a ban on export from or import to the UK for sale or hire, with some exceptions,[41] and it will introduce new penalties for those found guilty of breaching the ban, including fines and possible imprisonment. Furthermore, new legislation was drafted requiring CCTV in all abattoirs in England in 2018. Official veterinarians will have unrestricted access to footage.[42]

There have been further attempts at reform with the Animal Sentience Bill, in the advent of Brexit, where EU rules could be rescinded. However, the bill failed to pass all stages of the Parliament before the end of the session in 2019 meaning that it made no further progress. The draft bill would have done two things. It would have increased the maximum penalty for animal cruelty offenses from six months to five years of imprisonment, although this has now been achieved through the Animal Welfare (Sentencing) Act 2021. It would also have defined animals in UK law as sentient beings, though this will be achieved on the passage of the Animal Welfare (Sentience) Bill.

Overall, the Animal Welfare Act provides an improved framework for strengthening rules relating to animal welfare. With the AWA being primarily an enabling act, implementation depends on developing secondary legislation and appropriate codes of practice. Some of the weak points of the act include the exemptions, particularly those relating to animals used.

The Environment, Food and Rural Affairs Committee conducted a review into the effectiveness of the Animal Welfare Act 2006 in 2010, questioning its enforcement with regard to domesticated animals. Given the growing body of evidence regarding sentience, the omission of invertebrates has been raised as a concern.[43] Furthermore, there is a lack of public awareness regarding the new responsibilities placed on companion animal caregivers and the functions of the act, particularly the codes of practice.[44] The report states that the act has resulted in an improvement in animal welfare and does provide a suitable legal framework. Importantly, it is noted that the act has achieved its objectives of harmonizing farmed and companion animal welfare and consolidating animal welfare legislation.[45] However, it notes that further work is required to ensure higher standards of animal welfare in the UK.

In a more recent 2016 report, enforcement of the act was highlighted as an issue. Any individual, authority, or organization, such as the RSPCA, can bring a case for prosecution regarding an offense. Inspectors under the act are appointed by local authorities or by the secretary of state in England (the National Assembly in Wales). The RSPCA deals with the majority of cases relating to companion and domesticated animals. The 2016 report recommends that the government place a statutory duty on local authorities to enforce the AWA. The committee recommends that the RSPCA should continue its important work investigating animal welfare cases but should work alongside the police and statutory authorities. It is noted that the government must ensure that appropriate resources are made available to local authorities to ensure they can fulfill their statutory duties.[46]

THE IRISH APPROACH: ANIMAL HEALTH AND WELFARE ACT 2013

The Animal Health and Welfare Act 2013 (AHWA) was introduced in March 2014 and replaces the 1911 and 1966 acts. Previously animal welfare and animal health were seen as separate issues. However, this act recognizes that they are closely related and, in many cases, interdependent. In Ireland the welfare of animals is covered in short but significant language. Matters such as their health, disease, export, and disposal and animal marts (for animals used in agriculture) are of prime concern.

The aim of the act is to promote welfare and prevent harm, or "unnecessary suffering," to an animal. The objective of this act is to "revise the law relating to the health and welfare of animals and their protection and identification; to provide for the regulation of certain activities relating to animals; to prevent cruelty to animals; and to make provision for the licensing of animal marts and for levies for the purposes of animal health and the control of animal diseases."[47]

Scope of Protection

An "animal" under the AHWA is defined as a member of the kingdom Animalia other than a human being. A "farm animal" means an animal who either has been bred or is kept for the production of food, wool, skin, fur, or feathers. The act also covers animals used for breeding, sport, or the farming of land. A "protected animal" means an animal who is being kept for farming, recreational, domestic, or sporting purposes in the state, when the animal is in the possession or under the control of a human being, whether permanently or on a temporary basis, and who is not living in a "wild" state.[48]

Provisions of the Act

Anyone who has a protected animal in their possession or under their control must take a considerable number of their traits into consideration in their treatment of the animals. The persons themselves must be competent and humane. The duty to protect the animals' welfare is dealt with under part 3 of the AHWA, which puts the onus on the person to consider "the animals' nature, type, species, breed, development, adaptation, domestication, physiological and behavioral needs, and environment, in accordance with established experience and scientific knowledge." Such persons must take all necessary steps to ensure that animals in their care are kept and treated in a manner that safeguards their health and welfare and does not threaten the health or welfare of another animal. Moreover, all structures used to contain the animal must be constructed and maintained in a manner so that they do not cause injury or harm to the animal.

The language of this provision of the act is quite detailed, and if taken to its logical conclusion, it would put a considerable expense on many animal keepers. It also would seem to be somewhat at odds with policies that encourage farmers to increase their herds, thus potentially reducing the quality of accommodation and food that they are able to provide for the animals.

Cruelty toward animals is prohibited by the legislation. Under section 12(1), "a person shall neither do nor fail to do anything, or cause or permit anything to be done, to an animal that causes unnecessary suffering to or endangers the health or welfare of an animal." One cannot be neglectful or reckless regarding the health or welfare of an animal. Exemptions are granted in cases including the destruction of an animal, providing it is done in an appropriate and humane manner. Further exemptions are granted for "anything done under and in accordance with any of the enactments or regulations mentioned in section 10(5)." Other exemptions apply to anything done under or in accordance with the following legislation: the Animal Remedies Act 1993, the Irish Medicines Board Act 1995, and the European Union (Protection of Animals used for Scientific Purposes) Regulations 2012 (S.I. No. 543 of 2012).

Levels of Suffering

The term "unnecessary suffering" is defined in detail in the legislation and relates to an animal's physical or mental pain, distress, or suffering that is unreasonable or unnecessary.

While enforcement is often a problem—and bodies such as the RSPCA, or its Irish equivalent, the ISPCA, are often chronically underfunded, thereby hampering their ability to take prosecutions—where enforcement is not an issue, it is interesting to examine critically how this legislation applies in practice. Daly, O'Flynn, and O'Sullivan highlighted the plight of mink under this legislation, where there appears to be a disjuncture between the acceptance of a practice—fur farming—as legal and the practice's clear violation of the principle and letter of the act.[49] The authors examined the case of mink, who at the time were protected animals under the act and yet undoubtedly suffered harrowing lives and deaths. While the act was supposed to protect their nature, their nature is understood to be solitary, and therefore the keeping of these animals in close cages might have been necessarily cruel in order to farm them. The practice itself could only be viewed as unnecessarily cruel. The act failed to protect them. Adherence to other requirements, such as having regard for the animals' "type," would have been difficult for lawyers to assess—though wordy, the act was not necessarily helpful. Moreover, even after Veterinary Ireland had spoken out against the farming of mink as indefensible, the government responded only once it became apparent that its defense of the practice was swimming against the tide of public opinion. This became apparent after a long campaign by grassroots groups such as the National Animal Rights Association (NARA), which contacted different politicians weekly over a long period of time to drum up support for a ban. As commented previously, the government finally gave in once it realized that the legislature would take credit for the executive's lethargy should it fail to act. The then government was a minority administration.

Fur farming is now due to be phased out, although it is arguable that a compensation regime would be much more desirable. Should the government change, the phasing out of fur farming could be disrupted, and once it is accepted that a practice is to be discontinued, it is infinitely preferable to do so as fast as possible.

Exceptions

As is the practice in the UK, the Irish act also contains exceptions. These include fishing; the lawful hunting of an animal, unless the animal is released in an injured, mutilated, or exhausted condition; and the lawful coursing of a hare, unless the hare is hunted or coursed in a space from which the animal does not have a reasonable chance of escape.[50]

Hare coursing involves greyhounds chasing a hare. In Ireland this is a competitive activity in which dogs compete in pursuit of the hare and it is administered by the Irish Coursing Club (ICC) which consists of eighty-nine affiliated clubs from Ireland and Northern Ireland.[51] There is some controversy about this activity. The ICC operates under a license from the Minister of Arts, Heritage and the Gaeltacht, issued annually with a total of twenty-two conditions attached and therefore they contend that coursing operates in a highly regulated environment with stringent rules in place. However, there are also arguments that this type of activity is cruel and unethical. The Irish Council against Blood Sports holds that "hare coursing involves the terrorising of one animal by another and is full of unnecessary cruelty and killing."[52] It is argued that the capturing of the hares from their natural habitats and the trauma, suffering, and possible injury they experience during the coursing event are cruel and unnecessary.[53] Hares used in coursing are specifically excluded from the scope of protection granted under the 2013 act. The hare is protected under the 1976 Wildlife Act, but the same act also permits hare coursing; that is, it is illegal to trap or sell hares other than for the specific purpose of coursing them. Therefore, hares warrant protection by both acts unless they are being used or hunted for the purposes of coursing.

Codes of Practice

No codes have been developed under Ireland's Animal Health and Welfare Act. The Farm Animal Advisory Council has issued codes of practice, but these were developed prior to the 2013 act. Therefore, we have no codes under this act or any codes for non-farmed animals and must look for guidance from sources such as the ISPCA, which is unsatisfactory. Apart from anything else, this body is not well funded.

Punishment

The majority of offenses warrant a fine up to €5,000 and/or imprisonment for up to six months. Penalties including a €250,000 fine and/or five years of imprisonment may apply. A disqualification order can also be issued which prohibits the keeping animals for any period up to and including life. Furthermore, costs associated with both legal action and veterinary treatment can also be awarded against any person or organization convicted of offenses under the AHWA.

Recent Reform: Regulations Developed under the Act

A ban has been introduced on the use of undomesticated animals in circuses under the Circuses (Prohibition on Use of Wild Animals) Regulations 2017. These regulations have been made under the Animal Health and Welfare Act 2013 and came into effect in 2018.

In 2015, the Department of Agriculture, Food and the Marine introduced legislation requiring mandatory microchipping and registration of all dogs from March 2016 in order to strengthen controls and traceability. All new dog "owners" are advised to require the breeder to produce an official certificate of registration before purchasing a dog.

Tail docking and declawing also have been prohibited under S.I. No. 304/2017—Prohibition on Tail Docking and Dew Claw Removal (Dogs) Regulations 2014 (Amendment) Regulations 2017[54]—made under section 36 of the Animal Health and Welfare Act 2013.

Although the 2013 act has greatly improved the legal protections in place for animals by providing increased powers for authorized officers to investigate complaints of animal cruelty and by introducing stricter penalties on convictions, including five years of imprisonment and up to a €250,000 fine, in addition to owners having a responsibility to care for the well-being of their animals, there is a need for further improvements. For instance, no codes of practice for non-farmed animals have been introduced as of yet, there has been no comprehensive review of this act, and coursing is still permitted.

Prosecutions are occurring, but until recently, very low fines have been issued, and custodial sentences are rarely handed down, so do not serve as a deterrent. The ISPCA is under-resourced with only eight inspectors. There is a need for greater resources to enforce the legislation.

THE TREATMENT OF DOGS

A. Dog Breeding

Both the UK and Ireland have legislation relating to dog breeding. Ireland introduced the Dog Breeding Establishments Act 2010, and the Breeding and Sale of Dogs (Welfare) Act 1999 was brought into force in the UK. Ireland has been labeled the "puppy farm capital of Europe" due to the numbers of pups being produced.[55] Dog breeding is on an industrial scale in Ireland. Furthermore, Ireland is one of the leading suppliers of puppies for the UK market.

UK

The legislation in place in the UK is the Breeding of Dogs Act 1973 and the Breeding and Sale of Dogs (Welfare) Act 1999 (applicable in England and Scotland), which sets out the licensing regime under which local authorities license dog-breeding establishments.

Previously, a license was required for those breeding five litters or more in a twelve-month period. Dog breeders that have a breeding establishment and sell the animals are obliged to get a license from their local council. Dog breeders who do not sell their dogs are known as "hobby breeders": defined as producing less than five litters in any twelve-month period do not need to obtain a license.[56]

The grant of licenses is discretionary but local councils must enforce the legislation. Before granting a license, the council must ensure that animals have appropriate accommodation, bedding, food, and water. The animals must also be exercised and visited, and any diseases should be controlled and treated."[57]

There are also controls on breeding and female dogs' litters are restricted to six over their lifetime. They cannot have more than one litter a year and they must have reached a year old before being mated. Compliance must be shown through the keeping of breeding records and puppies at licensed establishments can either be sold there or at licensed pet shops. Moreover, puppies under the age of eight weeks can only be sold to a licensed pet shop keeper or in Scotland, a "rearing establishment."[58]

Reform

This area has recently been the subject of reform, with new regulations introduced in 2018. These regulations require that anyone breeding three or more litters and selling at least one puppy in a twelve-month period will require a dog-breeding license. This is a reduction from the previous requirement of five or more litters. (If none of the puppies or adult dogs have been sold a license is not required. Evidence must be supplied.)

Furthermore, a star rating system was introduced for breeders to encourage good welfare standards and to aid the public in identifying compliant breeders. Licensed breeders receive a star rating from one to five stars. The star rating has an impact on the license fee and rate of inspections. For example, breeders with a five-star rating will receive a three-year license and pay a lower fee. Furthermore, they will be inspected less frequently. In contrast, other breeders will only receive a one-year license and must pay a higher license fee and also be inspected on a more regular basis.

Further reforms were introduced in 2020.[59]A ban on the sale of kittens and puppies from third parties, known as Lucy's Law, was introduced.[60]The new law requires animals to be born and reside in a safe environment, with their mother, and to be sold from their place of birth. This law came into effect in April 2020.

Ireland

The legislation governing dog breeding in Ireland is the Dog Breeding Establishments Act 2010, which came into force in 2012. The purpose of this act is to regulate dog breeding. There are currently over 250 dog breeding establishments (DBEs) registered under Irish Dog Breeding Establishments legislation, but only seventy of these are considered to be commercial breeders.[61]

This legislation requires those who have six or more dogs capable of being used for breeding to register with their local authority and to comply with certain standards which include providing suitable accommodation, adequate care of the animals, and record keeping. The act covers registration, staff, animal care, hygiene, health checks, records and identification, and inspection. In addition to this act, guidelines were introduced to assist organizations to comply with the act. The Dog Breeding Establishments Guidelines[62] were put in place to provide further guidance around welfare standards required and to promote good practice in dog breeding throughout the country. They provide guidance on construction and maintenance of establishments, registration, operation, and management. The first set of guidelines was issued along with the introduction of the act. However, due to ambiguity and lack of clarity regarding the duties of operators, in late 2015, the then Department of the Environment, Community and Local Government began a process of reviewing the guidelines. A new set of guidelines came into effect in 2019.

Concerns

There are many welfare concerns with dog breeding in Ireland. First, there is the number of pups being bred. The aforementioned title "puppy farm capital of the EU" highlights the scale of puppy breeding in Ireland. Furthermore, more than fifty thousand dogs are exported to the UK annually.[63] A second concern is the poor welfare standards for breeding establishments, and third, there is a lack of enforcement given the poor resources available.

In addition to welfare concerns, there is no registration requirement for breeders and premises with under six breeding females, and therefore no local authority data is available on these breeders. The new Animal Health and Welfare (Sale or Supply of Pet Regulations) 2019 state that if a person *sells or supplies six or more puppies in a single calendar year*, then they must register as a breeder. However, they are not subject to the requirements set out in the Dog Breeding Establishment Act. Breeding mothers can be spread to other premises, often with relatives, in order to avoid registration requirements, local authority inspection, and compliance with the Dog Breeding Establishments Act 2010, which amounts to a very large number of unregulated puppies and transactions.

Compliance

The act allows local authorities to inspect premises where there are six or more female dogs capable of breeding to ensure that they reach certain standards. It further sets out the duties of operators. Premises that do not meet the standards set out under law can be issued a "fixed payment notice," an improvement notice, or a closure notice in very serious cases. If a closure notice is issued, the DBE operator must cease breeding or keeping dogs at the establishment. These notices are issued when local authorities are satisfied that there is a significant and imminent threat to an animal's health or welfare.

Local authorities issued thirty-one improvement notices and four closure notices to DBEs between 2013 and 2017.[64] Four of the ten improvement notices issued in 2016 by local authorities were appealed by DBE operators to the district court. The lack of clarity in the previous DBE guidelines has contributed to the high rate of appeal, and therefore, the new 2019 guidelines are a welcome addition.

Punishment

Fines of up to €5,000/€100,000 and imprisonment of up to six months or five years, depending on the severity of the breach, can be issued.

B. The Greyhound Industry

Commercial greyhound racing is legal in only six countries: the UK, Ireland, New Zealand, the United States, Australia, and Mexico.[65] Recent bans have been passed in Australia's capital city and across states in the United States—most recently in Florida. Additionally, the main track in China—Macau—closed in 2018.

Thus, Ireland and the UK share the fact that they are among only a few countries where greyhound racing is legal. Greyhound Racing Ireland, the governing body for the Irish coursing and greyhound industry, is a commercial semi-state organization. The Irish government supported the greyhound industry with a financial grant of €19.2 million in 2021. However, in the UK, clubs registered with the Greyhound Board of Great Britain may apply for funding through the British Greyhound Racing Fund (BGRF). The BGRF is supported by voluntary contributions from bookmakers.

UK

The relevant legislation in the UK is the Welfare of Racing Greyhounds Regulations 2010.[66] These regulations were introduced after mounting pressure from charities, MPs, the media, and the public to ensure adequate welfare of the dogs. The regulations were devised under the 2006 act and focus on licensing requirements only. Unlike in Ireland, greyhound racing in the UK is not state-funded.[67] As of 2022, there are twenty-one licensed greyhound racing tracks in England. The sport is divided into two sectors which includes greyhound racing tracks licensed by the industry regulatory body, the Greyhound Board of Great Britain (GBGB), and independent tracks that operate outside the industry regulator. Under the Welfare of Racing Greyhound Regulations 2010, greyhound racing tracks must be licensed by a local authority. As of 2022, there are nineteen greyhound racecourses managed by the GBGB and three independent greyhound racing tracks, which are licensed by local authorities.

Concerns

The UK faces similar concerns as Ireland. Over 75 percent of the greyhounds who are raced in the United Kingdom come from Ireland. The Greyhound

Forum, which represents eight major dog charities, estimates that 3,700 of a total 9,000 retired greyhounds are "unaccounted for" every year.[68]

Ireland

The governing legislation in Ireland is the Welfare of Greyhounds Act 2011,[69] which provides for the welfare of greyhounds, the establishment of a register, and the regulation and operation of greyhound breeding establishments. There are also general welfare provisions, which include rules regarding accommodation, food, bedding, exercise, and the control of infection/disease. There is additionally a requirement to keep records.

The Greyhound Racing Act 2019[70] amends and extends existing legislation. The purpose of the new act is to improve governance and tighten regulation in the greyhound racing sector. It is largely focused on the boards, functions, meetings, licensing, and sanctions in place. It also has a section on welfare and traceability of greyhounds to allow for further regulations to be made.

Concerns

In Ireland, the Irish Greyhound Board is a semi-state organization that receives government funding. A figure of €16.8 million was issued in 2019.[71] A 2019 Irish documentary, *RTÉ Investigates: Greyhounds Running for Their Lives*, uncovered many of the welfare concerns inherent in this industry. Welfare issues, overbreeding,[72] the treatment of retired greyhounds, traceability, and export of greyhounds were highlighted. Furthermore, dogs who "don't make the grade" and "disappearing" greyhounds are a prevalent issue in Ireland.[73] It is estimated that around 10,000 greyhounds are surplus to requirements every year, and there are good homes for only around 1,200 animals. This means that around 88 percent of unwanted greyhounds disappear to an unknown fate.

The Irish RTÉ documentary has raised many concerns among members of the public and sponsors.[74] However, subsequent to the release of this documentary, the government confirmed a subsidy of over €16 million for this industry in 2020, which further increased in 2021.

POLITICAL INFLUENCE IN THE PROTECTION OF ANIMALS

In the UK, the Green Party, the Labour Party, and the newly formed Animal Welfare Party all promote higher welfare standards for some animals for a plethora of reasons. It was a Labour government that introduced the ban on fox hunting, and the Green Party's environmental focus often brings different animals within its ambit. The Green Party's parliamentary representation is paltry in comparison with jurisdictions with a more democratic electoral system that does not eliminate all other candidates with a "first past the post" felling. For instance, the Green Party won six seats in a Parliament of (the then) 166 seats in Ireland in 2007.

Outside of Parliament, NGOs and charities include Respect for Animals, the RSPCA, Cruelty Free International, the League against Cruel Sports, the Horse Trust, the Dogs Trust, Blue Cross for Pets, the Donkey Sanctuary, and Battersea Dogs and Cats Home, to name but a very few. Of note are the policies of environmental groups such as Greenpeace and Friends of the Earth, which also include animals within the ambit of their concern.

In Ireland, several animal welfare parties have been formed in the recent past and present. These include the Irish Animal Welfare Party (now defunct), the Party for Animal Welfare, and Animals First (now defunct). There are also numerous NGOs and charities such as AFAR, LAW, the ISPCA, the Irish Council against Blood Sports, NARA, MADRA, My Lovely Horse Rescue, and PAWS.

CONCLUSION

The ongoing need for legislative updates and for the existence of charities, NGOs, and grassroots groups related to animals shows that our societies have problems in how we treat animals. We believe that a fundamental overhaul of how animals are treated should be conducted. All of our interactions with the animal kingdom should be based on science, and where information is not available, ideally we should have a precautionary approach. We should not assume that animals cannot suffer until proven otherwise; on the contrary, we should proceed with caution and assume that they can suffer until proven indisputably otherwise. Even then, this approach should not provide human beings with a free-for-all in their treatment of members of the animal kingdom. Even if we do not put animals at the heart of our consideration, we should at least be aware that human beings' disregard for the natural world may in the end terminate the existence not only of plants and animals but also of humans themselves. Legislation does well to pay heed to the ability to suffer. It is high time that legislation acknowledges animals' ability to suffer but that it also protects them from suffering by ensuring that it is enforced. We may then start moving from a solely welfare-oriented approach to animals to a more rights-based paradigm.

REFERENCES

Animal Boarding Establishments Act 1963.
Animal Health and Welfare Act 2013.
Animal Health and Welfare (Scotland) Act 2006.
Animal Welfare Act 2006.
Animal Welfare Act 2008 (Tierschutzgesetz [TSchG], 2008).
Animal Welfare (Licensing of Activities involving Animals) (England) Regulations 2018.
Animal Welfare (Sentencing) Act 2021.
BBC News. "Lucy's Law: Puppy Farm Ban Set to Be Confirmed." May 13, 2019. https://www.bbc.com/news/uk-48249333?.
BBC One. "Britain's Puppy Dealers Exposed." May 20, 2016. https://www.bbc.co.uk/programmes/b07cgscx.
Breeding of Dogs Act 1973.
Breeding and Sale of Dogs (Welfare) Act 1999.
Burke, R. "Further Protests Planned against Ireland's Greyhound Industry." *Echo Live*, June 30, 2019. https://www.echolive.ie/corknews/Further-protests-planned-against-Irelands-greyhound-industry-96466f94-fbed-4d1d-b3aa-d18e7cd9f49a-ds.
Cantillon R. "Budget Process Goes to Dogs." *Irish Times*, October 10, 2019. https://www.irishtimes.com/business/companies/budget-process-goes-to-dogs-1.4045522.
Daly, T., S. O'Flynn, and M. O'Sullivan. "The Infuriating Resilience of the Fur Trade in Ireland: Part 1." *Irish Law Times* 36, no. 11 (2018).
———. "The Infuriating Resilience of the Fur Trade in Ireland: Part 2." *Irish Law Times* 36, no. 12 (2018).
Department for Environment, Food and Rural Affairs (Defra). "Animal Welfare Legislation: Protecting Pets." April 9, 2013. https://www.gov.uk/guidance/animal-welfare-legislation-protecting-pets.
———. "CCTV Becomes Mandatory in All Abattoirs in England." Press release. May 4, 2018. https://www.gov.uk/government/news/cctv-becomes-mandatory-in-all-abattoirs-in-england.
———. "Codes of Practice for Non-Farmed Animals." March 27, 2012. https://www.daera-ni.gov.uk/publications/codes-practice-non-farmed-animals.
———. "Codes of Practice for the Welfare of Cats, Dogs, and Horses, Ponies, Donkeys and Their Hybrids." March 1, 2018. http://www.legislation.gov.uk/uksi/2018/310/pdfs/uksi_20180310_en.pdf.
———. "Codes of Practice for the Welfare of Gamebirds Reared for Sporting Purposes." April 8, 2013. https://www.gov.uk/government/publications/code-of-practice-for-the-welfare-of-gamebirds-reared-for-sporting-purposes.
———. "Post-Legislative Assessment of the Animal Welfare Act 2006." Policy paper. December 20, 2010. https://www.gov.uk/government/publications/post-legislative-assessment-of-the-animal-welfare-act-2006.

———. "The Welfare of Wild Animals in Travelling Circuses (England) Regulations 2012: Post Implementation Review 2018." January 2018. https://assets.publishing.service.gov.uk/government/uploads/system/uploads/attachment_data/file/683306/wild-animals-circuses-post-implementation-review-feb2018.pdf.

———. "World-Leading UK Ivory Bill Becomes Law." Press release. December 20, 2018. https://www.gov.uk/government/news/world-leading-uk-ivory-bill-becomes-law--2.

Dog Breeding Establishments Act 2010.

Elgot, J. "Puppy and Kitten Farming to Be Banned under 'Lucy's Law.'" *Guardian*, May 13, 2019. https://www.theguardian.com/world/2019/may/13/puppy-kitten-farming-banned-new-lucys-law.

Encyclopaedia Britannica. s.v. "invertebrate." https://www.britannica.com/animal/invertebrate.

Environment, Food and Rural Affairs Committee. *Animal Welfare in England: Domestic Pets.* House of Commons, November 11, 2016. https://publications.parliament.uk/pa/cm201617/cmselect/cmenvfru/117/117.pdf.

Greyhound Racing Act 2019.

Greyt Exploitations. "The British Greyhound Racing Fund." https://greytexploitations.com/the-structure-of-the-greyhound-racing-industry/the-british-greyhound-racing-fund/.

Hennessy, M. "Gardaí Investigating Complaint about 'Almost Dead' Hares Released Back into Wild." *The Journal*, June 3, 2013. https://www.thejournal.ie/gardai-hare-coursing-complaint-927338-Jun2013/.

Horgan-Jones, J. "Barry's Tea and FBD Insurance Pull Greyhound Racing Funding." *Irish Times*, July 2, 2019. https://www.irishtimes.com/news/ireland/irish-news/barry-s-tea-and-fbd-insurance-pull-greyhound-racing-funding-1.3944643.

———. "Minister Seeks to Ringfence Funding for Greyhound Welfare." *Irish Times*, June 28, 2019. https://www.irishtimes.com/news/ireland/irish-news/minister-seeks-to-ringfence-funding-for-greyhound-welfare-1.3940674?.

Irish Council against Blood Sports. "The Facts about Hare Coursing." Accessed November 3, 2019. http://www.banbloodsports.com/leaf-coursing.htm.

Ivory Act 2018.

Loughlin, E. "Ruth Coppinger to Meet Agriculture Minister over Plans to Ban Fur Farming." *Irish Examiner*, June 24, 2019. https://www.irishexaminer.com/breakingnews/ireland/ruth-coppinger-to-meet-agriculture-minister-over-plans-to-ban-fur-farming-932699.html.

Microchipping of Dogs (England) Regulations 2015.

O'Flynn, S. "Irish Animal Protection Laws: A Comparative Analysis." *Web Journal of Current Legal Issues* 4 (2011). http://webjcli.ncl.ac.uk/2011/issue4/o'flynn4.html.

O'Halloran, M. "Ireland's Reputation as 'Puppy Farm Capital of EU' Informs UK Bill." *Irish Times*, November 11, 2018. https://www.irishtimes.com/news/politics/ireland-s-reputation-as-puppy-farm-capital-of-eu-informs-uk-bill-1.3694223.

O'Rourke, R. "Protest outside Limerick Greyhound Stadium." *Limerick Leader*, July 25, 2019. https://www.limerickleader.ie/news/home/433947/protest-outside-limerick-greyhound-stadium.html.

Performing Animals (Regulation) Act 1925.
Pet Animals Act 1951.
Pope, C. "Protesters Urge End to State Support over 'Horrors' of Greyhound Racing." *Irish Times*, July 27, 2019. https://www.irishtimes.com/news/ireland/irish-news/protesters-urge-end-to-state-support-over-horrors-of-greyhound-racing-1.3969744.
Prohibition of Fur Farming Bill 2018.
Protection of Animals Act 1911.
Rannard, G. "Has a New Racing Ban in Florida Doomed These Dogs?" BBC News, November 13, 2018. https://www.bbc.com/news/world-us-canada-46145276.
Riding Establishments Acts 1970.
RTÉ. *RTÉ Investigates: Greyhounds Running for Their Lives*. June 26, 2019. https://www.rte.ie/player/movie/rt%C3%A9-investigates-greyhounds-running-for-their-lives/104051751967.
Ryan, C. "Greyhound Industry Over-Breeding by 1,000%." *RTÉ News*, December 17, 2019. https://www.rte.ie/news/investigations-unit/2019/0624/1057320-greyhound-industry-over-breeding-by-1000/.
———. "Thousands of Greyhounds 'Culled Each Year' for Not Being Fast Enough." *RTÉ News*, June 26, 2019. https://www.rte.ie/news/ireland/2019/0626/1057535-greyhound-rte-investigates/.
Ryan, O. "Vets Say New Dog Breeding Guidelines Need to Improve Standards." *The Journal*, June 17, 2018. https://www.thejournal.ie/dog-breeding-guidelines-4065232-Jun2018/.
Veterinary Ireland. "Ireland's Dog Trade and Breeding Establishments—What Next?" Media release. February 4, 2017. http://www.veterinaryireland.ie/images/Veterinary_Ireland_Media_Release_4th_February_2017.pdf.
Wedderburn, P. "Greyhound Racing: An Industry in Terminal Decline." *Telegraph*, August 31, 2016. https://www.telegraph.co.uk/pets/news-features/greyhound-racing-an-industry-interminal-decline/.
Welfare of Animals Act (Northern Ireland) 2011.
Welfare of Farmed Animals (England) Regulations 2007.
Welfare of Greyhounds Act 2011.
Welfare of Racing Greyhound Regulations 2010.

NOTES

1. First of all in 1922 and subsequently in 1937.
2. Protection of Animals Act 2011, https://www.legislation.gov.uk/ukpga/Geo5/1-2/27.
3. The bill from Ruth Coppinger, TD (Irish equivalent of an MP), the Prohibition of Fur Farming, was in the process of being debated in the Irish parliament, the Dáil. See E. Loughlin, "Ruth Coppinger to Meet Agriculture Minister over Plans to Ban Fur Farming," *Irish Examiner*, June 24, 2019, https://www.irishexaminer.com/breakingnews/ireland/ruth-coppinger-to-meet-agriculture-minister-over-plans-to-ban-fur-farming-932699.html.

4. Creed is a supporter of hare coursing and hunting.

5. RTÉ, *RTÉ Investigates: Greyhounds Running for Their Lives*, June 26, 2019, https://www.rte.ie/player/movie/rt%C3%A9-investigates-greyhounds-running-for-their-lives/104051751967.

6. R. Cantillon, "Budget Process Goes to Dogs," *Irish Times*, October 10, 2019, https://www.irishtimes.com/business/companies/budget-process-goes-to-dogs-1.4045522.

7. Some examples can be seen in national news reports in cities such as Cork and Limerick. See R. Burke, "Further Protests Planned against Ireland's Greyhound Industry," *Echo Live*, June 30, 2019, https://www.echolive.ie/corknews/Further-protests-planned-against-Irelands-greyhound-industry-96466f94-fbed-4d1d-b3aa-d18e7cd9f49a-ds; R. O'Rourke, "Protest outside Limerick Greyhound Stadium," *Limerick Leader*, July 25, 2019, https://www.limerickleader.ie/news/home/433947/protest-outside-limerick-greyhound-stadium.html.

8. C. Pope, "Protesters Urge End to State Support over 'Horrors' of Greyhound Racing," *Irish Times*, July 27, 2019, https://www.irishtimes.com/news/ireland/irish-news/protesters-urge-end-to-state-support-over-horrors-of-greyhound-racing-1.3969744.

9. O'Flynn has written at some length on this and subsequent legislation in S. O'Flynn, "Irish Animal Protection Laws: A Comparative Analysis," Web Journal of Current Legal Issues 4 (2011), http://webjcli.ncl.ac.uk/2011/issue4/o'flynn4.html.

10. Animal Welfare Act 2006, https://www.legislation.gov.uk/ukpga/2006/45/pdfs/ukpga_20060045_en.pdf. In Scotland the relevant legislation is the Animal Health and Welfare (Scotland) Act 2006. In Northern Ireland reform came in 2011 with the introduction of the Welfare of Animals Act (Northern Ireland) 2011.

11. Animal Welfare Act 2006, sec 2.

12. The previous legislation was the Protection of Animals Act 1911.

13. *Encyclopaedia Britannica*, s.v. "invertebrate," accessed November 2, 2019, https://www.britannica.com/animal/invertebrate.

14. Animal Welfare Act 2006, sec. 1(4).

15. Animal Welfare Act 2006, sec. 4.

16. Animal Welfare Act 2006, sec. 5.

17. Animal Welfare Act 2006, sec. 6.

18. Animal Welfare Act 2006, sec. 7.

19. Animal Welfare Act 2006, sec. 8.

20. Animal Welfare Act 2006, sec. 9.

21. Animal Welfare Act 2006, sec. 11.

22. Wales and Scotland have their own equivalent codes.

23. Department for Environment, Food and Rural Affairs (Defra), "Codes of Practice for Non-Farmed Animals," March 27, 2012, accessed November 3, 2019, https://www.daera-ni.gov.uk/publications/codes-practice-non-farmed-animals.

24. Defra, "Codes of Practice for the Welfare of Cats, Dogs, and Horses, Ponies, Donkeys and Their Hybrids," March 1, 2018, http://www.legislation.gov.uk/uksi/2018/310/pdfs/uksi_20180310_en.pdf.

25. Defra, "Code of Practice for the Welfare of Gamebirds Reared for Sporting Purposes," April 8, 2013, accessed November 3, 2019, https://www.gov.uk/government/publications/code-of-practice-for-the-welfare-of-gamebirds-reared-for-sporting-purposes.

26. Point 10 in the explanatory notes that accompany the act states, "The Act will apply to all inland waters (rivers, streams, lakes and ponds) and to estuaries. It will not apply to the sea."

27. Animal Welfare (Sentencing) Act 2021.

28. Animal Health and Welfare Act 2013, sec. 52.

29. Tierschutzgesetz (TSchG), Art. 26 (2008).

30. Animal Welfare Act 2006, sec. 10.

31. Animal Welfare Act 2006, secs. 18–20 and Schedule 2.

32. Animal Welfare Act 2006, secs. 22–23 and 52.

33. Animal Welfare Act 2006, sec. 33.

34. Animal Welfare Act 2006, sec. 34.

35. Animal Welfare Act 2006, sec. 35.

36. For example, the Welfare of Farmed Animals (England) Regulations 2007; the Microchipping of Dogs (England) Regulations 2015, made under section 12 of the Animal Welfare Act 2006, which came into effect on February 24, 2015; Animal Welfare (Licensing of Activities involving Animals) (England) Regulations 2018 under section 13 of the Animal Welfare Act 2006. The effect of the new regulations is to replace some existing licensing regimes and to put in place a new licensing regime to control "licensable activities," such as selling animals as pets; providing or arranging for the provision of boarding for cats or dogs; hiring out horses; breeding dogs; and keeping or training animals for exhibition.

37. The Pet Animals Act 1951; the Animal Boarding Establishments Act 1963; the Riding Establishments Acts 1970; the Breeding of Dogs Act 1973; the Breeding and Sale of Dogs (Welfare) Act 1999; and the Performing Animals (Regulation) Act 1925.

38. See Defra, "The Welfare of Wild Animals in Travelling Circuses (England) Regulations 2012: Post Implementation Review 2018," January 2018, https://assets.publishing.service.gov.uk/government/uploads/system/uploads/attachment_data/file/683306/wild-animals-circuses-post-implementation-review-feb2018.pdf.

39. Scotland has had a ban in place since 2017. In July 2018, the Welsh government announced that a bill to ban the use of undomesticated animals in traveling circuses would be brought forward within the next twelve months. The draft Wild Animals in Travelling Circuses (Wales) Bill was published on October 1, 2018, and aims to enforce a ban on using undomesticated animals in traveling circuses in Wales, on ethical grounds.

40. Defra, "World-Leading UK Ivory Bill Becomes Law" (press release), December 20, 2018, https://www.gov.uk/government/news/world-leading-uk-ivory-bill-becomes-law--2.

41. The five exemptions permitted under the Ivory Act 2018 are for museum sales, pre-1918 "high artistic" objects, items made before 1947 where the ivory content is less than 10 percent, musical instruments manufactured before 1975 where the content is less than 20 percent, and antique portrait miniatures backed in ivory.

42. Defra, "CCTV Becomes Mandatory in All Abattoirs in England" (press release), May 4, 2018, https://www.gov.uk/government/news/cctv-becomes-mandatory-in-all-abattoirs-in-england.

43. Defra, "Post-Legislative Assessment of the Animal Welfare Act 2006" (policy paper), December 20, 2010, https://www.gov.uk/government/publications/post-legislative-assessment-of-the-animal-welfare-act-2006.

44. Defra, "Post-Legislative Assessment," n43.

45. Defra, "Post-Legislative Assessment," n43.

46. Environment, Food and Rural Affairs Committee, "Animal Welfare in England: Domestic Pets."

47. Animal Health and Welfare Act 2013.

48. Animal Health and Welfare Act 2013, sec 2.

49. See T. Daly, S. O'Flynn, and M. O'Sullivan, "The Infuriating Resilience of the Fur Trade in Ireland: Part 1," *Irish Law Times* 36, no. 11 (2018); and "The Infuriating Resilience of the Fur Trade in Ireland: Part 2," *Irish Law Times* 36, no. 12 (2018).

50. Animal Health and Welfare Act 2013, sec 11.

51. See Irish Coursing Club available at https://irishcoursingclub.ie/about-us/.

52. Irish Council against Blood Sports, "The Facts about Hare Coursing," accessed November 3, 2019, http://www.banbloodsports.com/leaf-coursing.htm.

53. See M. Hennessy, "Gardaí Investigating Complaint about 'Almost Dead' Hares Released Back into Wild," *The Journal*, June 3, 2013, https://www.thejournal.ie/gardai-hare-coursing-complaint-927338-Jun2013/.

54. https://www.irishstatutebook.ie/eli/2017/si/304/made/en/print

55. See *BBC One*, "Britain's Puppy Dealers Exposed," May 20, 2016, https://www.bbc.co.uk/programmes/b07cgscx; and M. O'Halloran, "Ireland's Reputation as 'Puppy Farm Capital of EU' Informs UK Bill," *Irish Times*, November 11, 2018, https://www.irishtimes.com/news/politics/ireland-s-reputation-as-puppy-farm-capital-of-eu-informs-uk-bill-1.3694223.

56. Defra, "Animal Welfare Legislation: Protecting Pets," April 9, 2013, https://www.gov.uk/guidance/animal-welfare-legislation-protecting-pets.

57. Defra, "Animal Welfare Legislation."

58. Defra, "Animal Welfare Legislation."

59. BBC News, "Lucy's Law: Puppy Farm Ban Set to Be Confirmed," May 13, 2019, https://www.bbc.com/news/uk-48249333?.

60. J. Elgot, "Puppy and Kitten Farming to Be Banned under 'Lucy's Law,'" *Guardian*, May 13, 2019, https://www.theguardian.com/world/2019/may/13/puppy-kitten-farming-banned-new-lucys-law.

61. See Veterinary Ireland, "Ireland's Dog Trade and Breeding Establishments—What Next?" (media release), February 4, 2017, http://www.veterinaryireland.ie/images/Veterinary_Ireland_Media_Release_4th_February_2017.pdf.

62. They became effective from January 1, 2012, following enactment of the Dog Breeding Establishments Act 2010.

63. Figure provided by the Dublin Society for Prevention of Cruelty to Animals.

64. O. Ryan, "Vets Say New Dog Breeding Guidelines Need to Improve Standards," *The Journal*, June 17, 2018, https://www.thejournal.ie/dog-breeding-guidelines-4065232-Jun2018/.

65. G. Rannard, "Has a New Racing Ban in Florida Doomed These Dogs?," BBC News, November 13, 2018, https://www.bbc.com/news/world-us-canada-46145276.

66. Welfare of Racing Greyhounds Regulations 2010, https://www.legislation.gov.uk/ukdsi/2010/9780111489727/contents.

67. Greyt Exploitations, "The British Greyhound Racing Fund," https://greytexploitations.com/the-structure-of-the-greyhound-racing-industry/the-british-greyhound-racing-fund/.

68. P. Wedderburn, "Greyhound Racing: An Industry in Terminal Decline," *Telegraph*, August 31, 2016, https://www.telegraph.co.uk/pets/news-features/greyhound-racing-an-industry-interminal-decline/.

69. Welfare of Greyhounds Act 2011, http://www.irishstatutebook.ie/eli/2011/act/29/enacted/en/html.

70. Greyhound Racing Act 2019, http://www.irishstatutebook.ie/eli/2019/act/15/enacted/en/html.

71. J. Horgan-Jones, "Minister Seeks to Ringfence Funding for Greyhound Welfare," *Irish Times*, June 28, 2019, https://www.irishtimes.com/news/ireland/irish-news/minister-seeks-to-ringfence-funding-for-greyhound-welfare-1.3940674.

72. C. Ryan, "Greyhound Industry Over-Breeding by 1,000%," *RTÉ News*, December 17, 2019, https://www.rte.ie/news/investigations-unit/2019/0624/1057320-greyhound-industry-over-breeding-by-1000/.

73. C. Ryan, "Thousands of Greyhounds 'Culled Each Year' for Not Being Fast Enough," RTÉ News, June 26, 2019, https://www.rte.ie/news/ireland/2019/0626/1057535-greyhound-rte-investigates/.

74. J. Horgan-Jones, "Barry's Tea and FBD Insurance Pull Greyhound Racing Funding," *Irish Times*, July 2, 2019, https://www.irishtimes.com/news/ireland/irish-news/barry-s-tea-and-fbd-insurance-pull-greyhound-racing-funding-1.3944643.

Index

About the Editors and Contributors

Andrew Linzey (*Editor*) is director of the Oxford Centre for Animal Ethics and has been a member of the Faculty of Theology in the University of Oxford for twenty-eight years. He is a visiting professor of animal theology at the University of Winchester and a professor of animal ethics at the Graduate Theological Foundation. He is the author or editor of more than thirty books, including *Animal Theology* (SCM Press/University of Illinois Press, 1994); *Why Animal Suffering Matters* (Oxford University Press, 2009); *The Global Guide to Animal Protection* (University of Illinois Press, 2013); and *The Palgrave Handbook of Practical Animal Ethics* (Palgrave Macmillan, 2018).

Clair Linzey (*Editor*) is the deputy director of the Oxford Centre for Animal Ethics. She is a professor of animal theology at the Graduate Theological Foundation. She gained her doctorate in theology from the University of St Andrews and is coeditor of the *Journal of Animal Ethics* and coeditor of the Palgrave Macmillan Animal Ethics Series. She is coeditor with Andrew Linzey of *Animal Ethics for Veterinarians* (University of Illinois Press, 2017); *The Ethical Case against Animal Experiments* (University of Illinois Press, 2018); *The Routledge Handbook of Religion and Animal Ethics* (Routledge, 2018); *The Palgrave Handbook of Practical Animal Ethics* (Palgrave Macmillan, 2018); and *Ethical Vegetarianism and Veganism* (Routledge, 2018).

A. W. H. Bates is a coroner's pathologist working in Essex and London, where he is an emeritus consultant at the Royal Free Hospital and an honorary associate professor in pathology at University College, London. A fellow of the Oxford Centre for Animal Ethics, he has authored such books as *Anti-Vivisection and the Profession of Medicine in Britain: A Social History* (Palgrave Macmillan, 2017) and *The Anatomy of Robert Knox* (Sussex Academic Press, 2010).

Mariah Rayfield Beck, DVM, is a wildlife veterinarian practicing in Rhode Island. Dr. Beck graduated from Cornell University College of Veterinary Medicine in 2020 and is now the chief veterinarian at the Wildlife Clinic of Rhode Island. Dr. Beck also teaches marine conservation to a variety of age-groups, from elementary to postgraduate students.

Alice Collinson is a freelance consultant solicitor, and has most recently worked with Advocates for Animals, the first UK law firm dedicated to animal protection. She has a particular interest and background in animal protection law focused on free-living communities of animals and an international animal law master's degree (LLM) from Lewis and Clark Law School in Portland, Oregon.

Danielle Duffield practices international arbitration and litigation and is an adjunct animal law lecturer. She has been involved in animal law work in the United Kingdom, the United States, and New Zealand, including through law reform projects, litigation, and academic work. She cofounded and served as president of the New Zealand Animal Law Association and cochairs the Farmed Animal Welfare Working Group of the UK Centre for Animal Law. She holds a bachelor of laws with first-class honors from the University of Otago in New Zealand and a master of laws from Harvard Law School, where she was a recipient of a Frank Knox Memorial Fellowship and the Animal Law and Policy Program Writing Prize.

David Favre has been teaching and writing in the animal law area for forty years. He is a professor at Michigan State University School of Law, and he spent over twenty years on the board of the Animal Legal Defense Fund and was dean of the law college for five years. In addition to over a dozen articles, he has published five books, including *Respecting Animals* (Prometheus Books, 2018), *Animal Law: Welfare, Interest, and Rights* (2nd ed., Aspen Pub lishers, 2011), *International Trade in Endangered Species* (Martinus Nijhoff Publishers, 1989), and *The Future of Animal Law* (Edward Elgar, 2021).

Angela Fernandez is a professor in the Faculty of Law and Department of History at the University of Toronto. She is a fellow of the Oxford Centre for Animal Ethics, a member of the Board of Advisors for Animal Justice Canada, and a member of the Brooks Animal Studies Academic Network with the Brooks Institute for Animal Rights Law and Policy. Her publications include a book on the famous first-possession foxhunting case from early nineteenth-century New York, *Pierson v. Post, the Hunt for the Fox: Law and Professionalization in American Legal Culture* (Cambridge University Press, 2018). Her new book project is a coauthored work on a late-nineteenth-century overfishing case from the Supreme Court of Canada, *The Frederick Gerring*, which will appear in the University of British Columbia Landmark Cases in Canadian Law series.

Robyn Hederman, JD, is an associate court attorney in New York State Supreme Court and a fellow of the Oxford Centre for Animal Ethics. As cochair of the Animal Law Committee of the New York City Bar Association, she writes legal reports analyzing pending legislation and creates public programs examining issues affecting nonhuman animals. She has a Master of Arts in history and is a member of the Phi Alpha Theta History Honor Society. Her publications include "Gender and the Animal Experiments Controversy in Nineteenth-Century America," in A. Linzey and C. Linzey eds., *The Ethical Case Against Animal Experiments* (University of Illinois Press, 2018), and "The Cost of Cruelty: Henry Bergh and the Abattoirs" in A. Linzey and C. Linzey eds., *Ethical Vegetarianism and Veganism* (Routledge, 2019).

Lena Hehemann, PhD, is an associate fellow of the Oxford Centre for Animal Ethics and an independent researcher from Switzerland, where she collaborates, among others, with the Swiss animal protection organisation "Tier im Recht." She is also a member of a German committee on animal experimentation. Her publications include the book "*Die Genehmigung von Tierversuchen im Spannungsfeld von Tierschutz und Forschungsfreiheit*" (Schulthess, 2019) as well as several articles such as "Religious Slaughtering, a Stunning Matter: Centraal Israëlitisch Consistorie van België and Others" in *European Papers* (2021), "The Administrative Appeal in Animal Experimentation Law" in *Schweizerische Juristen-Zeitung* (2021; in German), and "The Protection of the Dignity of Laboratory Animals" in *Global Journal of Animal Law* (2018).

Oliver B. Langworthy, PhD, is a lecturer in the School of Divinity at the University of St Andrews and an academic editor working on the *St Andrews Encyclopaedia of Theology*. His research is focused on the theology and biblical interpretation of Greek writers in late antiquity and the impact of their reception especially in early-modern and modern sources. His recent work is focused on the pneumatology and soteriology of Gregory of Nazianzus.

Randall Lockwood, PhD, has degrees in psychology and biology from Wesleyan University in Connecticut and a doctorate in psychology from Washington University in St. Louis. After teaching at Washington University and the State University of New York at Stony Brook, he was with the Humane Society of the United States for twenty-one years. In 2005 he joined the staff of the ASPCA as a senior vice president. He retired from this position in 2019 but continues to serve as a consultant to the ASPCA on policy, response, and engagement. He is a fellow of the Oxford Centre for Animal Ethics and the Denver University Center for Human–Animal Interaction and an affiliate assistant professor in small animal clinical sciences at the University of Florida College of Veterinary Medicine. He is the coauthor of *Cruelty to Animals and Interpersonal Violence* (Purdue University Press, 1997); *Forensic Investigation of Animal Cruelty* (Humane Society Press, 2006); and *Animal Cruelty and Freedom of Speech: When Worlds Collide* (Purdue University Press, 2014) and the author of *Prosecuting Animal Cruelty Cases* (American Prosecutors Research Institute, 2006).

Stephanie O' Flynn, PhD, is a lecturer in law in the Department of Law and Criminal Justice at Waterford Institute of Technology, Ireland. Stephanie holds a BA (Hons) in legal studies with business (WIT), an LLM. (University College Cork) and a PhD (National University of Ireland, Galway). As part of her master's, she completed a thesis titled "Irish Animal Protection Laws." Her doctoral thesis is "From Animal Welfare to Animal Rights: Rethinking the Legal Paradigm." Stephanie's main lines of research focus on the legal status of animals, animal rights theory and EU and comparative animal protection law. She has a particular interest in the legal treatment of dogs, both as companion animals and in sport. Stephanie is an associate fellow of the Oxford Centre for Animal Ethics.

Maureen O'Sullivan, PhD, is a lecturer in law (above the bar) at the School of Law at the National University of Ireland, Galway, where she specializes in industrial and intellectual property law and animal rights and legal issues related to veganism and vegetarianism. She completed a PhD in 2017 at the School of Law at the University of Edinburgh, where her doctoral studies focused on patent system reform in the area of biotechnological inventions using devices of participatory budgeting from Brazil. She published a monograph titled *Biotechnology, Patents and Morality: A Deliberative and Participatory Paradigm for Reform* with Routledge in 2019. She has published an article on patenting human–animal hybrids and chimeras in the *Journal of Animal Ethics*. She is the author of a major article on artistic copyright law, published in the *Intellectual Property Quarterly* in 2015, and also has published widely in the area of free/open source and creative commons licensing. She previously taught at the University of the West of England, Bristol, and at Warwick University. She holds a research LLM from the University of Warwick and studied for her BCL and BA (philosophy and English) at University College Cork.

Solana Joy Phillips is a writer and mother. She was raised in Alaska but has spent many years since in England, Ireland, California, and Germany. She holds degrees from the London School of Economics and the University of California, Davis, but her keen interest in animal ethics stems from her experiences of growing up in the woods, working with the San Francisco SPCA, and schlepping around the world with her tabby.

Frances M. C. Robinson is an associate fellow of the Oxford Centre for Animal Ethics. She was a practicing veterinary surgeon from 1971 to 1989. She returned to academic study in 1996 and gained a BA in philosophy and environmental management (University of Keele, 2000); an MA in values and the environment (University of Lancaster, 2001); and an MPhil in philosophy with a thesis titled "Animal Experimentation, Complexity and Animal Ethics" (University of Lancaster, 2011). Her publications include a review of *The Costs and Benefits of Animal Experiments* by Andrew Knight (*Journal of Critical Animal Studies*, 2013); "The Relevance of the *Belmont Report* to Research Using Animals" (*Journal of Animal Ethics*, 2019); and, as a member of the working party, "Normalizing the Unthinkable: The Ethics of Using Animals in Research" in *The Ethical Case against Animal Experiments*, edited by Andrew Linzey and Clair Linzey (University of Illinois Press, 2018).

Rebecca Rose Stanton is an associate fellow of the Oxford Centre for Animal Ethics and is a member of the Vegan Society's Researcher Network and Campaigner Network. She is also the founder and head of the "Animals and Animation" group within the Society for Animation Studies. Rebecca gained her PhD from Northumbria University. Prior to pursuing her PhD, she also focused on animal rights during both her MA and BA dissertations at Loughborough University. She is the author of *The Disneyfication of Animals* (Palgrave Macmillan, 2021).

Kenneth R. Valpey (Krishna Kshetra Swami) is a research fellow of the Oxford Centre for Hindu Studies, a fellow of the Oxford Centre for Animal Ethics, and dean of studies at Bhaktivedanta College, Septon, Belgium. As a practicing monk in the Chaitanya Vaishnava tradition of Krishna-bhakti, he has been engaged since 1972 in the study and teaching of Indic cultural and religious ideas and practices. His publications include *Attending Kṛṣṇa's Image: Caitanya Vaiṣṇava Mūrti-sevā as Devotional Truth* (Routledge, 2006), two volumes with Ravi M. Gupta—*The Bhāgavata Purāṇa: Sacred Text and Living Tradition* (Columbia University Press, 2013) and *The Bhāgavata Purāṇa: Selected Readings* (Columbia University Press, 2017), and *Cow Care in Hindu Animal Ethics* (Palgrave Macmillan, Animal Ethics Series, 2020).

Matthew J. Webber is an ordained minister in the Presbyterian Church (USA) and is currently a doctoral student in the Study of Religion in the Joint Doctoral Program at Iliff School of Theology and the University of Denver. He is an associate fellow of the Oxford Centre for Animal Ethics. Matthew has served in churches in both Holland, Michigan, and Timnath, Colorado. After twelve years of ordained service, Matthew has stepped out from behind the pulpit to continue his education full-time. His emphasis in both ministry and philosophical study revolves around the ethical treatment of nonhuman animals. Matthew lives in Colorado with his wife Nicole and their cat Milo and dog Huxley.

Ruaidhrí D. Wilson read international relations and politics at the University of Sheffield and, as a British Council Scholar, at the University of Hong Kong. Upon graduating in 2012, he worked for HM Civil Service as a policy adviser. He left in 2014 to pursue an interdisciplinary master's degree at the Graduate Institute for International Development Studies, Geneva, Switzerland. His academic background is complemented by a range of practical experience working alongside nonhuman animals, including training Arab endurance horses in France and qualifying as a field guide in South Africa. He is involved in a number of animal and wildlife charities, serving as a trustee of Curlew Action and an adviser to We Are All Mammals. He is currently studying for an MPhil in conservation leadership at the University of Cambridge.

Steven M. Wise, JD, is president of the Nonhuman Rights Project, the mission of which is to attain fundamental legal rights for at least some nonhuman animals through litigation and legislation in the United States and throughout the world. He received a BS in chemistry from the College of William and Mary and a JD from the Boston University School of Law. He has taught animal rights jurisprudence at the Harvard, Stanford, Lewis and Clark, University of Miami, Vermont, St. Thomas, John Marshall, Tel Aviv, and Autonomous University of Barcelona law schools. He is the author of four books: *Rattling the Cage: Toward Legal Rights for Animals* (Perseus Books, 2000); *Drawing the Line: Science and the Case for Animal Rights* (Perseus Books, 2003); *Though the Heavens May Fall: The Landmark Trial That Led to the End of Human Slavery* (Da Capo Press, 2005); and *An American Trilogy: Death, Slavery, and Dominion Along the Banks of the Cape Fear River* (Da Capo Press, 2009). His work is the subject of the Hegedus and Pennebaker film *Unlocking the Cage*, which premiered at the 2016 Sundance Film Festival.

Made in United States
Orlando, FL
17 January 2025

57392268R00195